BACKSTORY IN BLUE

BACKSTORY IN BLUE

ELLINGTON AT NEWPORT '56

John Fass Morton

Rutgers University Press
New Brunswick, New Jersey, and London

Library of Congress Cataloging-in-Publication Data
Morton, John Fass, 1947–
Backstory in blue : Ellington at Newport '56 / John Fass Morton.
p. cm.
Includes bibliographical references and index.
ISBN 978–0–8135–4282–9 (hardcover : alk. paper)
1. Ellington, Duke, 1899–1974. 2. Newport Jazz Festival. 3. Jazz—Rhode Island—History and criticism. I. Title.
ML410.E44M67 2008
781.65079'7457—dc22

2007033644

A British Cataloging-in-Publication record for this book is available from the British Library.

Visit our Web site: rutgerspress.rutgers.edu

Designed by Isabella D. Palowitch, Artisa, LLC

Manufactured in China

For Gail, my esteemed partner for this dance

Contents

Contents

Foreword

Jonathan Yardley

In the summer of 1956 I was sixteen years old, living with my family in the cottage they'd just completed in Middletown, Rhode Island, spinning my wheels as a counselor at a nearby day camp while waiting for my senior year at prep school to begin. I was a nice enough kid, well schooled by my parents in the basic courtesies, respectful toward adults as teenagers still were in those days, but also resentful about being a scholarship boy at a rich kids' school, lazy and distracted in my studies, rebellious in any number of silly but to me deeply meaningful ways.

One of them took musical form. I played no instrument and had no technical understanding of music, but I loved melody and rhythm and was beginning to develop as much of an "ear" as a musical illiterate can hope to have. About four years earlier I'd somehow gotten my hands on a 45-rpm "album" that contained four selections by Jelly Roll Morton and His Red Hot Peppers. I'd immediately fallen in love, and had set out on what was to become a lifelong love affair with jazz, one that continues to delight and define me half a century later.

However improbable it may seem, Aquidneck Island was exactly the right place for someone of my tastes to be. As John Fass Morton describes in fascinating detail in this book, two years earlier the first Newport Jazz Festival had been presented on the grounds of the old Casino on Bellevue Avenue, no more than five miles from my family's house. My father loathed jazz, indeed had little taste for music of any sort, but had been kind enough to chauffeur me to that first festival. The next summer, when the event was moved to Freebody Park, I was able to drive myself in the family station wagon, thanks to the brand-new driver's license in my wallet.

For the jazz festival of 1956, I was joined by several of my classmates; I didn't much like my school, but that didn't stop me from having friends there. In all there may have been a half dozen of us, sleeping catch as catch can inside and outside the house. By day we headed to Middletown's Second and Third Beaches, by night to Freebody Park. My friends were less interested in jazz than I was, indeed some of them may have been beginning the drift toward rock and roll that so altered the musical landscape in the next few years, but a long weekend on sunny, beautiful Aquidneck Island was reason enough to be there and besides, hey, the jazz festival was a party.

We had no idea, of course, what kind of party Saturday night at that 1956 Newport Jazz Festival would turn out to be. The skies were still light as we found a parking space (God knows where) near Freebody and made our way onto the grounds. We managed to finagle beers—all of us were underage, but at the jazz festival no one seemed to care—and went to our seats. We were well in the rear, able to hear what was going on but not to see very well. Cursed as I am with an unreliable and highly selective memory, I recall scarcely a thing about the early parts of that night's program. I do remember that Ellington opened with "The Star-Spangled Banner" and followed with a couple of other numbers, promising to return later in the night with a full presentation.

At the time I didn't know much about Ellington. He was a formidable presence in the jazz galaxy, but one with which, at my tender age, I had yet to come to grips. I knew a modest amount about classic jazz, and thanks to the discovery of the lost tapes of Benny Goodman's 1938 concert at Carnegie Hall I'd developed a strong liking for the big bands, but I had yet to find my way to the bandleaders who ultimately would epitomize jazz for me: Jimmy Lunceford, Chick Webb, Count Basie, and, of course, Ellington.

Which is to say that when Ellington's orchestra came back on stage half an hour later than planned, I had no idea what to expect. I knew almost nothing about his ambitions to write at length so was essentially unprepared for the new three-part composition, the "Newport Jazz Festival Suite," that had its premiere that night. I wasn't especially impressed. By contrast with "Take the A Train," which opened the session, the suite struck me as stiff. It still does. It's Ellington, which is reason enough to pay attention, but at most it's minor Ellington.

As Morton's thorough account makes plain, Ellington was at a crucial point in his career, and around 11 P.M. on the night of July 6, 1956, it looked as if this latest effort to resuscitate it wasn't going to happen. Then it *did* happen, and if you're reading this book you almost certainly know *what* happened because you've listened—probably more times than you can remember—to "Ellington at Newport," the recording that ensured that night's permanent and lofty place in jazz history.

Except among the cognoscenti, there wasn't much crowd reaction when Ellington announced "Diminuendo in Blue" and "Crescendo in Blue," to be "separated by an interval by Paul Gonsalves," but it didn't take long for people in my part of the park to sense that something out of the usual was taking place. For the first time that night the band was swinging, and swinging hard. We didn't know, of course, that the great drummer Jo Jones was in the wings, pounding time with a rolled-up newspaper, egging the band on, but we certainly felt the change, felt the electricity. Most of us in the rear of the park were young, and ready for action. Gonsalves gave it to us.

The Columbia recording of the concert tells you, better than I can, what happened. As Gonsalves marched on from chorus to chorus, the intensity of the crowd became almost unbearable. On the recording the roar of the crowd (and in this case the old cliché is absolutely

Crowd before the stage during "Tulip or Turnip." Jonathan Yardley in center foreground. ::: *Photo courtesy of Bob Parent and Time-Warner.*

true: it was a roar) becomes a great wave that carries Gonsalves higher and higher. Desperate to be in the action, we moved as close to the stage as we could get. We saw a lovely young woman dancing passionately not far from the stage, in a space the crowd had opened for her; Morton tells her fascinating story in full. A few weeks later, when *Time* magazine published a cover story on Ellington, I saw my own face in the middle of a photograph of the crowd and felt that I too had been granted a place, albeit a very small one, in the history books.

When at last the "Crescendo" came to its high-voltage conclusion, all we wanted was more. You can hear it on the recording. But though Ellington toned things down thereafter—both he and the festival's producer, George Wein, feared that roar could degenerate into riot—there was little sense of letdown or anticlimax. In part that was because the two solos by Johnny Hodges were incredibly sensuous, in larger part because—so at least I think—all of us knew that we had been both witnesses to and participants in something genuinely momentous.

Now, more than half a century later, nearing my sixty-eighth birthday, my shaky old memory still recalls that night almost as keenly as if I were there. Oh, some of the details are fuzzy, but the incredible sensation remains of being lifted out of myself into some higher place. As I said to Morton when we talked about that night, I have been blessed in many ways, probably more than I deserve, with a richly rewarding private life and a small but gratifying public one, but that night in Newport stands alone and apart. That I was actually there is something to this day I can't quite believe, and that gives me undiminished joy.

Jonathan Yardley *is the book critic of the* Washington Post. *In 1981 he was awarded the Pulitzer Prize for Distinguished Criticism.*

Acknowledgments

This backstory owes its existence to virtually everyone I encountered on this journey. All wanted to talk about Newport '56; many insisted on referring me to others who had their own backstories to tell. As a result, what I had intended to be a magazine article became this book.

Thanks to all those whom I interviewed or with whom I had conversations. Thanks especially to those of you who played a part in bringing to life the America of the fifties. Called now the greatest generation, you are the ones who perfected a more perfect union, if only for a moment in time. History will judge. But for those of us who followed, you raised the bar for American culture and society and for what was expected of us once we grasped the baton. This work is a modest attempt at tribute and redemption.

I want to cite several folks who had an unforgettable impact on me personally and who collectively pointed the work in the direction it eventually went: Monsignor John Sanders, for your unique insights into the moment, the men, and the music; Michael James, truly a national treasure, a historian who was there, who knew and was friends with great men; Ron Barboza, for your perception into the Cape Verdean–American experience and for patiently taking time to make me a street-level part of your historic New Bedford, if only for a day; George Avakian, for making me aware early in the project that this story was epic; Rick Anderson and his family for revealing their personal story of a woman ahead of her time; and Newport '56 audience member Jonathan Yardley, for enthusiastically confirming that the performance of "Diminuendo and Crescendo in Blue" was an experience as life-changing as the original LP most definitely recorded.

Thanks as well to Stanley Crouch, for introducing me to Michael James, and to Clark Terry, for putting me inside the Ellington Orchestra, on the road, onstage and off.

Also I want to thank all the fine folks at Rutgers University Press who embraced the project above and beyond: especially my editor, Leslie Mitchner; her assistants, Alicia Nadkarni and Rachel Friedman; Marilyn Campbell, for her editing assistance; Joe Abbott, for copyediting the manuscript; Isabella Duicu Palowitch for design; Jennifer Holan for indexing; and the director of the press, Marlie Wasserman. Thanks also to Stuart Mitchner, for his help in fact checking, and to the Rutgers University Foundation's James Dawson, for his support and encouragement as we brought the manuscript to life as a book.

I also owe a debt of gratitude to Connie Buchanan, for her editorial support during the writing of the early chapters; my friends, fellow writer Chris Hunt, the ever-knowledgeable bookman Bob Lemstrom-Sheedy, fellow authors Jim Lester and Gus Russo, and Professor Barton Carr Shaw of Cedar Crest College—all for their wise counsel as I was conceiving the proposal and sharpening my focus; and Debbie Madigan, for her faithful transcriptions of the interview material.

For invaluable research assistance, thanks to all the staff at the Institute of Jazz Studies at Rutgers University, especially to Tad Hershorn for his work with me on the photos; Kay Peterson, Deborra Richardson, Reuben Jackson, and Wendy Shay at the Ellington Collection at the Smithsonian Institution for help also on photos and for familiarizing me with the collection; the most generous photo assistance from the folks at Sony BMG Music Entertainment, especially Natalie Nagulies, director of business and legal affairs in the Commercial Music Group, and Phuong Baum, as well as Che Williams, photo archive manager, and in earlier photo research, Marie Lin; the Motion Picture, Broadcasting, and Recorded Sound Division of the Library of Congress, in particular Larry Appelbaum; and the Nimitz Library of the U.S. Naval Academy for use of its astounding collection of jazz and African American cultural materials, which proved invaluable for secondary sources.

I should also thank James Fitzpatrick, the music director for St. Margaret's Church, Westminster Parish, who first made me aware of the musicological significance of Ellington's modulations in "Diminuendo and Crescendo in Blue" and the *diabolus in musicam* in the Gonsalves solo.

Finally, thanks to Ted Hudson, vice president of the Duke Ellington Society; Patti White, Lee Anderson, Michael Miller, and David Dizenfeld of Filmsters, along with Jennifer McGorry-McCormick and Suzanne McDonnell-Long, for their embracing of this backstory to take it to an entirely different level and audience. Per ardua ad astra.

JFM
July 7, 2008
Annapolis, Maryland

How We Got There

1

A Phrase with Six Tones—Apart, Yet Integral

"All across the U.S., in the summer of 1956, the people seemed to feel let out of school," read a July 16, 1956, *Time* piece wistfully titled "The Tranquil Time." "Never before had the nation been so prosperous; never before had wages been so high and jobs so plentiful."

This is a remembering song. It is the backstory of one of jazz history's epic performances—postwar pop culture's first certified and recorded happening. It's the story of who and what made this heroic event so compelling and how one performance reflected the feelings and shaped the sensibilities of the postwar generation, peoples of many diasporas, and testified to their arrival as Americans. It's a story of how one summer night anticipated the cultural epiphanies of the sixties.

This is a song sung as much by those who performed offstage as by those who performed on.

In proper perspective, the song begins later in time, on the far side of the continent, when one Thursday evening in September 1965, six notes soared from Harry Carney's baritone saxophone to the vaulted ceiling of San Francisco's Grace Episcopal Cathedral.

Each note filled the space, reverberating for perhaps as much as seven seconds. Carney's tones were the motif for the words "In the beginning God," the first six syllables of most English translations of the Bible. So began the opening section to the public debut of America's greatest twentieth-century composer's *First Sacred Concert*.

"If a man is troubled, he moans and cries when he worships," said Edward Kennedy Ellington in his program notes. "When a man feels that which he enjoys in this life is only because of the grace of God, he rejoices, he sings, and sometimes dances. That is what I am doing in this *Sacred Concert*. Now I can say openly what I have been saying to myself on my knees."

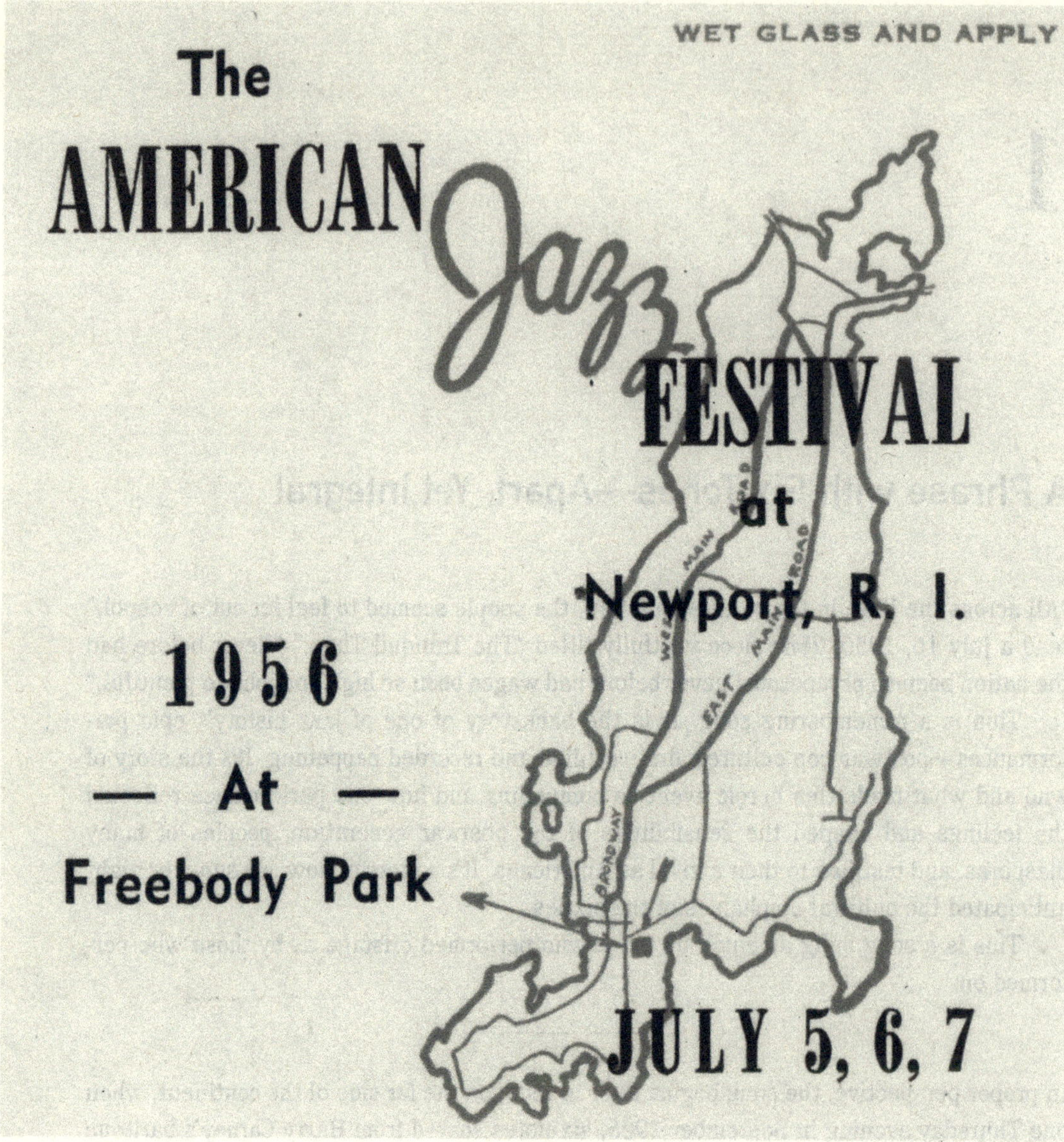

Decal for the Newport '56 jazz festival. ::: *Courtesy of the Institute of Jazz Studies, Rutgers University.*

Though very much given to the flesh, Duke Ellington always believed The Man was there for him, guiding his every step. From the time of his mother's death, in 1935, he had worn a cross given him by his much younger sister, Ruth Ellington Boatwright. Ruth Boatwright maintained that her brother read the Bible daily and on the road said prayers while kneeling on a pillow on the hotel floor. Ellington once claimed he had received two educations: one from the poolroom and one from the Bible. "The Bible is the most important," he said. "It taught me to look at a man's insides instead of the cut of his suit."

Over the course of his career, Duke's tones progressed from the guttural to the godly. In the forties he said that he had to know how an instrumentalist played poker before he could compose parts for him. And yet his direction was evident from the beginning. His early jazz compositions incorporated gospel-inspired antiphonies between brass and reed sections, heralding a desire to move his music from earthy entertainment into high art.

Ellington's historic *Sacred Concert* was one of many events held during 1965 as part of the consecration celebration to inaugurate Grace Cathedral. That September night, as his six-tone phrase voiced by Harry Carney reverberated over the congregation, Duke was celebrating his rebirth. His audience had come not to a jazz festival, nightclub, or concert hall but to the third-largest Episcopal cathedral in the nation, a French-gothic structure crowning Nob Hill. Invited guests and communicants alike had entered through the doors of the main entrance, whose gilded bas-reliefs were cast from Lorenzo Ghiberti's original molds for the Porta del Paradiso in Florence, Italy.

The particular resonance of Carney's phrasing energized the meditations of a striking forty-two-year-old blonde woman, a socialite from the East Coast, prompting her to reflect on Ellington's program notes and her own life to that point. An apparition from Duke's past and one of his personal guests that night, she was living across the bay in Tiburon, before the hills of Sausalito and Marin became dotted with houses and hot tubs.

A whole host of women had danced into Ellington's long life. Ruth Boatwright spoke of her brother's aesthetic delight in the opposite sex and how he regarded women as flowers, each one lovely in her own special way. Since the late thirties he had made a home in successive Harlem and Upper West Side New York apartments with the graceful and leggy chorine Evie Ellis. From 1960 to his death in 1974, his constant companion on the international road—who virtually managed his life on tour—was a different woman, a tall, blonde, sensuous, and cosmopolitan Portuguese chanteuse more than twenty years his junior, Fernanda de Castro Monte.

Ellington played to women in his every audience. On a pretty young admirer at the end of his piano, he could lay a hypnotic smile. Whatever she might return, in glance, gesture, or movement, would recharge his visceral batteries, electrifying his performance for all in a dance of intersubjective mood and fantasy.

At the time of the performance of his *Sacred Concerts* Ellington was choosing to identify himself as "God's messenger boy," the maestro of an orchestra that the great gospel singer Mahalia Jackson called a sacred institution. That night in San Francisco he had a message for this once-wealthy sophisticate sitting in a preferred pew with his other invited guests. When they were finally able to speak privately, he delivered it. His words transported them to that earlier time, the Newport Jazz Festival of 1956. This complex, enormously gifted, larger-than-life man allowed that she "was the force that put his band back on the jazz map."

In the years prior to Newport, Ellington and his orchestra had been languishing as popular musical tastes and the music business abandoned the big band sound of the thirties and forties. "There was no industry buzz on Ellington," said jazz impresario

George Wein of his booking Ellington for the 1956 festival. "To me he was always Duke Ellington, but to the press and to the jazz world he was on the way down. That's why Duke always said, 'I was born in Newport in 1956.'"

Duke's rebirth came during his orchestra's legendary late-night performance at the '56 festival of "Diminuendo and Crescendo in Blue," with its mythic interval by tenor sax soloist Paul Gonsalves. That night this same blonde socialite was in the box section in front of the stage. Early in Gonsalves's lengthy solo she jumped from her seat and performed a rapturously expressive dance that lasted throughout the rest of the interval. Some dozen photographers recognized the event as a "decisive moment" and captured it on film. One photo, freezing her in anonymous ecstasy, appeared on the back cover of the '56 LP, Ellington's best-selling record of his entire half-century career.

"Who caused the moment?" the heretofore anonymous Elaine Anderson would ask decades later. Gonsalves, or herself? "It's how you look at it. The glass was half-filled—I caused it. Or the glass was half-empty—Gonsalves did. Take your pick. They tell me I saved the night for the Ellington band and that I was the cause of a historic event in jazz history." The recorded evidence is unmistakable in the music and the cheers, which fed each other, on both the 1956 Columbia LP and the 1999 Sony Columbia/Legacy CD reissue.

"I am not playing jazz. I am trying to play the natural feelings of a people," Ellington said in a 1930 interview. "I believe that music, popular music of the day, is the real reflector of the nation's feelings."

As a young man, Ellington preferred to label his creative output Negro music, as opposed to jazz. He may have worn the label *Negro,* but whatever he said about his music and his own identity, he was expressing himself in the language of segregation. Postwar America would speak a new language beyond black and white. "American culture, even in its most rigidly segregated precincts, is patently and irrevocably composite," wrote the distinguished and prescient African American cultural observer Albert Murray in 1969. "It is, regardless of all the hysterical protestations of those who would have it otherwise, incontestably mulatto." That statement—reinforced by an archaic label wholly intended to shock—is especially remarkable given that Murray wrote it three years into the Black Power movement and a year after the Martin Luther King assassination and the riots that followed. That same year, Murray's Tuskegee friend and colleague Ralph Ellison, a trumpeter, better known as the author of the canonical 1953 novel *Invisible Man,* wrote in his essay "Homage to Duke Ellington on His Birthday": "Who, seeing and hearing Ellington and his marvelous band, hasn't been moved to wonder at the mysterious, unanalyzed character of the Negro American—and at the white American's inescapable Negro-ness?"

One view has held that jazz came into being during the latter half of the nineteenth century, as the cross-cultural music of a New Orleans Creole society transformed both by race mixing and foreign immigration. Early in the twentieth century, African Americans escaping Jim Crow segregation in the rural South took this music with them when they embarked on their Great Migration to cities in the North and Northeast. There they intersected with the so-called New Immigrants—Eastern European Jews, Italians, and Poles—all arriving from the Old World on their Great Wave. In cities like Boston and New York, these several peoples began to assimilate into an urban, working-class American culture that was forming shared values, ideas, and attitudes into common memories and reference points. African American music helped acculturate European immigrants. With its infectious appeal, jazz—the liberating musical expression of a once-enslaved people who had been in America for well over a century—provided the relative newcomers a song that was an obvious alternative to the exclusive and dominant culture of the white Anglo-Saxon Protestant establishment.

At the same time, David Sarnoff and William Paley, themselves immigrant entrepreneurs, created their revolutionary new industries—broadcasting, communications, and mass entertainment. Advances in sound recording and radio technology made their mass-communication empires technically possible. By the thirties, commercialized communications technology took jazz from a musical form catering to regional or racial tastes to one that appealed to a national audience. Into the mid-forties, swing music was the express ticket for second-generation immigrants into America. The swing lifestyle absorbed all American youth, regardless of background—black and white, Catholic and Jewish, Polish and Italian—melting them all in the same pot.

America emerged from World War II the preeminent world power that would inherit in fact—if not in name—the imperial mantle of Europe, where victor and vanquished alike lay prostrate. By that purportedly tranquil summer of 1956, the United States had become a confident, affluent society. Americans were becoming more and more mobile, and increasingly, family background accounted for less in determining social status. New money surpassed old; local society gave way to national society.

"The deciders and originators in matters of the highest fashion and style of life," wrote C. Wright Mills, popularizer of the postwar term *white collar*, "have definitely passed from the old families of Boston, Philadelphia, Baltimore and Newport to the stars of Hollywood and Radio City." For many, the new promised land was the white-collar suburb, enabled by the mass production of homes and the new interstate highway system. The growth of the service economy propelled working-class Americans into the middle class. The cumulative weight of these social trends and the demographic shift to the suburbs dissolved twentieth-century class structure in America and began to sideline the WASP establishment. Replacing it was a new corporate power structure. In the expansive postwar climate, corporations with new products to sell found that they could mold susceptible, uprooted suburbanites with "manufactured loyalties and distractions." American culture was becoming a fabricated culture, a mass culture imposed from above, a culture, above all, of consensus.

Those who resisted consensus in the mid-fifties were a mixed bag of Adlai Stevenson liberals, old leftists from the thirties, beats, blacks, and, in the words of philosopher Peter

Viereck, "nonconformist[s] in the Marlon Brando tradition"—anyone who was "unadjusted" and opting to dissent from status seeking. Unlike organization men in gray flannel suits and suburban housewives, fifties nonconformists chose not to enter the rat race. Instead they became teachers, social workers, artists. Disaffected WASPs and other unadjusted whites shared with most blacks a collective dissatisfaction with—or suspicion of—the American dream. And postwar jazz fed this attitude.

These were the audiences for bop and its West Coast successor, cool jazz, sustained by independent labels. A subculture was growing in which individuals in the lonely crowd began to share outlaw emotions in nightclubs where they and the performers could interact, re-creating, in cultural historian W. T. Lhamon's words, "a secular, vernacular rite that substituted for religious sacrament." It was the old call-and-response pattern from slave days in the South reborn in the midcentury North. The artistic statement calls: "*This* is what I am." An audience committed to that statement responds: "This is what *I* am." By its second year, 1955, Newport was fulfilling that ritualistic role on a grander scale as a three-day outdoor jazz revival meeting.

Behind the audience and musicians were those of the swing generation who had remained in the music scene as record producers, critics, and impresarios—in some cases acting in all three roles, regardless of any perceived conflict of interest. Among those who helped conceive or institute the Newport Jazz Festival were many who came of age in the swing era, among them Elaine Lorillard, George Wein, John Hammond, and George Avakian.

At different times Hammond and Avakian represented one of the midcentury's two prestige record labels: Columbia, whose powerful corporate parent was Bill Paley's CBS. Other swing aficionados formed the dozen or so independent labels whose professed noncommercial ethos provided their artists access to cosmopolitan audiences. But only a major label like Columbia had the corporate clout to reach and, if necessary, create a nationwide audience that hungered for its commercial product. Like its worthy rival, General Sarnoff's RCA Victor, the label relied on gifted artist-and-repertoire (A&R) men with intimate knowledge of the jazz world, who saw their role as messianic purveyors of a music of transformative longing. These producer-technicians could recognize a musician's potential and generate quality product for a mass market of record buyers. George Avakian signed to Columbia such stars as Dave Brubeck, Miles Davis, and finally Ellington himself. Taken with live performances and live performance recordings of Davis and Brubeck, Avakian planned a four-album Columbia release for the third Newport Jazz Festival that would include a recording of Ellington performing a specially commissioned work. It proved to be a recording of a happening.

The first generation of the rock era begins its cultural history with another song from 1956, when, in the words of Sun Records producer Sam Phillips, "a white boy who could sing like a black boy and catch the beat of black music" made his first TV appearances.

The Sunday before the Ellington performance, Elvis Presley appeared on NBC TV's new *Steve Allen Comedy Show* and that Monday recorded "Hound Dog" and its flip side, "Don't Be Cruel." In August his RCA Victor 45 shot to number one as a double A-sided single, where it remained for eleven weeks, selling seven million copies. The previous year, this other wind had begun to blow through the postwar music culture. Rock and roll, then a strictly teenage phenomenon, emerged from the subgenre of rhythm and blues. Whereas bop and cool had been about listening in the clubs, rhythm and blues was about dancing in the dance halls and other such venues. It did not exactly fit the idea of jazz as an art form that some of the middle-aged swing critics were proffering after the war. Many had refused to take seriously the honking saxophone solos, the grandstanding, and the pandering to the audience. Rhythm and blues was entertainment, not art.

Others saw R&B differently. Amiri Baraka (LeRoi Jones) identified the "screaming saxophone" solo as elemental. "The riff itself was the basis of this kind of playing, the saxophonist repeating the riff much past any useful musical context, continuing it until he and the crowd were thoroughly exhausted physically and emotionally." "The good jazzmen never wanted to get rid of the blues. They knew instinctively how they wanted to use it, e.g., Ellington," Baraka continued. "[Rhythm and blues'] very vulgarity assured its meaningful emotional connection with people's lives."

By 1955 Duke Ellington had already attuned himself to the musical momentum. *Blackboard Jungle* had opened in March, and by the time of the second Newport Jazz Festival, the song that opened this classic film on fifties juvenile delinquency, Bill Haley and His Comets' "Rock around the Clock," was well into its eight-week run as the nation's number-one hit song. Ellington wrote a piece for the 1955 festival's program titled "The Future of Jazz." Looking forward and back, he tantalized festival goers with a Janus-like ambiguity. "I have written a number of rock and roll things myself," he wrote, with a touch of the dramatic, "but am saving them for possible use in a show."

The blues of rival big band leader Count Basie was a seed for rhythm and blues; Duke Ellington's blues more frequently came across with rhythm and dissonance. His early biographer Barry Ulanov wrote of his once playing a dissonant chord, telling him, "That's the Negro's life, hear that chord. That's us. Dissonance is our way of life in America. We are something apart, yet an integral part." Yet at Newport in 1956, when Ellington launched "Diminuendo and Crescendo in Blue," he attacked his keyboard from the first bar, rhythmically vamping with dissonant chords to ride on a jumping R&B groove worthy of Basie. And thus did he masterfully set the stage for Paul Gonsalves to improvise and deliver the cathartic epiphany.

The Ellington Orchestra had opened its first set of the evening with the national anthem. The audience had stood, each ritually affirming solidarity with his or her notion of the American ideal of that tranquil time, which elsewhere was anything but. Yet "Diminuendo and Crescendo in Blue" conjured participation in an entirely different ritual, where Ellington's rhythmic dissonance reflected the feelings of some—including socialite Elaine Anderson—who were challenging social identities shaped or imposed by cultural forces not necessarily their own. For them, jazz was an expression of heady liberation and at times rebellion. Its blue notes acknowledged the burdens of the earthly here and now, whether slavery, discrimination, love lost, addiction, or suburban boredom. The blues asserted, "We are all under a yoke, but let's celebrate when, where, and while we can."

And so this song possessed the beautiful Elaine Anderson and compelled her to dance. As she continued, the focus shifted from performers to audience. Photographers left their positions at the front of the stage and elbowed their way through an ecstatic crowd toward her, clicking feverishly with their cameras. With every shot, every flash, they captured her body and soul, at a decisive moment that for Ellingtonians fifty years later is urban legend. The Newport audience that night in 1956 was seven thousand strong. All were on their feet, moving with Ellington, Paul Gonsalves, and Elaine Anderson, many brought to near riot before night's end. That is what one hears on the recording—mass release.

"The most neglected component of a successful concert," wrote jazz critic Gary Giddins, "is a good audience." For many who were in that audience, life afterward was not the same. America underwent a subtle change in 1956. The national focus on fighting the cold war did not obscure the truth that culturally defined identities were failing, in large measure owing to the power of the media—simultaneously reproducing and subverting old cultural hegemonies. That night, the Newport Jazz Festival had gathered together a heterogeneous crowd—from jazz fans to the just plain curious. "The audience expectation—with the exception of a relatively small minority who were the serious, seasoned fans—was to be entertained," observed jazz historian Dan Morgenstern, director of the Institute of Jazz Studies at Rutgers University. "They wanted to enjoy themselves. It was a show."

The tipping point, however, came with a tritone, an unexpected choice for the first note of a saxophonist's chromatic call in his wailing interval. This devil in the music propelled a blonde sophisticate in the audience to respond with her own solo, publicly shedding her inhibitions. Significantly, this decisive moment took place not in Harlem, not in Radio City, not in Hollywood, Las Vegas, or Miami, but in Newport, still regarded as the center of Anglo-American high society.

The deeper reality behind Ellington's two impromptu heroes is more nuanced, however. While Elaine Anderson may have been in Newport, she was not of it. And by contrast, while fifties America may have categorized Paul Gonsalves as a Negro, he was a Negro by choice. Both had adopted identities. And that summer night when the electric current arced between them, from stage into audience and back again, both were expressing arrival.

In 1956 something was in the air. It was a year of epiphanies, when new identities were forming and a culture teetered on the cusp of one popular music form to another. It may be that the hit song most baby boomers identify from that first week in July 1956 is a simple twelve-bar blues, hyped by a twenty-one-year-old and his handlers, and sold on nationwide TV to a teenage audience. But this remembering song, with its elongated fourteen-bar choruses of rhythm and dissonance, played on the night of July 7, 1956, by a fifty-seven-year-old and his big band, got *everybody* on their feet and moving as one. And some people still talk about it, whether they were there, or whether they heard the recording. Fifty years on, this other song says much more about America—how we got there, and where it all went.

2

Ellington's Long Road to Newport

Apparitions within the Music

Exactly thirty years before, Duke Ellington first played Newport. It was the summer of 1926. The town's opera house billed him as the Colored Paul Whiteman of America. The country was in the midst of the Jazz Age, and Whiteman was touted as the King of Jazz. Ellington's New England promoter was encouraging Newporters to infer that the band-leader was the colored King of Jazz.

Ellington once recalled that weekend, specifically a private dance he played the night before the opera house engagement. At the end of the performance a society woman who had listened from her wheelchair for the entire evening came rushing to the bandstand. "You have really given me something!" she blurted, before realizing she had left her wheelchair and was standing. "She said the music had gotten into her soul," Ellington exclaimed, "into her bones!"

At twenty-seven, Duke Ellington had already mastered the ways to reach into an audience on its own terms and transport it into his own world that was subliminally beyond black and white. Ellington-the-performer was drawn to communicate with dancers. The success of a performance was measured in getting a woman to dance—getting an audience to move.

Duke Ellington came of age as part of the Harlem Renaissance of the 1920s. He brought to it a sensibility honed by what his contemporary Langston Hughes, the esteemed African American poet and writer, once called the Oxford of America, the scene around the Shaw District of northwest Washington, DC.

Having the largest concentration of African Americans in the country, turn-of-the-century Washington had been African America's cultural capital, in part owing to the distinguished presence there of Howard University, founded in 1867. Howard attracted a professional caste. Its professors, along with doctors and government employees, constituted the top of a highly stratified African American society, a rigid hierarchy based on profession as well as income and pigmentation. Just below was the middle class of Pullman porters, butlers, and house servants to the best of white society. At the bottom was the working class of laborers.

Into this caste-conscious Washington world of 1899 was born Edward Kennedy Ellington. His father, James Edward, was a butler who for many years served a well-to-do Rhode Island Avenue doctor, through whom he landed a number of butlering jobs, including service at the Grover Cleveland White House. Later he would work in the blueprints section at the Washington Navy Yard. J. E. had a high-tone style that he imparted to his son. He also bequeathed an urbane and irresistible appeal to the ladies. Very early in life, J. E. married the beautiful but highly principled Daisy Kennedy, the daughter of a half-caste DC policeman, one of forty Negroes on the 1910 force, whose own father was a white Virginia senator. Daisy's mother was part Cherokee, and as a result she was very light-skinned. J. E., however, had a solid brown complexion. Although Ellington tended to move among men and women of light-brown skin, he didn't care for pigeonholing on the basis of skin color and refused to be categorized himself. A debonairly handsome six-feet one-inch, he was going to write his own script for his life. The legendary jazz producer and critic John Hammond, who once chided him for not taking more of an active political stance for the race, believed he "enjoyed mingling with the cream of any social circle."

Another preoccupation—refined early in life—was the pursuit of women. In mid-1918, at nineteen, he married his high school sweetheart, Edna Thompson. The daughter of two educators from the top drawer of their segregated society, Edna was a dancer who was captivated by Duke's early music. It was a shotgun wedding. Early the following year, their son Mercer was born.

Ellington had initially considered a career in fine art, but in early 1917 another ambition took possession. A piano player since age seven, he quit high school three months before graduation to start playing professionally. Capitalizing on the nationwide acceptance of public dancing based on African American steps like the foxtrot, made popular by Vernon and Irene Castle, Ellington soon started a youth dance band, complete with his own booking agency. As a leader of a band, he could mingle with highest society, not as a servant but as an entertainer, a vocation that would give him more control over his life. Whereas a butler could never hope to command attention, a society bandleader could. Should fame and fortune come his way, he might even command respect.

Ellington's band would indeed benefit from the dance craze that had arrived with pre–World War I ragtime, the music of the bordello and the antecedent of jazz. The instrument of ragtime was the piano, and Ellington himself said he was raised in the school of parlor piano playing. He never credited himself as a technically brilliant piano player, however. His art was a balance of instrumentalist, composer, and bandleader. Billy Strayhorn, his partner in composing and arranging, famously maintained that Duke's real instrument was his band.

As an entertainer, Ellington knew how to read and play to his audience. Fingers dancing on any keyboard, he fully appreciated how stage theatricality could enhance the liberating impact of his music. An early tutor in this regard was Luckey Roberts, a New York stride pianist who came through Washington in the early twenties. A successful society bandleader whose music was an influence on George Gershwin and who later wrote the Glenn Miller hit "Moonlight Cocktail," Roberts was a mannered showman who would throw his hands away from the piano to accentuate various moments in a passage. From Roberts, Ellington said, he got the idea to play with "flashy hands."

By the early twenties, Ellington and his up-tempo dance band were making significant money and garnering local fame playing society balls, embassy parties, and Virginia hunt club dances. Yet the real action for African Americans appeared to be happening somewhere other than in stifling Washington. As Langston Hughes wrote in his autobiography, as opposed to the segregated Washington, in the New York of the twenties he—a Negro—had "sat beside white people in theaters and movie houses and neither they nor I appeared to suffer." In New York, Ellington saw, he could be more than just a colored dance-band leader. After initial forays to Manhattan, he relocated in 1923, arriving just as the Harlem Renaissance was entering full flower. If Langston Hughes was Harlem's interpreter in word, Ellington would prove to be its interpreter in music.

In the 1920s, Harlem eclipsed Washington as the nation's African American population—and cultural—center. Whereas the rigid Washington caste system within the black community was entwined with the professions, Harlem was a magnet for those in the arts and letters and was thus more fluid.

Harlem was home to the so-called New Negro movement, espoused in a 1925 essay (and later book) entitled "The New Negro," by Howard professor, sociologist, and critic Alain LeRoy Locke. An Oxford Rhodes scholar from Harvard and later student of aesthetics in Berlin, Locke celebrated the African American heritage and promulgated the idea that the Negro elites in Harlem would lead their race into a new era through the transformative power of art.

Ellington's art was jazz, but for much of his early career, the American public regarded the music as a low-class form of entertainment, and as a result he didn't especially like the term. To his mind *jazz* represented discrimination and categorization that reinforced a racial and economic ghetto for African Americans. He preferred the term *Negro music* and saw his ultimate calling as that music's most serious composer. When white society came to Harlem in the twenties for its encounter with primitivist chic, however, the music was simply called jazz.

Writing on the 1955 Newport Jazz Festival for the *New York Daily News*, award-winning society reporter Inez Calloway Robb (a.k.a. Nancy Randolph) divined in the audience a long dormant intimacy with the jazz of those heady days of Harlem nights. "Some of Newport's middle-aged millionaires must have remembered how they enjoyed youthful excursions to Harlem, in the great days of the Cotton Club, the Nest, and the Sugar Cane on Fifth near 135th."

"The Sugar Cane Club is a narrow subterranean passageway about twenty-five feet wide and 125 feet long," wrote Wallace Thurman, an African American from Salt Lake City who was part of Langston Hughes's literary set:

> Rough wooden tables, surrounded by rough wooden chairs, and the orchestra stands, jammed into the right wall center, use up about three-quarters of the space. The remaining rectangular area is bared for dancing. With a capacity for seating about one hundred people, it usually finds room on gala nights for twice that many. The orchestra weeps and moans and groans as only an unsophisticated Negro Jazz orchestra can. A blues singer croons vulgar ditties over the tables to individual parties or else wah-wahs husky syncopated blues songs from the center of the floor. Her act over, the white lights are extinguished, red and blue spot lights are centered on the diminutive dancing space, couples push back their chairs, squeeze out from behind the tables and from against the wall, then finding one another's bodies, sweat gloriously together, with shoulders hunched, limbs obscenely intertwined and hips wiggling; animal beings urged on by liquor and music and physical contact.

In 1956, Ellington would come to Newport and play for an audience that would include scores of swells and flappers in their fifties and sixties, who still had similar music-inspired memories of the Jazz Age ready to be quickened.

Returning, though, to the 1920s: in 1924 Ellington's band, the Washingtonians, began to play dances on the New England circuit, which led to a number of society engagements. Spring and summer road trips continued into the rest of the decade in between their regular bookings in midtown where they played on Broadway and Forty-ninth at the Hollywood Club, later renamed the Club Kentucky. Here Ellington's regional reputation benefited from CBS broadcasts via a WHN radio wire.

In late 1926 Ellington secured a new band manager: song plugger Irving Mills, among whose clients was Hoagy Carmichael, best remembered for "Stardust," the most recorded song of the century. While Ellington had had some nine previous recording sessions as an accompanist, within the month Mills got him a studio date to record his first signature tune, "East St. Louis Toodle-Oo." That first issue, on the Vocalion label, was an electric recording with a microphone, a relatively new technology that was an advance over acoustic recording using a horn.

Ellington's 1927 summer road trip through New England brought him again to Newport. In July he played two nights at the Newport Beach Pavilion in a "battle of music" that on the second night was against Ray Stewartson and his Broadway Orchestra. The following night he appeared at the town's Colonial Theatre. On his return to New York, Mills landed the band a contract with Victor, a label that within two years would have significant reach by virtue of its acquisition by RCA, a corporate parent with its own radio network, NBC. The first session was in October.

Ellington was now enjoying a solid New York reputation. Bootlegger Owney Madden, a gangster from Yorkshire, England, with mob connections in Chicago, had been running a Harlem club since 1923 and needed a new band. He and his backers wanted Ellington's. A deal was arranged. In December 1927 Ellington opened his first show at Madden's establishment, the famed Cotton Club. The club was on the second floor of 644 Lexington Avenue at the corner of West 142nd Street. Its entrance motif was a log cabin. Inside, the decor aped a southern plantation with bales of cotton strewn around the walls. Viennese architect Joseph Urban, designer for the New York Metropolitan and Boston operas and the Ziegfeld Follies, designed the sets from which African American entertainers would emerge to entertain a high-tone white-only clientele. The Cotton Club was a segregated establishment. As such, it was not universally popular in Harlem, despite its international fame.

The club featured two floor shows a night—midnight and 2 A.M., when Harlem came to life. According to Lena Horne, who was a chorus-line dancer at the club in the early thirties, the shows "had a primitive naked quality that was supposed to make a civilized audience lose its inhibitions." Its singer-dancers were promoted as "the cream of sepia talent, the greatest array of Creole stars, supported by a chorus of bronze beauties." The girls were all tall and stunningly beautiful.

Ellington did not win immediate critical acclaim, however. Owners and audiences were not accustomed to what one critic characterized as his "weird" sounds. Capitalizing on the primitivist chic and the vicariously exotic floor shows, he quickly arranged and wrote what he repackaged as "jungle music," and eventually his performances began to take.

In his Cotton Club compositions, he refined the theatricality in his music to convey powerfully subliminal moods of sensuality and longing. Often he would color his arrangements by juxtaposing a growling trumpet with a dark sax. Behind these solos his orchestration would provide additional tone colors for development.

To separate him from other bandleaders, Mills fashioned a PR strategy around the Duke in Ellington and began presenting him as a composer-conductor of genius, with all the aristocratic airs associated with the name. The aura around him thus grew. In September 1929 Ellington was into his fifth Cotton Club revue. Among his regular patrons was William S. Paley, CBS radio network chief. Paley had CBS put a wire from WHN into the club before the year was out, and soon his network was carrying Ellington live coast to coast, as it had done with him regionally from the Hollywood several years before. By 1930 Ellington's orchestra was being broadcast by a number of different radio stations and networks, including New York's WABC and Paley's rival, NBC, on both its popular-music Red Network and the more upscale Blue Network.

Ellington's personal appeal extended to downtown Park Avenue women who, by the account of one Cotton Club chorus girl, could not keep their hands off him. It was, however, one petite dancer who performed in the opening duo in the fifth revue who succeeded in getting under his skin, an attractive and assured coffee-complexioned beauty from Boston whose name was Mildred Dixon.

Ellington's marriage to Edna was already on the rocks. Mercer Ellington later maintained that his father's 1929 affair with his costar in the short film *Black and Tan,* the gorgeous and talented mulatto actress Fredi Washington, was the real cause of the final breakup. In any event, Ellington left Edna for Dixon, and soon they were settled in Sugar Hill, the high-tone end of Harlem, where he brought Mercer, his parents, and his younger sister Ruth.

When not playing the Cotton Club, Ellington took to playing the vaudeville theaters around New York. His was the first colored band to play the Paramount Theater on Times Square. At the Brooklyn Paramount in 1932 and other such venues, he employed a scrim curtain behind which his band appeared as a shadowy form from another world—the Harlem of inviting mystery. "He was always very conscious of the need to make the listener *feel* experiences with the sound," wrote Mercer Ellington, "almost as though he were creating apparitions within the music."

Fredi Washington, with Arthur Whetsol (left) and Duke Ellington. Still from 1929 film *Black and Tan.* ::: *Courtesy of the Institute of Jazz Studies, Rutgers University.*

His Cotton Club engagements ran until early 1931, although he would return for limited runs over the next two years. That year he embarked on his first national tour, which included feature-film work in Hollywood. He and the band went by train on two private coaches, plus baggage car. At numerous stops fans familiar with his music from the radio broadcasts would meet the train. Ellington was a star by now, making almost as much money as white big-bandleaders Paul Whiteman and Guy Lombardo.

John Hammond in the thirties. ::: *Photo by New York swing era photographer Otto F. Hess. Milt Gabler Papers, Archives Center, National Museum of American History, Smithsonian Institution.*

In 1932 he released "It Don't Mean a Thing If It Ain't Got That Swing," a title that anticipated the swing era by several years. Once embraced, swing would become the commercial form of jazz that would be America's popular music for at least the next ten years. Ellington, however, was not at the cutting edge of the swing phenomenon, at least not for the Lindy Hoppers who frequented ballrooms such as Harlem's Savoy and the Roseland, on West Fifty-second Street. At the outset his band differed from the swing bands in his use of a rhythm section that served to color his music, not drive it.

By 1936, popular music was moving ahead without him, and new stars were rising. A thirty-year-old talent scout and producer with Columbia Records, John Henry Hammond II, a Yale graduate whose mother was a Vanderbilt, heard a band at Kansas City's Reno Club and later that year brought it to New York for a stint at the Roseland. The band was William "Count" Basie and his orchestra, whose All-American Rhythm Section featured drummer Jo Jones, bassist Walter Page, guitarist Freddie Green, and the Count himself on piano.

According to Hammond, Ellington felt threatened by Basie, whose beat was what the dancers wanted. For the most part they were kids and young singles escaping their homes for the ballrooms to cavort with members of the opposite sex. They were not into the musical subtlety proffered by the likes of Ellington, who had honed his craft playing for the Harlem sophisticates. Basie's rhythm section underpinned his great soloists, tenor saxophonist Lester Young and trumpeters Buck Clayton and Harry "Sweets" Edison, whom he allowed free rein to work unwritten head arrangements and blow for several choruses.

Duke Ellington at the 1938 Randall's Island concert, where his performance of "Diminuendo and Crescendo in Blue" generated a "riotous reaction." ::: *Frank Driggs Collection of Duke Ellington Photographic Reference Prints, Archives Center, National Museum of American History, Smithsonian Institution.*

Ellington's year to embrace swing was 1937. He reprised his Cotton Club engagements at the club's new location downtown on Broadway and Forty-eighth at what had been the Palais Royale, Paul Whiteman's famous venue. In a March battle of the bands before a record crowd at the Savoy, he matched house bandleader and drummer Chick Webb. Among the new songs he wrote that year was a two-side 78-rpm called "Diminuendo and Crescendo in Blue," recorded in September.

Eight months later, New York disc jockey Martin Block hosted a "Carnival of Swing," a six-hour outdoor festival at the Randall's Island East River Island Stadium. New York was in the midst of a swing frenzy, fresh from Goodman's earlier engagements at the Paramount and the "Battles of the Bands" at the Savoy. Among the twenty-five featured acts, a crowd of twenty-five thousand heard Count Basie, Chick Webb, Gene Krupa, Woody Herman, and Duke Ellington. Film footage of the event shows a mixed-race audience on their feet for Basie. The British music tabloid *Melody Maker,* however, labeled Ellington's performance of one number as the occasion's "biggest thrill," one that generated a "riotous reaction":

About ten persons jumped from the grandstands onto the field, and taking this cue, three thousand other enthusiasts swarmed the field from the tier seats in an effort to get near the stage, creating turbulent havoc with the field attendants.

At the conclusion of the selection, with hundreds more pouring from the stands, Martin Block announced that unless order was restored and people returned to their seats the concert would be concluded immediately. A call was put in for extra policemen and the session was delayed about ten minutes.

The *New York Times* reported the incident in a similar vein: "Then Duke Ellington began sending his 'Diminuendo and Crescendo in Blue,' and a pair of little Brooklyn girls, wearing beer jackets with swing jargon written all over them, ran screaming onto the cinder track to Lindy Hop. . . . Ivie Anderson tore off the 'St. Louis Blues,' leaping high into the air and smacking Duke on the back. The bull-fiddler 'smacked his doghouse' till it groaned, the boys were all jiving and the crowd was like jelly."

With his 1938 performance of "Diminuendo and Crescendo in Blue," Ellington proved he could deliver the goods to the swing generation—a new white audience altogether, younger, urban, less social, more democratic. He had returned to capitalizing on his primal ability: getting an audience to move.

Duke Ellington and Beatrice Evie Ellis. ::: *Duke Ellington Collection, Archives Center, National Museum of American History, Smithsonian Institution.*

Ellington's life was primed to move in other ways, as well. In 1937 he met another chorus girl, the beautiful Beatrice "Evie" Ellis. Originally from Chicago, she had joined the chorus at the downtown Cotton Club, where she appeared with Lena Horne; Louis Armstrong's wife, Lucille; and Johnny Hodge's wife, Cue. Ellington left Mildred Dixon for Evie, who would come to be his lifetime companion.

On tour through Pittsburgh that same year, Ellington encountered another who would play a central part in his life: a twenty-three-year-old composer, Billy Strayhorn. At once shy and confident, Strayhorn was polite, almost cherubic, a gifted composer-arranger whose maternal grandmother had been General Robert E. Lee's cook. Ellington was immediately impressed by Strayhorn's ability to play his music on the piano note for note, imitating even his inflections. The same

Billy Strayhorn. ::: *Duke Ellington Collection, Archives Center, National Museum of American History, Smithsonian Institution.*

appeared true for his compositions. In particular, he was struck by Strayhorn's lyrically poignant "Lush Life."

Strayhorn followed Ellington to New York. The relationship between the two was assured by Ellington's ultimate desire to transcend his origins as a dance-band leader to become a composer of long works. His compositions had always been collaborative, in particular with his musicians who, for example, would contribute the odd riff from which a song would spring with a shared credit. Strayhorn, who could provide much more with full orchestrations, would write Ellington's next theme tune: "Take the A Train."

In 1940 Ellington had reason to change record labels. His sometime nemesis, John Hammond, had come to Columbia/Brunswick/Vocalion the year before to lead its jazz division as part of the CBS acquisition of the label. Ellington not only chafed at Hammond's domineering manner, but he was especially resentful of his criticism that he distanced himself from "the troubles of his people or of mankind." Ellington thus left for rival RCA Victor, for which he had earlier recorded.

Over the next few years, he would find himself at what many critics regard as the musical peak of his career: the era of the so-called Blanton-Webster band, which would inspire many new compositions. In 1939 Jimmy Blanton, a twenty-one-year-old bassist, arrived with a youthful energy and fluid bass lines to put added drive into Duke's rhythm section. Ben Webster, a breathy tenor saxophonist, renowned for his textured vibrato, joined in 1940. Initially a Coleman Hawkins disciple, he came under the spell of Johnny Hodges to fashion his own voice. Said by his one-time pianist and arranger Dick Katz to be "as rhythmically sophisticated as Charlie Parker," Webster was the first and best of Duke's tenor soloists, one of the greatest swing tenor soloists of his day and often imitated. He was a quirky talent who was let go in 1943. One night Ellington had allowed him to play piano with the band, but he stayed too long at the keyboard, angering the maestro. When Ellington refused to discuss the matter, Webster took a knife, shredded one of Duke's best suits, and left. He would return briefly for a stint in 1948 and 1949.

The Blanton-Webster band could swing with riff patterns that rivaled Basie's. In March 1940, a week after Ellington's contract expired with Columbia, the band had its first two Victor sessions in Chicago. A third took place in Hollywood in May. One of the two songs recorded was "Cotton Tail." From the first bar Blanton's throbbing bass drove the swing piece, which featured along with a celebrated reed chorus a Webster solo that jumped and wailed. Webster's studio performance made him a star. Later at concerts, fans would demand that he reprise the solo exactly as on the record. Indeed, many reed players were so struck by Webster's attack that they learned the solo note for note. For some emergent New York jazz musicians, "Cotton Tail" was a bright marker on a musical trail that led beyond swing to a new kind of sound soon to be known as bebop.

Bop was born when Dizzy Gillespie teamed his trumpet with Charlie Parker's alto sax. Together they participated in after-hours Harlem jam sessions at Minton's Playhouse with Thelonious Monk, drummer Kenny Clarke, and others. Beboppers were a new generation of jazz musicians. Some twenty years Ellington's juniors, they did not aspire to appeal to dancers or to the larger music and entertainment industry. Their movement was a reaction to commercialization and World War II. They resented the perceived white theft of African American music, as well as a draft that expected them to risk their lives by fighting against a racist enemy in Europe while accepting continued segregation in America. Their music was highly introspective and aspired to communicate only to an intensely inner-directed set of jazz fans, never more than a fraction of the African American audience.

Ellington's music certainly had introspective elements, compared to other swing arrangements, but in the forties, riding the crest of a popular-music wave, he wasn't inclined to embrace bop and remain a leader of the jazz avant-garde. Wartime on the home front would not prove easy. Although the war years were lucrative for Ellington, touring a succession of one-nighters would become an increasing hardship. The military requisitioned Pullman cars for troop transports. The last Blanton-Webster recording session was in July 1942. Two days later, Blanton died from a lingering tuberculosis.

The following day, the American Federation of Musicians (AFM) instituted a recording ban in its effort to get its members royalties for each record sold. RCA Victor refused to settle with the union until November 1944. As a result Ellington, along with others in the Victor stable, did not record until December—a sixteen-month hiatus. To a degree he was able to keep in the public eye by recording sixteen-inch transcription discs for radio broadcast that included seventy-nine V-Discs for the Armed Forces Radio Service. The wartime ban and a subsequent union action in 1948 sounded the death knell for most big bands and for swing as the popular music form. Some eight major orchestras had folded in 1946. Only the Basie and Ellington bands and a few others survived.

When the war ended in August 1945, Ellington was forty-six, and popular music was moving in yet another direction: toward the big solo singer. Above all was the bobby-soxer idol and heir to Bing Crosby, Francis Albert Sinatra, the skinny kid from Hoboken, New Jersey, who excelled at investing a lyric with inviting emotion. The movement spread. In the mid-to-late forties and into the fifties, war-weary white adults embraced the nonthreatening and mellifluous music of the likes of crooners Mel Torme, Perry Como, and Dick Haymes, along with female singers Jo Stafford, Peggy Lee, and Patti Page—all of whom had sung for the big bands and then left for solo careers. By the start of the fifties, the top female soloists were the pretty blondes Doris Day, whose wartime classic "Sentimental Journey" had launched her career, and Rosemary Clooney, who entered the charts in 1951 with her first number-one hit, a rearranged Armenian folk song, "Come on-a My House."

Meanwhile, jazz segmented into traditional jazz and bebop. Throughout the forties young African American dancers were embracing the latest iteration of race music, going under the marketing label rhythm and blues and defined by jump R&B artists like Louis Jordan, Joe Liggins, Wynonie Harris, and the Orioles. The music trends notwithstanding, Ellington won in 1947 the tenth *Down Beat* band poll in the swing and sweet categories. He had also won the magazine's swing polls in 1940, 1943, and 1945. Yet he was now struggling to find an audience. His recordings were not in tune with the mass market. Now having to watch his bottom line, he needed royalties from recording to support payroll. After the war he had struggled to find a label to promote him and the right producer to capture his sound. When his Victor contract expired, he left in May 1946 for Oliver Sabin's Musicraft Records. A year later the label hit the wall financially. Ellington took a buyout and returned to Columbia, once more an attractive proposition, especially since John Hammond had left the year before. Unfortunately, once the second AFM recording ban went into effect, Ellington wasn't able to get into a studio for eight months, prompting some bitterness toward the label.

Another obstacle was changing demographics. In the 1950s fewer nightclubs and juke joints were operating because wartime swing audiences had matured and moved to the suburbs. Ellington's fans were aging with him. The suburbanites were raising children, donning their gray flannel suits, and becoming organization men. He was now in the midst of what would be almost a decade of hard slogging to keep his career and band going. The day-to-day dynamics of leading a band had changed. Before the war the band had traveled in Pullmans, with Ellington among the musicians, eating, drinking, and playing cards—just one of the guys. After the war the band went by bus, with Ellington riding separately by car. Initially he rode with his bop clarinetist Jimmy Hamilton until he shifted to traveling by Cadillac with his baritone sax player Harry Carney, who had been with him since the twenties. Knowing Carney to be steady, well-behaved, and organized, Ellington appreciated their long periods of silence on the road together, which allowed him to think and create. The shift was a manifestation: Duke was growing aloof.

As for his band, the older members had married. Emotionally, some were choosing to invest more in their families than in their music careers. In an editorial about-face in a June 1949 issue, *Down Beat* ran an article headlined "Duke Should Disband." His band, according to the author, was a "disgrace to the man who heads it and the men who play in it."

Most engagements were now one-night stands. Ellington would book his band into second-rate hotels to play gyms, Elks Clubs, African American college fraternities and sororities—even segregated gigs in the South. Two tours in 1951 drew bitter protest from local NAACP chapters. Ellington indignantly justified his segregated performances, citing his need to keep his band employed. Notwithstanding the bickering, he continued to send the national organization money.

Ellington paid his men guaranteed salaries, whether an audience showed or not. A raise, however, was not automatic, and his bandsmen had to pay their own expenses on the road. His sidemen, once they gained repute, could now make more money fronting their own small groups. Not surprisingly, the turnover of chairs intensified. For those who remained, the fatigue and the pressure could lead to the best performances—or the worst. At the beginning of the decade Ellington had finally lost Ben Webster. In 1951 the slide worsened. His signature alto saxophonist Johnny Hodges left, lured away by the dynamic jazz impresario and record producer Norman Granz. With him went trombonist Lawrence Brown, and together they teamed with another recent departure, Duke's longtime former drummer, Sonny Greer. Minus Webster, Hodges, Greer, and Brown, Ellington had lost much of his continuity and was forced to look to the future—and find a sound that was moving with it. The time had come to incorporate bop into his music.

The boppers had captured the intellectual college set. A predominantly white variant of bop had come to the fore on the West Coast: cool jazz. Its practitioners were incorporating classical elements into jazz and deemphasizing rhythm in an effort to get the music taken seriously by highbrows. On May 3, 1951, Ellington opened a three-week run at bop's home: Birdland at Fifty-second and Broadway. His was the first big band to play the celebrated bop venue, although he followed Basie, who had just played there with one of his reduced lineups. *Down Beat* tagged Duke's band "a powerful, rocking enthusiastic bunch of musicians." Other reviews were good, based on the critics' reaction to his new drummer, Louis Bellson, and Ellington was booked there again in late June, the first of a series of extended return engagements.

Ellington's abiding and ultimate aspiration was to create long compositions. Within the confines of popular music, such creations were "beyond category," the term Billy Strayhorn applied to Ellington himself. The long-playing record, Columbia's great postwar recording technology, he saw as a means to feature his longer works. "He always wanted a hit single again," said his Columbia producer of the time, George Avakian. "He never got one when he was recording at Columbia with me, but he also wanted to get more of his long compositions on record which the company had not been interested in before, because they didn't mean anything in record sales."

Ellington's first LP was the 1950 *Masterpieces by Ellington,* featuring uncut concert arrangements. The following year he recorded *Ellington Uptown*. Both releases gave him opportunities to feature extended works using high-fidelity technology. Avakian was producer for both albums. "I quickly realized when there was all this stuff about hi-fi, hi-fi, hi-fi that the most exciting sound in jazz could be the Ellington band because it was so rich in color, so I began exploiting that." The track that "really took off in that album was one that I didn't produce," said Avakian. It was of drummer Louis Bellson's showpiece "Skin Deep," a recording that was a "master purchase" from the Mercer label, which had many of Duke's "private catalog" recordings. Engineers recorded "Skin Deep" after hours in a Fresno, California, ballroom.

Unfortunately, sales on both were sluggish, and Ellington decided that only hits would enable him to keep his band. Avakian attempted to pitch the idea of Ellington as a hit maker to Mitch Miller, Columbia's singles director. Miller wasn't interested. When Avakian repeatedly asked Miller to release a single for promotional purposes, he would just say, "George, you're taking attention away from Rosemary Clooney [or Tony Bennett or Guy Mitchell]." Avakian would reply, "But you know this is a way we get air play for the albums." Miller was unmoved.

By now, Ellington was frustrated with both major labels—RCA Victor and Columbia—feeling that neither was prepared to promote him aggressively. He left Columbia with time still to run on his contract and in early 1953 signed with Capitol. Although more a pop than a jazz label, Capitol was known for aggressive promotion and contacts with disc jockeys. It was a hit-singles label that had worked well for the likes of Peggy Lee, Woody Herman, Frank Sinatra, and Nat "King" Cole. His new producer was Kansas City's Dave Dexter, who later as head of international artists and repertoire signed the Beatles to the label.

Ellington's first session for Dexter produced "Satin Doll," a song that benefited from a collaboration with Strayhorn and Johnny Mercer. It became a jazz standard, and the royalties helped support his band through the next three lean years. Ellington looked for another singles hit, but it was not to be. Taking a leaf from Mitch Miller's book of novelty-tune hit strategies, he and Dexter next thought of capitalizing on the then-current mambo dance craze. According to Ellington's nephew, Michael James, who toured with the band as a youth and remained personal friends with many of the band members, "Duke would pick up a trend and do his version of it." However, his short-lived mambo phase would prove to be a period of recording lows.

For the next two years, the Ellington band mostly played dances for older audiences and college proms. In a September 1952 *Metronome,* Ellington had conveyed his frustration with the shift: "It's getting to be more a business than an art, isn't it? 'Dance music' is now little more than what we have always called the 'business man's bounce.' We're getting instructions on how to play for dances from heads of college prom committees. They like medium dance tempos . . . not too loud. At least it's a change for us and that's fine. Sometimes though, our followers want to hear some of the things with which we have been associated. I refer them back to the committee. Usually some compromise is effected."

Throughout the early fifties the pace on the road had been exhausting, and the money was not what it had been. Biographer John Hasse noted that in 1954, for example, Chicago's Blue Note (one of his favorite venues) booked Ellington's band for $5,000 a week—the same fee as in 1931, when the cost of living was 43 percent less. Worst of all, Duke was getting scant public recognition.

In July 1955 Ellington was an emcee at the second Newport Jazz Festival. For that year's program he wrote a piece called "The Future of Jazz." In it he prophesied, "Rock and roll is the most raucous form of jazz, beyond a doubt; it maintains a link with the folk origins, and I believe that no other form of jazz has ever been accepted so enthusiastically by so many. . . . I have written a number of rock and roll things myself, but am saving them for possible use in a show." It would not be at that festival, however. While he was reportedly booked to appear at Newport that year, in truth he was playing elsewhere—at the Aquacades in Flushing Meadows, New York.

The Aquacades, an eight-thousand-seat amphitheater, was originally a feature of the 1939 World's Fair. Produced by famed impresario Billy Rose, it was the hit show with a water spectacular starring such swimmers as Johnny Weismuller, Buster Crabbe, and America's most famous aquanaut, Eleanor Holm. After the fair, the amphitheater served as a public swimming pool (named after Gertrude Ederle, a Flushing resident who was the first woman to swim the English Channel), as well as a venue for shows and concerts, including Eliot Murphy's Aquacade.

In June 1955 Ellington began a six-week stint as second on the bill to the water fountain display, "Dancing Waters." To his band, management added a women's harp and string section to provide background music for ice skaters, dancing exhibitions, and comedians. Four of his regular musicians were unable to play because they did not carry local union cards, and five New York studio musicians substituted. "The band had to be broken up," recalled trombonist John Sanders. "Britt [Woodman] went home to L.A., and Ward Silloway, a studio man, played first trombone." At the end of the two-hour evening, Ellington would come onstage, relieving his stand-in pianist Woody Kessler, formerly of the Sammy Kaye Orchestra, to finish the evening's performance playing a medley.

The Aquacades booking is generally regarded as the nadir of Ellington's career. It was, said trumpeter Clark Terry some years ago, a "stupid, senseless gig." In 2005, however, Terry recalled it differently. "The place was packed. It was a godsend, because we were glad to get off the road." Ellington's nephew Michael James had another take on the booking. "What the band didn't know was the reason why Duke took the gig. Maestro was trying to get a show on Broadway [an unproduced play script, *The Man with Four Sides*].

It was a place to park the band so he could be on the scene in New York for two months." In late August, in fact, Ellington got *The Man with Four Sides* aired on the NBC Monitor radio program.

Jazz historian and critic Dan Morgenstern offered a third view: "If you look at it from the perspective of the big band story in general, [Ellington] stands out . . . heroically because he kept on going. . . . That was the way that you survived. I mean, even Benny Goodman, he played in bowling alleys." At the Aquacades in the summer of 1955, Ellington was playing to those once-frenzied Brooklyn teenagers who seventeen years before had reacted riotously at Randall's Island but were now parents in their thirties in Flushing. Heroic or not, Duke Ellington's career was on life support.

3

Duke's Instrument

The '56 Band

Ellington's Newport '56 orchestra was as classic as his Blanton-Webster band of the early forties. This ensemble was anchored by the remarkable musicians who'd been with him since the twenties, thirties, and forties swing. At the same time it could foray into bop, rhythm and blues, and beyond, thanks to the gifted members of a second generation, who brought youthful energy and drive, all of which Maestro fashioned into compositions and performances that could take an audience anywhere.

As is well known, Ellington composed for the person, not the instrument. Through sixteen individual personalities and experiences, the '56 band could interpret and express the broadest of repertoires to refrain any time in jazz history. A night's performance featured each musician in moments where he could paint an image or picture to provide a texture, tone, or mood, which Ellington used to build an audience up or bring it down, to put it in a reflective frame of mind or make it expressive. Whether simply in phrases from their perches or in solos or full numbers at the mike, the musicians had opportunities to conjure apparitions of sophisticated ladies, tell stories about teas for two, or voice moods of having it bad. Throughout the evening they spoke, sometimes in whispers, other times in shouts, but always with tasteful theatricality. Whether in solos, ensembles, or the full band, they conversed in a dialogue akin to a stage play scripted by a master. Indeed, these great personalities in the '56 band were as varied and archetypal as the characters of Shakespeare's opus.

In August 1955, the day before his band's last performance of the Aquacades run, Duke Ellington got a call from a former band member, Johnny Hodges. Ellington's longtime alto

Johnny Hodges at the Savoy Ballroom. ::: *Duke Ellington Collection, Archives Center, National Museum of American History, Smithsonian Institution.*

sax star wanted to return to the fold. The return of Johnny Hodges can be said to be the beginning of Duke's comeback. The sharp edge of Duke Ellington, Hodges was the soloist who could cut to the quick of an audience and separate soul from body.

Hodges had been in the band the longest. Ellington had first met him while on his summer '26 New England tour. Born into a middle-class African American family from Boston's South End, he had studied at the New England Conservatory of Music. His style was influenced by one of Ellington's heroes, the uniquely inspired Sidney Bechet. In 1924 the New Orleans Creole clarinetist and soprano saxophonist had come to Boston, and Hodges managed to gig with him. Bechet recommended the gifted teenager to stride pianist Willie "The Lion" Smith, who offered him a temporary job in New York. For the next several years, Hodges moved back and forth between New York and Boston. Ellington routinely offered him jobs on tours and finally got him on his payroll in March 1928, three months into his first series of Cotton Club revues.

Hodges was known as Jeep. Duke called him by his nickname, Rabbit, or Rab. Some accounts have it that the tag came from his liking for lettuce-and-tomato sandwiches. He said it derived from his school days, when as a truant he was known for his fast running. Said by some to have no personality, he was a complex and contradictory individual. At times he was quite friendly; at other times he appeared shy, solitary, and inarticulate, a man of few words or outward emotions. He was, however, highly communicative with his instrument. Despite his conservatory training, he was not a fast read. It was his tone and phrasing that made him distinct and indeed great. Ellington wrote that "his tonal charisma [was] difficult to describe." His sound was lush, velvety, sweet, sensual. He had a poetic way of playing in smears that worked off a bluesy seventh note.

Charlie Parker once paid tribute to Hodges, tagging him "the Lily Pons of the saxophone," comparing him to their contemporary and expressive French coloratura. Others commented that he played to open a woman's bedroom door. At bottom his sound could exquisitely express a recurrent Ellington mood. "Writers talk about Johnny like he was another instrument that Ellington played," said his wife, Cue Hodges, "but he was his own man all the way—with or without Duke. When he made music, he made the music he wanted to, the way he wanted to."

By the mid-thirties Hodges was Ellington's biggest star. His great number was the sultry "Jeep's Blues" that dated from 1938 and was a jukebox hit. His rich alto would influence Ben Webster and complement the latter's tenor during the great years of the Blanton-Webster band. By the mid-forties he had become the highest paid of Ellington's band members, sometimes making even more than Duke himself. After Webster left, Hodges became very protective of his turf and stature. Onstage, when Ellington would recognize him for some display, he would mime the counting of bills. If a band member landed on his note one too many times or started borrowing a riff, he would snipe, "Come out of the kitchen; stop stealing my stuff."

In early 1951 Hodges succumbed to the temptation to make it on his own. The catalyst was impresario and Clef Records owner Norman Granz. Unabashedly, Granz admitted to pinching him, along with trombonist Lawrence Brown and drummer Sonny Greer. He wanted to feature Hodges, believing that Duke was preventing the saxophonist from realizing his full potential as a soloist. Granz was not fond of Ellington. "He was incredibly *égoiste* in the French sense," Granz observed. "So he was really piqued when I took Johnny away."

In their first Clef recording session, Hodges, Brown, and Greer landed a hit: "Castle Rock," a straight twelve-bar blues with a simple riff. Its author and soloist was not Hodges but the tenor sax player, Al Sears, another Ellington veteran. Hodges was more comfortable in the studio than handling the business aspects of fronting a band. Sears stepped into the breach but only for so long. In August 1952 he left the group to launch a solo career and later migrated to rock and roll.

Without Sears, Hodges found himself reverting to his past with Duke. In both studio and performance, he tended to work with other Ellington veterans playing Ellington and Ellington-style material. He was never able to repeat the success of "Castle Rock." "I had my own band and I had to scuffle, and when you scuffle you can't play what you like," he

Harry Carney in the studio. ::: *Duke Ellington Collection, Archives Center, National Museum of American History, Smithsonian Institution.*

Ray Nance. This photo was taken by Chicago photographer Don Bronstein, known for his work with *Playboy*, in addition to work for the Columbia and Checker record labels. Bronstein did some five *Playboy* gatefolds and seventeen LP covers in the fifties and sixties. ::: *Duke Ellington Collection, Archives Center, National Museum of American History, Smithsonian Institution.*

told the British *Melody Maker* in 1958, "but when you are famous and popular you can." Band leading was too much headache for him, and when he lost Lawrence Brown, it was time to quit.

In the spring of 1955 Hodges disbanded and did a stint on "The Ted Steele Show," a dance-party format on New York's WOR-TV. Steele was a songwriter, singing bandleader, and disc jockey, later best recalled as orchestra leader on the TV show "Cavalcade of Stars." He was not progressive. In 1946 he had been the music director at Hollywood radio station KMPC, where he refused to play jazz on the grounds that it contributed to juvenile delinquency. One of the first records banned by the station was Harry "The Hipster" Gibson's "Who Put the Benzedrine in Mrs. Murphy's Ovaltine?"

In short, 1955 was Johnny Hodges's nadir, as well as Ellington's. Whatever his complaint about the money, he was ready to return. Norman Granz made it easy for him. He renewed his recording contract, giving him two to three small-band sessions a year at a rate higher than Ellington's. The saxophonist thus would return to the band with his head held high.

In 1956 Hodges controlled Ellington's sax section and demanded his share of solos. He never played any of the first half of a concert and would give tenor saxophonist Paul Gonsalves the throwaways. Once the night had built, he would come forth to deliver the last word with "I Got It Bad (And That Ain't Good)" and his defining "Jeep's Blues." Making more than any of the band's other musicians, and with his additional income from Granz, he was in no way beholden to the bandleader, and he flaunted the fact. "Johnny was in the spotlight again," recalled valve trombonist John Sanders of the alto's return. When Rab rejoined the band, said bassist Jimmy Woode, "it was a reborn world."

The only member of the band who had logged more years with Duke than Hodges was his fellow South End Bostonian, Harry Carney, three years his junior. Carney was raised some four blocks away, yet their two paths didn't cross until they attended the New England Conservatory of Music, where they had the same teacher. Carney was a clarinet and alto sax player who would later master the baritone sax. In 1926 Ellington and his band were in Boston during their annual summer tour of New England. Duke needed a musician for his booking in nearby Salem, and Carney's teacher recommended the sixteen-year-old. That summer, the youth toured briefly with the band and eventually followed Ellington to New York, joining the reed section permanently for the 1927 New England summer tour.

The baritone sax in the hands of the tractable Carney would anchor the band throughout Ellington's career. By the mid-forties, polls would honor his recognizably weighty baritone. One of the first jazz musicians to master circular breathing, he could hold notes seemingly forever.

In 1940, the year the great Blanton-Webster band entered its stride, Ellington had lost his talented trumpeter Cootie Williams to Benny Goodman. To fill the void, Ellington found a huge stage personality in the versatile Ray Nance, a Southside Chicagoan who had been performing for a few months as a solo act after a couple of years with pianist Horace Henderson. Nance had also played with Henderson's more famous brother, Fletcher, and for pianist Earl "Fatha" Hines. A singer and dancer, Nance played the open, muted, and growl trumpet, as well as the violin.

Jimmy Hamilton later in his career. This photo was taken by Norwalk, Connecticut, photographer Victor Kalin, whose credits also include illustrations for John Coltrane's *A Love Supreme*. ::: *Courtesy of the Institute of Jazz Studies, Rutgers University.*

Immediately on joining the band, Nance gained stardom for blowing the trumpet chorus to "Take the A Train." Given to twirling his instrument onstage for effect, Nance was a cocky star, dubbed Floorshow by fellow band members. His other sobriquet was the Captain. In the fifties he was often in the company of the younger, drug-using

Lucky Millinder (white suit) and his band in 1937. ::: *Courtesy of the Institute of Jazz Studies, Rutgers University.*

members of Ellington's band, tagged the Air Force. Nance was always loose and could get a crowd on its feet and jumping.

Clarinetist Jimmy Hamilton joined Ellington in April 1943 as the bebop movement was gathering steam. Hired to replace Ellington's longtime soloist Barney Bigard, Hamilton had recorded with Billie Holiday and played with alto saxophonist Benny Carter, swing pianist Teddy Wilson's sextet, and the Lucky Millinder Orchestra.

In the 1940s Lucky Millinder's group was a key link in the chain between big band swing and the rhythm and blues influences that would subliminally creep into Ellington's fifties performances via Hamilton and two other Millinder veterans, trombonist Quentin Jackson and trumpeter Cat Anderson. Rhythmically exciting, the Millinder band was a particular hit in Harlem as it moved from swing to jump blues and R&B.

Classically trained, Jimmy Hamilton played with minimum vibrato, using the modern Boehm fingering system. Known among musicians as the author of the arrangements for the bebop standard "How High the Moon," Hamilton was a bop clarinetist with a cool technique, the opposite of the hot New Orleans sound.

To retain some New Orleans color in his reed section, Ellington hired Russell Procope, a lead alto sax man and clarinetist, in April 1946. Procope, raised next door to Benny

Carter in the San Juan Hill district on Manhattan's West Side, had recorded with pianist Jelly Roll Morton and had had successive big band stints with Carter, Chick Webb, and Fletcher Henderson.

With Johnny Hodges taking the lion's share of the alto solos, Procope had to be content serving as a section player. Occasionally he would get clarinet solos. In contrast to the cooler Hamilton, Procope used the older and less familiar Albert fingering system, which added a warm tone to the orchestra. Though rarely in the limelight, he was secure, appreciative, and apparently quite happy with his lot.

Russell Procope. ::: *Photo by Parisian photographer and cellist Herve Derrien. Duke Ellington Collection, Archives Center, National Museum of American History, Smithsonian Institution.*

In 1949 Ellington signed trombonist Quentin "Butter" Jackson. An expert with the plunger mute, Jackson was Ellington's best "wah-wah" trombonist after thirties star Tricky Sam Nanton. He had played with Don Redman's Orchestra and later, for eight years, with Cab Calloway, as well as for a time with Lucky Millinder. Occasionally soloing for Redman and Calloway, Jackson was effective for Ellington equally as a soloist and in his ensemble work.

Ellington had entered the fifties struggling to find a sound that would keep him in tune with the tastes of his public. To that end he began to seek younger musicians from a new generation. In September 1950 he booked Paul Gonsalves, a tenor saxophonist fresh from a year with Dizzy Gillespie and who had also played with Basie.

Quentin "Butter" Jackson. ::: *Photo by Parisian photographer and cellist Herve Derrien. Duke Ellington Collection, Archives Center, National Museum of American History, Smithsonian Institution.*

"When Hodges left," said Duke Ellington's eldest nephew Michael James, "Paul got the extended soloing. And when Rab returned, he would get the ballads again, but [Hodges] was older and had stopped doing the up-tempo pieces. So those stayed with Paul."

A Cape Verdean American from Pawtucket, Rhode Island, Gonsalves had an extroverted saxophone style with a solid drive. "Paul's idol was Hawk [Coleman Hawkins] for his breathing," said James, who was sometimes his roommate during many of his times on the road with the band. "He always told me that his main influences were Hawk, Ben [Webster], and [Don] Byas." The latter tenor star, equally seminal, but less well known, succeeded Lester Young in the Basie band, also had a stint with Millinder but expatriated to Europe in 1946, where he was a most influential on-scene presence. At heart Gonsalves was into romantic ballads and played with a warm breathiness reminiscent of Webster. Gonsalves himself reckoned that Duke hired him because he knew all Webster's solos.

Although he had a great love for Basie's swing and Gillespie's modernism, Gonsalves soon found that he could explore the full range of the jazz genre with Ellington. Appreciating how the Ellington opus could stretch him as a musician, he once referred to his early years with the bandleader as his "jazz class."

Gonsalves's solos were harmonically advanced, and his swing solos could incorporate some phrasing from rhythm and blues. This drift acquired some urgency in late 1955, when Johnny Hodges returned to the Ellington fold and started reclaiming his lock on ballads. Gonsalves then sought to distinguish himself from Hodges by drawing on the influence of Cannonball Adderley, an alto sax player who could play in a wailing style that excited dancing and celebration.

Three months after signing Gonsalves, Ellington rehired the high-note trumpet player William "Cat" Anderson, who had been with his orchestra from 1944 to 1947. Orphaned at age four, Anderson first learned trumpet while at the Jenkins Orphanage in Charleston, South Carolina, where he acquired his nickname from his fighting style. Going professional, he toured with the Carolina Cotton Pickers, with whom he made his recording debut, and from there gravitated to Lucky Millinder, Lionel Hampton's band, and later Boston pianist and bandleader Sabby Lewis.

With Ellington, Anderson—like many others—came into his own. Now he could play the full range of his instrument, using half-valve and various plunger-mute techniques and achieving fine tones in both the lower and upper registers. He was best known as a high-note player, and Ellington often used that pyrotechnic skill to predictable effect on an audience, perhaps to a fault. Anderson could hit a double C on his solos. It was said, "one note higher and only a dog could hear him." At Newport '56 it was his trumpet that finished "Diminuendo and Crescendo in Blue."

In February 1951 the band was playing the Thunderbird in Las Vegas when Ellington found a trombone replacement for Lawrence Brown. Britt Woodman was a musician from L.A.'s Central Avenue jazz scene. He had played for the Les Hite Orchestra, once the house band for the Culver City Cotton Club, which sported the same kind of theatricality as its New York namesake. From a musical family, Woodman was an adept technician and interpreter, both as a section player and a soloist, and knew his way around a variety of subgenres. He had a lifelong association with virtuoso Charles Mingus that began before the war, when as a teenager the future bassist came to him for tutoring on the trombone.

Clark Terry. ::: *Photo by Don Bronstein. Duke Ellington Collection, Archives Center, National Museum of American History, Smithsonian Institution.*

After launching into bop at Birdland in May 1951, Duke hired Clark Terry, an accomplished musician who had versed himself in the genre. A trumpeter from the trumpet-playing town of St. Louis, the versatile Terry fashioned his first wind instrument from a funnel and a garden hose. His inspiration came from the "King of the Cornet," the flamboyant Charlie Creath. Having trained for the ring with turn-of-the-century middleweight contender Kid Carter, Terry had thought of becoming a professional boxer before the war, until he found that lip injuries hampered his trumpet playing. In wartime he continued developing his chops as a bandsman for the U.S. Navy, emerging in the late forties to play for Basie until he folded his big band. A soloist in both bop and swing, he was a member of the youthful side of the Ellington band and could articulate a happy sound with his horn, reflecting his own light and witty disposition.

Four days after hiring Terry, Duke attracted bop trumpeter Willie Cook, another veteran from Dizzy Gillespie's band. Nicknamed Ool-Ya-Koo after a Gillespie record, Cook was born in Tangipahoa, Louisiana, and had moved with his family to East Chicago when

John Sanders. ::: *Photo by Roy DeCarava. Duke Ellington Collection, Archives Center, National Museum of American History, Smithsonian Institution.*

he was a child. Even though Cook was not yet thirty when he joined Ellington's band, he had played lead with such jazz heavyweights as Count Basie, Earl Hines, Jimmy Lunceford, and B. B. King, as well as Ella Fitzgerald. When Ellington hired him, he had left the music business, after a year with Billie Holiday's band and a tour as her musical director.

Like Terry and Gonsalves, Cook valued his education with Ellington. "You could see how jazz had evolved from the very beginning up to the point where we were at the time," he once said of his stint with the band, "and you could also surmise how it might be in the future." Cook mixed with the band's younger set and was a mainstay of the band's aforementioned Air Force.

More conventional was trombonist John Sanders, who joined in February 1954. Mercer Ellington had seen the twenty-nine-year-old from Brooklyn while he was playing at the Savoy with tenor man Lucky Thompson. During the war Sanders had played in the U.S. Navy Band and then studied at Juilliard. He replaced valve trombonist Juan Tizol and with his encouragement switched from slide to valve trombone.

Tizol had been Ellington's copyist for orchestra arrangements, and Sanders undertook those responsibilities as well, translating basic melodies into ensemble statements or to solos with brass accompaniment. Typically, Ellington would write on score paper the parts for each instrument section on separate staves. He did not need a piano to do his scoring; he could score anywhere he had a pencil and paper, whether in his hotel room, in a coffee shop, or on the band bus. Sanders and Ellington had a professional friendship such that if the trombonist needed clarification on a score, he could interrupt the maestro any time, whether in his hotel room or on the road. Sanders's seat on the bus was right behind Ellington, whenever he opted to ride with the band. Returning from a gig, others would sleep, but the pair would remain awake, working on scores well into the wee hours.

Though partially disbanded during the 1955 Aquacades run, the Ellington orchestra was noteworthy for its individual musicians who more than capably represented the range of genres, hot jazz, swing, bop, and R&B. It was the arrival of the last two members that would make the '56 band the great aggregation that it was: the key members of the rhythm section, bassist Jimmy Woode and drummer Sam Woodyard.

In early 1955 Ellington hired Woode, whom he knew when the bassist was a child through his uncle, the songwriter Henry Woode, cowriter of the Basie hit "Broadway." Born in Philadelphia, Woode had studied both piano and bass. The draft and the war delayed the start of his professional career until 1946, when he formed his own band. Woode worked with such names as Boston pianist and arranger Nat Pierce and tenor sax soloists Zoot Sims and Flip Phillips, one of Jazz at the Philharmonic's later wild men. He also accompanied leading vocalists Ella Fitzgerald and Sarah Vaughan. After future Newport impresario George Wein opened his Boston club Storyville in the early fifties, Woode played in the house band, where he would gig with many visiting groups. At the time, Ellington was struggling with a succession of stand-in bassists. When he played Wein's club in the spring of 1954, the impresario suggested Woode; Ellington hired him, and Woode remained for five years.

Woode was youthful, energetic, and very sophisticated. "I loved to play in the rhythm section," he once told Phil Schaap, the well-known New York jazz disc jockey and reissue producer. Able to draw on his early piano training, he knew how to integrate the bottom pulse in his bass playing into his section to put drive behind a solo. All that now remained for the Duke was to find the right drummer.

Sam Woodyard, with Butter Jackson (foreground). ::: *Photo by Roy DeCarava. Duke Ellington Collection, Archives Center, National Museum of American History, Smithsonian Institution.*

Just after Hodges's return, while passing through Atlantic City, Ellington found his man in Woodyard. A self-taught rhythm ace, the youthful Woodyard had Woode's energy and swing but was initially unnerved by the Duke's orchestra, having never before played with a big band. He had started in the forties, gigging with local groups in New Jersey. Sometime around 1950 he was playing rhythm and blues with a Louisianan, Paul Gayten. Later, Woodyard would play and record with the Sicilian-born tenor saxophonist Joe Holiday during the mambo craze, trumpeter Roy Eldridge, and pianist Milt Buckner. From the jumping Buckner, Woodyard learned to lock into a drive.

Woodyard's playing was thought to be at times erratic, but his bass partner Jimmy Woode saw him differently. Woode explained to Phil Schaap that Ellington wanted to have his drummers interpret the eighth note. As a result the pair conferred a lot about how their rhythm section could best support the horns on, behind, and ahead of the beat. Woodyard's great back beat, said Woode, would play "right where Maestro would stomp it off and not move ahead or favor any section. And eventually the sections became accustomed to our pulse, and that is what started this band swinging in another direction."

Woodyard also had a good right hand to ride the cymbals, Michael James remembered. "He could swing a band with just the cymbal." From his immediate predecessor in the band, Louis Bellson, he learned to play with a double bass drum and sometimes would drum barehanded. For Woodyard, anything was a drum.

Once with Duke's band, Woodyard fell in with the younger musicians. His closest companion was the gentle Paul Gonsalves. Once Gonsalves started to wail, Woodyard could sustain the drive behind him for as long as the saxophonist could blow.

This, then, was Ellington's orchestra at Newport:

Trumpet section: Willie Cook, Ray Nance, Clark Terry, and Cat Anderson

Trombone section: Butter Jackson, John Sanders, and Britt Woodman

Reed section: Johnny Hodges, alto sax; Harry Carney, baritone sax; Russell Procope, alto sax and clarinet; Jimmy Hamilton, clarinet; and Paul Gonsalves, tenor sax

Rhythm section: Duke Ellington, piano; Jimmy Woode, bass; and Sam Woodyard, drums

At Newport '56 the old guard included a forty-eight-year-old Hodges, forty-six-year-old Carney, and forty-seven-year-old Procope. The younger members were Gonsalves and Terry, both thirty-five; Woodyard, thirty-one; and Woode, twenty-seven.

The reed section—the downstage face of the orchestra—had been stable. Hodges had returned to Harry Carney, Russell Procope, and Jimmy Hamilton. These four, together with Gonsalves, would be the front line of Ellington's team that night.

Accompanying for one number was vocalist Jimmy Grissom, a West Coast blues artist who had been touring with Ellington throughout the spring. From late 1951 Grissom had sung with the band off and on with songs like "Balling the Blues," "What More Can I Say?" and "Ain't Nothing Nothing, Baby." "Duke tried to get some juke box hits with Jimmy," said

Michael James. One notable occasion was the March 1953 Pasadena concert, another instance when Paul Gonsalves soloed his wailing interval for "Diminuendo and Crescendo in Blue."

So with these most-proficient musicians, who represented every genre from hot jazz, to swing, bop, and R&B, the '56 band was the veritable Cadillac of sound, powerfully purring as it would when it accelerated full throttle over Newport into the "Crescendo in Blue."

The confluence of events that led Ellington portentously to a Newport showcase began in the autumn of 1955, sometime after Johnny Hodges had actually started performing again with the band, when Ellington's longtime publicist, Joe Morgen, sensed the alto star's return was a promotion opportunity. Morgen conceived an idea that *Time* magazine should do a cover story on the bandleader. His great notion was not far-fetched. The middlebrow *Time* had an editorial predisposition to jazz and was another quarter that had long been pushing the music as an American art form deserving recognition. The magazine had featured jazz cover stories before, notably a 1949 issue with Louis Armstrong titled "Louis the First."

Joe Morgen was a stocky, rough-hewn character, short on sophistication, who did publicity for the Hickory House steak restaurant on Fifty-second Street, a favorite eatery for jazz personalities. Dogged and thus effective, he worked his idea through *Time*'s music editor, Carter Harman, who had been responsible for *Time* cover stories on Rosemary Clooney in 1953 and Dave Brubeck in 1954, as well as those on ballet choreographer George Balanchine and opera diva Maria Callas.

Harman was an Ellington fan. He had first heard him on radio in 1934 and had seen him in person at the Cotton Club. As a Princeton undergrad he had even met Ellington, when he played at a dance pavilion in nearby New Brunswick, New Jersey. Morgen kept nudging Harman to listen to the new Ellington, and when he finally did, he was particularly taken by drummer Sam Woodyard. The experience motivated him to write a short bellwether article titled "The Duke Rides Again," which ran in a January 1956 issue. Sam Woodyard, Harman wrote, "sits, lean and still, behind his battery, neatly punctuating every phrase, coming as close as any man could to playing a tune on his four side drums and three cymbals (he actually squeezes pitch changes out of one drum by leaning on it with an elbow), while keeping a rhythm as solid as Gibraltar. When the band appeared bored with a number, he seemed to get under and above—and the band came alive."

That January, Ellington and his orchestra had been in Chicago's Universal Studios for their last recording session under Duke's Capitol contract. Ellington had opted to leave Capitol without a contract with another label. Returning to New York, he and the band opened at the Café Society. There a second opportunity came the bandleader's way: Columbia Records had been sniffing. Pop album producer George Avakian saw a means to segue Ellington's possible return to the label by linking him with the nation's golden girl pop singer, Rosemary Clooney, the darling of Mitch Miller and his pop singles department.

"When I reissued Bessie Smith on four LPs, Rosie wanted to do some of that repertoire in an album," Avakian said. "I told her that the incompatibility with her image and voice was too great, whereupon she asked me if I thought Duke would be willing to do an album with her. 'That I can hear,' I said, and Duke agreed." Avakian assigned his assistant, Irving Townsend, to the task. At Duke's opening night at Café Society, Townsend discussed the project with him and was put together with Billy Strayhorn.

Strays was looking for a project, having just returned from Paris, where he had immersed himself in the expatriate American scene. Working with Clooney had its challenges. At the time, the singer was at home in Beverly Hills, pregnant with her fourth child and unable to travel. Avakian conceived the novel idea of recording separately. The Ellington band would record first in New York at the Thirtieth Street Studio; Clooney would overdub later in Los Angeles. Strayhorn's job was to go to California to work on material with the singer and prepare her for her session. He would then return to New York to join Townsend and the band for their recording. The result was the album *Blue Rose,* with Townsend's liner notes. Although some now regard the release as a classic, sales never caught fire. While the effort may have fostered his reassociation with Columbia, Ellington remained in a wait-and-see mode. Indeed, he had other recording dates immediately to follow.

In early February the band returned to Chicago's Universal Studios, this time to do two albums for Bethlehem. A three-year-old label started two years before by one Gus Wildi, Bethlehem was known for recording East Coast hard bop, West Coast cool jazz, some Dixieland, and many vocal sets, notably featuring Nina Simone. Later, in March, the band returned for another session. These dates resulted in two very satisfactory recordings: *Historically Speaking* and *Duke Ellington Presents*. . . . Some, however, were not entirely satisfied. Savaging the first LP, French jazz composer/arranger/critic André Hodeir notoriously wrote, "This is not just another bad record; it is a sign of a dereliction which confirms once and for all the decadence of a great musician." Hodeir was writing an ocean away and not exactly in tune with Ellington's acceleration. That spring Ellington shoehorned into his busy schedule a handful of small-group sessions for Mercer, his son's label started with jazz critic Leonard Feather. After a fallow time of more than a year, 1956 was proving a fruitful recording season.

Meanwhile in New York, along the corridors of Time, Inc., Joe Morgen's cover story idea was beginning to bud. Carter Harman had shopped the proposal to editors Robert Manning and Otto Fuerbringer, who supported him. In the end Roy Alexander, *Time*'s managing editor, gave Harman the go-ahead. The sudden interest in his career coming simultaneously from two media titans like Columbia and now *Time* dramatically raised the stakes and held a promise that 1956 could be a pivotal year for Ellington.

From mid-May to early June he was in Las Vegas for an extended run at the Flamingo Hotel. Harman would fly to Las Vegas to live with him for three or four days, during which time he taped the interviews, with Joe Morgen hovering in the background. As for the cover portrait, logistics suggested a local talent. In late May *Time*'s Otto Fuerbringer felt

Paul Gonsalves (foreground), Jimmy Hamilton, Johnny Hodges, and Russell Procope in the studio. The reed section, minus Harry Carney. ::: *Photo by Roy DeCarava. Duke Ellington Collection, Archives Center, National Museum of American History, Smithsonian Institution.*

he had one: southwestern artist Peter Hurd, a rancher from San Patricio, New Mexico. Fuerbringer telegrammed Hurd to gauge his interest.

Hurd was an establishment free spirit. He had spent two years at West Point, followed by another at Pennsylvania's Haverford College, before making his way to nearby Chadd's Ford to mingle with the elect painting circle around N. C. Wyeth. In time he married Wyeth's daughter Henriette and became a close friend of his brother-in-law and fellow artist Andrew Wyeth. Recognizing in Ellington a fellow free spirit from another art, Hurd agreed.

With all this attention Ellington was feeling his oats. Moreover, the '56 band was now hitting its stride and generating considerable heat. *Saturday Review* ran a positive piece, "Celebration for the Duke," and a May article in *Down Beat* said it all: "My Biggest Thrill? When Duke Roared Back: Basie." Duke's rival, who had hit it big with his early 1955 release of "April in Paris" on Norman Granz's Clef label, was now by popular reckoning the top big band. In April 1956 a nationwide *Cashbox* poll of jukebox operators had voted his aggregation the best rock and roll band in the country, which was announced during disc jockey Alan Freed's first regularly scheduled network rock and roll broadcast, "Rock 'n' Roll Dance Party," when it premiered on CBS Radio. The Count's words carried weight. From on high Basie told *Down Beat* that his "biggest thrill as a listener" was at Ellington's 1951 opening at Birdland, when he heard his rival big band leader knock the socks off "the so-called progressive jazz" audience. The self-effacing Basie said Ellington's orchestra was "the greatest band of all time," then added, "I mean that Duke Ellington is the greatest of them all."

Immediately following the Las Vegas engagement, Ellington and his orchestra went to San Francisco for a ten-day booking at the Macumba Club on Grant Street. In his San Francisco hotel, the Beverly Plaza, Ellington sat in an adjoining room for Peter Hurd's portrait. At times, Hurd wrote to Fuerbringer at *Time*, the musician would be "wearing a silk kerchief of olive green wound around his head which gave the immediate impression of some royal personage out of the Middle East. . . . There was a more or less steady stream of phone calls and visitors to the hotel room where we worked, and though I had known for years that California is over its quota in strange individuals I was amazed at the numbers and variety that turned up in my quarters to pay homage . . . to the Duke. I was delighted for they served to entertain him and keep his expression animated during the sittings."

From all appearances Duke Ellington had returned to the charmed life. What remained was a news peg for Carter Harman's story. For whatever reason, possibly because the booking was not yet a done deal, Ellington wasn't thinking of Newport. When Harman asked, Duke suggested that he peg the cover story to an upcoming mid-July date with the New Haven Symphony Orchestra.

Whether by serendipity or divine providence, the course of Ellington's career would run through Newport that summer. In the recent years it had been all labor in a vale of dry bones, and now a distant breath appeared to be joining them bones together. Writing with the benefit of hindsight, Mercer Ellington chose to interpret his father's festival appearance in terms of an answered prayer.

4

The Tiffany Label

Columbia Records

Toward the end of June 1956, about the time that the Newport Jazz Festival booked him for that year, Ellington was moving to sign with Columbia Records. The label was preparing to leverage its premier status in long-playing record technology to record its artists live at Newport. It would be a seminal and technically bold undertaking, the fruits of which only Columbia could promote and deliver to a mass audience. In so doing, Columbia would further define a continental, countercultural identity for sympathetic listeners.

A consummately successful company among the three major labels, Columbia was by name also the oldest. By the mid-fifties it had arrived, largely as the result of the determined drive and consuming interest of two generations of mainly immigrant Americans. At the top of the corporate hierarchy stood an older generation, born before the First World War, whose competitive vision was to combine taste with the decision to implement advancing technology for market dominance and profit.

Columbia was, after all, a division of the Columbia Broadcasting System, the "Tiffany Network." Its popular-music department had attracted and fostered directors and producers of a second generation born after the Armistice of 1918, who came of age in the swing era, matured during World War II, and remained committed to jazz almost as a lifestyle.

Columbia competed most directly with RCA Victor. Together the two leaders outpaced an also-ran, American Decca. Close behind these were three companies dating from the forties: Capitol, MGM, and Mercury. By some reckonings, there were also two hundred independent companies of varying sizes specializing mainly in niche and regional markets.

Columbia and Victor benefited tremendously from the powerful corporate parents behind them in a race to determine broadcast and record industry standards that would further drive profits—and make and sustain stars. Although the prewar nationwide audience was shaped by radio, by the mid-fifties the medium of choice had become television. In 1954, the Newport Jazz Festival's debut year, for example, there were almost 33 million TV sets among a population of more than 162 million Americans. That year CBS doubled its advertising billings, making the network the largest single advertising medium in the world. CBS was awash with cash, talent, and prestige.

Iron sharpens iron. CBS and RCA had arrived at such heights through the rise and rivalry of two immigrant titans of the broadcast industry, William S. Paley and David Sarnoff. "Competition brings out the best in products and the worst in men," Sarnoff once said. Born at the turn of the century, both he and Paley were young men in an even younger industry when they started their careers and charted the direction broadcasting would take. Both were strong-willed corporate leaders, but they were temperamental opposites.

Sarnoff was the son of an impoverished Russian immigrant to New York. Early in his life he wanted to be a rabbi, but to help support his family after his father died, he hit the streets as a nine-year-old, selling Yiddish-language newspapers. When the nation began to adopt wireless telegraphy, Sarnoff landed a job with American Marconi Company. On a fateful night in April 1912, Sarnoff was Marconi's telegraph operator atop John Wanamaker's Manhattan department store. For seventy-two hours he received and sent messages following the *Titanic*'s SOS. This heady experience inspired his decision to make his mark in the communications industry.

Three years later—although some say it was much later still—Sarnoff began promoting to his bosses a concept of a radio music box consisting of a radio receiver and phonograph in the same cabinet. In 1919 General Electric formed the Radio Corporation of America when it acquired American Marconi, by which time Sarnoff was undoubtedly pushing his idea. RCA was slow to hear, however. Although amateur radio operators had been on the air broadcasting for several years, history generally regards November 2, 1920, as the date of the first commercial radio broadcast. That evening, Westinghouse's Pittsburgh station KDKA broadcast the election results of Republican candidate Warren G. Harding's presidential victory.

The event gave Sarnoff the support he needed to prod RCA to launch into broadcasting. In 1921 it entered the game with blow-by-blow coverage of a major boxing event, the Jack Dempsey–Georges Carpentier prizefight. The broadcast of this early Jazz Age happening garnered for its time an enormous audience; the result was a demand for radios that RCA was pleased to manufacture. Five years later, as RCA's general manager, Sarnoff formed the National Broadcasting Company as a subsidiary. The growth of radio was explosive. By the end of the decade and the onset of the Depression, radio sets were in a third of all American homes.

Whereas an early rival, Westinghouse, based its broadcast network on building and owning radio stations, Sarnoff took the position that RCA was first and foremost a product manufacturer. Fulfilling his vision for his radio music box, in 1929 he bought Victor, the manufacturer of the legendary Victrola phonograph. Victor, of course, also had a record company, giving Sarnoff three related products in the RCA line for which his network could generate demand. In 1930 he became RCA's third president. Sarnoff was thirty-nine.

Bill Paley would take another approach altogether. Unlike Sarnoff, he began life in relative privilege. His father, the son of a prosperous Jewish businessman who had immigrated from the Ukraine, built a successful family business, Chicago's Congress Cigar Company, and sent Paley to Pennsylvania's Wharton School of Finance and Commerce. Paley returned to work for the family in sales just as broadcasting was starting to boom. With a notion that radio advertising could increase cigar sales more effectively than print, he bought time on a Philadelphia radio station, WCAU, which began airing the "Miss La Palina Hour," so named after one of his cigars. Sales of the cigar correspondingly skyrocketed. When the family later opted to sell the business, his father gave Paley $400,000 to purchase the failing network with which the station was affiliated. Thus in 1928 he acquired CBS and its network of sixteen affiliates. Paley was twenty-seven.

By this time Sarnoff's NBC was the dominant network, charging its forty-seven affiliates to carry its programs. Paley and CBS, on the other hand, opted to charge only advertisers and gave the programs to affiliates with the proviso that they had to clear time for the advertisers. The approach was obviously popular among stations. Not always able to afford to produce their own programming, nor to sell time to local advertisers, they could rely on free network programming and ads to fill air time. The strategy reflected Paley's distinctive approach to business: its essence was sales and promotion, not product. His was a merchandising genius that was realizing a new concept—the idea that a mass medium could profit mightily by enabling advertisers to sell to a national audience in the home. Paley proved his concept decisively. He took CBS from gross earnings of $1.4 million in 1928 to $28.7 million in 1937, while expanding his network from 16 to 114 stations. In Sarnoff's relatively conventional view, however, Paley was an upstart. By temperament the RCA head was not a salesman but an engineer who came into business. His personal ambition, it seems, was to create a communications empire over which he would rule like a Henry Ford—a traditional industrialist who built things. Paley was not interested in technology per se, only in how he could use it to sell other people's products. Whereas Sarnoff viewed media as a means to an end, Paley saw it as an end in itself. His approach put him at the center of the 1930s revolution in communications and advertising that created a national market. In the postwar boom CBS would capitalize in that market, proving Paley to be truly one of the early visionaries in mass entertainment.

Sarnoff was not comfortable around entertainers and kept his distance from them. It was said that he never met his number-one NBC radio star, comedian Jack Benny. Nor was he particularly interested in programming. "Basically, we're the delivery boys," he was quoted as saying, reflecting his earliest vocation as a newspaper vendor. Sarnoff's predisposition was an

Achilles heel that Paley appears to have exploited right into the fifties. Paley, who had a critical eye, could recognize talent and was genuinely engaged by programming. He enjoyed raiding Sarnoff's stable—Benny being one notable postwar prize—particularly when it enabled him to boost RCA's technology developments. After all, advancing technology was what would drive corporate profits.

Sarnoff had a record label. Paley wanted a record label. Having successfully challenged RCA in radio broadcasting, Paley-the-programmer was now positioned to take a shot at its claim on the upscale record market, served nationally by Victor's Red Seal label classical music catalog. In 1938 CBS acquired the American Record Company, which included the original Columbia label along with Vocalion and Brunswick. Prompting Paley's buy was the former general manager of RCA's Victor division, a very courtly thirty-nine-year-old, Edward Wallerstein. For some three-quarters of a million dollars, Paley acquired control and in early 1939 installed Ted Wallerstein as president of the new Columbia Recording Corporation.

When Wallerstein left Victor, he went with knowledge of a recording technology that would help Paley realize his goal for Columbia Records. It was the technology that would replace the ten-inch 78-rpm shellac disc, the standard recording vehicle since the turn of the century, when it had emerged as an alternative to Thomas Edison's wax cylinder. Though certainly an advance on the cylinder, the 78 was breakable, and furthermore it imposed limitations both on what engineers could record and what home listeners could hear. The disc could only hold some four minutes of music on a side. Although the 78 was a satisfactory standard for popular songs written for sheet music—previously a main avenue for distribution along with rolls for the player piano—it would not do for classical pieces. Upscale listeners were not the sort of folk who particularly wanted to rise from their comfortable chairs to change records every four minutes—especially in the middle of an extended adagio.

In the mid-twenties the Edison Record Company developed a technology for a long-playing, microgroove twelve-inch 78 capable of holding twenty minutes of music per side—the Edison Diamond Disc. By the early thirties RCA Victor had introduced its own version, a modified transcription disc for recording masters on wax used to impress the stampers that would ultimately press the shellac 78s. The Victor engineers kept the groove size and the twelve-inch format but slowed the speed to 33⅓ rpm.

Although Wallerstein strongly believed in the technology, in 1933 he pulled the plug on the effort for reasons that were both technical and commercial: the grooves quickly degraded with every playback, and the record market had simply collapsed with the Depression. Sales had peaked in 1929, when annual record sales exceeded 100 million discs. By 1932 they had fallen to a scant 6 million. People were now getting their music free—from the radio. Reluctantly, he was left to conclude that long-playing record technology was not commercially mature.

When he came to Columbia, Wallerstein initiated mastering at 33⅓ rpm on 16½-inch lacquer discs of cellulose nitrate. His idea was eventually to replace the 78-rpm shellac disc as the industry standard. Developing the LP technology would provide him with a challenge to RCA Victor's Red Seal classical catalog, certainly one of Paley's objectives in his personal contest with Sarnoff.

By 1947 Wallerstein's engineers had finally perfected a microgroove vinyl record capable of holding fifteen minutes on a side in a ten-inch version and twenty-two minutes on a side in a twelve-inch format, yielding playing times suitable for the classical market. The following year Columbia made what it regarded as record history, introducing the first twelve-inch LP, Mendelssohn's *Violin Concerto in E minor,* with violinist Nathan Milstein and the New York Philharmonic Orchestra, Bruno Walter conducting.

Within a year and a half of the introduction of the LP, Columbia had sold twice as many Masterworks as RCA was selling of Red Seal. RCA had begun to lose its artists. Some, like opera tenor Ezio Pinza, would go to Columbia and join such staples of the Masterworks department as the New York Philharmonic and Chicago symphonies and the Philadelphia, Pittsburgh, and Cleveland orchestras.

Sarnoff, however, had secretly started work in 1938 on another vinyl option to replace the 78. The RCA Victor rollout of its rival 45-rpm system was not-so-surprisingly quick. In June 1949 it released the first seven-inch 45-rpm singles, "everything from a bebop bash to a minuet" plus a 45 record changer. Like the LP, this vinyl medium was lighter, cheaper, easier to manufacture, and far less breakable than the 78. The 45, however, also had the same limitation as the 78: it was only capable of holding three to four minutes of music.

RCA technology was in fact targeting the singles market in a format that was perfect for the pop songs dominating the airwaves and the jukeboxes. In 1950, capitalizing on the success of the format, jukebox manufacturer Seeburg introduced the first jukebox to play 45s. Jukeboxes would quickly become ubiquitous wherever teenagers gathered. That year Columbia started releasing 45s. Two years later RCA adopted the LP format.

Columbia was late getting into the pop-singles market, because in the forties Paley had committed the company to the LP. Even though his label's pop department at the time had Benny Goodman, Mary Martin, Frank Sinatra, and society bandleader Eddie Duchin, he was perhaps not as interested in pop as in classical. RCA appeared to be making a strategic play for pop music, while Columbia continued its quest to dominate the classical market.

Columbia actually had a two-phase strategy: first, to target the classical record buyer and, second, to introduce the LP to the pop music audience—of which jazz listeners were a subset. To further establish the industry standard, Columbia, through retailers, supplied new 33 1/3 long-play Philco phonographs below cost to listeners, in exchange for a commitment to buy a certain number of Columbia LPs. In 1951 it ceased producing 78-rpm classical discs.

The following year, Columbia released *Beethoven Symphonies Nos. 2 and 4* with Bruno Walter and the Philharmonic on a disc that contained more than sixty minutes of music. In 1953 it introduced the 360 model high-fidelity phonograph. By the time that hi-fi arrived, with all the attendant hoopla, the label had already positioned itself to exploit the technology to appeal not just to the classical market but also to a new generation of jazz listeners.

Columbia Records earned its entrance into the postwar jazz record market by means of reissues, second releases of previously issued recordings. The strategy would take time to bear fruit—in fact, not until the second generation of swing enthusiasts had moved decisively into positions of power and influence in the record business.

In the mid-thirties the hippest of high school and college youth were into jazz casualties like white Chicago trumpeter Bix Beiderbecke, who at the age of twenty-eight died of pneumonia and bootleg liquor, and blueswoman Bessie Smith, who died in her late thirties from injuries in a car crash. For the thirties generation Bix represented youthful alienation from a bourgeois society that was attracted to the emerging urban jazz subculture. After his death he captured the imagination of youth in a manner similar to that of James Dean, Jim Morrison, and Kurt Cobain later in the century.

Some single 78s memorialized Beiderbecke and Smith's deaths, creating a demand for earlier records of the jazz masters—notably trumpeter Louis Armstrong—that were out of print and consequently rare. "Hot collecting," a hip and entirely fan-driven movement, developed early in the swing era. It was a craze, especially on such campuses as Yale and Princeton, and records by Bix were the hottest.

The young were attracted to the buzz, led there by the infectious excitement generated by swing phenomenon Benny Goodman. The fad emboldened young enthusiasts to seek entry to the otherwise closed circle of jazz musicians, in some cases on the pretext of collecting. "Since the advent of the jitterbug type of music, newspaper feature stories, the *Life* photographic section," wrote one disparaging commentator of the day, "people who do not even own phonographs have been bothering musicians on every pretext under the sun. Musicians call them all collectors."

The more conservative swing audiences would derisively call the young men who would crowd the bandstands and bop with the rhythm—as opposed to dancing—ickies. This thirties generation would have a major impact on postwar American culture by opting to stay in the jazz scene and parlay what they knew as collectors, writers, and critics, as well as entrepreneurs, distributors, and founders of new labels, to capture the potentially profitable reissue market. They started journals like *Hot Jazz* and *Swing Music* and later the East Coast's *Down Beat* and the West Coast's *Tempo*. French collector Charles Delaunay's *Hot Discography* was probably the most useful book on jazz for hot collectors. His first two editions appeared in 1936 and 1938 and listed all the records made by hot artists, giving labels, titles, and record and master numbers. To a great degree, the noise made by hot collectors helped propel swing forward to broad public attention.

At the time, no album-length reissues existed as such, but a few organizations emerged from the movement. Notable was Commodore Records and the related Hot Record Society, which arguably pioneered the reissue movement. In 1933 a young man

Milt Gabler (fifth from left) stands beside Louis Armstrong at the Commodore Music Shop with fans from Public School 2. Armstrong is present to autograph copies of his biography *Horn of Plenty,* by Belgian critic Robert Goffin. ::: *Photo c. 1947, by New York photographer Bill Mack. Milt Gabler Papers, Archives Center, National Museum of American History, Smithsonian Institution.*

from Harlem, Milt Gabler, the proprietor of East Forty-second Street's Commodore Music Shop, New York's first jazz specialist store, launched his Commodore label with a reissue of some of trombonist Jack Teagarden's traditional jazz records from the twenties. A sponsor of the 1946 edition of *Hot Jazz Discography,* Gabler would eventually join Decca's A&R staff and produce a fifties song by a New Jersey–based combo given to rhythm and blues imitations. That band was Bill Haley and His Comets; the song was "Rock around the Clock."

Although Paley may have been predisposed exclusively to classical recording, Ted Wallerstein looked well into the future and saw jazz as a burgeoning field where someday Columbia Records should have an equally commanding presence. About the time CBS acquired Columbia, Wallerstein read a ten-page *Life* magazine article about the roots of swing, famous musicians, big bands, jitterbug dancers, and recording sessions and got the idea of reissuing some of the jazz records mentioned in the story. In 1940 he found an expert to undertake the job and offered it to him. That man was John Hammond. In addition to bringing Count Basie to New York, Hammond had discovered Billie Holiday and guitarist Charlie Christian, among his other early contributions to jazz. Hammond, however, demurred on Wallerstein's offer. Too involved with his own agenda and efforts to move jazz forward, he recommended a Yale undergrad, knowing that his alma mater was one of the hippest centers for hot collecting and that a student would be closer to the hot collector market and thus better suited to selecting the most popular titles.

His recommendation was George Avakian. A hot collector who epitomized his generation, this college student had already gained a reputation in reissue circles and come to the attention of the label earlier via correspondence and published writings. The Tiffany Label was about to get hip.

5

George Avakian

From Hot Collecting to Live Recording

In 1940 Jack Kerouac attended the Riverdale, New York, Horace Mann School for Boys as an athlete prepping for Columbia. Idyllic, with its ivy-covered granite, the school overlooks Van Cortlandt Park and was known for its tweedy instructors who taught their charges to think and write in the classical tradition.

In his autobiographical novel *Vanity of Duluoz,* Kerouac describes it as an "exceptional school" where, he continued in wildly exaggerated prose, "ninety-six percent of the students are Jewish kids, and most of them are very rich: sons of furriers, famous realtors, thissa and thatta, and here come mobs of them in big black limousines driven by chauffeurs in visored hats, carrying large lunch boxes full of turkey sandwiches and Napoleons and chocolate milk in thermos bottles."

Kerouac wrote of a character that Jack Duluoz (his alter ego in the book) befriended at Horace Mann: "Chuck Derounian the Armenian kid playing me old Bix records in Washington Heights." Derounian was none other than George Avakian.

George Avakian was born in Armavir, in southwestern Armenia just north of the Turkish border, shortly after the Great War. His father's family were Armenian cloth manufacturers from western Iran who had relocated to Georgia. His father applied for a U.S. visa and in January 1922 arrived in New York, a move that shifted the family into the business of importing oriental rugs. A year and a half later George and his mother and sister joined him; the family eventually settled in an Armenian enclave in Washington Heights.

As a Horace Mann student in the mid-thirties, Avakian discovered swing through two weekly radio broadcasts: the CBS *Camel Caravan,* with the Casa Loma Orchestra, and NBC's *Let's Dance* program, with Benny Goodman, sponsored by the National Biscuit Company (Nabisco). He quickly became a fan and a member of the United Hot Clubs of America. At the time he wore horn-rim glasses that gave him the appearance of being the King of Swing's kid brother. Goodman was especially meaningful to the Horace Mann set. Like many of the students, he came from Russian Jewish immigrants, and his career offered a profound lesson: swing was a hip ticket into the heart of America. Avakian applied that lesson his senior year as editor of the school newspaper when he started authoring swing record reviews.

In late 1936 a classmate invited Avakian to his house to listen to some of his older brother's Satchmo records on the Okeh label. "That was my real introduction to Louis Armstrong," recalled Avakian. "Before that, I had heard him on the radio and had started buying some of his Decca records, which were the only ones available." Disappointed that his friend's recordings were out of print, Avakian wrote the first of two letters to Brunswick, which had acquired Okeh, suggesting a reissue program, but nothing happened.

That autumn Goodman had arrived in New York for an engagement at the Hotel Pennsylvania's Manhattan Room. The mother of another of Avakian's school friends was able to arrange an interview with Goodman after a performance. The bandleader was impressed, and during his lengthy New York stay, Avakian and his school chum were frequently found among the bandleader's entourage as unpaid helpers to Dwight Chapin, Goodman's one-man support organization.

The following year, as a Yale freshman Avakian joined the university's chapter of the United Hot Clubs of America. The founder and secretary of the UHCA was a Yale postgrad, Marshall Stearns. Avakian quickly became a prominent figure among the circle that surrounded Stearns, who had one of the most extensive collections of jazz records in America, later the basis of the holdings of the Institute of Jazz Studies, which he founded in 1952. Every Friday Avakian and his cohorts would gather at Stearns's apartment and listen to early records by such greats as Armstrong, Bessie Smith, Eddie Condon and the Chicagoans, Bix, and Ellington. When Duke played New Haven, a UHCA undergraduate and friend of Avakian invited him for a meal at one of Yale's dining halls, an occasion Ellington never forgot.

Avakian's link to Stearns yielded a significant writing opportunity. In 1938 Stearns had him write his monthly New York news reports, and the following year he began writing a column for the West Coast jazz publication *Tempo.* It was in early 1938, however, that Avakian got his first lead into the record business. The Brunswick Records factory in Bridgeport, Connecticut, some twenty-five miles down the road from New Haven, finally replied to one of his letters, expressing interest in his reissue idea but saying that it had referred the notion to the advertising department in New York.

Though Avakian heard nothing further, the smattering of interest led him to push another idea, this time on Chicago record entrepreneur Jack Kapp. In 1934 Kapp had left

Marshall Stearns at the Music Inn, Lenox, Massachusetts, 1952. From 1951 to 1960 the Music Inn, near Tanglewood in the Berkshires, put on concerts, roundtables, and workshops led by Stearns, focusing particularly on African American music. This photo was taken by Dr. Edmond Souchon, New Orleans ragtime and Dixieland guitarist and historian. Souchon was one of Stearns's roundtable panelists that year. That July Stearns launched the Institute of Jazz Studies with George Avakian and John Hammond. ::: *Courtesy of the Institute of Jazz Studies, Rutgers University.*

Brunswick to found the American label of the British company Decca, taking with him singer Bing Crosby and making him an even bigger star.

Avakian had the conviction that jazz should be represented on annotated albums, "not just singles, because it was best understood in wider terms than a three-minute 78 side. The basic inspiration was Victor's opera and symphony Red Seal albums." He proposed to Kapp a series of three reunion albums, new recordings with annotations, to document the "original pioneers of the three great centers of jazz development, New Orleans, Kansas City, and Chicago, and have the musicians play in their original styles."

Bingo. Kapp took a chance on the idea. "The acceptance came in the form of a postcard, which was typical of Decca Records. It was a penny postcard, and I wish to God I'd saved it, because it was [a] great example of how chintzy they were with money. It was a thirty-five-cent label."

Remarkably Avakian, still an undergrad, got to produce his first album, arguably the first jazz album ever recorded. "In the first meeting, Jack Kapp turned to his brother Dave and to Bob Stevens, who was the recording director—that was the title that A&R guys were given in those days—and said, 'Well, I don't think we quite know what this young man is talking about, but *he* seems to know. So let's do it, and Bob, you show him the ropes in the studio.'"

Although Avakian was not sure how to discuss payment with Kapp, he managed to cut his technical teeth with Stevens, producing two sessions in New York and one in Chicago. Titled *Chicago Jazz* and consisting of a packet of six 78s, it reunited guitarist Eddie Condon, clarinetist Pee Wee Russell, and others from the late twenties Chicago scene. Decca released it in March 1940. Avakian thus became the producer of the first jazz album to record sessions with the specific intent of issuing them together and not as singles, in short, a concept album in which the annotations and recordings were one.

When it came time to discuss the next two albums, Avakian finally raised the issue of money. Kapp offered him "six bits"—$75—not enough to cover his travel to Chicago and expenses. He walked from the deal, intent on focusing on his remaining college courses. Handing Kapp all his material for the rest of the project, he recommended Kansas City writer Dave Dexter to do that album and Steve Smith, who had contributed to the seminal 1939 book *Jazzmen*, for the third release.

In 1939, after CBS acquired the American Record Company divisions Columbia, Vocalion, and Brunswick, it had introduced the new Columbia Records label. The timing was propitious for Avakian, who had been in touch yet again with the Bridgeport factory regarding his perennial reissue idea. In early 1940, shortly after turning his back on the Decca offer, Avakian took a day-trip to Bridgeport, where he met with none other than Columbia Records president Ted Wallerstein and his staff. Acting on a recommendation by John Hammond, whom Avakian had met during his time with the Goodman entourage, Wallerstein had read one of his *Tempo* columns and decided to call him to the plant. During the meeting, factory manager L. J. Morrison said that the public had indeed been writing to ask for reissues. "He read one of those letters," Avakian recalled in 2002, "and it sounded very familiar. I said, 'Excuse me, but I think I wrote that letter in 1938, and was promised an answer from the advertising department.' "

"Did you ever get that reply?" Wallerstein interrupted.

"No, sir," Avakian replied.

"Well, you have one now," Wallerstein continued and promptly offered him a job.

The Columbia president asked him to research and catalog the factory's stored masters and then assemble a reissue series of classic hot jazz recordings in a format based on Avakian's original proposal. The label would pay him $25 a week. From that point onward, after his one Thursday morning class, Avakian made the trek to Bridgeport until he finished the task. Soon after, Columbia launched its first *Hot Jazz Classics* album to stake a position in the hot jazz collector market.

In an industry first for a major label, Columbia reissued these late twenties and early thirties recordings, not just as singles but as complete albums with Avakian's annotations explaining the importance of the musicians and the material and its history. His selections included Armstrong and his Hot Fives and Sevens, Bix Beiderbecke, Bessie Smith, Fletcher Henderson, and Ellington. In the process he became the first producer to discover and issue unreleased alternate takes. His choices would influence jazz writing just as the music was receiving its first serious criticism. In effect, this student from Yale had produced a short history of jazz to 1940. With this first regular series of reissue albums for a wider audience—beyond just the hot collectors—Columbia was in the early stages of positioning itself to dominate yet another music industry niche.

Avakian graduated in 1941 and was soon drafted into the army. Believing that the reissue program was still a long-term winner, Wallerstein told Avakian, "George, when you finish your service, if your father will let you work for me instead of going into the family business, then I'd like to have you back." Avakian remained in uniform until early 1946,

George Avakian (right foreground) as GI, with friends, c. 1945. ::: *Courtesy of the Institute of Jazz Studies, Rutgers University.*

when he came home eager to talk to his father about contacting Wallerstein regarding a return to Columbia. On his receipt of the patriarchal blessing, his way was clear for a career in recording.

During the war Wallerstein had come to see a powerful potential in the conjoining of record recording and radio broadcasting. Since October 1943, the Armed Forces Radio Service had distributed eight million "V-Discs" exclusively to American GIs. The program, which would continue until 1949, offered the only released recordings available during the two American Federation of Musicians bans. The records were twelve-inch vinyl 78s, six and one-half minutes; the few V-Discs of radio broadcasts were on sixteen-inch transcription discs. These recordings were the first to replicate the excitement of live radio broadcasts in the twenties and thirties. They featured extended numbers and improvised solos, unbridled by the typical 78 format that was restricted to three to four minutes.

The impact on radio was dramatic. Most radio programmers had broadcast music live. "Disc jockeys" were a rare breed, the two most notable being Al Jarvis in Los Angeles and Martin Block in New York. Jarvis originated the record-playing broadcast format with his "make-believe ballroom" programming. Block adopted the format in 1935, when his station, WNEW, was broadcasting the sensational trial of Bruno Hauptmann, accused kidnapper of Charles and Anne Morrow Lindbergh's infant son. During an extended lull in court proceedings, Block started playing records. Listeners flooded the station, requesting that he continue the format as a regular program. He did, and it lasted well into the fifties.

After the war, stations shifted wholesale to broadcasting recordings. Block and other deejays had enormous power to make or break a hit record. If one radio station in the twenties could exponentially propel Miss La Palina cigar sales in the Philadelphia market, it was a sure bet that national airplay of familiar recordings would make for significant postwar demand for records.

Wallerstein could see ripening consumer potential for, among other things, an extended series of jazz reissues. Avakian met with the Columbia Records chief in his New York office, hoping that his prewar offer of full-time employment still held. Aware that John Hammond had just returned to civilian life and was rejoining Columbia, he asked Wallerstein about the potential for conflict within the popular music department if he hired both returning veterans. He got a surprising answer: "John Hammond will never work for Columbia again as long as I'm president." Avakian didn't probe. Later he learned that

Wallerstein had caught Hammond moonlighting to help start the Majestic label. After the Columbia chief discovered that he had steered singer Mildred Bailey and other artists to Majestic, he fired him.

Thus Avakian, at twenty-seven, had landed in a position without peer, in a company that was poised to explode, where he could do something he loved: produce quality jazz records both with the greats and the potentially great.

In the first years after the war Avakian was getting a reputation as an expert. In 1946–47 he helped revise the first U.S. publication of Charles Delaunay's *Hot Discography,* the widely acknowledged bible for hot jazz collectors. Like John Hammond, he had become a prolific jazz writer, with critical pieces initially appearing in *Mademoiselle, Pic,* and *Esquire's Jazz Book,* then later in the hip, news-oriented *Down Beat* and the more intellectual *Metronome.*

Into Avakian's second year on the job, Wallerstein paid him a surprise visit. The Columbia president told his charge that he wanted to do something new in the way of expanding the popular album catalog and offered him the job. The assignment was but one aspect of Wallerstein's grand plan for the label based on development of long-playing record technology. He wanted Avakian to research the pop single catalog to see what eight-song packages he could assemble if the LP became a reality.

West Coast jazz impresario Norman Granz (right) in 1946. Granz founded the Jazz at the Philharmonic (JATP) series and was a renowned crusader for racial justice. ::: *Courtesy of Tad Hershorn.*

In advance of Wallerstein's introduction of the LP, Avakian put together his list for transfer to ten-inch LPs. All pop albums prior to the LP were four-disc packages, each 78 with a single on each side. Now four 78s could be translated directly onto a two-sided ten-inch LP, usually with four songs on each side. Avakian's task was easier than for classical transfers, which often required the technically tricky synchronizing of the original sides to make one extended track on the LP. Pop transfers simply involved three-to-four-minute songs—one song, one track.

The Columbia LP hit the streets in June 1948. Avakian's first hundred pop LPs entered the market in 1949 following the end of the second AFM recording ban. The series included such major sellers as Harry James's *All Time Favorites* and *Trumpet Time, Dance Parade,* and

Your Dance Date. Decca was the first to follow with a ten-inch pop-album format. Twelve-inch pop albums would not appear until much later.

Sometime before the end of the second AFM strike, when Josef Zamanzind, Columbia's international director, retired, Avakian got that added responsibility "because nobody else wanted it." Soon after the end of the strike, he recorded the phenomenal 1949 hit that sold more than 4 million records: "Blue Skirt Waltz," by the world's most popular polka band, Frankie Yankovic and his Yanks. Suddenly Avakian was a big hero.

In 1950 Columbia embraced 45s, signaling its readiness to compete in the pop-singles market. The label chose to keep Avakian's focus on albums and opted to raid Mercury Records for the head of its pop department, Mitch Miller. As Columbia's A&R for pop singles, Miller would remain in the forefront of entertainment into the sixties, recording light pop singles and hosting his own TV show, *Sing Along with Mitch*.

Miller's approach to records was formulaic and allowed for no departures. When rock and roll entered the scene in the mid-fifties, he ignored it, finding the genre not to his taste. Miller's preferred formula was the novelty tune. With his group, Mitch Miller and His Gang, he recorded such hits as the Weavers' Israeli folk song "Tzena, Tzena, Tzena" and later "The Yellow Rose of Texas." As for Avakian, his pop focus was entirely on jazz. In 1951 he expanded many of his earlier 78 reissues to the LP format with the release of a four-volume *Louis Armstrong Story* and other LPs. He also led the Columbia effort to release its first twelve-inch pop LPs with the Gray Label 500 series for maturing collectors. The first were a couple of Goodman offerings, followed by a four-volume set of Bessie Smith and a three-volume edition of Beiderbecke. In 1950–51 his first recordings and issues of Duke Ellington were released.

Still in his early thirties, Avakian was becoming a major force within the company.

LP technology made possible a different kind of record for a different kind of listening experience that was, for some, infectiously vicarious: the live recording. In late 1950, live recording enjoyed a boost when Columbia released its first issue of a recording of one of the most fabled happenings of the swing era: Benny Goodman's 1938 Carnegie Hall concert. The decision to release arose after his sister-in-law found misplaced acetates of the concert and Goodman put them in the hands of Ted Wallerstein. Not knowing exactly what he had, the Columbia chief played a disc for Avakian, who immediately recognized it and its import. With the *Carnegie Hall Jazz Concert* in 1950, Columbia was the first major label to issue a live jazz recording, but one independent, Clef, had already developed the market.

The inspiration behind live recordings came from a rising West Coast jazz impresario. Born in 1918, a native of south central Los Angeles, Norman Granz was yet another committed jazz collector, as well as a frequenter of the hopping African American club scene along Central Avenue in West Los Angeles. During the early war years, Granz had worked on a labor crew at MGM studios. After a short stint in the army, he returned to Warner Bros., where he got into film editing. Film was, however, merely his means to an end. His passions

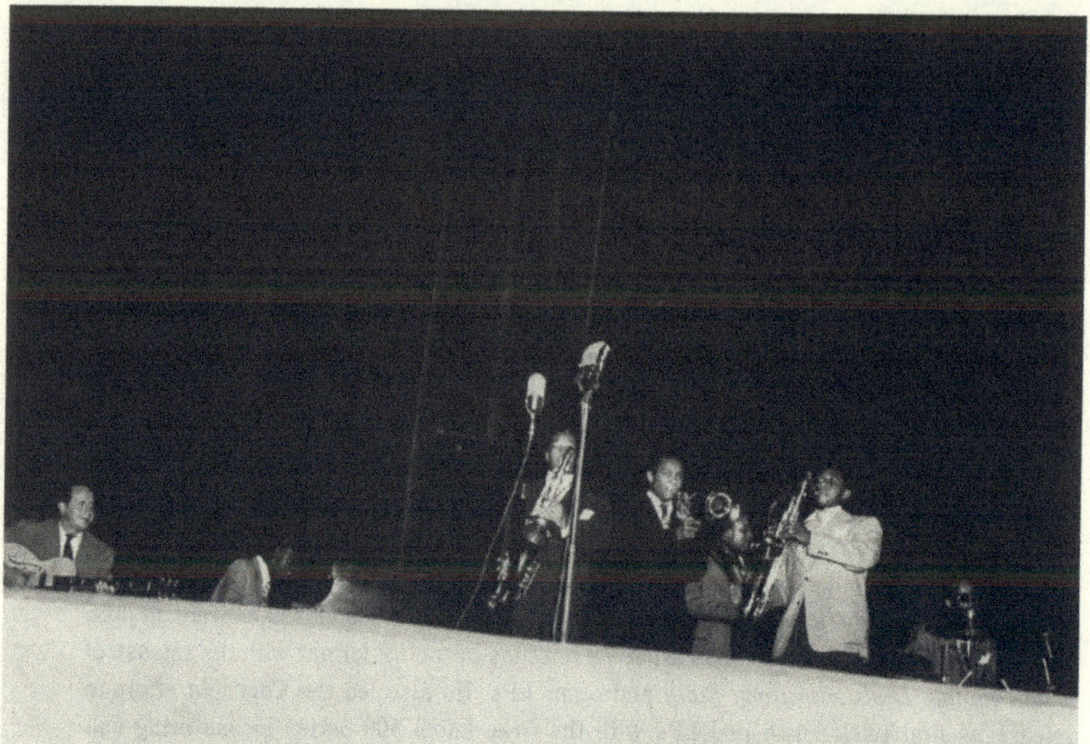

The first JATP concert, July 2, 1944. Left to right, Les Paul, guitar; Nat Cole, piano; Illinois Jacquet, tenor sax; J. J. Johnson, trombone; Johnny Miller, bass; Jack McVea, tenor sax; Lee Young, drums. ::: *Courtesy of Tad Hershorn.*

were jazz and promoting racial justice through the music. Granz parlayed his access to the jazz community to produce a benefit concert that was seminal, featuring improvised jam sessions, a familiar part of most live performances during the swing era. Jams allowed musicians to stretch beyond the written arrangements and dazzle an appreciative audience of listeners and dancers. As often as not in a jam session—at least in the context of swing, if not in bebop—the musicians were improvising in response to an audience as much as to one another. Granz found this combination both fascinating and marketable. In July 1944, almost a month after the D-day landings on the beaches of Normandy, Granz presented his first in a series of jam session concerts known as Jazz at the Philharmonic, or simply JATP. *Down Beat* heralded the event as L.A.'s "first full-scale jazz concert."

The Armed Forces Radio Service had recorded the concert on acetates for broadcast to GIs, as it had done with other live transcriptions throughout the war. One of the musicians, guitarist Les Paul, was said to have played in uniform but didn't. The energy between wartime audience and musicians was intense. Fans were standing on their seats. Musicians grandstanded. Serious jazz critics, then more attuned to the frenetic introspection of bebop, groused. One either loved or loathed JATP.

Nonetheless, Granz, a natural promoter, was sure he was onto a good thing and packaged JATP into a regular series. In 1946 the management of the Philharmonic Auditorium ostensibly refused to continue the events because they appeared to lead to unruliness. Granz maintained that the cancellation was really about performances before racially mixed audiences. He was already one step ahead, having taken JATP on the road the previous autumn. By the end of 1946, he had produced fourteen JATPs in and out of town, as far east as Pittsburgh.

In the jam sessions Granz could see immediately that the AFRS acetate recordings had captured a real energy and excitement that were throwbacks to the heyday of prewar swing. Musically, he may not have been breaking new ground, but his audience was taking off. Granz would feature a number of bop artists as well, later tagging one of his 1949 JATP sessions "danceable bop at last."

Regardless of the critics, for many fans participatory excitement was vital to the jazz experience. Granz was disturbed by the thought that his jam sessions, like other live performances of the era, would survive only in the memories of those present. Radio stations, networks, and the AFRS had made transcriptions of remote broadcasts from ballrooms, but only for later broadcast, never with a record release in mind, given the constraints of the three-to-five-minute limit of a 78-rpm record side. Granz acquired the master from the first AFRS broadcast, recognizing the import of having documented an exceptional concert that also had potential as a live music product for record buyers.

"Norman is very articulate on this," stressed his biographer Tad Hershorn, "because what he said is that the concept of live recording just went over the heads of these people who thought you make recordings in studios and were critical of the crowd noise, clinkered notes, and stuff like that. Norman pretty much said, 'Well, this is a documentary of an event.' It captured the spontaneity that is something else than just going into a studio and recording."

Granz would not be the first to release a live recording. In November 1941 Britain's HMV had released two 78s with extended performances from a live jazz concert. Granz was nonetheless ahead of the curve in the United States. Neither Columbia, Decca, nor RCA would prove responsive to his overtures. Eventually, he made his way to Moses Asch, the founder of the folk music label Folkways Records. In 1946 he came to a deal with Asch to issue and distribute the first JATP concert on the Disc label. The original ten-inch 78s offered home listeners the novel experience of hearing extended solos, with the musicians propelled forward by the roar of the audience. One song, "Blues," featured a slick Illinois Jacquet on tenor sax, Nat "King" Cole on piano, Les Paul on guitar, and J. J. Johnson on trombone in a blistering ten-minute jam that filled three sides and was titled "Blues Parts I, II, and III." The piece was an orgy of improvisation, and reviewers were critical, complaining that the soloists were pandering to the crowd.

When Columbia introduced the LP format, Granz recognized immediately that the technology was perfect for release of live recordings. Eager to issue more live JATP volumes and not wholly satisfied with Asch's distribution capabilities and business ethics,

Illinois Jacquet in the late 1940s. This photograph was taken by William "Popsie" Randolph, New York jazz and rock photographer, who got his first camera from Benny Goodman. ::: *Courtesy of the Institute of Jazz Studies, Rutgers University.*

he aligned his Clef label with the two-year-old Mercury Records in 1947. The following year, he signed a five-year distribution contract. It was just a matter of time before Granz, who maintained ownership of the masters he produced for Mercury, would merge the very successful Clef, Norgran, and his other niche labels into Verve Records.

Norman Granz and his JATP releases accustomed the jazz public to extended live performances on record. It was the introduction of magnetic tape recording technology to a live concert, however, that brought live recording to Columbia and George Avakian. Nazi Germany had developed tape recording technology during the war. In 1945 a Columbia engineer was one of the first to see a German AEG Magnetophon in newly liberated Luxemburg. Quickly, he packaged and shipped it to CBS for study. Shortly thereafter both Ampex and EMI introduced their first models, and Columbia engineers placed orders for both. Ampex proved to have better machines; Columbia returned the other recorders to EMI.

In 1949 one Columbia studio installed monaural—one channel—tape machines and simultaneously recorded on tape and disc. Six months later the engineers concluded that tape could handle the job, and Columbia discontinued direct disc cutting and switched to all tape recording in early 1950, thus becoming the first U.S. label to do so for master recording. Of the label's initial LP releases, about 40 percent were from tape originals.

Once engineers had determined that tape could provide fidelity relatively equal to that of disc, they saw immediate practical advantages. Tape eliminated what had been previously a major problem for extended live recording: synchronizing the minor variations of the recording speeds and equalizing the relative qualities of 78 acetate masters. In studio, tape enabled Avakian and his engineers to replay instantly passages just recorded. With the ability to edit performances and make cuts on the masters for lengthy movements, editors could contribute to the recording process more than just technical skill—they could exercise their artistic sensibility as well.

If tape could revolutionize studio music recording, it could do the same for live concert recording. The first jazz performer fully to capitalize on this truth was a young San Francisco pianist making waves in the Bay Area—Dave Brubeck. In 1953 Brubeck happened to play a concert at the very bohemian Oberlin College in Ohio. The date became the stuff of legend, thanks to engineers from the college radio station, who recorded the event with magnetic tape. Brubeck's San Francisco label, Fantasy, later obtained the tapes and produced his breakthrough album, *Jazz at Oberlin*. The Brubeck concert started a trend across the country as other jazz artists started to play the hippest college venues.

The excitement of the student audience that came through the *Jazz at Oberlin* recording caught the attention of George Avakian and Columbia Records. Avakian was especially intrigued when he found that Brubeck's standard policy for college tours allowed student engineers to record a concert for use on their college radio station as long as he retained masters of the tapes and the rights to the material. Brubeck was similarly intrigued by Avakian. He knew the name by way of the producer's wife, violinist Anahid Ajemian, and her pianist sister Maro, who were by this time internationally renowned and had regularly come to Berkeley and played the Bay Area. Brubeck would later tell *Time* magazine interviewer Carter Harman, who would write a cover story on the rising jazz star, "If George Avakian is smart enough to marry Anahid Ajemian, then that's the guy I want to have record me."

Avakian signed him and subsequently produced all of Brubeck's studio and live recordings from 1955 to early 1958. The first was *Jazz Goes to College,* recorded by student engineers at the universities of Ohio and Michigan. Avakian had signed Brubeck for $6,000, a price set by the musician based on what he still owed on his family ranch in California. The deal was a risk, Avakian recalled, because Brubeck was "very unproven in terms of real sales." The album earned more than that amount in its first twenty-four days on the market and eventually would sell more than one hundred thousand copies. In November 1954 the pianist made the cover of *Time*. "What people hear and cheer in Brubeck is not only a new type of jazz," read Carter Harman's article. "It is the same exuberance that is causing a tremendous boom in all types of jazz—the birth of a new kind of jazz age in the U.S."

With Brubeck, Columbia and Avakian had one of the best young performers, and the label was growing hotter. Record sales and the pace of product release at Columbia were building dramatically. Jazz recordings fell under pop. "We didn't consider that we separated the jazz releases from the pop releases," said Avakian. "They all came out in one release. . . . Once a month, we put out maybe fifteen to eighteen albums." Avakian's two departments were now the most important moneymakers in the company, giving him a freer rein to pursue projects of his own choosing.

After Brubeck, he began to look at live recording more seriously. He had produced live before: Harry James at Uptown Chicago's Aragon Ballroom in 1953 and Lionel Hampton and others performing dance music in similar ballroom settings. The most significant live recordings, however, were two Louis Armstrong albums.

In mid-1954 Avakian released a studio album, *Armstrong Plays W. C. Handy,* followed the next year by *Satch Plays Fats*. Pops was going to Europe that autumn. Avakian thought the tour might provide a recording opportunity. Columbia's new European partner, the Dutch label Philips, had excellent engineers, and Avakian opted to use them on the roadwork for recording the 1955 Armstrong tour. The tour album drew from October dates in Amsterdam and November dates in Paris. Avakian titled it *Ambassador Satch.*

When Armstrong returned from overseas swings in the spring of 1956, Avakian recorded him in June, producing additional live material that he would release as *The Great Chicago Concert, 1956.* Although in that latter recording, he had to overcome serious miking problems with Armstrong's unanticipated stage movements, the Columbia producer was determined to advance live recording as an art. What he needed was the right time, place, and performance.

He would find all at Newport '56.

6

Outdoor Live Recording

Columbia Goes to Newport

In a 2002 interview impresario George Wein reflected on the early years of the Newport Jazz Festival and its impact: "It created this incredible public relations viewing for jazz. It created the focus on jazz that had never happened before, [at least] not since Benny Goodman. That was the importance of the Newport Jazz Festival, and of course it really started everything that's happening today." George Avakian was a charter advisory member of the festival board. He owed his position to Wein, who in 1954 was a Boston jazz producer and pianist and the board of directors' vice president. Wein's role was already key to the festival's success. He booked talent and managed the event and was thus the board's interface with the jazz and record business and key players like Avakian.

In 1954 the *New Yorker* characterized Wein as a "stocky man of twenty-eight who seemed to be filled with a controlled frenzy." The son of a plastic surgeon and an heiress to a paper-bag company, he was born in Lynn, Massachusetts, on Boston's North Shore. Eventually the family settled in Newton, a suburb west of Boston. "I grew up in a very musical home," Wein once told the *Boston Globe*'s John Koch. "My father and mother loved show business; they loved Al Jolson. I used to sing at Saturday kiddie shows on WHDH radio in Boston—I was a bit of a ham."

Wein began studying classical piano at age eight and later, as a teenager, turned to jazz, making forays to New York to witness the late thirties jazz scene. In the summer of 1948 he took private lessons at the Juilliard School in New York with the great swing pianist Teddy Wilson.

After he graduated from Boston University with a history degree in 1950, he opened a jazz club, Storyville, which would have a variety of locations before returning to its original venue at the Copley Square Hotel in Boston's Hub. Drawing on his childhood connection to WHDH, Wein was able to get deejay John McLellan to do live Tuesday night broadcasts from the club. In late 1953 he launched Storyville Records. By this time the club featured progressive jazz musicians such as Charlie Parker, and sometimes Wein himself would play with a group he had put together. In the summertime he began running summer Storyvilles in Gloucester and Magnolia on Cape Cod. In early 1954 he was asked by upper-crust Newporters Elaine and Louis Lorillard to help put together a jazz festival, and today the name George Wein is inseparably identified with the annual event.

George Avakian was one of a number of jazz names that Wein and others assembled to advise the Newport Festival board. The role afforded Avakian box seats to the concerts, invitations to all the off-site parties, and easy access to talent—whether signed by Columbia or looking to be signed. In its first two years the Newport Jazz Festival had become a camp meeting for musicians and fans. The event was very intimate. Almost anyone could get close to the music and the musicians.

"I remember it was so wonderful to be backstage at Newport and watch musicians who hadn't seen each other in years greeting each other," recalled the jazz historian Dan Morgenstern. "Because after all, if you are a professional jazz musician, you don't move in necessarily the same circles. It was like a reunion and also a getting acquainted. Here people would be listening for the first time to younger musicians whom they had never encountered, and the younger musicians would suddenly have a revelation—'Boy, Ellington, Armstrong! Is that what they are all about?!' So it was a great thing, and it was the same thing for the audience."

At the 1955 Newport Jazz Festival, the second, Avakian could attend to his official festival duties and also joyfully participate as a fan. He scouted for talent for his label and supported his latest artist, Dave Brubeck, whose *Jazz Goes to College* was only a month into becoming—to that time—the best-selling album in jazz history. Brubeck would be in the company of other progressive jazz musicians such as baritone sax man Gerry Mulligan and pianist Thelonious Monk, as well as traditional and swing staples like Armstrong, Basie, and Woody Herman.

At this Newport Avakian would find another big name, although one not scheduled to perform: Miles Dewey Davis. The son of an eminent African American dentist in East St. Louis, Davis had burst on the scene in 1945–46 as a nineteen-year-old trumpeter, sitting in the Charlie Parker Savoy and Dial sessions that yielded the first definitive bop recordings. Beginning in about 1953, Davis had it in mind to record for Columbia and to that end several times approached Avakian, who politely declined. His was not a label prepared to bet on Davis, who had been struggling with a heroin addiction for some three years. By the beginning of 1954, however, Davis employed supreme willpower to kick his habit—cold turkey. He also continued to harbor thoughts about recording for Columbia. In some ways the motivation was envy. Chet Baker, a young Oakie from Los Angeles, was another trumpeter who would wrestle lifelong with his own heroin addiction. A key member of the Gerry Mulligan Quartet, Baker was suddenly the darling of cool jazz. His rise and temperament had parallels to Davis's.

What impressed the egotistically driven Miles Davis about Baker's career was the commercial marketing behind him. The succession of brooding photos that had appeared in print with predictable regularity had made him a national jazz poster boy akin to the early fifties movie icon James Dean. Davis wanted the same, and he was convinced that Avakian and the powerful Columbia label—with CBS, its corporate parent, behind it—could make that happen, just as they had done with Brubeck. His work was still irregular, his attitude was gratingly unpredictable, but he had been clean for a year. That summer, Miles Davis had made his way to Newport determined to prove himself to the suits.

On the final night of the '55 festival, George Wein wanted to give his stage crew the opportunity between the last two scheduled performers—the main events, Basie and Brubeck—to clear the stage. Wein agreed to let Duke Ellington introduce a pickup group to fill time. Davis was there in the backstage tent. Said Wein, "I put him together in the jam session." As the musicians assembled on the stage, Ellington told the crowd, "It looks like these gentlemen live in the realm that Buck Rogers is trying to reach." The aggregation was certainly stellar: Thelonious Monk, Gerry Mulligan, tenor sax man Zoot Sims, bassist Percy Heath, and drummer Connie Kay.

They opened with Monk's "Hackensack." The second song was the enigmatic pianist's best-known classic " 'Round Midnight." To the absolute surprise of the crowd, Miles Davis joined the group as a walk-on and proceeded to improvise a brilliantly haunting solo that hushed the fans. When the song finished, the applause was rapturous. The group closed with Charlie Parker's "Now's the Time," and a now keenly interested Avakian made his way backstage. When Davis saw him by the musicians' tent, he shot him a knowing grin. Producer and trumpeter agreed to meet at Lindy's for lunch the following Tuesday.

Avakian offered Davis $4,000 to join Columbia—an offer accepted. However, Avakian had trouble selling him to one Columbia VP, Albert Earl, who, in the producer's view, was "a real square." Davis still had a year and a half to run on his contract with Prestige, which included a commitment for four more records. "George, think about this," cautioned Earl; "this guy may be dead before you can record him." Avakian prevailed without further argument, however; his blazing success with the Brubeck album was sufficient leverage to secure Al Earl's sign-off.

After Miles Davis's performance at Newport '55, George Avakian realized that the festival was a venue for the potentially, and unpredictably, momentous. Whether such an event was a jam or an improvisation, whether it featured an old star or a young one, a new direction or a comeback, it would be a one-time happening—intense but fleeting, with electricity passing back and forth between performer and audience, then no more. For many who were there, "'Round Midnight" had transformed the Newport stage into the mercy seat of jazz.

Sometime after the festival, Avakian found himself musing over the presence of the U.S. government's Voice of America, which attended the whole weekend to make recordings for broadcast overseas. On tape VOA engineers had recorded three nights of concerts live—not inside a concert hall but rather in the open air. Given the limitations of prestereophonic, single-channel recording from one omnidirectional microphone challenged by the acoustic impact of wind, barometric pressure, echoes, and ambient noise, it was technically bold.

When 1956 came, Avakian decided he didn't just want to be there—he wanted to be intimately involved. Avakian-the-artist wanted to capture the ephemeral. Avakian-the-sound-engineer, a proven producer backed by the number-one entertainment combine in the world, was going to propose something even more technically demanding: outdoor live recording—not for broadcast, but for LP release.

"Nobody had ever recorded [for record release] at a jazz festival before," Avakian said. "The whole idea of recording live was considered kind of scary, although I had done it." Whether he would get an opportunity to record at a third Newport was in doubt, however. At one postfestival board meeting, George Wein and the organizers met and determined that they might have to fold their enterprise—sellout crowds, critical success, and acclaim notwithstanding. The festival was just not able to cover its costs. For Avakian the news was a shock, but it also afforded an opportunity.

"Part of my desire to do live recording was to raise money for the Newport Festival," Avakian said. "I thought if I could persuade the company to let me do that in 1956, we could make a payment to the festival for the recording rights, which of course wasn't necessary. The festival would have paid anybody if they had the money to record, because the publicity would be so great." He pitched the notion to Wein. The idea was a simple one. "Whatever I paid the artist," recalled Wein, "Columbia paid me, and they could record, and in effect we had the artist for nothing, which I thought was a great deal. And it turns out, it wasn't such a great deal, but I didn't know any better in those days."

Avakian didn't have to twist Columbia's arm. "I had a very free hand," he said. "I didn't even have a recording budget, because the pop albums, once they really got started, were so successful that I could do anything I wanted—literally. . . . 'George knows what the hell he is doing. Look at the money that's coming in.'" He planned to record every Columbia artist that Wein contracted, produce three or four complete albums, and then package them as the festival. When he got the Columbia sign-off, Avakian got back to Wein.

For Newport '56 Columbia expected Wein to book a number of its artists, certainly Louis Armstrong, the Dave Brubeck Quartet, the Eddie Condon All-Stars, and veteran Basie trumpeter Buck Clayton. It hoped he would take trombonists J. J. Johnson and Kai Winding, who were performing together. Avakian and the label also wanted Wein to include one more, whose debut at Columbia was imminent: Duke Ellington.

Before discussing any details with Wein, however, Avakian needed to resolve the repertoire issues with his artists, particularly Armstrong and Ellington. Understandably, on the road these longtime jazz stars would cater to their audiences who were paying to hear them play their favorite songs. "To record Louis Armstrong live, I had discovered in '55, was a real problem," said Avakian, "because he played the same basic program in those days. He did that all the time with his all-star group." "Please, I need some fresh material," he told Armstrong when he presented his Newport proposal. "I can't put out what you've put out on Decca and also put out on Columbia." "Yeah, Daddy, yeah Daddy," Pops replied offhandedly, "we'll do something."

In late June Avakian put a call into Ellington, who was finishing his spring '56 road trip out West. Remembering his failure to get his singles counterpart, Mitch Miller, to agree to release any Ellington single, Avakian realized that "the obvious thing would be to get Duke to write a long composition." "Do you have anything at all in the works that would be ready in time?" he asked. "No," Ellington responded, "but Strayhorn and I always have something going, and I'll work something up for sure." "We can't have 'Mood Indigo' and 'Take the A Train,'" Avakian pressed. "They're in the Columbia catalog three times over, plus other catalogs. We're going to have to have some fresh material." "Yeah, I know the problem," said Ellington. "We'll work on something." "Could it be called something like the 'Newport Jazz Festival Suite?'" "There is no other title."

In his liner notes to the original 1956 *Ellington at Newport* issue, Avakian wrote that it was Wein who asked Ellington to write a composition. Apparently, Wein and Ellington had been discussing directly a possible Newport appearance. A few days after their talk, read the 1956 liner notes, Ellington played in New York and was finishing a piece that he and Strayhorn were writing, the "Suite."

After his own discussion with Ellington, the Columbia producer returned to Wein to negotiate the terms of the recording contract—how much his label would pay and what Columbia artists would perform. "George," said Avakian, "do you ever think you would be interested in hiring Duke again for this?" Whatever he had discussed with Ellington directly, the Newport impresario was unsure whether Duke was still a draw. He had already agreed to front the costs of one big band, the sixteen-member Count Basie Orchestra, and he didn't automatically see a place for another. Said Wein, "As far as the press and the jazz world [were concerned], he was on the way down."

When Wein and Ellington had talked about the possibility of a Newport gig, apparently the bandleader was nonchalant. Asked what he was planning to perform, he demurred, telling Wein that he would present one of his medleys. The offhanded pronouncement was not what the festival impresario wanted to hear.

"Well, I wasn't planning to hire Duke, but I will," Wein conceded to Avakian. "But he can't play his medley of hits." "I don't want him to do that either. Duke says he'll have fresh material. Don't worry, I'll arrange it with him." "Okay," Wein said, "we'll put Duke on the program."

Some have suggested that Columbia pressured Wein to put Ellington on the bill. "I put Ellington in the program myself, and nobody ever had to browbeat me to put Ellington anywhere," said Wein forcefully, notwithstanding his reservation. "I worshiped Duke Ellington."

Wein then agreed to the other Columbia artists also, "which basically he was going to do anyway," recalled Avakian.

So Ellington came to Newport as a Columbia artist, even though he did not yet have a signed contract with the label. For its package of artists, Columbia paid Wein $25,000.

With Columbia on board, Avakian had to scramble. "The preparations were made for all the artists, and contracts were drawn up and so forth. The planning was kind of crazy. The whole thing was done in kind of a hurry. I think that Duke was entirely off Columbia's artist roster at the Newport festival. I don't think we had a signed contract, but it wasn't necessary with Duke. After all, we'd had a relationship for years and years, going back to when I was a student at Yale."

Ellington was anxiously happy. He wanted a record. The indisputable industry giant in popular and jazz LPs, Columbia had broken Brubeck live, had signed Davis and that year released the trumpeter's first Columbia LP, and was going great guns with Armstrong. Knowing that the world's greatest label was recording him live at Newport, Ellington would be performing before the assembled multitude of jazz fans, personalities, and the national media. His *Time* magazine cover story now had a solid and sexy news peg. All the elements were in play. Like his first Cotton Club booking almost thirty years before, Newport suddenly seemed to have the potential to be a major career opportunity, an occasion to which he would have to rise. It was also one that—at fifty-seven—might be his last.

As for his Columbia recording package, Avakian was feeling confident in the second week of July 1956, the immediate run-up to the Newport weekend. "Everything was set up, and on Tuesday before the festival—I had the check [for Wein] in my pocket—we had a meeting in Goddard Lieberson's office."

Columbia Records' gifted and flamboyant president who had succeeded Ted Wallerstein, Lieberson had once been the head of its Masterworks department. He was another who had written his own life's script. Born in England, he had immigrated to the States with his family and been raised in Seattle. He studied at the Eastman School of Music in Rochester, New York, hoping to become a composer. By 1939 he had written more than a hundred compositions and managed to have several of his works performed by orchestras funded by the Works Progress Administration. This New Deal relief program supported struggling musicians during the Depression through conductor Nikolai Sokoloff's Federal Music Project, which sponsored orchestras across the country and provided work to more than ten thousand musicians.

In 1938 Ted Wallerstein hired Lieberson to head artists and repertoire at Masterworks. The following year, Lieberson assumed the title of assistant director of the department. Throughout the forties his focus was on classical and operatic works. Riding on the success of the introduction of the LP, he advanced to become Columbia's executive vice president in 1949. Considering Decca's success with its 1943 release of the smash hit musical *Oklahoma!* on 78s, history's first original cast recording, Lieberson saw that the LP format could capitalize on the success of Broadway musicals, arguably homegrown

American opera. Recognizing the commercial potential in marketing original cast recordings, he launched a new Masterworks line by recording the hit musical *South Pacific.* The LP took New York by storm, became a smash hit, and was for seventy straight weeks the number-one-selling album, a record still unbroken.

Inspired by his success with *South Pacific,* Lieberson had the daring to invest in Broadway musical productions on behalf of the label in order to gain recording rights. His other award winners were *Flower Drum Song, Camelot, West Side Story, Mame, The Sound of Music,* and *My Fair Lady*. He had been so impressed by Lerner and Lowe's score that he persuaded CBS to become the sole investor, hence the holder of all rights to *My Fair Lady,* unique for a record label. In this particular arena Lieberson was very hands-on. He loved to run the recording sessions of the original Broadway cast albums. He was able to play this role because he had the respect of the label's vocalists and musicians, who valued a senior executive who understood the creative process and could actually read and write a musical score.

Less formal than Wallerstein, Lieberson "fancied himself as a bon vivant," recalled Columbia photographer Don Hunstein. He was sophisticated, well connected, good looking, and affable. John Hammond called him the wittiest man he ever met, although "not particularly a jazz fan." Lieberson surrounded himself with competent directors and senior staff and gave them the freedom to think creatively and independently. For pop music—beyond his domain of cast albums—he relied on the sensibilities of his department heads: Mitch Miller, a fellow student from his days at Eastman, was given free rein in pop singles, and George Avakian enjoyed wide latitude in pop albums.

Another critical member of the team was Columbia's gifted publicist Deborah Ishlon. In large measure Lieberson's position in the company was enhanced by his relationship with the sharp, assertive Ishlon, who reported to him directly and with whom he was very close. Unpopular with the "boys club" in sales, "she kissed Lieberson to keep the job." Single and thirty, Debbie Ishlon was perhaps the only woman who had risen to the top of any record department in the fifties. Hers is a story in and of itself. The daughter of a Latvian Jewish refugee who became a Pittsburgh doctor, Ishlon was a short, bespectacled brunette, a theatrical person whose dark eyes penetrated from under bushy eyebrows and a beret. "She was famous for her hats. She always had a hat on." Her personal taste was classical music, which aligned her perfectly with Lieberson. She revered Igor Stravinsky and Glenn Gould, for whom she managed publicity and "had a lot to do with Glenn's success."

Until she hired Hunstein in early 1956, the publicity department was herself, an assistant publicist, and a secretary. Interviewing him for the job, she said, "I need someone I can rely on to edit photographs and make sure this publicity outfit gets what they want or need." Reporting directly to her, Hunstein started by refining the catalog of jobs, organizing the photo files and archives. He then moved to shoots, hiring freelancers as necessary. Ishlon was among the first to supply photographs with the press releases. Avakian remembered that she was wildly talented and only gradually became a jazz fan.

When he took her to see Miles Davis perform at the Bohemia in 1955, she immediately recognized that she could work with him. "With the Italian suits and Cole Porter with a mute," she told Avakian, "I'll get a full page in both *Time* and *Newsweek*." And she did.

"Debbie knew the record business was going to expand," said Hunstein. "She was shrewd enough to see that it wasn't only going to be the crooners with the orchestra behind them." Ishlon was possibly the first person working for a major label to appreciate the explosion of photography and the importance of label design for the record business. Until 1955, LP cover art was minimal, tending toward line drawings, if anything. All these efforts on the part of the independents inspired Ishlon to move her label—the major label—in a more creative visual direction. Among her first successes was getting photos onto all the album covers in Avakian's Armstrong series. "Debbie was forward looking and knew how to hire pretty good people," Hunstein recalled, "art directors who were part of a new generation: Neil Fujita and later Bob Cato, who was a well known designer and painter who went to *Redbook,* and then John Berg from *Esquire,* the best of all designers."

Suddenly Ishlon's office was expanding, and she was gaining clout. At the same time that she hired Hunstein, she brought onboard a third publicist. Her brash style, however, would eventually be her undoing at Columbia. According to Hunstein, eventually her rivals in sales "might have gotten her fired." Her departure probably had more to do with her 1960 novel *Girl Singer,* which reflected insights into her own world, which she labeled a "perfumed tar pit." Her record-business exposé told a familiar tale about a small-town girl caught both in the swirl of pop music star-making and a relationship gone wrong with the A&R man who created her public personality. Ill-advisedly she based the relationship on that between Columbia's enduringly powerful Mitch Miller and Jill Corey, one of his finds.

Debbie Ishlon was always a significant voice in Lieberson's weekly Tuesday meetings. Another was Hal B. Cook, Columbia's vice president of sales. Cook would later become a publisher with *Billboard.* Still later, he would develop the concept of "Music in the Air," the first in-flight music program, launched in 1964 by American Airlines. And so, on that Tuesday before Newport '56, Ishlon, Cook, and Avakian took their places before Lieberson's desk and began the routine of discussing the week's business. When they turned to Newport, to Avakian's amazement, the Columbia chief announced that he had cooled on the recording project. Well adept at balancing commerce and art, he had weighed his responsibility to both and at this late juncture found the scales tipping in favor of the corporate interest.

"Look, George," Lieberson said, "it's a big risk. I mean, what if the weather is bad, and the performances aren't good? Why don't we just tell the artists you're planning to record to come into the studio, and we'll tie it into the festival?" Avakian was stunned. "Goddard! It won't be the same thing." Lieberson was unmoved. "Let's cancel out. Let them keep the money, but don't go and record."

Avakian's technical arguments fell on deaf ears. Lieberson's mind was set. With the project about to eighty-six, Avakian began to ponder how to phrase his apologies to George Wein, Ellington, and the other Columbia artists.

"Goddard," Cook interrupted unexpectedly, "I think George should do it. It's a risk, but if it succeeds, it's something that has never been done before. George is convinced that the performances will be more exciting and more saleable, and I'm inclined to agree." Lieberson looked to his publicist. Ishlon had no doubt that the festival would present Don Hunstein with hundreds of photo ops she could use effectively to promote company product. She was fully behind going to Newport and said so. Cook, the label's distribution ace, added a final word calculated to play to Lieberson's executive ego. "Look, after all, we are Columbia, and we do things that other people don't do. George has already done a lot of that, and it has always worked out. Let's do it." Lieberson's eyes darted back and forth as he reached for his final answer. When at last they settled on Avakian, the Columbia executive made the pronouncement. Green light.

Louis Armstrong and Bing Crosby on the set of the film *High Society*, 1956. ::: *Courtesy of Dan Morgenstern, the Institute of Jazz Studies, Rutgers University.*

7

From the Masses to the Classes

Newport and Elaine Lorillard

At the time of the third Newport Jazz Festival, the great trumpeter Louis Armstrong was the most famous jazzman in the world. In addition to continued engagements in America, Pops and his All Stars had recently toured Europe, Japan, and Australia. In early May 1956 Ambassador Satch was in Great Britain giving a command performance for the royals. Later that month, the CBS network and its august broadcaster Edward R. Murrow sponsored and helped arrange a last-minute trip to the Gold Coast. In Accra, Armstrong blew his horn for an afternoon crowd at the polo grounds. The scale was staggering: a hundred thousand people spread over a space as large as three football fields. For Africans Louis Armstrong had become more than a bandleader. He was America's international ambassador of jazz.

He had also been shooting a feature film, *High Society,* in which he played himself. A remake of *The Philadelphia Story,* it was a musical with songs by Cole Porter and, along with Armstrong, featured Bing Crosby, Frank Sinatra, and Irish American beauty Grace Kelly. *High Society* opens with Pops introducing the story while en route with his band to exclusive Newport, Rhode Island, to play a jazz festival sponsored by the Bing Crosby character. Kelly played the part of his ex-wife, a feisty socialite who is about to remarry. Newport legend has it that Grace Kelly modeled her performance on one Elaine Guthrie Lorillard.

The August 14, 1954, issue of the *New Yorker* ran a delightfully evocative article on the first Newport Jazz Festival titled "You Dig It, Sir?" The reporter was the witty Lillian Ross, who would be the romantic partner of the magazine's otherwise married editor, William Shawn, for forty years. Ross introduced Elaine Lorillard to her cosmopolitan readers simply as "an attractive, titian-haired woman" while sprinkling her piece throughout with Lorillard's observant bon mots. In his 2003 autobiography, *Myself among Others*, none other than jazz impresario George Wein wrote, "There is no doubt that the driving force and inspiration behind the festival was Elaine."

Born in 1914, the elder of two children, Elaine Guthrie lived with her family in an upper-crust southwest suburb of Boston on the road to Wellesley: Brookline, Massachusetts. Elaine described herself in the Ross piece as coming from a longhair family and being raised on classical music. Her father, Walter E. Guthrie, hailed from a Maine family of colonial Scots. Handsome and athletic, Guthrie had gone to New Hampshire's Phillips Exeter Academy. Initially he attended Harvard, but "he left," said Elaine, "because he wanted to be a painter; so he went to Yale." Guthrie would take a job as editor and cartoonist for the *Boston Advertiser* and eventually would go into the printing business, establishing a family firm, Boston's Guthrie Printing.

Elaine and Louis Lorillard (right), founders of the Newport Jazz Festival, with Columbia producer George Avakian (far left) and Boston jazz impresario George Wein, at one of the 1956 festival's after-performance gatherings at the Lorillard mansion, where musicians and the jazz world commingled with Newport society ::: *Photo by Don Hunstein. Courtesy of Sony BMG Music Entertainment.*

While at Harvard Guthrie met Lida Pray, a young soprano who had come to Boston to study at the New England Conservatory of Music. The Pray family were also colonials from Maine, Congregationalists who had mixed with a line of Quakers, the denomination that Elaine claimed as her own. Lida was the niece of Lillian (Norton) Nordica, the famous Wagnerian soprano who recorded for Columbia records, appeared in early Coca-Cola advertising campaigns, and later died on Java following exposure after a shipwreck. When Elaine turned seven, her mother enrolled her in a piano class at the conservatory, and in that same year she performed her first concert, playing one of Edvard Grieg's piano concerti. As she matured, she showed an interest in art, eventually studying art history at Boston University's College of the Arts and becoming an artist. But she continued her study of classical piano into her early adult life.

At seventeen, Elaine's first real beau was the young Jimmy McHugh, son of the well-known jazz composer. The elder McHugh had been the partner of song plugger and Duke Ellington manager Irving Mills. In 1927 he teamed with Cotton Club lyricist Dorothy Fields. Altogether, McHugh composed for nine Cotton Club shows. With Fields he scored the all-black Broadway hit musical *Blackbirds of 1928,* famous for such hits as "I Can't Give You Anything but Love, Baby." Exposed to such liberating musical influences via the McHugh family, Elaine lost interest in playing classical music and switched to jazz. "My family was furious," she commented. "I had to hide everything, all the sheet music Jimmy gave me, which I would play when nobody was around."

After her breakup with Jimmy, she moved to New York. A modern, independent woman, she started modeling and frequently posed for artists, then got steady work as a department store display designer. Among her early assignments was a stint at Macy's. Elaine was moving in downtown bohemian art and literary circles where she soon met her first husband, a young Dutch architect, Adriaan Pieter Hocke van Moolenburgh, the son of the governor of the Dutch East Indies. In 1939 they married and moved into a Greenwich Village townhouse apartment just off Fifth Avenue. Six months later, the Germans invaded Poland and van Moolenburgh went off to war.

Jazz remained Elaine's keen interest. Two Dartmouth grads lived in the apartment across the hall. As hot jazz collectors, they had the records; she had the record player. "We would sit around listening to old jazz sides, and then we would go over to Nick's, the Dixieland jazz stronghold where Sidney Bechet, Muggsy Spanier, and some of their cohorts usually were in residence," she wrote in a 1956 article for *Collier's* magazine. "If it hadn't been for those Dartmouth boys, I probably would have remained a square." Soon she grew close to a number of jazz personalities in the New York scene, notably Chicago guitarist Eddie Condon, with whom she remained close for decades.

After her design for a Fifth Avenue window display advertising Red Cross bonds received an award, the charity invited her to go overseas to restore buildings at Bagnoli, a coastal suburb northwest of Naples that the Allies had captured in 1943. The Bagnoli site was a compound where Benito Mussolini had billeted his officers; American GIs would be using it for R&R and as a bivouac. Once her team had finished the rehab, her attention turned to entertaining the troops, for whom she managed to borrow instruments and put on jazz concerts. There she met a fellow New Englander from Newport, Louis Livingston Lorillard, who had enlisted in the army and risen to be a finance officer on General George Patton's staff. Born in 1920, Louis Lorillard was a direct descendant of the nineteenth-century tobacco tycoon Pierre J. Lorillard. Another in his line helped to found Newport's Casino Tennis Club in 1879, the birthplace of American lawn tennis. Although the Lorillard name is more famous, it was in fact his mother Edith Norman's family who possessed the wealth and stature that enabled him to move among the very top of Newport society. The Normans were a distinguished and successful Rhode Island line. Her father, George H. Norman, was one of the co-owners of the *Newport Daily News.* Norman, who had nine children, was also a property tycoon who invested in waterfront acreage and waterways.

Elaine and Louis fell into a wartime romance, and Lorillard proposed that they marry while still in Italy. Elaine, however, was still married to her Dutch husband, though she had no idea where he was. As soon as he was able, Lorillard returned to Newport to make arrangements. Once his plan to enable the marriage was set in motion, he sent for Elaine, who was still in Bagnoli. In 1946 Elaine got her divorce in Cora, Wyoming, where she and Louis were married before returning to Newport to start a new life together in nearby Middletown. For a number of years they also had the use of Paradise, a bird sanctuary and farm that belonged to a Norman aunt, Mabel Cerio, an artist who had married an Italian count.

In no time the young couple became fixtures of the Newport scene and started a family, Elaine giving birth to a daughter, Didi. Unlike so many other Newporters, they weren't just seasonal residents but lived there year round. Louis went into the travel business, and after his grandmother died, leaving him another six houses, Elaine went to work for her husband, throwing herself into interior decorating.

Having such a heavyweight lineage, Louis Lorillard would serve on virtually every committee and board of directors in Newport, including the cliquey Bailey's Beach, the Reading Room, and the Casino Tennis Club. By 1952 Elaine and Louis Lorillard had become the acknowledged leaders of Newport's younger set, even if its ranks were ominously thinning.

"There were very few young people who wanted to come back to live here," Elaine said, "and that's why the houses were going for nothing, or being torn down. This town was like a desert. Some of the old people were still here in the mansions, but they came only in the summer. I remember seeing the big trucks that would bring all their furniture."

When Elaine became pregnant with her second child, she realized that the family would soon outgrow the house in Middletown. She started looking at properties in Newport and found a "cottage" at the end of Bellevue Avenue just opposite Rough Point, the estate of the eccentric philanthropist Doris Duke. They named it Quatrel, French for "four Ls," one for each member of their family.

In the eighteenth century Newport had been a major seaport, a cosmopolitan city on Aquidneck Island that rivaled more prosperous Boston, New York, Philadelphia, and

Charleston. From its founding in 1639, the city had enjoyed a climate of religious tolerance that attracted Quakers, Baptists, Congregationalists, and Sephardic Jews. Notwithstanding its reputation for tolerance, Newport had its contradictions. A shipbuilding center, it was also a point on the triangular route of ships carrying West African slaves to the West Indies, where they were traded for sugar and molasses, which in turn was traded for Newport rum. The price of each male slave was one hundred gallons of rum. In the Gilded Age Newport acquired its mythic image as the playground for the Vanderbilts and other great commercial families who had amassed wealth as the United States industrialized. From the perspective of the old Newport families, these robber barons were the nouveau riche. By World War I the formerly nouveau riche had become the Newport establishment, and by World War II much of that establishment was no longer creating wealth. The real money was being made elsewhere. By the 1950s many old-guard colonists would resist the idea of a Newport jazz festival. They wanted the drawbridge raised on their exclusive island colony. For many others living in Newport, however, the prospect of a jazz festival seemed intriguing. Many of these were local businessmen who had prospered not so much from the profligacy of the summer colonists but rather from the predictably wanton spending of sailors.

Newport and Narragansett Bay, with its natural harbor, had long been an important naval training center. In 1941 the Newport Naval Base was built, along with new facilities across the bay, the Quonset Naval Air Station and the Naval Construction Battalion Center at Davisville. Thousands of officers and other men received their training at Newport schools, and Quonset became the largest of the navy's airbases and home port to a number of aircraft carriers. At the war's peak in 1944, the number of naval personnel at Newport was a whopping 162,000. During the Korean War the navy established an Officers Candidate School at Newport. Throughout the fifties navy men and their families continued to swamp the town. Sailors packed notorious dives like Leo's First and Last Stop at the end of Long Wharf, Blood Alley on West Pelham, and the Blue Moon on Thames. The sheer scale of mobilization in back-to-back wars had transformed all in Newport—including the society that Elaine Guthrie Lorillard had joined.

The wealthy summer colonists who had once accounted for the lion's share of Newport's taxes now contributed less than 10 percent, and some colonists had to sell their cottages to pay those taxes. Some cottages were leased; others were boarded shut or destroyed by fire or vandalism. The old social aristocracy was dying, while the younger generation was summering elsewhere. Yet colonists still went through the motions of the summer season. They enjoyed their luncheons at Bailey's Beach and golf at the Country Club. Gentlemen would unwind with cocktails at the Reading Room, the town's oldest men's club, and rejoin their families for dinner at the Clambake Club. On Fridays and Saturdays colonists would host private dinners for up to thirty people. Debutantes would have their dances at Bailey's or the Clambake. In addition to these and other private dances, the social season would include the Country Club costume party, the White Elephant Ball, July Fourth and Labor Day formals, and finally Tennis Week, the season's climax. For Elaine Lorillard, a prescient outsider who had joined Newport society only by marriage, this annual whirl of activity was a bore. Certain it wouldn't survive much longer, she set herself a task to revolutionize the Newport summer season with music.

The idea of a music festival had come to Newport in the thirties, when the town rejected a proposal that eventually led to the Boston Symphony Orchestra's summer offering at Tanglewood in Lenox, Massachusetts. In 1952 the Lorillards became part of a group called the Newport Music Committee, which campaigned and raised money to bring the New York Philharmonic to Newport. According to Elaine, the state government in Providence gave their committee a $5,000 grant. The plan was to have the Philharmonic play an annual summer season. The following summer, the orchestra opened at the Casino for a two-night engagement. The concerts were sparsely attended, and bad weather forced the program inside, where the acoustics were poor. The backers were reputedly out almost $30,000, losing sixty-seven cents on the dollar.

A number of accounts have it that shortly after the failed attempt at a classical summer season, John Maxon, director of the Rhode Island School of Design's museum, suggested to Elaine that she launch a jazz festival. The claim that he first had the idea for a jazz festival originated in her 1956 *Collier's* piece. However, in 2003 she maintained that although the article went under her byline, much of it was actually written by her coauthor, Richard Gehman, and that the account of Maxon as instigator was false. Maxon's name, however, appears on Newport Jazz Festival letterhead as advisory member for the 1954 and 1956 offerings. Elaine credited instead the U.S. Navy as the catalyst behind her idea for the jazz festival.

In the early fifties, still an unabashed jazz lover, she had discovered that the navy's Coasters Harbor Island Officers Club hosted weekend jazz events. "On Saturday nights in the winter here, there was nothing going on, no place to hear jazz music, and so we would go out to the officers club. They had a big ballroom, and we loved it." Until that point, music for Louis Lorillard had been Meyer Davis, the society bandleader who played for Jack Kennedy's 1953 Newport wedding and was famous for his quip, "What we provide is atmosphere." A few Saturdays at the naval station in Newport opened his eyes, and soon Louis was a fan. Elaine, energized by her Saturdays at the officers club and recalling how successful her jam sessions had been in wartime Bagnoli, started toying with the idea of doing a summer concert series focused not on classical music but jazz.

"We really ought to do something other than classical," she remarked to her jazz convert one night. "Well, I don't want anything to do with it," said Louis, "but I'll back it." Elaine thus entered the world of jazz promotion.

Initially, the Lorillards were not sure what kind of event they were proposing. "We didn't look ahead at all, because of the bad luck we had with the classical festival." Newport had held a few two- or three-night lecture series. "We wanted something more than just a concert. We wanted to make it bigger and do it again every year."

Harking back to her years in Greenwich Village, Elaine Lorillard wanted to introduce new music into her social circle. As Cleveland Amory, a friend of the Lorillards and a proper Bostonian who was the ghostwriter for the Duchess of Windsor's autobiography, put it, "To take jazz from the masses to the classes was an extraordinary idea in itself—but hardly less so was Mrs. Lorillard's choice of Newport as a festival site."

Whether it was in Newport, Providence, or Washington, Louis Lorillard was in the habit of using his social position to slip through the back door and make things happen. The Lorillards pitched their jazz proposal to Providence and were refused a grant. The Casino's board of directors was more open to the idea. A year before, the Casino had wanted Lorillard to be its president, but Louis wasn't a tennis fan and so had proposed James H. Van Alen. Now Louis placed the notion before the board and Van Alen, making the case that the number-one tennis court would be ideal. "We had used it the year before [for the classical concert]," said Elaine, "and so it was already an easy thing to do." The Casino bought the Lorillards' idea and agreed to charge them a nominal $350 for the use of the grounds.

With a venue secured, the Lorillards now needed a jazz manager who could book talent and manage the event. In January 1954 Elaine was in Boston having dinner with her brother Tom Guthrie, who was running his father's printing business as its president. "Where's there a good jazz place?" Elaine asked him. "Well," he replied, "I'll take you over to Storyville."

Later that night they arrived at the upstairs bar, where Guthrie spotted his former English professor from Boston University, Donald Born, a jazz fan and Storyville regular. Guthrie grabbed Born and had him join them for a drink. Born began telling Elaine of his last trip to Europe and his jazz studies. "You know what this country needs?" Elaine offered. "It needs a jazz festival." "There's somebody here who can help you with that," Professor Born replied. "The guy who owns this club." According to Elaine, he left the table and came back with "a great big heavyset guy" and introduced them. That heavyset guy was George Wein.

Wein often heard wealthy swells in his club spin grand ideas about taking jazz into their social orbits, but they never took concrete action. At first blush, Elaine and her brother, whom Wein remembered erroneously as Louis Lorillard, must have appeared to be yet another society couple with a mere passing interest in jazz.

"Elaine talked a little more about the jazz festival and so forth. George Wein didn't say anything," Guthrie recalled. "He just stood there. So that was the end of that."

"I'm not interested," Wein said abruptly, then turned on his heel and walked away. "We were kind of shocked," Elaine added.

Elaine's trail seemed to have come to a dead end. Undaunted, she next turned to a New York contact she had known since the forties: Sylvia Marlowe. A world famous harpsichordist, Marlowe was married to the well-regarded Russian painter Leonid Berman. She was a "real New Yorker," said Elaine.

Marlowe and Berman moved in music, art, and literary circles. Among their closest friends was the poet Robert Penn Warren. Her parties of the thirties, forties, and fifties were legendary mixers for the New York intelligentsia and provided an introduction for Elaine. Among her party tricks, Marlowe would play boogie-woogie on the harpsichord.

When Elaine called to get leads for a festival manager, Marlowe and Berman were living in an apartment on East Sixtieth Street. "Listen," said Marlowe, "I've got just the right person for you: John Hammond." Her friendship with Hammond dated from 1932, when they had worked together at New York's top Yiddish radio station, WEVD. Marlowe was also close to Hammond's second wife, Esme O'Brien. Elaine had actually met the Hammonds earlier at one of Marlowe's parties and remembered Esme, whose first marriage had been to David Sarnoff's son Robert. Elaine was delighted with the lead and soon met with Hammond at Marlowe's apartment.

On hearing Elaine's proposal, Hammond's initial reaction was to express doubt that Newport could handle the racial implications of a jazz festival, specifically the matter of accommodations for African American musicians, their families, and fans. Ironically, considering his Vanderbilt family background—or perhaps because of it—Hammond would later claim to have "no particular love for Newport," adding that it was "a kind of society and a kind of life" that was "everything I abhor."

Hammond was in conflict about his own background. Later in the fifties, once he, Esme, and the Lorillards had become friends, they frequently got together in Newport. Hammond had his own social ax to grind. Elaine believed it came from his Vanderbilt mother, who "was interested in all kinds of very strange people. There was an island that she went to and took care of the natives, and I think John had that in him, to break away. He was scorned by the rest of the family. They called him a communist."

Aware that he was too busy with his own recording projects, Elaine didn't approach him to run the festival, although in the end he agreed to serve on the committee's advisory board. Instead, she drew on a list of people that Hammond supplied her. At the top was Eddie Condon, whom Elaine knew well. Already engaged with his own jazz club on West Third Street, Condon declined, telling her that he would soon be too busy with an uptown club in which he had just acquired an interest. Another on Hammond's list was producer Ernie Anderson, famous for his jazz concerts at New York's Town Hall, who passed because "he was on his way to Europe." So it went.

A short while later, Hammond called to see how her search was going. "I'm discouraged," Elaine replied.

"You should have somebody near you in New England," Hammond said. "You need somebody in the area. There's a young guy who opened jazz clubs in Boston, and his name is George Wein."

Given her initial foray to Storyville, Elaine was unsure how to proceed. Hammond, however, may have gotten to work behind the scenes, for soon she received a letter from George Wein's assistant, Terri Turner. "George has told me that you came in about the jazz festival," Turner wrote. "I've convinced him that we should come down and see you."

Not wanting to handle the business end of the festival, Elaine asked Louis to do the talking to Wein and then placed a call to Turner accepting the proposal.

A couple of days later, Wein arrived in Newport with Turner and his Storyville publicist, Charlie Bourgeois, to meet with Louis at the Casino. In his autobiography Wein wrote that Louis gave him a $20,000 budget for the first year's effort. Lorillard had a second meeting with Wein in Boston. When he returned to Newport, he announced to Elaine, "Well, pull in your belt. I just gave George Wein $40,000." "But Louis," she replied in astonishment, "do you have anything in writing?" "No, we just shook hands." Seeing her skeptical expression, he added, "Well, this means I have shares in his record company." A week later, Elaine got a phone call from Terri Turner. "I don't believe it, Elaine, but I have another check from Louis for $40,000!"

Whatever Storyville's apparent success, Wein was having financial problems. In his autobiography he wrote that Storyville Records "was barely surviving. In 1955 the only thing keeping the company afloat was a loan from Louis Lorillard."

Once he decided to embrace the Lorillards' effort, Wein's initial thought was to produce a summer season around another Storyville, as he had been doing in Gloucester and Magnolia, to capture the Boston and New York winter audiences that vacationed in Cape Cod. The other possibility was to put together a jazz equivalent of the Tanglewood Festival. In mid-April 1954 Elaine and Louis moved ahead to legalize their decision to do the festival. Lorillard turned to his friend and Newport lawyer Richard Sheffield to draft articles of association to incorporate "The Jazz Festival of Newport, R.I., Inc." On April 28 the Lorillards and three signatories from Sheffield's firm filed the paperwork. Louis and Elaine then departed for their annual two-week trip to oversee the management of a family villa on Capri.

The officers for the first festival were Louis Lorillard, president; Wein, vice president; Jeremiah P. Maloney, Lorillard's banker at the Newport National Bank, treasurer; and Providence PR man Russell Jalbert, secretary. The board of directors included these officers, plus Elaine, with no title; Sheffield, lawyer; and Charles Bourgeois, assistant secretary.

Early on, Charlie Bourgeois proved to be a key player in the festival's success. Bourgeois knew Wein from his Boston University days. As students both he and Wein had been organizing jazz concerts. Before Boston had jazz critics, Wein said, Bourgeois would bring classical critics like the *Boston Globe*'s Cyrus Durgin to the club. After a time he asked to be the Storyville publicist, and Wein put him on his payroll, where he has remained to the present day. Bourgeois soon undertook many of the promotion duties associated with the festival. "He knew what he was doing," said Dan Morgenstern, "and he was very good at getting [reporters] from literally all over the world to cover Newport. This was covered like a major sports event, photographs and behind the scenes, you know, talking to the audience."

Elaine gave Bourgeois high praise for engaging the Boston media and jazz fraternity, as well as for providing a number of the advisory members for the 1954 board: "He had taste. He was the one who knew who was good and who should be on the program. He really did the programming, because George was the business man, the one who made the arrangements and did the contracts." However, she credited Jalbert for generating the publicity and maintained that she was the one who worked the New York press. Her great coup was to get the *New Yorker*'s Lillian Ross to cover the weekend. Although it was a classic in reportage, the festival organizers initially objected to the wry tone of the Ross piece.

The festival's 1954 advisory members were a hefty lot that included sponsors, leading classical and jazz personalities, and, perhaps most significant, print media. In addition to Sylvia Marlowe, John Maxon, Jimmy Van Alen, and Cleveland Amory was one especially key sponsor, Carl W. Haffenreffer, the Rhode Island beer baron. The Haffenreffers bought two boxes at $100 apiece. His Narragansett Brewing Co. was known for its postwar slogan, "Hi, Neighbor, Have a 'Gansett." Haffenreffer clearly saw the value in getting the beer concession at the festival and thus identifying his product with a mass of fans devoted to another spectator event aside from Boston baseball. By 1955 his was New England's best-selling beer.

A second sponsor was longtime Newport colonist George Henry Warren, a financier-turned-philanthropist, whose wife, Katherine, started the Newport Preservation Society. Described by Lillian Ross as "a gracious, jolly, pink-cheeked man wearing tortoise-shell glasses," Warren was one of only two Newport colonists who accepted the Lorillards' approach to invest in their project. Sixty-three others refused.

"As I remember, nobody gave more than $200 [the cost of two six-seat boxes]. We had three people that did that." They were Haffenreffer, who actually lived in Bristol, Warren, and one other Newport investor, a successful Providence newcomer named Edward J. Capuano. "Everybody was against Capuano, because he was Italian and a working person," said Elaine, "but he was quite rich. He owned a factory in Fall River and was new in Newport. And was ignored, of course, by everybody." The Lorillards were the exceptions. Capuano lived at their end of Bellevue Avenue, and his daughter was a close friend and playmate of the Lorillards' daughter, Didi.

Eddie Capuano was one of a trio of Fall River, Massachusetts, jazz fans in the clothing business who helped sponsor the first festival. The other two were his partner Ted LeSavoy and Larry Anderson. The latter owned Anderson Little, a factory-direct-to-you operation initially for men's suits. He was also the husband of Elaine Anderson, the anonymous platinum blonde whose photograph would grace the back cover of *Ellington at Newport*.

Among the rest of the festival's advisory members was jazz historian Marshall Stearns, George Avakian's old music mentor at Yale, by this time Hunter College professor of medieval English literature. Stearns would run the festival's discussion panels featured in the afternoons. Providing further intellectual horsepower and context was African American author Ralph Ellison, whose first novel, the best seller *Invisible Man,* had been published in 1952. From Boston were that city's Art Festival director Peter Temple and Donald Born. Joining Born was a fellow Storyville regular, Norman O'Connor, the Paulist chaplain of Boston University's Newman Club. Dubbed Boston's jazz priest, Father O'Connor would serve as sometime festival emcee. Along with George Avakian were other jazz names—Norman Granz, Louis Armstrong, Duke Ellington, Benny Goodman, and Stan Kenton. Other musical voices came from folk balladeer Richard Dyer-Bennet; conductor-composer Leonard Bernstein, in some ways heir to the music-popularizing tradition of George and Ira Gershwin; Boston Pops conductor Arthur Fiedler; African American conductor Dean Dixon; and composer Aaron Copland.

As an aside, Elaine recalled, "I had met [Copland] one time at Bailey's Beach. A woman brought him for lunch. I could see she was sitting way over at a table, and she waved at me and then came over and said, 'Would you come over and join us and have a drink?' Well, I was sitting next to Claiborne Pell [a future Newport board advisory member and Rhode Island senator] and all these friends of Louis' at a big round table, and I said, 'I'd love to.' So I rushed over and sat next to him, and he was charming. When I came back to my own table, somebody said, 'Who was that Jew?'" Like John Hammond, Elaine abhorred Newport's narrow-mindedness and wasn't one to be bound by the prejudices of others. Copland, however, was not an advisory member through any action on her part. "I think Charlie [Bourgeois] had him put on," Elaine said. "I wrote a letter thanking Copland [for being on the board], and he wrote me back a very sweet letter saying, 'Mrs. Lorillard, I was never invited to be on the board.'"

As with many boards, especially those serving nonprofit organizations, some of the many names on the first and successive Newport Jazz Festival letterheads were lent by noteworthy individuals who may not have attended a single meeting. Apparently Copland was not even aware that he had lent his name, leaving Elaine to speculate about the accuracy of other names on the letterheads. Some advisory members, however, were especially significant, at least from a promotional standpoint: media representatives Cyrus Durgin, music critic for the *Boston Globe;* Rudolph Elie Jr., columnist and music critic for the *Boston Herald;* Nat Hentoff, New York editor of *Down Beat;* jazz critic and author Leonard Feather; Jay Harrison, critic for the *New York Herald Tribune;* Alan Morrisson, editor of *Ebony;* Barry Ulanov of *Metronome;* and Arnold Gingrich, publisher of *Esquire.*

The presence of press advisers on the board enabled the organizers to manage both what was said and what was not said about many aspects of the festival. From the very beginning the Newport Jazz Festival had advance media buy-in. This kind of clout conveyed credibility in media circles and, after the second festival, was used to bring pressure on none other than the *New York Times* when it was deemed to be insufficiently supportive, if not downright critical, of the festival. Beyond those colonists who served on the festival boards, few in Newport society were rushing to buy festival tickets or boxes in advance. Elaine Lorillard said at the time that she had early support from the Vanderbilts, "one or two Astors," and a Mrs. Leroy King, whose husband was Louis Lorillard's godfather. One doyenne who bought a box was a Mrs. Harold Brooks. Another box went to the Count and Countess Reventlow, whose son was a close schoolmate of young Pierre Lorillard. A third would go to the John Barry Ryans. Their son John, who had worked in New York as a stage manager for Sammy Davis Jr., would be Newport's stage manager.

Among the Rhode Island Democratic Party establishment represented in the boxes were Claiborne Pell, who at one festival would introduce Elaine to the audience; Pearl Mesta, minister to Luxemburg from 1948 to 1953 and later Washington hostess; and the octogenarian U.S. senator Theodore Francis Green. With members of New England society and the arts, along with New York, Boston, and jazz media and nationally known classical and jazz names on its letterhead, the Newport Jazz Festival was launching with an imposing cachet that would command attention.

Friday, July 16, 1954, was festival eve. That night, George Henry Warren and his wife, Katherine, gave a dinner party in their garden to celebrate the coming event. Among the many they invited were sixty-five neighboring colonists, including those sixty-three who had refused the Lorillard offer of sponsorship earlier in the spring: the *New Yorker*'s Lillian Ross reported that all sixty-five invitees accepted. Entertainment was provided by blonde show-tune singer Lee Wiley and swing pianist Teddy Wilson. Colonists were relieved to hear something other than predictably staid bandleaders like Guy Lombardo or Meyer Davis. Teddy Wilson, pronounced one older woman in a black lace dress with a high collar, was "musically somehow or other more frolicsome." By the end of the weekend, these and other colonists would find themselves digging a musical argot way beyond a playful mischief. Driven and inspired by Elaine Lorillard, Newport was on the verge of yet another social and cultural transformation.

8

The Most Unlikely Place

Newport to '56

On the evening of Saturday, July 17, 1954, music industry VIPs and Newport society in formal dress took their box seats at the Casino Tennis Club for the opening night of the first Newport Jazz Festival. Some colonists were unsure what they were about to hear. When the wife of the elderly president of the Clambake Club had bought tickets thinking it would be a symphony concert, she was told it was jazz. Perplexed, she asked, "What is a *jazz* festival?"

Initially, the Lorillards had only expected one or two thousand serious students of jazz to travel to Newport. A lot more than that arrived. Workers who had set out chairs for an audience of five thousand did some last-minute scrambling to provide additional seating, and in the end the Casino was able to accommodate seven thousand, many of them standing. As Elaine Lorillard made her way to her seat, Theodore Francis Green shouted enthusiastically from his box, "Magnificent undertaking! Bold enterprise!" At eighty-eight the oldest sitting U.S. senator, Green was a blue-blood Democrat who appreciated social change. His fellow Democrat, Newport mayor John J. Sullivan, kicked off the 1954 festival after a delay of some thirty minutes to allow for the overflow audience to settle on the lawn or find a perch on the gabled roof. It was the biggest crowd he had ever addressed.

The festival took place on the Casino's number-one court. The bandstand was bracketed by a stiff cardboard shell designed by MIT-trained architect Hsio Wen Shih, future publisher of the *Jazz Review*. Between the stage and the first line of boxes, George Wein allowed space for what he called a photography pit—a prescient innovation by Charlie Bourgeois and Elaine Lorillard that enabled photographers to snap across the footlights. It also afforded the opportunity for the more youthful and exuberant to leave their seats and mass in front of the stage apron, and they did.

Eddie Condon opened with his traditional jazz band. Condon and clarinetist Pee Wee Russell wowed the crowd with the Dixieland classic "Muskrat Ramble." They were followed by swing legends Lester Young, Buck Clayton and Jo Jones, Teddy Wilson, Ella Fitzgerald, and Gene Krupa's trio, as well as such modern artists as Dizzy Gillespie's quintet, Gerry Mulligan's quartet, the Modern Jazz Quartet, Oscar Peterson's trio, pianist Lennie Tristano, alto saxophonist Lee Konitz, George Shearing's quintet, and Erroll Garner's trio. While Duke Ellington may have been conspicuously absent, in truth, the '54 festival didn't have the funds for a big band like his—hence this profusion of small groups.

John Hammond and Marshall Stearns didn't want the festival to be identified with any one school of jazz—be it swing or bop, traditional or modern, hot or cool. To ensure the full range of genres, Wein and the Lorillards relied heavily on their input to use the festival as an opportunity to promote jazz as an art form. Stearns was principally responsible for putting together a Sunday afternoon panel discussion, "The Place of Jazz in American Culture," that drew a thousand people.

Newport '54 blossomed as a gloriously freewheeling affair. In his piece for the *New York Times*, entertainment critic Howard Taubman wrote: "Led by Mr. and Mrs. Louis Lorillard, one of the gold karat names, Newport now has chosen to align itself for the future with vigorous, youthful, democratic art. . . . And a Newport audience reacted like jazz aficionados the nation over—with pounding of feet, beating of hands, rocking of bodies and ecstatic cries of 'go, go, go.'"

After the opening-night show, the Lorillards hosted a party at their home, Quatrel, which included some of the musicians, staff, and Newporters. One attempt at a rival party was a "dismal failure." The entire party—with hostess—was said to have repaired to the Lorillards. "Tonight Newport went back to its beginning," Cleveland Amory told Lillian Ross of the *New Yorker*, "back to a time when it hummed with artists, writers, school-teachers, ministers, and freedom."

On the second night the heavens opened with an unrelenting downpour. "The national media was interested in Newport from the time that they saw people sitting in the rain in 1954 listening to jazz," said George Wein. "The international news service paid attention. Those wire photos of people sitting under umbrellas listening in the rain went all over the world; that was a big thing." Both nights at the Casino were sellouts. A total of some fourteen thousand attended the two offerings. The Newport Jazz Festival had launched with great fanfare and promise. "Jazz has made the grade," said one scholarly looking man whom Lillian Ross found leaning against a doorway at the Lorillards' home after the first night. "From Storyville to Newport in fifty years."

Notwithstanding these auspicious signs, the future of the festival was in doubt. Financially, the enterprise was only just in the black. Louis Lorillard wanted festival proceeds to go to the Institute of Jazz Studies, which Marshall Stearns, with help from John Hammond and jazz critic Leonard Feather, had founded in 1952. Until Stearns found a permanent home for his institute, it existed as an extensive collection of recordings, sheet music, writings, and other archive materials in his townhouse in Greenwich Village. Sometime after the festival, Louis gave Stearns a check for $1,000. He later said that what was left "in the kitty" to put toward the 1955 festival was a mere $8. Wein's reckoning put the profits a little higher, at $142.50.

Moreover, Newport was divided over the issue of hosting another festival. While local merchants were pleased with the profits they had reaped from the first festival, Newport had not been able to cope with traffic congestion in the streets, bottlenecks at the ferries, and the swarm of fans, photographers, and intrusive reporters. The old guard mobilized in opposition to future festivals. "The one that really disapproved of us," said Elaine, "was Jimmy Van Alen's mother, Mrs. [Louis] Brougiere. She said that she would spend $10 million to keep the festival out of Newport. She came down to three million according to *Vogue*." Although the son himself had been a staunch ally, pressure mounted on him as Casino president to withdraw support. Nevertheless, Van Alen continued to be seen at many festivals.

The club was understandably worried about damage to its lawn tennis courts. In her article Lillian Ross quoted Charlie Bourgeois telling George Wein, "They're fixing the chairs so that each blade of grass curls around each chair leg. That's what we get for putting on a show on sacred grounds." In Louis Lorillard's absence the Casino board voted to refuse use of its site for another festival.

Meanwhile, Lorillard had his eye on an empty three-acre estate, the derelict Belcourt Castle and its stables, as a venue not for the festival but for a jazz school. Following the Casino decision, he opted to purchase the estate for $22,000. Styled after a Versailles hunting lodge, Belcourt was at the far end of Bellevue Avenue, close to Bailey's Beach. Its grounds had held one of the first automobile races in the United States and had belonged to the late Perry Belmont. The last time it had been open to the public was in the twenties, when Belmont's sister-in-law, Alva Vanderbilt-Belmont, suffragist leader and financier, threw a party for her fellow voting-rights activists. Since Perry Belmont's death in 1945, Belcourt had been a white elephant, a storage space for Waterman Belmont's collection of automobiles.

In the *New York Daily News,* society reporter Nancy Randolph reported that the 1955 Newport Jazz Festival would be at the fifty-two-room lodge and its grounds. In her 2003 interview, however, Elaine Lorillard said that despite the press reports her husband never intended the three-acre estate as a site for the festival—it wouldn't have been big enough for the crowds—but only for a school for jazz music. Whatever the truth, more than forty families of the old guard rose in protest against the supposed plan. Although Louis was its president, the Newport Improvement Society campaigned against his plan while he and Elaine were away for their annual trip to Capri. Others of the old guard attempted to oust him from the Reading Room but failed.

Edith Wetmore and her sister were among the protestors. They "were two very rich old maids," said Elaine. "They had a mansion [Chateau-Sur-Mer] on Bellevue Avenue and were related to Louis in some way. The sad thing is that Pierre [Elaine's son] was just a little boy, and they saw him someplace. One of them shook her finger in his face and said, 'Your father is a naughty man!' Of course, Pierre didn't know what they were talking about. They scolded him because we had a jazz festival!"

Later that year, when the festival committee discussed the pros and cons of moving the festival out of state, one board member asked, "How about Elaine's personal preferences? I think that should be considered."

"I would like to see it out of Newport as far as my social existence is concerned," she replied. It had gotten to the point where her children were no longer "invited to certain parties."

While the Lorillards were overseas, the old guard petitioned the Newport City Council to rule that Belcourt could not be a venue for commercial activity, notwithstanding the festival's nonprofit status. In June the council met and arrived at a compromise. The festival could use Belcourt for Marshall Stearns's forums but not for commercial use as a concert venue. Finally, with support from small-business interests, the festival was able to secure Freebody Park and its municipal stadium for the concerts. Many years before, a Mrs. Freebody had left the park to the town of Newport with the idea that proceeds of any use would go to the poor. The stadium was across the street from the Casino. Ironically, part of Mrs. Freebody's bequest was land on which the Casino had constructed its number-one court and several others. And so, the second festival was finally good to go as planned for mid-July. As the festival approached, it became apparent that not all the old guard was resistant. In the July 15 *New York Daily News*, Nancy Randolph wrote, "Hurriedly getting on the jazz bandwagon at the last minute are a number of . . . socialites, taking boxes, rows of seats, arranging concert parties."

Meanwhile, Elaine hastily pulled together her opening night party at Belcourt. As a decorator and display designer, she wanted to ensure that her parties would be artful affairs. "There were fittings for sixty flags in that building, and I got big flags to go down the main room. We went to some antique shops, and I found all kinds of big things that filled up the place." As a finishing touch, she would have Belcourt's stained-glass windows lit from the outside to cast cathedral light on the revelers as they moved from room to room.

Logo for the 1955 Newport Jazz Festival. The same logo was used on passes for the VIP section at Newport '56. ::: ***Courtesy of Dan Morgenstern, the Institute of Jazz Studies, Rutgers University.***

Music aficionados of a new sort began pouring into Newport, a postadolescent audience whose appearance quickly overtook the self-absorption of the town's upper crust as a matter of cultural significance. John Clellon Holmes had already written about what came to be known as the beat generation in his 1952 novel *Go:* "In this modern jazz, they heard something rebel and nameless that spoke for them, and their lives knew a gospel for the first time. It was more than a music; it became an attitude toward life, a way of walking, a language and a costume; and these introverted kids . . . now felt somewhere at last." In her *New York Daily News* article, Nancy Randolph wrote, "These fans sleep in parked cars, don't spend any money, don't eat meals, live on benzedrine which everyone is selling to them right over the counter." Bohemia and the drug culture had made their festival debut. "We had only one case," said Elaine, "where we got information on a young man who flew in from Canada and was trying to sell marijuana." The would-be peddler was given the boot. For the first festival, at least, the drug problem had been manageable, but by the second festival clearly the postwar counterculture had arrived. In Newport its members found an opportunity to congregate and shake loose societal shackles to the beat of music.

Newport '55 was broadcast to foreign listeners and particularly those behind the Iron Curtain by the Voice of America, the U.S. government's overseas radio service. The VOA had been a supporter of jazz since 1949, when it broadcast the opening night at New York's Birdland. The VOA was unpacking its recording equipment at Freebody Park to broadcast the festival as one of Washington disc jockey Willis Conover's new *Music USA* series. George Wein had put the deal together after meeting Conover while playing a DC jazz club, Olivia Davis's Patio Lounge, some months after the first festival.

According to George Avakian, the musicians union had granted VOA the right to record certain events for shortwave broadcast only. "The agreement was that they didn't have to pay the musicians, and the material could never be used for any commercial purpose whatever—it was just for the Voice of America." They would tape both the concerts and Stearns's forums promoting jazz. By the 1956 festival, Conover would have a six-man team that included linguists; he would also serve as emcee for the opening. Press reports would say that he had a worldwide weekly audience of an estimated thirty million listeners and got two thousand letters a week.

The press momentum was building. *Variety* reported that Duke Ellington had invited President Eisenhower to attend. "Pop music was very dull," Wein commented. "Patti Page, you know. There was no rock and roll. Elvis Presley had not come on the scene. Jazz was in. It really moved. So by '55, we were covered by lots of magazines: *Holiday, Collier's*. I was interviewed, and Elaine was interviewed. *Playboy* asked me to write a piece. Lots of different things happened very quickly." Elaine's British friend Patrick O'Higgins, who was a PR man for Helena Rubenstein, arranged for fashion photographer Richard Avedon to do portraits of the musicians for a costly program that included extended articles by jazz luminaries and other commentators.

Hsio Wen Shih's shell was used again at Freebody. Wein wisely insisted on keeping the innovative photography pit. Ever sensitive to visual presentation, Elaine put plantings in front of the stage to mask the raw look of the supporting struts covered by chicken wire.

Reportedly, Freebody Park could accommodate some ten thousand folding chairs and two rows of forty boxes, each with six seats. The concrete stands could seat another eighteen hundred.

Newport '55 opened on Friday, July 15. Addressing the audience, Senator Green proclaimed jazz to be "a revolutionary force" and compared "its impact and music with the impact and politics of the revolutionists of 1776." Elaine Lorillard wrote his speech. "He didn't know anything about jazz, so he asked me to help," she said.

Wein had put together a balanced lineup of traditional and modern jazz similar to that of the year before and with many of the same musicians. This time, however, he had the budget to book two big bands: Woody Herman's and Count Basie's. Another big attraction was Louis Armstrong. Featured on opening night, he "brought down the house" and had the fans "dancing in the aisles," according to the press. The Sunday night emcee was Duke Ellington. For the modernists, the event of that evening was the unannounced walk-on appearance of Miles Davis and his ethereal " 'Round Midnight" solo. Said Wein, "Miles Davis returned with a lot of sparks—getting a lot of attention both for Newport and for Miles."

After the opening-night concert, Elaine hosted her Belcourt Castle party. Four hundred attended. Once again, the old guard tried to give their own rival parties but failed, one reason being that Elaine had rented all the gold chairs in town. For Saturday night she had announced a small after-concert soirée, only for musicians and their friends. Eight hundred people showed up.

The crowds flocking to all the events were a measure of how popular the festival was becoming. The total audience for the weekend was twenty-seven thousand—almost double the turnout for the previous year's festival. With the whopping turnout, media attention, not surprisingly, was legion, but it wasn't all sweetness and light. Harold C. Schonberg, the *New York Times*'s opera critic, was highly critical of the Sunday night progressive fare, which included Davis's fabled return: "And one young man said plaintively to his young lady, during a particularly abstruse and long-winded riff, 'D'ya dig this stuff?' In many cases it took a lot of digging, and after the excavation the listener would come up with precious little. A lot of modern jazz, the festival amply demonstrated, is having a love affair with a lot of modern music. Both can be dissonant, light, over-intellectual and nonmelodic." Schonberg's scant praise was reserved for Basie and his cohorts: "Anti-intellectual, no doubt, but a real emotional experience, backed by a solid rhythm, delivered by superb instrumentalists who were turning their techniques to something else besides abstractions in jazz. . . . An earnest young group featuring Mulligan and Brubeck had the misfortune to follow directly after. They sounded like anemic esthetes by comparison." It was, however, his remarks about the style of a jazz icon of the day, pianist Erroll Garner, that ignited a firestorm. Of Garner's "descending double thirds" and "vague impressionistic ramblings," Schonberg wrote: "It's not good music—or good piano playing for that matter—and it certainly isn't jazz."

The criticism outraged Garner's manager and companion Martha Glaser. A veteran who had worked for Norman Granz in the early days of Jazz at the Philharmonic, "Martha was tough, very smart and drove a very hard bargain for Erroll," said Dan Morgenstern. "She built him into the top jazz/classical concert attraction in the world—bar none." Glaser immediately organized a letter-writing campaign to the *Times*. The editors not only yanked Schonberg from the jazz beat but issued an apology. "His reviews created such a consternation with the jazz world," said Wein, "that the *Times* hired John Wilson the next year—'56—who was the first permanent jazz critic on a major. So the next thing you know, a lot of papers started to hire jazz writers."

Another highbrow critic remained as unfazed as Schonberg. A Princeton graduate, music reporter Roger H. Maren took the festival to task in a September issue of the slightly left-of-center magazine *The Reporter.* Dismissing the modernists, Maren wrote, "Players often give the impression that they are members of a metaphysical cult rather than simply entertainers." He accused Erroll Garner of being an "impish cocktail-hour pianist" and equated the modernist piano technique with that of French impressionist composer Claude Debussy, citing the predisposition to thirteenth chords. "Since such chords include—theoretically—all the notes in a scale, a bewildered improviser has a rather good chance to be with the correct harmony no matter how lost he gets." Several months later, an angry Marshall Stearns fumed at the "insidious criticism," characterizing one example in the *Chicago Review* as the "worst tripe."

Tripe or not, Newport's apparent success was breeding scrutiny.

And then there was the matter of race.

The influential glossy *Ebony* also reviewed Newport '55. Although its African American editor, Alan Morrisson, was a festival advisory member, the magazine was critical of the discrimination that some African American musicians and fans encountered in Newport. Race and Newport were among several issues addressed at the noteworthy December 9, 1955, meeting of the so-called Newport Festival Jazz Committee—the officers and directors of the board, plus for the first time many of the members of the advisory committee. The site was Marshall Stearns's Waverly Place townhouse in Greenwich Village. The three-hour meeting convened with President Louis Lorillard in the chair.

In the months following the '55 festival, the state of race relations had moved to the forefront of national consciousness. Throughout that autumn the newspapers and airwaves were full of the successive miscarriages of justice in the Emmett Till case, in which two whites were acquitted for the brutal murder of a black Chicago teenager who was said to have whistled at a white woman while he was visiting Mississippi. The race issue in Newport launched the committee into the discussion of whether and where to move the 1956 festival. Several press members were disturbed by the antagonism toward African Americans openly expressed by Newporters and even some former committee members. Jazz critic Leonard Feather took the position that the festival could attract more attendees at a New York venue and suggested Randall's Island or the Lewisohn Stadium, two well-known outdoor sites.

Supporting him was Alan Morrisson. While he was careful to say that he did not associate the Lorillards with Newport's "racial mores and its treatment of Negroes," he agreed with Feather. "There was a general feeling [primarily among Negro musicians and Negro jazz bands] that there was hostility there manifested in many ways. . . . Many Negroes were unable to find accommodations." New York, he said, would give them "greater leeway in which to move and operate." The Lorillards had provided beds to many musicians, both at Quatrel and at their farm.

Wein was against taking the festival to New York because he felt that it would have less impact in a big metropolis. "For the first time in my life I was in a town with thousands of people who were very much interested in jazz," he said. "No matter where I went that is all I heard. This was terribly exciting and I think very good for jazz." Wein saw accommodations as less of a problem than some of the other board members did. Wein recalled in 2002 that for the first year festival organizers had had to "break down a few racial barriers" by approaching hotels like the Viking that "didn't relish bringing in blacks, but [once organizers talked with them] we had no more problems with the hotels in town."

John Hammond was the most outspoken advocate for staying put. Newport was the most unlikely place for a jazz festival, he argued—which was one reason for its success. Moreover, they should take advantage of the publicity already built up during the past two festivals. Newport had been responsible for promoting jazz's reputation as an art form: "Because of the Newport Jazz Festival Louis Armstrong in Newport gets on the front page of the *New York Times*. . . . I think if we had tried to have this festival any place else we would find that eighty percent of our publicity value from the past and our good will would be dissipated." Unable to resist injecting politics, Hammond maintained that the festival had "brought democracy to Newport." Surprisingly, *Ebony*'s Morrisson responded crisply that he was against using the festival to abolish racial prejudice in Newport. As for the Lorillards, they did not appear to take a position on moving the festival. Although Louis was at the helm during the meeting, he did not insist on a course. Expressing his philosophy as festival producer, he said, "Basically my job is to pull things together. I don't intend to keep this job forever. . . . Then I can go back to the travel business where I belong."

In truth, the festival was becoming a personal financial liability. Lorillard was sinking a great deal of his inheritance into festival operations, and both he and Elaine were using the equity in their respective life insurance policies to help in paying salaries to Wein and his staff and other festival employees, as well as covering musicians' fees.

Elaine pointed to the experience organizers had already gained at Newport, plus all the money already thrown into the festival, and the support of the Newport and Providence newspapers, as reasons to keep it in town. She acknowledged, however, that she had suffered personally and would be delighted to move the festival. Interest had been expressed in relocating it to the symphony hall in Providence, Rhode Island; to Princeton, New Jersey; and to Wellesley College, in Massachusetts. John Hammond offered Tanglewood.

However, he cautioned, the travel problems associated with Lenox, Massachusetts, would be worse than with Newport, and talent managers might be wedded to booking Newport only. Wein responded that he could only book talent if the festival remained within a hundred miles of Newport. Lorillard resolved the discussion by appointing Hammond, Feather, and Morrisson to study site options. (Early in 1956, Hammond, Feather, and Morrisson would report their conclusions on site options, and the board would agree to keep the American Jazz Festival in Newport.)

On the technical side, all agreed on the need to improve the sound system. In his autobiography Hammond wrote that the sound at Newport '55 was the worst he had ever heard in an outdoor concert. The vaunted band shell tilted up, sending various frequencies into the sky, and the concrete stands to the back of the field seating produced an echo that was especially bad for the box seats. For 1956 the festival would contract with a different sound services company. Hammond had already been fully involved in festival business. When Lorillard asked him to join the board of directors, recognizing that Wein was overwhelmed and wearing too many hats, he agreed.

The matter of money was also discussed at the Greenwich Village meeting. Lorillard reported that the total cost of the 1955 festival was $75,588. While the city had contributed $4,000 for police, fire, and cleanup, the program, with Richard Avedon's splashy portraits, lost the organizers $8,000. The talent budget had been $15,400, but the festival spent close to $17,000 on musicians. Lorillard reported a profit of $942. In his autobiography George Wein reckoned that the Newport '55 festival actually lost $6,000. For the '56 festival Lorillard wanted to hold the talent budget at $15,000. Having underwritten two losing festivals, he would continue to seek support wherever he could. The festival would apply for a state grant. He was also preparing to solicit support from the Rockefeller and Ford foundations, among others.

At every opportunity, the festival was endeavoring to promote jazz as an art form, even the American art form. The issue was not simply a question of dignifying a folk music perhaps not grounded in the European tradition. "Every time we go and approach a foundation," Lorillard told his committee, "they say, 'What is jazz?' We have to prove it is an art form. They don't believe it is an art form." In considering the future, he had the committee look at taking the festival "to Europe and perhaps behind the Iron Curtain." "As you know," he observed, "the Voice of America wired our entire jazz festival the last time in Europe and I understand it was well received." The Lorillards had been communicating with officials of the State Department and Senator Green, a long-standing member of the Senate Foreign Relations Committee, which authorized the department's budgets and which he would chair in 1957.

At the time, Elaine was looking beyond Newport, selling a proposal for an international tour under the Newport brand that would give international recognition to Rhode Island. Louis and recent Newport advisory committee member Robert Schnitzer, director of the American National Theatre Academy, were exploring a way in which ANTA would provide funds for art "forms" such as the festival to tour the Far East and perhaps elsewhere. The Lorillards and John Hammond were also intrigued by the possibility of going to the Soviet Union. The international situation in 1956, however, would not prove to be hospitable for a jazz tour of the Soviet Bloc.

A few months before the opening of Newport '56, the Rhode Island General Assembly rejected a resolution to appropriate $10,000 to the festival, whereupon Louis Lorillard told the press that he would front the money—for the third year in a row. Over the course of the spring, George Wein completed his contracting with the talent. Early on Armstrong, determined to be the big draw in 1956, had been booked for Friday night. By late June, however, some degree of uncertainty still remained. At the June 22 meeting of the advisory board at Marshall Stearns's Waverly Street townhouse, Wein reported his attempts to finalize the billing to the advisory board. While earlier they had been able to agree on the composition of Stearns's panels, they could make no decisions on emcees because of uncertain availability. They decided to put Viennese pianist Friedrich Gulda on the Saturday afternoon bill before that day's panel discussion and to add cool jazz reedman Bud Shank to the Saturday night roster. Still to be determined was ailing pianist Art Tatum, whose Saturday appearance was in such doubt that the group agreed to make overtures to Dizzy Gillespie and his big band as a replacement.

The following day, the press reported the lineups to date. One local Newport paper began, "The great importance of the American Jazz Festival at Newport, Rhode Island . . . was attested to last week by the announcement that the Voice of America would send a six-man team of engineers and linguists to cover the event for the world." The article announced one emcee, presumably confirmed: the VOA's Willis Conover, the host of *Music USA*. In his year and a half as VOA broadcaster, this childhood army brat, whose idol was Duke Ellington, had built a committed audience behind the Iron Curtain. Many of Conover's young Eastern European listeners were among those ready to protest against their Stalinist puppet governments.

One of those listeners would one day end up on the stage at Newport. On June 27, in Budapest, members of Hungary's jazz elite gathered for a recording session at the Qualiton Studio. Numbered among them was a twenty-year-old guitarist who had learned his chops from Willis Conover's broadcasts: Gabor Szabo. Later in the autumn, when Hungarian students led the revolt against Soviet rule, Szabo became a freedom fighter. The movement was violently crushed. While twenty thousand Hungarians died, Szabo joined two hundred thousand others who fled to exile, crossing the border into Austria with only his guitar. Two years later, Gabor Szabo was on the Newport stage performing with the International Youth Band.

"*Music USA* certainly had an impact as the music of freedom," said Conover's VOA boss, Barry Zorthian, as he speculated on the effect in Eastern Europe of the VOA broadcast of Newport '56. "*Music USA* encouraged that type of public expression, individual expression. And a big concert with a name like Duke Ellington had to be a spike in that influence." Much later as the Soviet empire entered its last decade, Russian Nobel Prize-winning author Alexander Solzhenitsyn told the *Wall Street Journal*, "American broadcasts are the mighty non-military force which resides in the airwaves and whose kindling power in the midst of Communist darkness cannot even be grasped by the Western imagination."

Solzhenitsyn's pronouncement was not entirely true. Of the generation that had come of age with jazz on the airwaves, Elaine Lorillard, John Hammond, George Avakian, and some of the other festival organizers had grasped this truth. Having moved from urban juke joints to immigrant enclaves to the festival grounds in tony Newport, jazz—the American art form—had the liberating power to move the world.

Newport '56

From the stage, Freebody Park awaits the start of Newport '56. ::: *Photo by Don Hunstein. Courtesy of Sony BMG Music Entertainment.*

9

Newport '56

A Gathering Primed to Move

As soon as he got his green light from Columbia Records president Goddard Lieberson to do a live recording at the '56 jazz festival, George Avakian gave the thumbs-up to his engineers, Adjutor "Pappy" Theroux and his young assistant, Edward "Buddy" Graham. The pair promptly cased all their recording gear in a station wagon and left for Newport to begin the equipment setup. The following day, July 3, Avakian hit the open road to join them. In the car with him was his assistant, Calvin Lampley. An African American who was a trained concert pianist, Cal Lampley had been a so-called editing musician reading scores in the classical department. On joining Avakian's pop LP department, he promptly produced two albums for February 1955 release. Avakian and Lampley had become close friends and an expert team. With them was a third passenger, an inquisitive and alienated seventeen-year-old daughter of immigrants who had just graduated from high school in Ridgewood, New Jersey. Before beginning her college studies at Alfred University in upstate New York, she was making the epic journey to her first Newport jazz festival.

Her name was Arlene Avakian, and she was George's young cousin. Her parents had fled the Armenian genocide and come to America, settling in Washington Heights at the northern tip of Manhattan. Twenty years younger than George, she was in awe of his urbanity. "He was much more in the culture than anybody else in my family," she recalled. "He seemed very American to me. That's how I thought in those days. I wanted to be regular American."

In the late forties and early fifties, Arlene's immediate America was the Armenian community and church around 190th Street. As she grew older, she came to perceive the glimmers of the great beyond. "I identified with Americans through a couple of things: the

Arlene Avakian, George Avakian's young cousin, a teenage jazz fan who made her first trip to Newport in '56. ::: *Courtesy of Arlene Avakian.*

Irish, because the Irish were in the movies like crazy at that time, and jazz. Jazz made me very American. It was kind of a rebellion against my parents." At a young age Arlene started listening to jazz on the radio, "surreptitiously in my room." When her cousin recognized her budding interest, he would bring her records.

In 1954 she got her wish to be as American as she could be when her family moved to New Jersey, but the American life she encountered there wasn't all she'd thought it would be. In Ridgewood, as in New York, the teen musical taste tended toward pre–rock and roll, Johnny Ray and "the top 40 stuff." On weekends Arlene would return to New York. "None of my friends liked jazz," she said. "There was one guy I knew in New Jersey that I was dating who loved jazz, and we shared that. It was a rebellion to like something identified with black people." Whether through her boyfriend, her cousin George Avakian, or New York deejay Symphony Sid, she "was in contact" with Billie Holiday, Lester Young, and "the cool sound, the newest stuff that was coming up." Arlene reflected a sentiment quite common among older teenagers in the mid-fifties, if not in Ridgewood: "I thought that rock and roll was just dumb music."

After her high school graduation, her parents agreed to let her go with her cousin to Newport. "It was amazing. I mean, I was very, very carefully monitored. I don't know why they let me go, but they did." As they drove through the Connecticut countryside that July day, Arlene was ecstatic. For the next three nights, she would find herself among the thousand or so youths in the Newport audience and one of but a handful who were blessed with front-row seats. "I can remember driving to Newport. There was a beautiful road, and I was thinking, I'm getting to the beach, and I love the ocean. I was so excited, and then I was thinking, oh, this is not this little child's anticipation of going to the beach. Something else is going on that is much more important. Oh, my God, I am going to a jazz festival!"

When they arrived in Newport they went straight to the Hotel Viking, the festival headquarters where most of the staff, management, and performers stayed. "I was pretty unsophisticated," Arlene said. "I was around very famous people. I remember seeing that blues singer, Jimmy Rushing, in the elevator and thinking, Oh, my God, I'm in the elevator with Jimmy Rushing!" Later when she attended the Lorillards' party with George Avakian, she was amazed by "the opulence of the place, and all the jazz musicians. Erroll Garner was there. Louis Armstrong was there! I never saw the beach, and I didn't even care."

Newport was preparing for record crowds. City and state officials believed that they had resolved the travel problems. Coming from the west and New York, fans would be taking the ferry from Jamestown for their last leg to Aquidneck Island and Newport. For those with accommodations on the Jamestown side, the Jamestown Ferry Company agreed to continue runs into the morning to handle the expected loads. The same was true for the Short Line Bus Company, handling the run for fans coming from Providence to the north. For those attempting to stay in Newport, the Chamber of Commerce was still working on accommodations.

Freebody Park itself was expecting record numbers. Fans would be buying all tickets at the Freebody box office, built into the sides of the surrounding stone wall on Freebody Street adjacent to the west entrance, as well as on the Middleton Street side by the east entrance. The park was continuing a policy of reserved and numbered seating: that year, eight thousand chairs on the field, including the forty boxes, and another two thousand seats in the concrete stands.

Columbia's senior recording engineer, Ad Theroux, in the backstage tent with his equipment. ::: *Photo by Don Hunstein. Courtesy of Sony BMG Music Entertainment.*

The city staff had been busy scrubbing surfaces to remove the chalk and crayon markings that still adorned the stadium from the annual Thanksgiving Day football game. In their place the U.S. Information Service, which had camped there to film the event, painted its own marks to indicate camera positions.

George Avakian had done no formal reconnoiter of the site at Freebody Park. Having been to the two previous festivals, he was familiar with the setup and had briefed his senior engineer, Ad Theroux. Experienced in location recordings for Columbia, Pappy Theroux was a "wonderful looking guy" with

George Avakian's assistant, Cal Lampley, stands beside Buddy Graham, Columbia recording engineer, at the central board for the live recordings of the '56 festival. ::: *Photo courtesy of Sony BMG Music Entertainment.*

a shock of white hair, Avakian recalled affectionately. He and Buddy Graham had long worked together on mike setups on the road. "So I knew perfectly well what they would be able to handle and under what conditions, including what I described to them."

Once again, Hsio Wen Shih's shell bracketed the stage. Wooden steps with railings led from both sides of the stage to the rear, where a blue-and-white-striped tent served as a green room and dressing area for the artists. Its main entrance faced forward on the stage-left side.

Inside, the Columbia and Voice of America engineers placed their recording equipment. Columbia's area was in the rear corner of the tent, stage-left side. VOA was in the other corner, just in front of a curtain that provided a small dressing area for female vocalists. The accommodations were primitive. Erroll Garner's manager Martha Glaser remembered trash cans everywhere and no toilets backstage for the talent. There wasn't much in the way of a food concession.

Over the course of the weekend, VOA would record twenty hours of concerts and thirty interviews conducted by opening-night emcee Willis Conover in a mobile studio parked in the backstage area. The team consisted of Harold Boxer, chief of the music section, and one assistant. The VOA mike was on the same stand as the festival mike that fed the public address system, providing the amplified sound that the audience actually heard. On Saturday night that stand would have a third mike that fed a broadcast for Pat Weaver's NBC weekend radio program *Monitor*, a fact totally forgotten in all previous recounting of the Newport '56 recording story.

With its own mikes on separate stands, Columbia would record independently, and only its artists, most of whom were performing on Friday. The only exceptions were Eddie Condon, set to play on Thursday, and Ellington, on Saturday. The press reported at the time that the label's plan was to release the recordings in September as a four-record boxed set.

Pappy Theroux would be on the controls at Columbia's portable board. He would mix according to what he heard on small fold-back speakers in front of him. "He couldn't see anything," said Avakian. Theroux would mix for two tape recorders that ran at exactly the same speed. For the most part Buddy Graham's job was to start and stop the two machines. The second tape recorder was essentially backup. "When it came time to change reels," Avakian said, "the tapes were staggered, so that there was plenty of time for Buddy to change reels while the recording was going on. The mikes were all coming into the board, and the board was feeding to two tape recorders with essentially the same signal—monaural."

Theroux's miking was fairly standard for all three nights. For the Ellington sets on Saturday, four mikes did most of the work. By the mid-fifties, Ellington's normal stage setup had his rhythm section stage right. Downstage right, he would lead from his grand piano, facing his band. Looking upstage of his piano top, cocked fully open to project the sound toward the audience, he could see his drums on a riser and bass just below on another riser, both angled toward the center. Looking straight ahead through the open piano, he could see the rest of the band. From stage left to center, three lines of cream-colored music stands, each with Ellington's con brio signature logo, faced the audience. The downstage riser housed the five-instrument reed section. On the second riser behind were his three trombones; on the third to the very back were his five trumpets. Paul Gonsalves would be the reed closest to Ellington's piano. To his left was a narrow space between the reeds to allow trumpeters and trombonists to come downstage and solo at the microphone.

Columbia had one mike on a stand downstage pointing upstage toward the piano. "We had a microphone set up in front of the brass. It was to get the presence on the brass. Although the trombones were in front of the trumpets, the trumpets would carry anyway," Avakian said, recalling his thought process. "There was another mike for the bass, and that was also close enough for the drums—so we didn't have to worry about setting up anything special for the drums. A fourth was in front of the musicians, capturing the overall sound and doubling as the mike for the instrumental soloists and vocals." All Columbia's mikes were directional because they wanted to record the sounds as cleanly as possible.

To capture ambient and crowd noise, Avakian also suspended two mikes on wires high above the stage. "Remember, we were recording monaurally, so I couldn't manipulate the crowd noise afterwards. We would have to add crowd noise to cover up the splices. It was an absolute necessity, because everything can go wrong with two monaural tape machines overlapping."

During the performances Avakian's post would be near the top of the stage-left steps, which gave him a view around the side of the shell without making him too obtrusive. Lampley remained by the entrance of the backstage tent both within sight of Avakian and earshot of Theroux and Graham. Avakian communicated with the engineers through Cal by foot, running up and down the stairs.

On Thursday morning the weather was foreboding. At noon, the rains started and the temperature dropped. Undaunted by the inclement conditions, fans were eager to see their favorites among the hundred artists on the bill. Advance sales for Thursday night had been a solid five thousand tickets, and umbrella-toting aficionados purchased an additional fifteen hundred at the Freebody box office.

Despite the brisk ticket sales, as the 8:30 curtain-up approached only thirty-five hundred fans chose to brave the cold and rain. Drenched and shivering under umbrellas and blankets, the crowd settled into their chairs that in turn settled into the mud. A rain check was not in the cards. From the first night of 1954, Louis Lorillard's policy had been that the show would go on rain or shine.

"The weather was weird that whole festival," said Avakian. "I wanted to make everything sound as though it took place under the same weather and aural conditions. But every single recording had a different quality because of the clouds and the moisture in the air."

Just after 8:30, Count Basie and his band assembled on the rainy, windswept stage. Throughout the night wet gusts would soak both musicians and instruments; John Barry Ryan's stagehands had to drape blankets over the piano, even during the performances. The Count opened with the national anthem. The crowd rose and stood at attention. Basie then hit them with "Jumping at the Woodside" before yielding the stage to Louis Lorillard

Two young fans watch Basie through the first night's rain at Newport '56. ::: *Photo courtesy of Bob Parent.*

and Theodore Francis Green. After a few words, the pair passed the mike to the night's emcee, *Music USA*'s Willis Conover, and the program was under way.

The first part of the evening included the Modern Jazz Quartet and singer Sarah Vaughan. Following the intermission, Dixieland leader Eddie Condon appeared in a raincoat with his All-Stars and relayed a comment from George Avakian: "This is the first jazz concert ever done under water."

The Charlie Mingus Jazz Workshop followed Condon, and then Basie returned for the final set of the evening. He finished on a high, leaving innumerable pockets of huddled, soaked, but ecstatic jazz loyalists howling after eight repeat choruses of his big 1955 hit "April in Paris."

This Newport seemed to have an energy that bad weather couldn't dampen, a youthful energy that could only build through the weekend. The "concert performed under unbelievably bad conditions," reported the *Newport Daily News* in its Friday edition. "Incredibly it was one of the festival's best musical evenings in three years."

On Friday the uncertain weather continued. The fans, however, were undaunted. Soggy stragglers, mainly young, from the night before had found accommodation in private homes, at the fire station, in police jails, and in cars parked on obscure streets and back roads. In neighboring Middletown to the east, across Eastons Pond, the police moved car cat-nappers to the Second Beach parking lot farther east of town. The navy offered to house the Friday concert in its gym at the naval station, but in the end Wein and Lorillard took their chances on the weather and declined. The managers of the Casino Theatre volunteered their nearby venue without charge for Marshall Stearns's Friday panel, "Jazz as Communication." Although the rain wasn't falling, throughout the morning the skies had remained dark and cloudy, and the air balmy. Hedging their bets, Wein and Lorillard took up the offer and moved the forum inside.

Stearns got a nonpaying audience of eight hundred, dressed in Bermuda shorts and toting umbrellas. During the course of the discussion, panelists addressed commercialism in jazz and the timeless trade-off that performers must make between art and entertainment. At one point panel member George Wein got onto the subject of Louis Armstrong. Wein ascribed Pops's success to his ability as an entertainer, not to his technical achievement, and blamed the public for not allowing stars like him to play up to their ability. In his view, rather than accepting good music, the public only accepts "a gimmick, a new sound, a new approach." Wein reportedly urged fans to "go to hear what the musician is trying to play . . . not what you want to hear."

While the panelists analyzed the jazz scene, stage staff and technicians at Freebody Park dried equipment and prepared for the second night. George Avakian and his team readied themselves for what would be their most demanding night: the taping of the entire evening's fare, save Ella Fitzgerald, who was with Norman Granz's Verve label. In the midst of his prep, word came to Avakian that an agitated Duke Ellington was on the line at Wein's backstage headquarters.

Notwithstanding Wein's remarks at the Stearns forum, earlier in the week he had called Ellington to reiterate his position on the bandleader's program: no medleys. "I told him he better come in there swinging," recalled Wein, "or he was going to have a problem. Because the Ellington band could swing, but a lot of time Duke didn't play swinging numbers. He wanted to play his songs."

Ellington was due to arrive on Saturday morning. As Avakian made his way to take the call, he was certain that the Duke was phoning about his new composition. "George, I'm worried about the 'Suite,'" Ellington announced. "It's not well prepared. We haven't had enough rehearsal time. The guys are goofing, but we can't afford to cancel the recording, because it's been announced. Everybody's waiting for it, and on top of that, it's been years since I've had one of my long works recorded. This is an important occasion. So we've got to get a good recording that we can release." Avakian was unfazed, knowing that Ellington made last-minute changes in the studio all the time. "We'll just do the best we can," he replied, in an attempt to reassure him. Duke wanted insurance: "What's happening in the studios on Monday? Because we have Monday off. Can we go into the studio and make any repairs that we want? Can you patch it in and make it sound as though it happened at the festival?" "Yes," Avakian said confidently. "It can be done, but I don't know if there is a studio available." Ellington suggested, "Call up and find out, and call me back."

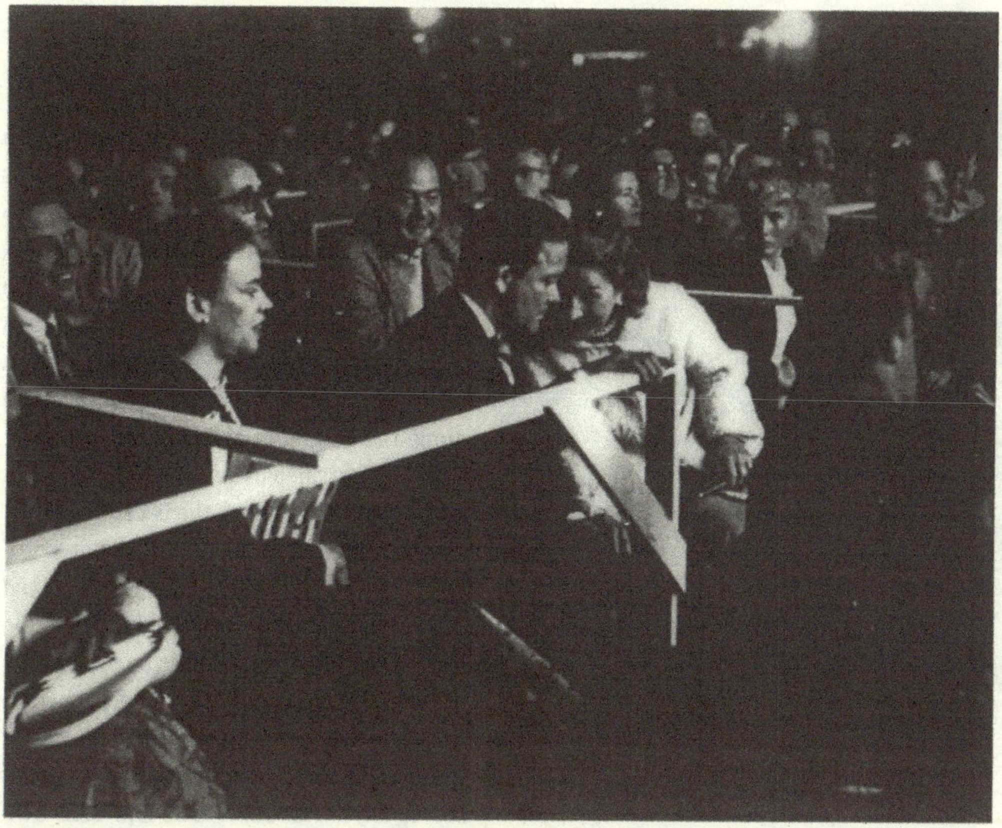

Elaine Lorillard talks to Eddie Condon on the second night of the 1956 festival. Louis Lorillard smiles in the background. John and Esme Hammond are to the left of an unidentified man with glasses. ::: *Photo courtesy of Bob Parent.*

Avakian contacted Columbia and found that the big Thirtieth Street studio, with a room quality ideal for his needs, wasn't available. Fortuitously, a small studio, Studio D at the top of 799 Seventh Avenue, was free. Avakian had used that studio to record other bands of comparable size. He phoned the Studio D technicians. "We're going to have to go in there first thing in the morning and listen to everything that was done and decide what to repair with Duke's band. Be sure that Chappy is available," he added, referring to Harold Chapman, one of the engineers who had recorded Duke and knew his setup.

Avakian phoned Ellington the news: "Okay, we're covered." "That's good," the bandleader said, breathing a sigh of relief. "Now," he continued, referring to the "Suite," "I'll have Strayhorn with a score, listening as the performance takes place. He'll mark all the things that he hears bad. Afterwards, we'll review it in the studio. After I decide what we have to do with the musicians, I'll call them at the hotel. They'll be standing by." "Okay," said Avakian. "We can do it."

On Friday night the weather was still chilly when Louis Armstrong opened with the national anthem. Although the Thursday night crowd had left the field as lacerated as a circus

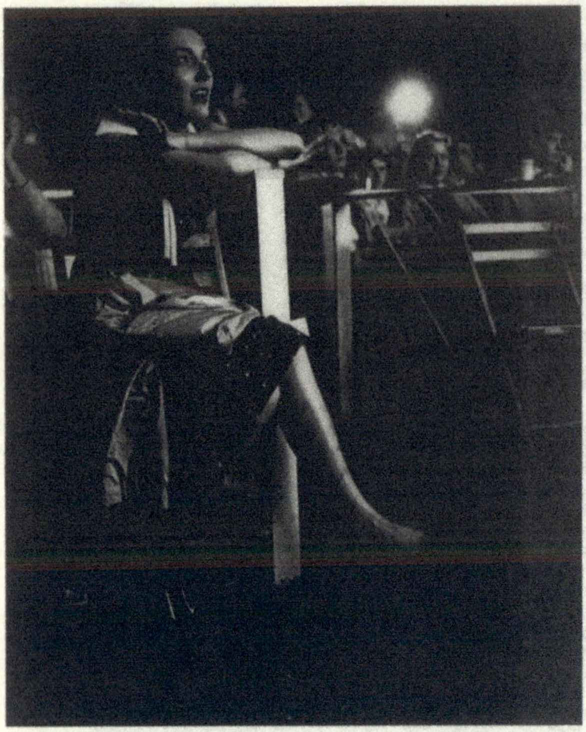

A photogenic fan keeps time during a Friday-night performance. ::: *Photo courtesy of Bob Parent.*

ground after a weeklong engagement, it had practically dried. Eleven thousand fans were assembling—a near sellout.

Eager but restless, this crowd was not one to sit. It moved about the grounds throughout the evening. Those less into the music socialized in the open area behind the seating or in the stands to the very rear. The Kiwanis beer concessions were raining forty days and nights' worth of 'Gansett. One was quite near the stage along the stage-left aisle against the blue-and-white-striped canvas fencing that separated the seating from the backstage area.

By the end of the night, hundreds of the most enthusiastic fans had moved forward along the side aisles that led to the photography pit between the boxes and the stage area. Scores of them had packed to the right and left of the box seats, among dozens of photographers positioning themselves for shots. Some fans had their own cameras and were mingling with the professionals who were perching their gear on the edge of the five-and-a-half-foot stage for their shots across the footlights.

While the need was not glaring, security was becoming a consideration. At one of the early festivals, the staff had put a wooden snow fence across the field to separate the boxes from the rest of the seating. Horrified by the visual suggestion of social stratification, Elaine Lorillard ordered it immediately removed. Still, increasing crowds required greater control, and after the '55 festival Elaine had concerns. "I was told that at the end of one of the nights a woman went out to one of those rented artificial toilet things in the back and gave birth to a baby," she said. Especially chastened that year by the knowledge of the marijuana bust, she persuaded Louis to contract with the local Pinkerton office. At the 1956 festival the Pinkertons began stationing plainclothesmen along with city police throughout the grounds. Elaine recalled that two Pinkertons were always positioned on either side of the stage. In addition to crowd control, in the unlikely event that it should be needed, they served to provide a liaison for Louis Lorillard with security backstage, where sometimes a fracas would occur involving the musicians.

"They always came to him from backstage," said Elaine. Louis "was the one who would go tearing backstage if things were wrong, because he was a big husky guy, and he could take care of himself. He could beat you up very quickly, but he was very good to work with in situations like that. He had a way to be authoritative, and they knew that."

Louis Armstrong storming through his second Friday-night set, July 6, 1956. ::: *Photo by Don Hunstein. Courtesy of Sony BMG Music Entertainment.*

The Friday lineup included Coleman Hawkins, Buck Clayton, J. J. Johnson and Kai Winding's quintet, and Dave Brubeck. It was Verve artiste Ella Fitzgerald who took the fans to intermission, and according to one review she "tore the place apart." Ella knew how to deliver a good thing. She chose to include in her set a number that played to a rock and roll sensibility by now markedly present in the audience. The song was the Tennessee rockabilly Carl Perkins's "Blue Suede Shoes." Sun Records had released the song that January, and by February it had reached number one on the country charts. Later in the spring, it had soared to number two on the rhythm and blues charts. Although it never made number one on the rock and roll charts, it remained high on that list for almost five months into the summer, the only song ever to be a monster hit in all three markets.

Following the break, Armstrong returned and played for an hour. The highpoints were "Mack the Knife," a huge hit which he had first recorded for George Avakian the previous September, and Chick Webb's oft-covered swing classic "Stompin' at the Savoy." Pops pumped an audience already primed by Ella. Read the *Providence Journal* the following day, Armstrong's " 'Kokomo,' smacking strongly of rock and roll, was one of the hits of the evening."

The audience response to Basie in the rain on Thursday night and to Ella and Armstrong on Friday forcefully suggested that this year's Newport audience wanted to move. Should the weather warm on Saturday, it could very well explode.

Saturday dawned auspiciously, to warm, partly sunny conditions.

In midmorning the Ellington bus pulled into the park, slowly made its way to the backstage area, and parked among the dozens of trucks and trailers. On the sides read "Duke Ellington's Orch / Mr. Hi-Fi of '56." The door hissed open and various band members descended along with a dapper Billy Strayhorn, who had been working on the score of the "Suite" up to the last moment. Duke arrived separately in Carney's Cadillac. Columbia photographer Don Hunstein's photos show a wary Ellington, wearing a light-colored suit, his shoulders tense. He was anxious to find Avakian.

The Columbia producer was with his engineers by the equipment in the backstage tent. When Avakian heard Duke had arrived, he dropped what he was doing and went to meet him. They met halfway between the tent and the festival's field office. "Right away of course," Avakian recalled, "we began talking about the problems that might come up." Ellington was distracted. "I'm still worried about the performance," he confided to Avakian. "I'm glad you have that studio time reserved." "You're covered," Avakian assured him. "Duke, I'm not going to ask you for anything. We've worked together for years; you just choose what you want as a program. I don't know how much we'll use, but the chances are

A tense Ellington (right) in the backstage area with Billy Strayhorn (center) and Teddy Wilson just after his Saturday arrival, July 7, 1956. ::: *Photo by Don Hunstein. Courtesy of Sony BMG Music Entertainment.*

A performance precedes the Saturday-afternoon panel discussion on the Newport '56 stage. ::: *Photo courtesy of Bob Parent.*

the 'Festival Suite,' according to what you're telling me, will make up one side. Then I'll probably want another side. What ends up on it depends on how much I can use from the other artists, and whatever else you play that will round out an even number of LP sides."

Ellington had so much riding on the night: a successful recording of a memorable performance of a new extended work would seal his band's comeback. He wanted to rehearse the "Suite" in the afternoon, but it was impossible. The clearing weather meant that the Saturday panel could convene at Freebody Park. As the sun began to stream onto the field, Avakian remained on-site through the afternoon sessions, from time to time joining Ellington as he and Strayhorn were left to greet Teddy Wilson and other musicians circulating in the backstage area. Any sort of rehearsal would have to wait.

For that afternoon Wein had arranged for an experimental piano offering, two hours of stage time that featured Memphis newcomer Phineas Newborn, Friedrich Gulda, and Mario Patron, a young Mexican who was Doris Duke's beau at the time and promoted by Elaine Lorillard initially and later by John Hammond. Following the music, *Metronome*'s editor Bill Coss and *Down Beat* associate editor Nat Hentoff moderated their panel, "The Future of Jazz." The panelists included a young composer and arranger, Quincy Jones, who was working in New York after returning from Dizzy Gillespie's tour of the Middle East.

The panel ran sometime past its scheduled finish at five, after which Ellington was able to get his band onstage for a brief rehearsal—or at least, most of it. According to

Avakian, "Some of the guys goofed off and disappeared." Ellington was missing four: trumpeters Ray Nance and Clark Terry, bop clarinetist Jimmy Hamilton, and bassist Jimmy Woode, three of whom were set to play solos in the "Suite." Terry, in fact, had a key solo in the third section.

The rehearsal was "kind of a disaster," Avakian recalled, "but we had no choice. He wanted to get a good performance of the first long work that he had written in years. And it was being talked about [in the press]. So it was a big deal." Whatever worries Avakian harbored of his own, he kept them from Ellington, whose well-honed cool was perhaps masking a deeper anxiety over what the night could mean for the rest of his career. In the year when rock and roll was manifestly beginning to shake the nation, Newport '56 had arrived as the epicenter of jazz. For three days the media had been there to report and record the tremors. If his sixteen-piece band were to remain in the game, its Saturday-night performance had to be nothing short of a quake. "Look, don't worry," the producer kept telling the anxious maestro. "We'll get it right in the remake."

When the band finished the rehearsal, Avakian and his engineers got a bite to eat at one of the food stands, the musicians repaired to the bus, and Ellington and Strayhorn went their own way. Anxious but happy, Duke fully grasped what was riding on the coming night's live recording with Columbia. The year before, the label had broken Brubeck—live. It had signed Davis and released his *'Round about Midnight* LP. It was now going great guns with Armstrong and his live recordings. In a little over an hour, Ellington would be performing before the assembled multitude of jazz fans, personalities, and the national media. As for the prodigal four, they were still nowhere to be seen.

10

The Saturday Night

Converging on the Decisive Moment

As the sun began to set behind the stone wall along Freebody Street, the sky was crystal clear. It was now evident that despite the first night's deluge, the festival had indeed logged a record crowd for the weekend: twenty-five thousand fans.

"Everyone was *up,*" said *Providence Journal* photographer Paul Hoeffler of that Saturday evening. "Buck" Hoeffler, whose photos from that night would appear in the 2001 Ken Burns PBS series *Jazz,* was assisting the paper's ace photographer, Winfield Parks. "I was eighteen and had been shooting assignments for several years in a freelance capacity." That July 7 with Ellington "had a significance few evenings ever have. There was a special energy in the air on arriving at Freebody. The weather was excellent, a lovely evening, with people flowing into the open air park. It was enjoyably respectful, but not stiff. The audience, some young people, but mostly adults, were civilized and attentive, nicely dressed," and the security people did "their part well, without being overbearing."

Hoeffler was struck by the number of African Americans in the crowd that night—and by the size of the press corps. "The media, the writers, were out in full force, and you can see all the photographers around the stage, in my shot of Ellington pointing to the band, just out of view, and the crowd thick and full around the stage."

Hoeffler, a lover of baseball, trains, and music, had studied at the Rochester Institute of Technology and was one of several photographers there that night who had been inspired by the great French photojournalist Henri Cartier-Bresson, known in America as the exponent of the decisive moment. In French the term was *images à la sauvette*—images of free spirits caught in the act.

Bob Parent was another Cartier-Bresson disciple who was on the shoot that night. Parent, a freelancer who had been shooting in jazz clubs in Boston and New York for a decade, was at Newport '56 supporting *Time* magazine's cover story that it was preparing on Duke Ellington and awaiting a news peg. One of his photos would also accompany Whitney Balliett's *Saturday Review* piece. Another would feature prominently above Leonard Feather's report in *Down Beat*. Early in his career Parent had designed his own lighting equipment. By 1953 he was working purely with available light, a technique made famous by Cartier-Bresson. At concerts he was legendary for working with several cameras slung over his shoulder at the same time, "mainly so he would not have to change lenses," said Columbia's Don Hunstein.

Another Cartier-Bresson admirer, Hunstein was at Newport shooting the promotion photos and artwork for Avakian's boxed set. Originally from St. Louis, Hunstein had gotten into photography in the early fifties while he was in the air force and stationed in England. On the odd weekend he would frequent London's jazz clubs. Later while on leave in Paris, he discovered Cartier-Bresson's work and determined to go professional once he returned to civilian life.

Hoeffler, Parent, and Hunstein were among the dozens of photographers and journalists crowded into what George Wein called the photography pit. Around them the shadows were lengthening. The stage lights brightly illuminated Duke Ellington's bandstand and concert piano to stage right. Into the descending darkness the band shell reflected a soft glow, warming the air that wafted across the footlights to caress the faces of photographers balancing their cameras on the edge of the stage apron, marking their turf in advance of Ellington's first set. For Hoeffler, Parent, and Hunstein, the top priority was getting shots of both stage and crowd that would capture and perpetuate the unanticipated mystique of what was about to happen.

Just behind the photographers Newport colonists, celebrities, musicians' families, and other VIPs were making their way forward to box seats. Front and center were Louis and Elaine Lorillard, enjoying the vibe with John and Esme Hammond, who were always houseguests at Quatrel during festival weekends. Just to the rear, Larry Anderson, the factory-direct-to-you magnate, and his wife, Elaine, arrived with the LeSavoys and the Capuanos, all energized by cocktails they'd had at the Capuanos' Ocean Drive mansion.

Sitting in what she remembered as the "rarified space" of the Columbia box among all the "jazz business people," was George Avakian's cousin Arlene. "I was in seventh heaven, so beside myself," she recalled. "That was kind of a liberation. The music had already been so transporting. We were taking Newport over and transforming it for the weekend."

Another teen was equally transported. On the field far to the rear sat sixteen-year-old Jonathan Yardley, future literary critic for the *Washington Post Book World*. Wearing his own uniform—khaki slacks, a madras shirt, and loafers—and accompanied by some of his friends from the Groton School in Massachusetts, Yardley eagerly awaited the evening lineup. "For a while among the prep school, the Ivy League, the spoiled-kids crowd, to go to Newport was kind of a hip thing to do," he recalled.

Yardley's father was rector of the fashionable girls' school, Chatham Hall, in southern Virginia. "My father strongly disapproved of jazz, although he really didn't know anything about music of any kind," Yardley said. But his mother loved the big band swing music of the thirties. One Christmas she gave him the first Glenn Miller LP set, awakening what would become a passionate interest in jazz from its roots, all the way from Jelly Roll Morton to bebop. "I was a scholarship boy at Groton. I was there primarily because my father was a private school headmaster, so I felt a fairly considerable gap between the haves and the have-nots, and I tended to hang out with the have-nots."

Yardley attended the first Newport Festival in the summer of '54 and returned the following two years with his friends from Groton. Having bought a used Rolleicord camera, he wangled a press pass for the '55 festival and one night pushed through the crowd right up to Wein's photography pit, where he snapped through one performance after another and got a tremendous rush.

Differing backgrounds aside, Yardley shared Arlene Avakian's attitude to rock and roll. "I was a jazz purist, and I just wasn't interested in that stuff." At the time he thought Elvis Presley was "ridiculous." Yardley loved big bands, and though he didn't know much about Duke Ellington, he approached the evening with great anticipation. "Ellington was a big band, and that was enough for me." He wouldn't be disappointed. "Listen," he would say many years later, "I remember Ellington in '56. That's what I remember above and beyond *everything* else."

Shortly after 8:30, the Duke Ellington Orchestra took the stage, the audience still filing to their seats. Ellington had changed into a loose-fitting houndstooth suit. The band was in white dinner jackets. Exuding an understated class, they played—with just a hint of swing—the national anthem.

Avakian did a quick check with his engineers. "We got quite a bit of echo on the brass bouncing back from the concrete grandstand," he recalled. "The sound of the brass bounced back in a different way according to what the weather was like. That was minor, but it was something that we had to compensate for."

The emcee for that evening was Father Norman O'Connor. He announced an Ellington band that was still without Nance, Terry, Hamilton, or Woode and mistakenly identified plunger style trombonist Quentin "Butter" Jackson as the stiffly formal Lawrence Brown, who had left in 1951 when Hodges took his hiatus.

Ellington was able to cover Woode's absence with bassist Al Lucas, who would be playing in two other sets later that night. Thus, without two trumpets and his bop clarinetist, Ellington chose as his first warm-up number his twenties-era "Black and Tan Fantasy."

Ever attuned to his audience, Ellington's well-considered introduction would subtly cut to the quick, without intruding on any sensibilities. One view holds that the title "Black and Tan Fantasy" refers to Harlem clubs that allowed African Americans and whites to mix. Whatever the truth of that interpretation, no doubt the piece was emotionally

The Duke Ellington Orchestra plays the national anthem at Newport '56. ::: *Photo courtesy of Paul "Buck" Hoeffler.*

stirring for those Newporters in their fifties who had come of age in 1920s and done their clubbing in Harlem. It must have been emotionally stirring for Ellington, too, calling to mind one of the apparitions from his past, one-time lover Fredi Washington, his co-star in the nineteen-minute short *Black and Tan*.

Musically, the piece evoked the African American experience with a sultry mix of themes and styles: urban and rural, sacred and secular, gospel and blues, Chopin and Africa. That night, Cat Anderson covered co-composer Bubber Miley's famous growl trumpet solos in the piece. Russell Procope doubled on alto sax and New Orleans clarinet.

The second warm-up stirred other long-buried memories: Broadway composer and producer Vincent Youmans's "Tea for Two." Older Newporters would have remembered it from the 1925 hit musical *No, No, Nanette*. Deceptively light fare, the musical told the story of New York ingenue Nanette, a flapper ready to rebel against her father, a publisher of Bibles.

"Tea for Two" would have been familiar to younger Newporters as well, via the 1950 film version starring Doris Day as Nanette. The fan magazines had fallen all over themselves to repeat the studio press release and report that Day, at the peak of her singing career, "dances for the first time on the screen." Wildly popular in its time, this Technicolor extravaganza depicted Nanette as a New York heiress who aspired to be a Broadway singer and dancer—an appealing fantasy for a postwar Newport deb finding herself raising children but subconsciously wishing that she had taken a different course in life.

That night Ellington had Willie Cook handle the "Tea for Two" trumpet solo. For some reason Cook wasn't listed with the orchestra on the festival's final mimeographed handout circulated to the press. Instead, the handout credited four in the trumpet section: Nance, Terry, Anderson, and one Nelson "Cadillac" Williams who had toured with the band in late 1949 and recorded with Hodges. Perhaps Ellington, not expecting Cook, had secured Williams and submitted his name for the program lineup. That April, during a run at Basin Street East, Williams and another trumpeter, Jesse Drakes, had covered for Cook and Nance, who had been arrested and jailed on narcotics charges. However, Williams left for France sometime afterward. Upset by the craze for rock and roll and R&B, he had said jazz was dying.

With "Tea for Two" Ellington introduced the song's familiar phrases ever so briefly and immediately brought into the beat Woodyard's cymbals and Lucas's bass lines. The piece jumped. An Ellington growl, a subtle Woodyard drum roll, and then lazily, Cook slid into the groove to run his solo. "Alright, alright, alright, alright, alright," Ellington confidently

The VIP section. ::: *Photo courtesy of Paul "Buck" Hoeffler.*

Ellington and the band during the second set, July 7, 1956. ::: *Photo courtesy of Paul "Buck" Hoeffler.*

interjected, leaning forward over the keys, hands flashing, goosing the band to join on Cook's second go-round. The trumpeter was now on a roll and hit it again. "Go, go, go," Duke shouted, jumping to his feet. Soloist and band went around for a fourth, whereupon Cook finished on a high note.

"Yeah," sighed Ellington with relieved satisfaction. For some in the audience, it was his first invitation to dance. "Do we stay up?" one band member asked over the mild applause. No. Father O'Connor started his segue remarks. "The Duke will be back later with lots more music, and consequently don't any of you go away mad because the Duke is not coming back."

Ellington may have been relieved, but Yardley wasn't too impressed. "It didn't start out propitiously," he remarked. "I remember being sort of restless. The band was pretty stiff."

Ellington and his band left the stage, but not prematurely, as some have suggested. Wein had established that each night's closing act would play the national anthem and one or two numbers to warm the crowd, then hand the mike to the emcee and return later to close the evening. Hence, the four prodigals may have decided that their presence in this first set was not all that vital. Ellington nephew Michael James maintained that they were most likely with other musicians at a favorite watering hole just over the wall around

Freebody Park. Willie Cook, in a 1994 interview with Phil Schaap, similarly suggested that the four were at a "good bar" about a block around the corner from Freebody Park. Ellington was certainly used to no-shows among his troop, but given the import of that particular evening, he certainly would have been peeved.

Heading down the stage stairs past Avakian, Ellington may have already been pondering how to cover Terry's trumpet parts for his "Suite," since it appeared that he might have only Cook and Anderson. He needed another trumpet, just in case.

Photos of the Ellington band during the second set clearly show a figure in a black suit in the trumpet section among the rest of the musicians in their white dinner jackets. According to Ellington's longtime publicist Patricia Willard, who studied one of Buck Hoeffler's photos, that heretofore-unidentified trumpeter was an accomplished thirty-year-old composer and arranger from Miami, Herbie Jones. He had once been a member of the Lucky Millinder Band, the rhythm and blues–oriented organization that graduated the other two Ellingtonians in the '56 band: Jimmy Hamilton and Cat Anderson. Herbie Jones wasn't listed anywhere in the advance mimeographed handout. According to Michael James, who traveled extensively with the band, Ellington sometimes brought extra musicians on the band bus as a backup. A good section man, Jones conceivably could have accompanied the aggregation as Duke's insurance, particularly given the drug habit that dogged trumpeters Nance and Cook. In *Music Is My Mistress,* Duke recalled the most reliable Jones as "a great asset to the band," "a good reader," who was "neat and clean, neither smoked nor drank."

Herbie Jones, the heretofore unidentified stand-in trumpeter for the evening. This photo was taken by London photographer, writer, reviewer, and interviewer Valerie Wilmer, who was associated with the Soho jazz venue Ronnie Scott's and author of *As Serious as Your Life* and coauthor of *The Jazz Scene*. ::: *Duke Ellington Collection, Archives Center, National Museum of American History, Smithsonian Institution.*

As if missing players weren't enough of a headache, Ellington had to endure additions to the scheduled lineup. For Saturday evening the handout had listed only the Duke Ellington Orchestra, Chico Hamilton Quintet, Bud Shank Quartet, and Anita O'Day. Last minute, however, George Wein had added three acts: his former piano teacher Teddy Wilson, West Coaster Jimmy Giuffre, and Friedrich Gulda. Presuming that each act would be onstage for twenty minutes, that decision added at least an hour to a program that was supposed to start at 8:30 and finish at midnight. Six acts with changeovers and an intermission would now follow before Duke would reclaim his seat at the keyboard to comp the first bars of "Take the A Train."

Already sixteen minutes into the evening and pushing 9:00, Ellington came offstage, did the math, and wasn't happy. Newport audiences had come to expect their final acts to blow the lid off the evening. Clearly this revised lineup posed the risk that his "Suite" would fall flat. No matter who was in his band, nor how well it played, the fans would be too satiated to appreciate the music.

The Bud Shank Quartet appeared next. A practitioner of West Coast cool jazz, Shank played a thirty-minute set with flute and alto sax, putting the audience into a wholly different vibe. More attuned to the intimacy of a club venue, his was not the kind of music to reach the folks in the stands. Teddy Wilson's trio with Lucas and drummer Jo Jones followed, with Jones getting a big hand from the crowd when introduced by Father O'Connor. Inexplicably, the trio launched their set with "Tea for Two," during which Jones put down a beat with the lightest of touches. Wilson then gave the audience his "nimble interpretations" of Goodman and Basie and "old show tunes," wrote one critic later, and finished with "I Got Rhythm," eliciting shouts for more. He encored with "Birth of the Blues" and finished to rousing applause and whistles. It was now pushing ten o'clock.

Father O'Connor acknowledged the Lorillards and the "assistance" from George Wein. Sensing the mood of the appreciative crowd during the changeover, he spoke of the significance of the swing era in his introduction of Jimmy Giuffre, unconvincingly making mention of his time with Woody Herman. (Shank in fact played with the Charlie Barnet and Stan Kenton big bands.) Almost apologetically, he added, "We have an awfully long program," as he segued his remarks to give a nod again to the West Coast school of jazz. Giuffre began his set, in which he would play clarinet as well as baritone and tenor saxes, with a new composition tagged by O'Connor as "reflective." To a man, Giuffre's sidemen were the same three who had played earlier with Bud Shank, prompting O'Connor to plug Nesuhi Ertegun's Atlantic jazz catalog. George Wein himself had recorded the previous year an album for Atlantic titled *Wein, Women & Song*. Shank left the stage swinging with "East of the Sun" and got a good hand for his effort.

Handicapped by sudden mike trouble, Father O'Connor did his best to manage a long three-minute changeover for Chicago veteran Anita O'Day, a self-proclaimed "swing chick." Born Anita Colton, she changed her name to O'Day, allegedly because it was Pig Latin for the dough that she said she wanted to earn. Her career had started during wartime when she sang with Gene Krupa, whose trumpeter was then Roy Eldridge. In her big hit of the time, "Let Me Off Uptown," an exuberant paean to Harlem, she did a duet with Eldridge during which she ad-libbed "Blow, Roy, blow!" It was a daring move: in the segregated forties, a white female singer dueting with a black trumpeter violated a fundamental social taboo.

Mid-decade, O'Day went with bandleaders Woody Herman and later Stan Kenton. In 1947 she wrote and sang "Rock and Roll Blues," becoming the first major singer to record a title with the phrase *rock and roll*.

A favorite of Elaine Lorillard, Elaine Anderson, and other equally sophisticated jazz fans, O'Day was ironic and hip, but living that persona had taken its toll. For years she struggled with a heroin addiction. Musicians always enjoyed working with her, nonetheless, because she was so rhythmic. "All I know," she once said, "is there are four beats to a bar and a million ways to phrase a tune."

O'Connor gamely plugged O'Day and her label, Verve, Norman Granz's consolidated label launched earlier that year. With a false start O'Day opened with "Pick Yourself Up," concluding with a scat finish that returned the audience to the here and now after Giuffre's more cosmic meanderings. The mike problems persisted, with her Boston pianist Don Ritter covering while the engineers did the fix. O'Day continued with two numbers and then went into "Honeysuckle Rose," where Lucas blew two intros. She then tackled "Ole Devil Moon," giving an aside that it was in "the same key, unfortunately." She had to key the band for a medley and then was ready to leave the stage. "Is that enough?" "More!" the crowd shouted back. She then gave a Gene Krupa number, "Boogie Blues," finishing with another scat. "Alright?" Shouts for more. "No more time," said O'Connor. It was now well past 10:30.

O'Connor announced an abbreviated ten-minute interval. "We're running just a wee bit late." He said they were not giving "pass out checks" and told the audience to stay in the grounds.

Going into the break, the audience remained up. The sky was still clear. The air was warm and carried the smell of the sea. Yardley and his friends made their way through the crowds to the rear, where the Kiwanis were selling massive amounts of 'Gansett. "There was a lot of drinking beer," Yardley remembered. The effect was tidal. The men's room under the concrete stands was awash and so crowded that "guys would be peeing in the wash basins." Midway through the evening, the social inhibitions in a number of the youthful quarters high in the stands had already begun to float away.

Meanwhile, George Wein made his way backstage, still harboring fears about Ellington's intentions for the program, fears heightened by the uncertainty resulting from the absent band members. Unbeknownst to him, sometime during the first half of the program, Nance, Terry, Hamilton, and Woode had returned from their adventures. Eager to ride the crest of O'Day's lift, Ellington was in an icy simmer over the lateness of the hour. It was all but inside 11:00, and still to go were Gulda and Chico Hamilton.

When Wein appeared, Ellington was conferring with his mid-twenties band boy, Bobby Boyd. "What are you going to play?" Wein pressed him. "I don't know." Wein persisted, offering a number of selections that, according to Boyd, "went in one ear and out the other." "I'll have something," Ellington kept saying dismissively. Exasperated at the prospect that Duke might play a tired medley, Wein finally broke. "I've worked my fingers to the bone to help the Ellington legend, and I'm not getting any help from you." Coping with a restless band and seeing the sands of the evening rapidly running to the bottom of the hourglass, Ellington vented. "What are we—the animal act, the acrobats?" "Don't worry," said Wein, "you'll be on in a few minutes." Duke answered: "I don't want to play exit music."

The Ellington band in the backstage performers' tent, ready to return to the stage. ***Left to right:*** **Sam Woodyard, Willie Cook, Paul Gonsalves, Jimmy Woode, Ray Nance, Clark Terry.** ::: *Photo by Don Hunstein. Courtesy of Sony BMG Music Entertainment.*

Clearly Wein had no intention of shortening the program for Ellington, who was left to pace. Sometime around 10:45 classical pianist Friedrich Gulda and his septet opened the second half. Characterizing Gulda as "an arrogant young man," *Metronome* panned him and his accompanists as an "often dull bop group." Gulda ill-advisedly repeated most of what he played during the afternoon panel sessions, and the critics called him on it. It was an unnecessary waste of precious running time. The audience received him coolly and soon grew bored. "Play one more?" someone asked. "No," O'Connor replied. It was now just past 11:15.

Innovative drummer Chico Hamilton came to the stage, taking more than three minutes to manage and mike his setup. In the forties he had played with Count Basie, Lionel Hampton, and blues guitarist T-Bone Walker. In 1952 he was a Pacific Jazz recording artist who backed Chet Baker and Gerry Mulligan, and a few years later he formed his own unusual group with cello, flute, guitar, bass, and his drums. On flute at Newport was the transcendental Paul Horn, who in the next decade would become famous for *Inside*, his recording inside the Taj Mahal. "A high spot of the festival," wrote one critic, "with new sounds . . . or, at least, the newest sounds of the event."

The quintet worked through a very satisfying set to a "bewitching" finish. "I thought Chico Hamilton's 'Blue Sands' was the most amazing thing I had ever heard," Arlene Avakian recalled. "I have never ever forgotten that. He had this incredible beat, a very complicated rhythm. It was just electrifying for me."

It was a mystical, Eastern beginning with a flute and tom-tom beat. Collette did a solo that got a hand some four minutes into the number. Working to a frenzy with the guitar, Hamilton rhythmically tapped on his blocks, which the PA system amplified, sending sharp clicks into the damp atmosphere, echoing off the grandstands and throughout the park, cutting the now rapt audience to the quick. Switching his beat to the tom-toms, Hamilton ebbed to light applause and then moved into a drum solo that yielded another round of applause followed by dissonant guitar chords and flute and cello. The group finished with the cello, agitated into stillness as the cellist worked up the frets. "Blue Sands" was a twelve-minute tour de force that took the lid off the audience. They finished to loud applause that was sustained for thirty seconds.

"Thank you very kindly," said Hamilton.

"That was very good, Chico," someone said. "Well put."

Collette, a founding member of Chico Hamilton's quintet, recalled the group's performance of the spellbinding number. "We played for about ten minutes, giving it our best shot. And at the end, as we'd do, we just tapered off, and everything just stopped. And for eight or ten seconds nobody moved, and then they jumped up and screamed; they went wild, and it went on and on."

During Chico Hamilton's set, the backstage scene in the musicians' tent ebbed and flowed as performers and others with passes came, mingled, and went. The Ellington band began to stir in anticipation, each engaged in his own routine. Some were slaphappy, some were focused, and some were angered by the long wait in a spartan tent that passed as a green room. Johnny Hodges, cigarette dangling from his mouth, nursed his instrument, and kept quietly to himself. Ellington realized that he needed to rally his band.

Avakian and his engineers were standing by the Columbia tables and recording gear. Nearby, Billy Strayhorn was arranging his score sheets for the "Suite," preparing to follow the performance and circle the bad notes. In the far corner, the VOA team continued monitoring their machines as the tapes rolled to capture the music of the Hamilton Quintet. Ellington called his men together in the middle of the tent.

"Look," said the bandleader, addressing them in a subdued tone, "we've all worked very hard to make this happen, and George [Avakian] has stuck his neck out, because nobody has ever done anything like this before. I know we're all worried about the fact that we haven't had adequate rehearsal, but I want you to know that there is nothing to be afraid of. Just go and play, because Strayhorn has a score sitting next to the engineers, and he will mark anything he hears that is bad."

Dave Brubeck (left) and Jo Jones share a moment backstage in the performers' tent at Newport '56. ::: *Photo by Don Hunstein. Courtesy of Sony BMG Music Entertainment.*

"I've asked George to reserve some time in a studio on Monday," Ellington continued, "and we can go in and fix anything that we have to fix. So just go ahead. We'll go straight through it no matter what happens. Don't worry."

George Wein had said all along that he'd better swing, better not play the medleys. Ellington took the point. Swing he would.

"After we finish [the 'Suite'], let's just relax and have a real good time. Let's play the 'Diminuendo and Crescendo.'"

Some of the musicians started buzzing about it. "Gee," Gonsalves interjected impishly, "I don't think I know that one." "B-flat," someone told him. "All you do is blow the blues."

"Gonsalves was the super goof of the group," Avakian recalled, "always high." As if to reassure himself, Avakian leaned toward the sax player. "Oh, sure you know," he whispered.

"Paul," Ellington said, "it's the one where we play the blues and change keys. I bring you on, and you blow until I take you off, and we change keys. Enough. It's number 107 and 108 in the book." "Oh yeah, I remember." He knew.

By now, Chico Hamilton was finishing his set. Ellington's band concluded their last-minute preparations, oiling slides, clearing valves, checking reeds. Hodges was still by himself, quiet.

As the band continued to mingle, ready to file from the tent and walk up the stairs to the stage, Avakian launched into a little speech that he had given all the Columbia artists before they went onstage. "Now look, you see the stage. Originally, we had a white handkerchief tied to the Columbia microphone. Well, that was too obtrusive. When you play a solo, go up to the microphone that has white tape. That's our mike. Next to it is the Voice of America and the PA system mikes. They'll pick you up alright, but for the sake of the recording, please blow directly into the microphone that has the white tape."

Avakian turned and chatted with Harry Carney and a couple of other musicians who had joined the band backstage, notably sax man John Coltrane and drummer Jo Jones, who had been hanging with Clark Terry after his appearance with Teddy Wilson.

Chico Hamilton was finishing his set. It was time.

"Let's go up and hit," Ellington finally said.

For jazz historian Dan Morgenstern, whether the band was angry for being delayed is irrelevant to the performance. "The amazing thing about that band is the professionalism. You could be on the bus, or you could be backstage, with the guys not talking to each other, having some kind of tiff, not wanting to sit next to each other. God knows what. And they would get on stage finally, and Duke would start something, and the rhythm section would lock in, and there they were. I mean, it was a band. It was a band, and it was a unit. They were all working together, and they'd get off."

The band filed from the tent into a starry night, as "Blue Sands" tapered into silence and then an eruption of applause. Ellington's musicians quietly passed along the twenty-odd feet to the foot of the stage steps.

Once there, Ellington and his men stood quietly, awaiting the cue for the changeover onstage. Duke's gaze lifted skyward as he pondered through the dying applause the high stakes riding on his follow-up.

Chico Hamilton's reedman, Buddy Collette, recalled the moment. As he and his fellow musicians were leaving the stage, he passed Ellington on the stairs. Duke smiled and said, "Well, you sure made it hot for me."

As band members filed by him at the bottom of the steps, Cal Lampley murmured, "Now, don't forget, it's the mike with the white tape." Avakian, now at the top of the stairs, reiterated the message: "Be sure you play into the Columbia mike, the one with the white tape." "Yes, yes."

When the band finally finished settling into their seats, Duke crossed the stage and took his place at the piano. The hour was 11:45, fifteen minutes prior to what was supposed to be curtain time.

Ellington hit some quick phrases; Jimmy Woode started his bass line with Sam Woodyard stroking a cymbal, and they eased into "Take the A Train." Ellington took his time romping over the keys, and then leaning away with an "Ahhhh!" invited the band to join. The musicians attacked the beat, purring like a well-tuned engine. Ray Nance came to the mike and competently worked his trumpet solo, then moved to his exchanges with the band. Into the finale, however, he inexplicably lost steam, finishing on a dying fall. The applause was not what it should have been. "Everybody!" cried Ellington. "Let's have it," he added, inviting the band to stand. Crediting Nance for his signature solo, Ellington tried to coax further applause. "Come on, come on." Polite ripples faded quickly into the night.

Backstage, the Columbia team readied themselves: behind the tables, Theroux and Graham at the controls, tape recorders rolling; Lampley, standing to their side, near the entrance, an ear cocked in Avakian's direction; Billy Strayhorn, sitting at another table facing the engineers, pencil in hand, his score sheets spread before him.

Just offstage left, down a few steps on the stairs, George Avakian, now feeling the pressure, ran a visual check, his eyes darting from mike to mike. The next three songs would be Duke's main event, on which all was riding.

Catching his breath, Ellington announced to his audience, "We have prepared a new thing, and we haven't even had time to title it yet. Of course, it's done especially for the Newport Jazz Festival, and so temporarily, I think we'll just call the first part of it," he added, looking for words, " 'Festival Junction.' Jimmy Hamilton will state the theme."

After Hamilton's brief solo wafted into the air, Ellington began chording in triplets that built into a beat, leading Woodyard into his cymbals, then Woode into his bass line, and finally the rest of the band. Now Ellington was punctuating with growled triplets. Willie Cook took the next solo, then came Gonsalves, unleashing riffs he would use later that night. Following him in sequence were Woodman's smooth trombone, Carney and his baritone sax, Jackson's plunger-style trombone, Procope's alto sax, and finally Anderson, attacking with his trumpet, finishing with one of his famous high notes. Standing before his piano, Ellington waved his arm with a flourish. "Everybody!" he shouted, before introducing his soloists. There, standing on the apron of the stage, was the Duke Ellington Orchestra.

The audience responded appreciatively. Not a bad start.

"The next spot, or rather the second section, will be tentatively titled 'Blues to Be There.' " Ellington played his introduction, Woodyard supporting and Woode's bass following. Duke worked through some effective blues wrinkles. The reeds entered, followed by the trombones. Procope then hit his New Orleans–inflected clarinet solo and took his thank you. The movement had a lazy feel. Nance returned with his muted trumpet, Duke from time to time purring his "Ahhhs" as the piece began to build, then faded to Woodyard's finishing drumbeat. "Yeah," Ellington exclaimed with a smile, eliciting all but a subdued response from across the footlights.

Ellington crossed to the downstage mike. "The third section of the Newport Special will be 'Newport Up,' " he announced and then turned to his musicians. "Newport Up," he whispered. He began humming the beat and with a quick grunt cued the band. Woodyard and Woode drove it, as Ellington crossed to the piano to join with his fills.

Hamilton drifted forward and started soloing into the VOA mike. Avakian gesticulated wildly, pointing to Columbia's microphone on the clarinetist's left. Looking across the stage, Ellington caught the gesture. "Other mike! Other mike!!" he shouted to Hamilton, who seamlessly recovered. Then came Terry, followed by Gonsalves, who rolled through a short bop solo, prompting Ellington to eject a long "Ahhhh." And then the soloists traded. The audience's response was still far short of enthusiasm. For jazz fan Jonathan Yardley, the "Suite" was a letdown.

Ellington read the audience and plowed into the rest of his set. Dropping the energy level, he introduced his baritone sax, Harry Carney, to solo on "Sophisticated Lady." Carney played the 1933 ballad with a thoughtful, boozy feel. To be sure, Ellington would have known that many of the ladies in the audience knew the lyrics and found them apt: "No, sophisticated lady / I know, you miss the love you lost long ago / And when nobody is nigh, you cry." A safe choice, perhaps, but the crowd hadn't caught fire. The hour was late. Some in the boxes were calling it a night. As Carney drifted away, Ellington faded with a sequence of chords that yielded only lukewarm applause.

Then the bandleader crossed to the mike and introduced Jimmy Grissom to sing Johnny Mercer and Rube Bloom's 1939 standard "Day In, Day Out." Punctuating the opening bars with another "Ahhhh," Ellington led the band from downstage before crossing back to his chair. Grissom and the band carried the song. Not playing—no comps, no fills—Ellington sat upright, looking exhausted as he cast his eyes anxiously over the crowd. To the rear he could see the audience exiting, some evidently assuming that the evening had already climaxed, others hastening to beat the exodus from town.

For an instant a despondent Ellington worried that his career had dwindled to the point where he was indeed playing exit music. "Day in, day out / The same old hoodoo follows me about," crooned Grissom. The unfinished aspects of the "Suite" haunted the composer-bandleader. The audience hadn't bought it. He was fifty-seven, and it had been a long road. Since coming onstage for the second set he had been playing full tilt, pushing himself and the band for almost half an hour, and the hour was well past twelve. Did he have anything left? A Bob Parent photo captured the moment from a seemingly defeated Ellington, catatonic. He was spooked. From Aquacades to acrobat, perhaps it was indeed all over.

Reacting to the photo, Michael James was more positive. "When Duke's looking like that, that's Duke listening and absorbing what's going on. He always got that expression when he's looking around and hearing what the band's doing. That's a common Duke expression when he's listening or even when he's humming at the piano."

"He had to change the energy," Clark Terry said, vividly recalling the competitive stakes of the moment, raised by skeptical music critics and audience members prepared to dismiss a big band. "Those cats were giving him a real tough battle, you know. When you get into a fight, and a cat is kicking your ass, you got to figure some way to get out. Maybe he was bewildered there for a minute, but he knew how to come out of it. That tells you he's normal. He's human. He's putting it all together. Like Joe Lewis, he knew what he had to do. His work was cut out for him. He was prepared to do it and he did it. He knew when he was in trouble, he knew when he had to do something. He didn't always look beautiful out there with all of his opponents. Some of these opponents were worthy opponents, and they were slinging leather."

Grissom finished and received tepid applause.

"Yeah," Ellington bestirred himself to say.

Recalling her mounting impatience in her second-row box, Elaine Anderson said, "Frankly, it was boring."

Ellington had died. But, by God, he wasn't going to go gently into that good night. He was going to return—return and hit them with the power of the blues.

He lifted himself from his chair, and crossing to center stage, he murmured an aside, almost teasing the photographers and crowd just across the footlights, "Don't go away." At the microphone he called his next number, written in 1937, to be sure, but one that summoned another apparition from '38, a Sunday in May when, as a thirty-nine-

Duke Ellington studies the audience during Jimmy Grissom's performance of "Day In, Day Out."
::: *Photo courtesy of Bob Parent.*

year-old entering his best years, he had literally stopped the show at New York's Randall's Island.

"And now, we would like to play some of our 1938 vintage 'Diminuendo in Blue' and 'Crescendo in Blue.' These are separated by an interval by Paul Gonsalves."

For many careers, for many lives, that interval would be the decisive moment.

11

A Leading Voice Supported by Many Parts

Paul Gonsalves

He was tagged Mex, by Basie trumpeter Harry "Sweets" Edison. One week into his two-year stint with the Basie band, Edison told him, "You may look like a Mexican, but you sure don't sound like one." Because of his light skin color and the Latin name, the label seemed appropriate. In truth Paul Gonsalves was a Cape Verdean American. Cape Verdeans were heroic people of the sea, who took great pride in their ancestry. It was this specific heritage that defined Gonsalves as a jazz interpreter and soloist.

"The Cape Verdeans were the only people of color who came from Africa to America willingly," said Ron Barboza, a historian, researcher, and photographer of the Cape Verdean community in New Bedford, Massachusetts.

The islands that make up the Cape Verde archipelago lie several hundred miles off the Senegalese coast. According to Barboza, Africans had fished the waters around the islands for centuries. Around 1460 explorers serving Portuguese prince Henry the Navigator were the first Europeans to settle the islands and subsequently brought slaves from West Africa. Cape Verdeans trace their ancestry to Portuguese settlers and some twenty-seven African tribes.

The Gonsalves line came from Brava, the smallest of the nine inhabited islands. Lying to the southwest and facing the open ocean, Brava—Portuguese for "brave" or "rough"—is a five-by-five-mile postage stamp in the sea. "At one time it was the most densely populated area in Africa," said Barboza. The peak population was more than nine thousand, but that number started falling when natives, weary of the famine and drought that plagued all the islands, began leaving for America.

Cape Verdeans first came to America in the eighteenth century on New England whalers. The ships would chase whales down the Atlantic, restock with provisions in the Azores, then proceed to Cape Verde for more supplies and to find shelter from storms. Brava became the most popular stop, said Barboza, because it had good bays where whalers could anchor. In time Cape Verdeans started shipping aboard, first as deckhands and later as harpooners. Dodging conscription into the Portuguese army, they would descend from the country under the cover of night, board the vessels, and leave for five or six years at a time. Around 1860 Cape Verdeans started coming ashore in greater numbers to New Bedford and arranging for their families to join them. By the turn of the century, they were banding together to buy old whalers and rig them as packet ships—Brava packets—that returned to the islands to collect those escaping poverty, famine, and drought. Between 1860 and 1920 some nineteen thousand Cape Verdeans came to America aboard packet ships. Ninety percent passed through New Bedford, what Barboza called "the Ellis Island for Cape Verdeans," and many would settle in the Water Street area alongside the Jewish community.

The epic crossing by Brava packet was a wholly unique immigrant experience. "Unlike centuries before when Africans were shipped to America on slave ships," said Barboza, "Cape Verdeans in the nineteenth century were entirely in control of their destiny." Of the hundred or so packets, a number were owned, captained, and crewed by the islanders. Most were whalers; some were schooners, but all were under sail. The men and their dependents traveled in one class—no steerage. The ships were jam packed, often carrying more than a hundred souls along with live animals that provided food. Passengers spent their weeks at sea cooking Cape Verdean food, playing cards, swapping stories, and making music.

Paul Gonsalves in New Bedford, Massachusetts, 1940. ::: *Photo courtesy of Joseph Livramento ©.*

Eventually the whaling era declined, but well into the 1950s, many young Cape Verdean men would return to the sea as a rite of passage, either in the merchant marine or the navy. Far from separating Cape Verdeans from their ancestral home, the sea bound them to it—as Cape Verdean music does today.

"In Cape Verde, musicians are like sports stars," said Barboza. "They are idols."

To this day, most Cape Verdean Americans sing and play instruments. In 1917 Cape Verdean musicians founded New Bedford's Ultramarine Band Club, a seventeen-member marching band for some thirty communities throughout New England. Members of the Ultramarine Band Club also played music for weddings, baptisms, and funerals. Other traditional musical forms were the *choraguiza* for wakes and *canta ris* for celebrations. Recorded by Columbia Records in 1931 and 1932, this music relied on guitars, violins, and violas. It was the music of kitchen dances, the New Bedford equivalent of the Harlem Renaissance rent parties.

Kitchen dances continued into the forties. "Sometimes you would have a kitchen dance to celebrate a baptism. It could be a fund-raiser for a family, or just a neighborhood dance, if there wasn't a hall available," said Barboza. "The kitchen was the social center of the house. People would move their furniture aside, they would get a number of musicians to perform, and they would dance, visit, and eat Cape Verdean food, *cachupa*, a one-pot meal, the national dish."

First-generation Cape Verdean Americans "knew tough times and would pour their feelings into their music. They would bare their souls," said Barboza, "and that was passed on to many of the next generation like Paul Gonsalves. That's why he played the way he did."

In the 1930s one of the leading lights in the Cape Verdean music scene was the dapper Isadore Oliveira, whose Anglicized stage name was Duke Oliver. With the universal popularity of swing, he migrated from straight Creole music to the big band sound. Oliver's dance band unit of the Ultramarine Band played swing material in the Ellington vein. His venue of choice was a Portuguese dance hall in New Bedford called the Monte Pio, which was upstairs from a grocery at the corner of Acushnet Avenue and Holland Street.

Though Duke Oliver never recorded, by the 1950s other Cape Verdeans were recording, some on their own labels. Dan Morgenstern recalled that the Institute of Jazz Studies has a 45 that was made on a small local label by trumpet player Phil Edmund Barboza. Paul Gonsalves is a guest on it.

As the swing era declined after the war, many Cape Verdean big bands returned to an older musical tradition, the *morna,* now a well-known genre thanks to the success of 2004 Grammy winner Cesaria Evora. Others would go on to achieve crossover fame in pop. Hard bop jazz pianist Horace Silver wrote the sixties bossa nova classic "Song for My Father," and the five Tavares brothers achieved international fame for "More Than a Woman," featured in the 1978 disco film *Saturday Night Fever*. The Tavareses were also the first Cape Verdean Grammy winners.

Cape Verdeans are justifiably proud of their pop-music achievements. But the most significant musical milestone in their American odyssey has nothing to do with pop. "One of the great moments in jazz history," said Ron Barboza, "was the single greatest Cape Verdean artistic feat of the twentieth century." He was referring to Newport '56 and the Paul Gonsalves solo.

Although Pawtucket, Rhode Island, just north of Providence, is generally regarded as the saxophonist's hometown, Barboza has established that Paul Joseph Gonsalves was born in Brockton, Massachusetts, some fifteen miles south of Boston. The date was July 12, 1920. His parents, John and Maria, were first-generation Cape Verdean Americans who spoke *Crioulo*, the Portuguese/African argot. They had separately made the Atlantic crossing by Brava packet. Maria had never been to sea before and crossed with their first child, Joseph, aged three months, on a voyage that lasted forty-two days.

In the thirties, Cape Verdean youth in Pawtucket had few outlets other than sports and music. Gonsalves was an athlete, playing high school baseball, basketball, and football. He inherited a love for Cape Verdean music from his father, an accomplished chef who taught him and his brothers, Joe and John, to play guitar. The brothers bought records, refined their skills, and formed a Cape Verdean Creole band. Gonsalves proved to be a natural soloist, as was Joe, who played rhythm guitar, and who introduced a nine-year-old Paul to Ellington music via his records.

Around the age of sixteen, Paul went with Joe to a midnight show at the RKO Theater in Providence to listen to swing showman and reed man Jimmie Lunceford and his two-beat band ensemble. One of the top swing/dance bands in the country, Lunceford's orchestra was fresh from a year's stint at the Cotton Club. America had embraced swing, and the Lunceford band was a hot crowd pleaser with its Sy Oliver arrangements and the instrumentalists' flashy, choreographed stage movements. The band was at its most exciting in fast tempo, but it could dig deep into a ballad as well. With the bandleader in the reed section was tenor man Joe Thomas, whose expansive, melodious tone helped shape up-and-coming sax men; however, Lunceford favored the alto sax played by Willie Smith, whose solos Gonsalves later memorized.

The concert was Paul Gonsalves's awakening to American popular music. Lunceford's music moved him and prompted him to want to move others. That night in Providence inspired Gonsalves to switch from guitar to saxophone. Shortly thereafter, his father bought him his first tenor sax for fifty dollars. Later he took lessons from Joseph Piaccatelli, who had taught at the Boston Conservatory. After a couple of years, Gonsalves decided to chuck his ambition to become a commercial artist and go professional in Providence, where he doubled on sax and guitar for a local band, Henry McCoy's Jitterbugs.

His future as a musician lay elsewhere. In 1937 the three Gonsalves brothers had entered a Creole talent contest at New Bedford's Monte Pio. The competition was keen. The local favorite that night was the Don Verdi Orchestra, whose clarinetist was the talented Joe Livramento. But it was the Gonsalves trio that came away the winner.

In the thirties, New Bedford was the Cape Verdean Harlem, the center of a hopping scene that was embracing swing. Hoping to capitalize on his success at the Monte Pio, Gonsalves started hitchhiking from his home in Pawtucket to play with musicians in New Bedford. "Joe was one of his first friends, and he eventually invited Paul home to stay with us on weekends," recalled Florence Almeida, Livramento's younger sister. "I was in high school at the time and used to cook for them." Joe and Paul became lifelong best friends. Livramento was moving from clarinet to alto sax. According to John Monteiro, a first-generation Portuguese American friend and fan of Paul's, Livramento had a fused left elbow which he could position perfectly to play the alto, and he and Gonsalves would sit next to each other whenever a section formed. Other New Bedford pals were the bass player Frank Monteiro and his trombonist brother, Pete, who were with Duke Oliver. Frank Monteiro remembered spending hours with Gonsalves understudying Coleman Hawkins records.

Although Gonsalves would gig with a variety of groups and sub in others, when the Jitterbugs folded, he joined the Phil Edmund Band, where he would play regularly with Livramento. Phil Edmund, a regular on the Cape Verdean kitchen dance circuit, played Creole as well as swing, and Gonsalves would occasionally play guitar for those engagements. But as a jazz aggregation, Edmund's band hit all the New Bedford hot spots, played the summer boats from Providence to Martha's Vineyard, and traveled the New England college circuit. Edmund also played a little jazz with national stars like Louis Armstrong and Count Basie.

Paul Gonsalves (second from right) in the Phil Edmund Band. A late-thirties performance at the New Bedford Country Club. ::: *Photo courtesy of Joseph Livramento ©.*

Paul Gonsalves, an army quartermaster at war, c. 1945. ::: *Photo courtesy of Joseph Livramento ©.*

New Bedford musicians all aspired to play with Basie and Ellington. But something in Gonsalves set him apart. "He was so shy," said David Reis, a Dartmouth, Massachusetts, deejay. "It was his horn that exposed him."

A seventeen-year-old John Monteiro saw Gonsalves jam at the Band Club: "He was a good-looking guy, and when he played, he used his body to express emotion. He would give you chills."

A regular guy who was into jazz performances, not musicological critiques, Monteiro, now a Springfield, Massachusetts, insurance broker, recalled seeing Gonsalves later play with a Boston territory band led by pianist and bandleader Sabby Lewis at the Eastern Star Temple, a former Protestant church (now the Verdean Vets Hall) that was a good-sized dance hall on Purchase Street. "All the chicks went there for his ballads. He had a nice way about him, nice smile," said Monteiro. "He wasn't a showman. He was just playing that soul. It was like the music was coming out of him all the way from his head to his heart, right out through his fingers. He was born to play that horn."

Like all great saxophone interpreters, Gonsalves gave a human voice to his instrument when he covered a ballad, personalizing the piece by putting his own gentle stamp on it. "His favorite was 'Stardust,'" said Monteiro. "It was so breathy you could feel it coming off the floor. You had that nice chick in your arms, and it was just stardust. It was all romanticism then."

Already, before the war, twenty-one-year-old Gonsalves had mastered how to capture American popular music for his Cape Verdean audience, and in the process he helped transform his generation of Cape Verdeans into Americans.

That transformation was sealed by war. When it came, Gonsalves joined the Army Quartermaster Corps. He was stationed in the China-Burma-India Theater between December 1942 and November 1945. It would not have been easy duty. The 1,079-mile road through mountainous jungle was a tremendous feat of engineering. More than 60 percent of the troops who served as road builders, truckers, and support were African Americans.

Gonsalves was a truck driver who rose to technical sergeant, fourth class. His unit was probably one among many that convoyed supplies during and after construction of the Ledo

Road from India into northern Burma. It was the only logistics supply line to General "Vinegar Joe" Stilwell's American and Nationalist Chinese forces fighting the Japanese in China.

While in theater Gonsalves gigged with pianist Teddy Weatherford in Calcutta, India's eastern port city linked by rail to the Ledo Road. Weatherford was a Virginian virtuoso who played in New Orleans and Chicago, where in the twenties he was a rival of Earl Hines. In 1926 he toured Asia, where he essentially remained for the rest of his career, leading bands in jazz haunts from Bombay to Singapore, Manila, and Shanghai. From 1941 to 1944 Weatherford was resident in Calcutta leading a band that played broadcasts for the Armed Forces Radio Service.

Along with millions of other GIs, Gonsalves demobilized at the end of 1945. Although he returned to New Bedford to resume his music and his association with Phil Edmund, the war had broadened his horizons. His eyes were now fixed on Boston, where the postwar jazz scene was thriving.

Boston jazzmen lived in the southwestern suburb of Roxbury, a community where there were numerous pickup bands, and African American musicians had their own union, Local 535. Living in a segregated world, they couldn't play the local hotel dance circuit. Most of their work was in South End nightclubs around Columbus and Massachusetts Avenues, Boston's Fifty-second Street, home to famous venues like the Hi-Hat, Wally's Paradise, and the Savoy.

Soon after returning stateside, Paul Gonsalves ventured north for a stint with Sabby Lewis, with whom he had played briefly before the war. A local institution, the Sabby Lewis Band launched many a jazzman in the Boston scene. It was a hot band, an eight-member group that included Joe Booker on trumpet and Jimmy "Bottoms Up" Tyler on baritone and alto. During his time with Lewis, Gonsalves doubled on alto and played at Wally's and the Savoy.

Paul Gonsalves (left) and Joseph Livramento in their Boston apartment, late forties. ::: *Photo courtesy of Joseph Livramento ©.*

Monteiro caught the Sunday afternoon jam sessions at the Savoy to hear him and the Lewis band. "He was the mainstay of that band," Monteiro said, "the most electrifying musician I ever saw in my life. Every time he played, it packed the house." On one particular Sunday the band was playing "Flying Home," Lionel Hampton's wartime signature tune, popular with GIs and famous for its Illinois Jacquet solo. Gonsalves launched into the interval with "so much soul, so much feeling, an intensity that was indescribable," Monteiro vividly recalled. In the middle of the solo he left the stage, marched through the audience with the band in his train—including Lewis—and out the door to the sidewalk along Massachusetts Avenue. Still playing, and now followed by the Savoy audience, he made his way down to the corner of Columbus and continued playing for the gathering crowd. Then Gonsalves led the pack back to the club and finished the number onstage.

It was this level of intensity that gave Gonsalves street credibility. According to Monteiro, African American musicians would claim him as one of their own and heap praise, saying, "Paul Gonsalves, he's mean. He's mean."

Gonsalves made his first records with Sabby Lewis. In late 1946 an opportunity came his way when Count Basie needed to replace his tenor, Illinois Jacquet. New Bedford bandleader Phil Edmund arranged for Basie to hear Gonsalves play in Atlantic City, where the Lewis band was engaged. "Paul didn't want to leave Sabby," said Ron Barboza, "but the people in the band told him, 'Oh, you should really take this opportunity and go with Basie.'"

It was his big break, catapulting his career. Although swing was becoming passé—that December, eight big bands folded—Basie kept his orchestra going for another three years by moving into pop, bebop, and rhythm and blues. Drawing on musicians like Jacquet and trombonist J. J. Johnson, he now fronted a flashy lineup very different from his wartime aggregation. Key to his rhythm section, as always, was the tremendously influential swing percussionist Jo Jones. In addition to Jones were two other geniuses of drive: Buddy Rich and J. C. Heard, said to be Dizzy Gillespie's favorite drummer.

The Count let his soloists blow the blues. If the Basie band was a machine in the fifties, in this earlier era it was uninhibited, allowing soloists like Jacquet and Gonsalves to move around a bar. Drummers Heard, Rich, and Jones and the rest of the Basie rhythm section would move the beat away from two-beat syncopation to an evenly accentuated four-four time.

Jones, who had both swing and touch, was hugely influential. A trained trumpeter and pianist, he had toured with carnivals and performed as a tap dancer. Some say that his touch as a drummer came from his experience as a dancer. He was among the first jazz drummers to set meter on a high-hat cymbal, as opposed to keeping time on the bass drum, which he used along with his other cymbals and snare for punctuation. He was also known for subtle brushwork that provided dynamic shading. Sidemen would say he played like the wind. He was expert in feeding time and ideas to his soloists by building a controlled intensity. A passionate musician-mentor, Jones liked to reach people and inspire them. He also knew how to milk an audience and rejoiced in getting a result.

Having been a guitarist himself, Gonsalves would find himself acutely attuned to Basie's rhythm section. As a sax soloist he was at his best when he could ride a tight rhythm, but his introduction was overwhelming. "Paul told me," Ellington nephew Michael James recalled, "for a while he was so hypnotized by the rhythm section, he forgot to come in." Once he settled in the saddle, he had two years to ride on Jo Jones.

An exciting ride it was. In February 1947 Basie had a number one hit with the R&B novelty song "Open the Door, Richard." Recording with Basie, Gonsalves "made a nice

Jo Jones. ::: *Photo by New York photographer George A. Douglas. Milt Gabler Papers, Archives Center, National Museum of American History, Smithsonian Institution.*

impression," said Morgenstern. One is a 1948 live set, a transcription from New York's primo bop venue, the Royal Roost, then actively hosting radio broadcast recordings during the second American Federation of Musicians strike. Fifty-second Street pianist Sir Charles Thompson's graceful "Robbins' Nest" featured Gonsalves, who also did some background guitar work on the recordings.

In late 1949 financial pressures forced Basie to cut his numbers to a nonet. Gonsalves returned to play with Sabby Lewis for a brief spell before joining Dizzy Gillespie's band. Since 1946, Gillespie had managed to survive with a big band by incorporating bop and Afro-Cuban musicians into his lineups. Dizzy was still hot. His early 1948 European tour carried the controversial banner of bebop across the Atlantic. That summer, the band proselytized California with its fusion of bop and Afro-Cuban material, though Gillespie found that many fans still wanted to dance.

Dizzy opted to go with "bop with a beat." Returning to New York, he added new players, including future Ellingtonian Willie Cook as his lead trumpet. (When Gonsalves joined the band, he and Cook would be roommates on the road.) Later in the year, his band played a series of engagements at the Royal Roost. The venue promoted its bookings by pushing the bop scene, catering to listeners—not dancers—by allowing standing crowds to crush around the bandstand. With his goatee, horn-rimmed glasses, and beret, Dizzy came to epitomize jazz modernism. By the end of 1948, deejays voted Dizzy Gillespie's band the number-one big band in the country.

Hip as he was, Gillespie still struggled to maintain his audience and find the right combination of musicians to sell records and tickets. In the autumn of 1949 he added two bop modernists: a rising twenty-three-year-old John Coltrane and his colleague, Jimmy Heath. At the time, both were alto saxophonists who were migrating to tenor. With them came drummer Specs Wright.

Gonsalves arrived a little while later. Although he immediately recognized that he had joined a band with sizzle, he was perplexed by Gillespie's interest in him. He did not consider himself a bop modernist. Whatever Dizzy saw in him, Gonsalves eventually carried the reed section and got most of the sax solos. Along with Cook and Coltrane, he played on some Capitol releases in late 1949 and the first half of 1950. These were reissued together as *Strictly Bebop*. Gonsalves made an impression. He told Michael James that Trane made the final switch to alto only after learning from him the nuances of the tenor sax.

Gillespie's band certainly had attitude—the cool, exciting swagger of bop alienation. The down side was the drug and alcohol use that came with it, introduced in large measure by Coltrane and Heath. "Dope was a whole way of life," wrote counterculture chronicler Martin Torgoff of the bop brotherhood during America's first heroin epidemic, "like living inside a walled city with those of your own kind, where you could make up your own language and create your own set of rules." Sometime during this period, Gonsalves—who earlier in his career had avoided drugs and alcohol—entered into this brotherhood.

In June 1950, when the financial burden of carrying so many players grew too heavy, Dizzy let Gonsalves go. Through the summer of 1950, he was out of work. After four years of sustained, high-octane energy generated by Basie and Gillespie, the comedown must have been a challenge. However, Gonsalves managed his habits with some degree of control. He was living in Phil Edmund's two-bedroom apartment in Manhattan with his friend Joe Livramento and fellow Basie alto saxophonist Earl Warren. Joe had returned to New York after several years of fronting his own band in New Bedford. Livramento was clean and remained so all his life.

Their apartment building was at 50 West 106th Street, home to many members of the jazz fraternity. Many other famous or soon-to-be-famous musicians, singers, artists, and actors could be found on the surrounding blocks. It was an intimate life there with musicians migrating nonstop from apartment to apartment to trade and practice new ideas and to jam.

By September, Gonsalves had exhausted his savings and had moved from the Edmund flat to the Alvin Hotel on Fifty-second Street, just opposite Birdland. One night while he was at the renowned bop nightspot, he saw Duke Ellington at a nearby table surrounded by a crowd of people. In his 1961 account to Stanley Dance, he maintained that after "a few drinks" he approached Ellington as he was preparing to leave. Recognizing him, Maestro said, "Hey, sweetie, I've been looking for you. Why don't you come down to the office tomorrow?" Gonsalves joined the band the next day.

Leon "Chu" Berry (right) and Roy Eldridge in front of the Savoy Ballroom, 1935. This photo was taken by Danish baron Timme Rosenkrantz. John Hammond took Rosenkrantz to the Savoy; in the thirties Rosenkrantz wrote of Harlem, and in the forties he was the first to record Erroll Garner. ::: *Courtesy of the Institute of Jazz Studies, Rutgers University.*

"The first thing that turned Duke on was that Paul was a Ben Webster fan and knew all of Ben's solos," said Morgenstern, referring to the oft-cited musical thread that linked Gonsalves's ballad interpreting to the great tenor soloist of Ellington's early forties Blanton-Webster band. "But Duke quickly realized that there was more to this guy than that."

He must have seen that he was, to use Morgenstern's words, "one of the great underrated tenor players, one of the primary tenor saxophone stylists of his generation," who was "great on ballads and great on up tempo, great on the blues." In addition to Ben Webster, Morgenstern speculated that Duke heard other influences on Gonsalves's style—Lester Young and Hawk disciples Don Byas and Leon "Chu" Berry. A very fluid tenor player, Berry was also a great interpreter of the tenor ballad. "Gonsalves told me he loved Chu Berry for his sound projection," said Morgenstern, "and the way that he would breathe. He said Chu Berry took some of the longest breaths of any tenor player. He really filled up that horn."

Michael James spoke of Gonsalves's use of note ride. "He got it from Lester Young and the way he would swing on one note, like he did in places in the solo after the 'Diminuendo,'" said James. "But Paul had a phrasing of his own, and what separates him from the others were the advanced, inventive runs, the inversions that come from his being a guitar player with the tricky licks." "Paul was a marvelous guitar player," said Clark Terry, recalling how his Cape Verdean friends used to say he had "a good 'fing-fing.'"

Paul Gonsalves in the studio. ::: *Duke Ellington Collection, Archives Center, National Museum of American History, Smithsonian Institution.*

Gonsalves would stay with Duke almost continuously for the next twenty-four years. He had his first recording session with Ellington in November 1950 for Columbia. They recorded "Build That Railroad (Sing That Song)," "Love You Madly," and "Great Times." Occasional Ellingtonian Nelson Williams was in the trumpet section. Gonsalves was back in the studio in December with Williams when they recorded "The Tattooed Bride," "Mood Indigo," "Sophisticated Lady," and "Solitude."

The following April Gonsalves did a New York recording session for Mercer Records with the Coronets, made up of fellow Ellingtonians Cat Anderson, Juan Tizol, Willie Smith, Billy Strayhorn, Wendell Marshall, and Louis Bellson, among others. In that session the

Coronets recorded one of Gonsalves's own compositions: a bright jumping piece with a culturally prophetic title, "The Happening."

Ellington, between labels, was working hard to keep his band busy. Having left Columbia in late 1952, he would not record with Capitol until April 1953. So for three weeks in February 1953, Gonsalves went to play with trombonist Tommy Dorsey, who after some six years had reformed his band. In some respects he appreciated his three-week stint with the sentimental gentleman of swing. Sy Oliver, who had left Jimmie Lunceford in 1939 to do Dorsey's arrangements, gave the band pulse, and Dorsey liked to balance ballads and dance numbers—a disposition that fitted Gonsalves perfectly.

Michael James said, however, that he went with Dorsey because he offered him more money. He soon returned because "Duke's music was more interesting." " 'I'm with you,' he told Duke; 'just take care of my family.' "

He rejoined the Ellington band in time for its spring tour. While in Los Angeles, the band had its first Capitol recording session in April that included the hit single "Satin Doll." On the same date, he soloed on "Warm Valley." He was hot: in succeeding sessions that summer, Ellington featured him with solos on six tracks.

When the band was on the road in southeast New England, he would rendezvous now and then with Joe Livramento, who would make arrangements for him to play after-hour gigs with local Cape Verdeans in the region—in particular, saxophonist Jimmy Lomba and Frank and Peter Monteiro. He thus maintained close contact with his family, friends, and the Cape Verdean community. When in the area, he would gig at such venues as The Kettle in Acushnet, with its Sunday afternoon jam sessions, as well as New Bedford's Picadilly Lounge, the Cape Verdean Band Club, and Sharpshooter's Hall. John Monteiro especially remembered many such jams in venues in Lincoln Park and Acushnet Park.

Well into the fifties New Bedford remained a jazz hotbed. Gonsalves preferred playing the hometown New Bedford gigs to New York engagements, where audiences took the musicians for granted. Thrilled New Bedford fans were easily aroused and thus drew more from musicians, inspiring them to cut loose.

At Newport '56 Ellington appreciated that Paul Gonsalves was virtually on his hometown turf. He knew his history as a crowd pleaser, a soloist who was more than just an introspective balladeer. More specifically, he was well aware of what he could do to bridge the two sections of "Diminuendo and Crescendo in Blue."

The extended composition is based on blues chords, written in two parts with no improvisation. In its 1937 recorded form, preferred by purists, it had no interval. The "Diminuendo" was on side 1 of the original 78, the "Crescendo" on side 2. While critics in the thirties were "puzzled by it," in the words of the early Ellington biographer Barry Ulanov, others, like classical composer Aaron Copland, praised the work.

Later, by including an improvised interval, Ellington made it a bluesy or swinging piece that enabled him to cater to every taste. In the recorded broadcasts of the forties it had swing. Writing in 1946, in the middle of the bop era, Ulanov observed that "the basic lines of the 'Diminuendo and Crescendo' are if anything more effective, our ears having become accustomed to more vigorous experimentation on the part of jazz bands."

Ellington would introduce the "Diminuendo" on his piano with wrinkles of agitated dissonance that jumped. Another Ellington biographer, A. H. Lawrence, speculated whether he wrote the composition in anticipation of his father's death in late 1937. Somewhat heavy-handedly, swing musicologist Gunther Schuller wrote of "the struggle, the torment, and the anguish" in the piece. Whatever the mood through the piece, the "Crescendo" climaxes in an orgy of positive glory.

Ellington had aptly demonstrated the power of the piece as a showstopper at the 1938 Randall's Island concert, where he played an interlude on piano. The first recorded instance on which Gonsalves played the interval was during the last night of his second 1951 Birdland gig, June 30. The performance was recorded by Jazz Anthology and Stardust. Having just come from the bop-infused Gillespie big band, he appreciated the value of his bop associations when playing a bop venue. He asked Duke for permission to do the break in place of the piano interval. Ellington agreed.

That night he played twenty-six choruses, rocking both the band and what audience happened to be there. "On many occasions," Clark Terry recalled, "Paul Gonsalves played more than twenty-six choruses, when Duke would just inspire the band with his growls, vibrating, and carrying on. The band would respond, and the tune would go on and on." After Birdland he may have performed the interval some fifteen times prior to Newport '56. One such occasion was at a concert at the Pasadena Civic Auditorium in March 1953, one of the Just Jazz series recorded by the GNP (Gene Norman Presents) label.

Three years later, in April 1956, the band performed the number again at an African American engagement in Durham, North Carolina. "Some promoter had booked a one-nighter at a dance hall," trombonist John Sanders recalled. "It wasn't big, wasn't anything fancy. It was a hot night, and it was crowded. A steaming hall, and I remember we took off our jackets. When we played 'Diminuendo,' it just took off. The guys were relaxed. The band was cooking. It was a dance hall beat that really caught on with the dancers."

Of that Durham night, the band's road manager Bobby Boyd recalled that Ellington played several choruses before the band got into a groove. When it came to the interval, Gonsalves stepped forward, played a staggering thirty-six choruses, and "the crowd went wild."

By 1956 African American audiences had been dancing to rhythm and blues for almost a decade. White Americans were two years into its derivative, rock and roll. Some would argue that the saxophone, most often the lead solo instrument in a rhythm and blues lineup, was the original rock and roll instrument, as opposed to the guitar. In the fifties many R&B and early rock and roll singles were sax-driven. In 1951 Red Prysock's tenor drove Tiny Bradshaw's "The Train Kept a-Rollin'," and tenor sax man Raymond Hill energized Jackie Brenston's "Rocket 88," a paean to the Oldsmobile model that at the time was supposedly the fastest car on the road. "Rocket 88" was an R&B classic for Ike Turner that some regard as the first rock and roll recording. Three years later, blues shouter Joe Turner featured another honking sax solo in his "Shake, Rattle, and Roll," also covered by Bill Haley and His Comets, who introduced the wild sound to white teenage audiences. R&B sax men were as often as not crowd-pleasing entertainers who would titillate their audiences by such displays as playing on their backs.

"During the rock and roll period, there were times when tenor saxophonists could get a group going with their physical exhibitionism," John Sanders observed. "But Paul was all musical. He wasn't out to exhibit any tricks, or say, 'Look what I'm doing' to get them excited. He was pure music."

On the back of the '56 LP, George Avakian would tag Gonsalves's sax solo during the interval at Newport "a leading voice supported by many parts." Far from Webster-inspired ballads, his choruses to "Diminuendo and Crescendo in Blue" had become solid, rocking R&B. At Newport this Cape Verdean American was about to step forth to take a ride on a monster groove and rock his loyal hometown fans and whoever else happened to remain. In so doing, he would fulfill for Ellington his 1955 prophecy that he had been "saving" his "rock and roll things . . . for possible use in a show."

12

The Rhythmic Groove of the Century

The Gonsalves Solo

"I was feeling concern," said trombonist John Sanders recalling the Ellington band's second set at Newport '56. "We got started late. We got off to a rough start. We were putting things together as we went on. We were just trying to get through it. The audience applauded, but it was just applause."

Ellington well knew the meaning of lukewarm applause. "If a guy plays something and nobody digs it, then he hasn't communicated with his audience," he once said. "And either he goes somewhere to an audience that does dig him, or else he adjusts what he's doing to the audience he has." With the "Newport Jazz Festival Suite," he had tried to communicate to the crowd as composer. To save the evening, he had to communicate as entertainer with "Diminuendo and Crescendo in Blue."

Ellington "had the knack of handling a disaster without blowing up," Sanders said. "We always brought all our music with us—the whole book, two parts that filled the music stand. So, intermission time, Duke said, 'We're going to do "Diminuendo." It's in the book, 107, 108. We're going to play something that I think the people would like to hear.' Duke was going to play a piano interval, to set the pace between diminuendo and crescendo, then he would call Paul."

By going with an interval by Paul Gonsalves, Ellington could build an audience around fans like John Monteiro. Earlier that evening, the New Bedford native had packed his car with cousins and friends. When they arrived at the concert venue, they "ran into a lot of other New Bedford people." Monteiro's carload had paid top dollar that night and somehow managed to get a fourth-row box just to the right of center, between Ellington and the solo mike. They came for one reason and one reason only: to hear their hometown star.

In a box on the right side was New Bedford theater manager Bob Zeitz, his sister Elaine Anderson, and her Fall River husband's business associates and their wives, all of whom had been box-seat holders since the first festival. Fresh from a cocktail party, the Anderson contingent was in high spirits. Just behind their box sat dozens of fans from New Bedford's Cape Verdean American community, among them musicians, friends of Gonsalves, whom Zeitz had booked from time to time: Jimmy Lomba, Eddie Stack, and Frankie Monteiro, all within shouting distance of the stage.

Farther afield, between rows of seats and the grandstand, was another local crowd, of younger people, many holding paper cups with beer sloshing through their fingers, who seemed more absorbed by the opposite sex than the music. On previous evenings this same mob had raised the ire of jazz critics.

In that crowd—but not of it—was the athletic and engaging Bill Farmen, a rising high school senior from Rochester, New York. Making $36 a week as a Falmouth, Massachusetts, lifeguard, Farmen was saving for college. In 1957 he would go to the University of Connecticut, attend ROTC, and eventually make a career in the U.S. Army, capping a distinguished career as the two-star NATO logistics commander during the Bosnian Joint Endeavor operation in 1996.

Earlier that evening Farmen and three of his lifeguard buddies, Falmouth locals, had piled into a 1952 Buick Dynaflow convertible and headed to Newport in search of girls and music. A hot-rodder and an unabashed fan of rock and roll who owned all of the Bill Haley records and loved Chuck Berry, Farmen was also genuinely into jazz. After parking and finding a bite to eat, the foursome bought a six-pack of 'Gansetts under the counter and made their way to the park.

All around, families and young folks who chose not to pay the entrance fees were sitting on porches or camped on folding chairs on sidewalks, listening to the music. Some one thousand fans had crowded the streets around Freebody Park that night. To catch a glimpse of the onstage action, many had climbed trees, while others had paid $2.50 a head to rent second-floor window spaces in the houses of various locals. Sometime early in the first set, Farmen and his friends, themselves unwilling to deplete their pocket money on tickets, jumped the wall. Late into the second set and Chico Hamilton's performance, the boys figured it was time to hit the road. Hamilton's mesmerizing "Blue Sands" appeared to be the appropriate climax to a good evening. Sunday would come early on their Falmouth beach, and in the spirit of adventure, the boys decided to exit over the wall instead of going through the turnstiles.

Farmen recalled scaling the stones at the very moment the first recognizable bars of Duke's intro to "Take the A Train" floated through the air. "It was a favorite of my mother's," he said, "and it drew me back." His buddies were not so taken. But once the full orchestra attacked and the wave of sound hit the wall with force, their tune changed, and they drifted back to the field. For Farmen, Duke had connected early, and his set built from there.

Ellington revived. Newport. July 7. 1956. ::: *Photo courtesy of Bob Parent.*

The audience that night was varied. As John Sanders observed, "There was the older group, and there was the younger. Rock and roll had taken over. The jazz rhythm had taken the backseat. The bebop rhythm was not the same as before, where you just wanted to tap your foot, let your body sway with the rhythm, feel a joy, and say, 'It's wonderful.' I think that was lost. At Newport, maybe Duke reached back and put back what was missing. Possibly the older audience came to hear a big band, a jazz performance, and others experienced something they had never heard before."

There comes a time in exceptional musical performances when one inexplicably feels the beat without hearing a thing—as if it were there before a single note was played. And so it was with "Diminuendo and Crescendo in Blue" at Newport '56. Duke Ellington's piano playing was always the "rhythmic energizer" for his musicians, said Gunther Schuller. "His tone and projection were such that with one chord or a few fill-in notes he could energize the entire orchestra."

Upon announcing the number, Duke crossed the stage to his chair and kick-started the "Diminuendo" with some vamps, setting a Basie-like tempo with his jumping discords and growls. Sam Woodyard entered with his sticks, crisply high-hatting on his cymbals. From his first stroke, he was locked into the drive.

Then came Jimmy Woode, his fingers working nimbly on his bass, and a musical conversation began. Shifting focus from his stick work on the cymbals, Woodyard began to click a stick rhythmically against the rim of his snare. Woode started his walking bass. "Cut! Cut! Hold it!" Ellington shouted to Woode, and the bassist extended his cut, further stretching tension. Still using his keyboard only for fills, Duke conversed by ejecting notes in his satisfied growls, expressed again and again. After four choruses, it was a cue to the rest of the band: "We're locked, baby, get ready to hit."

From his post at the top of the steps offstage left, Columbia producer George Avakian immediately sensed the energy. "Before they got started and cooking," he recalled, "I thought to myself, man, there is a beat going on here. I hope the guys [his recording engineers in the backstage tent] are catching it."

Ellington called his band. "Om pa!" The five trumpets—Cat Anderson, Ray Nance, Clark Terry, Willie Cook, and Herbie Jones—jumped into the drive, followed by the reeds, Gonsalves, Johnny Hodges, Jimmy Hamilton, Russell Procope, and Harry Carney on the end stage left, and the trombones, Britt Woodman, Sanders, and Butter Jackson. It was up, light, tight. The Lucky Millinder vets—Hamilton, Anderson, and Jones—well tutored in his brand of incipient R&B, were in their element.

"The rhythm ignited the band, all of us," said Sanders. "We were with it, because we were listening to this wonderful buildup."

Sitting at the edge of the stage on the step below Avakian was former Basie drummer Jo Jones, who had played earlier that night with Teddy Wilson. Once the full band had joined the conversation, Jones jumped to his feet and started thumping a rolled newspaper, reputedly a *Christian Science Monitor,* in the palm of his hands.

"I was aware of Jo because he was next to me," said Avakian. "He was there for the entire performance of Ellington, and I don't remember when he arrived. He must have been backstage. It was pretty loose. Musicians were allowed to wander in, but he was there for the whole thing."

Since leaving Basie, the forty-four-year-old Jones had became a regular with Granz's early Jazz at the Philharmonic tours and then recorded with Wilson and other swing artists like Billie Holiday, Buck Clayton, and Lester Young. In *Music Is My Mistress,* Ellington devoted a half-page section to his role that night. "Jo Jones was the driving force behind our big success at Newport in 1956 . . . slapping a back beat with a newspaper, talking to us, he prodded us into a 'Go, Baby!' drive that developed into the rhythmic groove of the century, with Paul Gonsalves down front at the microphone."

Johnny Hodges sharing the joy with fellow reedman Russell Procope. Just behind, trombonist Britt Woodman. ::: *Photo courtesy of Paul "Buck" Hoeffler.*

"Jo Jones was just elated with what he was hearing," recalled Sanders. "He was cheering the band on. Musicians respond to that. They respond to another musician listening to them and saying, 'Yeah, go on. Let me hear more.'"

By all accounts Woodyard was oblivious to Jones's shouts and the backbeat he was laying down on his palm and railing. However, Woode said he was able to respond from his perch. Clark Terry, who was just to the bassist's left in the first trumpet chair, also remembered glimpsing Jones's enthusiastic poundings.

Avakian had no doubt that an exceptional performance was unfolding onstage. "I would say that I became really aware of it when the ensemble was going full blast. Maybe two choruses before Ellington played his first interlude, I began to feel, hey, this is really something." Suddenly he bolted from the stage, heading backstage to make sure his engineers were capturing the moment. Brushing past Jones, he ran down the steps and burst into the tent. Ad Theroux handed him the earphones. By this time the trumpets were trading with the reeds. "Ear to ear, joy and happiness," Avakian recalled of the sensation, hearing the Ellington orchestra coming through the cans. "It was just so beautiful."

"Hey, this is great!" he shouted to his engineers, hands still pressed to the earphones.

The orchestra was still in full with Woode and Woodyard driving the beat. "Sam Woodyard," recalled trumpeter Willie Cook in his interview with Phil Schaap, "was just driving away that night." Ellington's chording remained well under the force of the band. Then the trombones entered, followed by the reeds, trading with Nance's growl trumpet. Ellington continued to rely on spare punctuation to energize the drive.

More relaxed now, Avakian made his way past Jones back to his perch at the top of the steps.

Three minutes into the performance, Duke rejoined the conversation, entering with his two-chorus piano interlude and concluding the "Diminuendo" with gradually diminishing ripples of notes, which grew softer and softer, preparing the way for Gonsalves. Someone's clap resonated in a microphone.

The musicians rested their instruments on their knees, some calling out to Jones. Most of the yelling in the recording, Avakian recalled, "is the sax section yelling at Jo and laughing, because they were digging Duke and Jo. He wasn't showboating, but he was very much there."

Ellington growled, his cue for Gonsalves to come downstage to the solo mikes. On the first line of perches, just next to the maestro's piano, it was a straight shot, only a few steps to the limelight.

"We didn't know Paul was going to go out and play a tenor solo of unlimited proportions," observed Sanders. "Maybe Duke told Paul. We didn't hear it. He went to the microphone. And Jo Jones, he was just elated with what he was hearing, still cheering the band on."

Some four minutes into the piece, Gonsalves arrived at the solo-mike stand. In his hands was the jazzman's quintessential solo instrument, his horn, his ax, a symbol of independence. For Gonsalves in 1956 it was his Selmer MK with its Otto Link metal mouthpiece that enabled him to make a living by producing a sound that so expressed his identity and gave him his own voice. In the audience Gonsalves's breathless Cape Verdean fans from New Bedford nudged each other. Those standing in the side aisles crowded forward, eagerly awaiting his familiar, sonorous sound. Woodyard and Woode were carrying the pulse behind him, while Ellington chorded underneath.

Gonsalves closed his eyes and began to blow, bouncing along with his trademark licks. Wincing, Avakian watched him angle the horn of his instrument toward the wrong mike. He had completely forgotten the instructions Avakian and Cal Lampley had conveyed to every band member as they ascended to the stage. Eyes screwed tight, Gonsalves was blowing into the Voice of America microphone. No amount of gesticulating would have effect. Oblivious to all but the beat, the saxophonist plowed ahead, eyes shut, digging into his solo with every sinew of his body.

Avakian was now frantic about the taping. Pushing past Jones a second time, he flew down the steps and collided with Lampley, who was racing toward him. "What's going on?" Lampley screamed to his boss. "We're not getting enough of Paul!" Not answering,

Paul Gonsalves from stage right. Note the apparent distance from the mike stands. ::: ***Photo courtesy of Paul "Buck" Hoeffler.***

Paul Gonsalves wails during his solo. ::: *Photo courtesy of Paul "Buck" Hoeffler.*

Avakian grabbed him, and together they ran to the tent and burst through the flap. Ad Theroux and Buddy Graham were on their feet, totally absorbed with their machines, checking the equipment and running through various attempts to fix the problem. "Can we save it with equalization?" Avakian pressed them. "Who knows?" came the reply.

Theroux made some adjustments, which Avakian said could be heard on the raw tape. "Ad pulled up the front mike as much as possible," he recalled, "and put the rest of the band in the subsidiary role. There was nothing much he could do, because there was an awful lot of sound going on, but he did manage to preserve some of the balance by reducing the recording level of the microphones that were feeding the band and now the saxophone. That was apparent by about the third chorus."

Onstage, Gonsalves was flying, Ellington was growling ecstatically, and Woodyard started to swing. Whenever Paul started to wail, Woodyard could sustain a drive behind him for as long as the sax man might blow. And Gonsalves could blow forever. This night was no different. A rhythm section stalwart on guitar, he was a master who had ridden the beat of the percussion greats—Jo Jones, J. C. Heard, Louis Bellson. Now perhaps he was sensing Jones offstage to his immediate left, urging him forward to dance on that improvisatory precipice and attain for himself a defining moment for all time. "Yeah!" he may have felt Duke shouting from his right. "Work on it! Work on it! Oh, yeah! Work on it!"

Six minutes into the performance, the audience caught fire. Someone was clapping double time. Shouts connected with the microphones. The performance broke wide open. Gonsalves began to rip into some R&B riffing. "Oh, yeah!" Ellington shouted as he chorded underneath, at times hitting the low register. More shouts from the band. "Go!"

"Usually when a solo ended, the soloist would glance at Duke to see whether he should sit down or continue. But that night Duke didn't cut him off," said Sanders, "and I think Paul just decided he'd play until he felt that was enough, then he'd leave. It was all spontaneous. It just happened."

The photographers were crowding around the stage. Columbia's Don Hunstein was snapping one shot after another of Gonsalves at the mike, eyes shut, brow furrowed. Among the countless others were freelancer Bob Parent, shooting for *Time,* the *Saturday Review,* and *Metronome,* and Buck Hoeffler for the *Providence Journal.*

The audience had quickened, and many were rising to their feet. Younger members who had been standing in the aisles to the right and left of the stage began to fill voids, crowding into vacated boxes whose ticket holders had left earlier. Others boldly advanced to the pit with the photographers. Some of the remaining VIPs in box seats stood up, craning their necks to see over the gathering throng.

Just behind the boxes in the middle of the crowd, one New York couple, Jack Heaney and his date, Eileen Farrell, saw the happening begin. Heaney, a former UPI man from Oklahoma City and then writer for Shell Oil's corporate magazine, was an Ellington, Basie, and Goodman fan who came to jazz as a teen via Bobby Hackett's solo in "String of Pearls." "As the mood swelled like a wave, sweeping up from the stage," he vividly recalled, "the crowd began to stand. Everyone began rising from their seats at about the same time."

"Oh, did we stand up! It was a roar!" said John Monteiro, who was with his New Bedford friends in the boxes just in front of Ellington. "I mean, Sam Woodyard was just drumming like crazy, man. It was dynamite." Mesmerized, Monteiro could see Duke

George Avakian savoring the moment from his offstage-left position. ::: *Photo by Don Hunstein. Courtesy of Sony BMG Music Entertainment.*

watching the crowd intently, as though he were beckoning any and all to approach.

Farther back, toward the rear of the main seating sections, Jonathan Yardley and his Groton contingent were also pressing forward. Well to the rear, where Bill Farmen and his fellow lifeguards were standing along with the drinkers and talkers around the 'Gansett barrows, people with dates began dancing. Without partners of their own, Farmen and his crew quickly made their way down the stage-right aisle to get as close to the music as possible.

Back at his post onstage, oblivious to the audience frenzy, Avakian was still focused on the performance, worrying whether Theroux and the Columbia team were going to capture what was turning out to be Gonsalves's thoroughly remarkable tour de force. "All through the solo," Avakian recalled, "Duke was trying to get Paul's attention about the mike, and all through the solo, Paul simply kept blowing away, either his eyes closed or staring straight ahead. He never turned his head toward Duke or anything. He couldn't hear Duke, and of course there was nothing I could do."

At this point, it was still just Gonsalves with the rhythm section behind him. Paul was wailing. Avakian had to accept that the success or failure of the recording was in the lap of the gods. Finally he let go and got drawn into the moment. "It was fantastic," he said. The night was on fire.

Sitting in her box in front of Avakian and Jones, Elaine Anderson recalled the moment. "Let's get this thing going," she remembered hearing someone say. Teddy LeSavoy, one of her husband's business associates and a family friend familiar with her cocktail-induced propensity to dance, then rose from his seat, pulled her from hers, and pushed her into the aisle. "Go Elaine!"

It would be her defining moment.

13

Elaine Anderson

"The Gal Who Launched 7,000 Cheers"

Only a very few in jazz circles ever discovered her name. For half a century she has simply been known as the platinum blonde in the black cocktail dress whose dance that night both expressed and inspired the Gonsalves solo.

Her maiden name was Elaine Zeitz. Her passage to that box seat amid Newport's upper crust that July 7 night may be said to have begun five years before she was born, when a certain British freighter rounded Cape Cod in the waning days of the Great War.

On November 1, 1918, the *Port Hunter* left Boston for New York to join a convoy bound for Europe, carrying materiel for the American doughboys serving on the Western Front. The *Port Hunter* never made it. The following morning, in the darkness off East Chop, Martha's Vineyard, she was rammed by a tug. Her captain managed to maneuver his fifty-five-hundred-ton ship to Hedge Fence Shoal, three miles off Vineyard Haven, before she wrecked, her superstructure just above water.

A hatch cover came loose and cargo began floating away. With boxes washing onto the north shore of the island, word spread quickly. After retrieving everything from lined leather jerkins and vests to soap and trench candles, fishermen entered Vineyard Haven and began conducting wharfside sales from their boats.

Attracted by the commercial potential, New Bedford merchants arrived by boat, eager to make deals with the locals. Eventually the Coast Guard intervened and took charge. In February the federal government awarded salvage rights to one of these merchants, Barney Zeitz.

Barney Zeitz was the eldest of eight brothers and two sisters, second-generation immigrants from Prussia. The family home was in New Bedford's South End, adjacent to

Elaine Anderson at Newport '58. This photo, placed below a close-up of Duke Ellington performing at the piano onstage, ran with a story on the festival in the July 5, 1958, issue of the *Newport Daily News*. The caption read, " 'I ADMIRE HIM. I NEED HIM'—That's the evident reaction of the lady patron in a front-row box at the Newport Jazz Festival, as she casts restraint to the winds and applauds merrily, to the sympathetic accord of the men on either side." ::: *Photo by Ron LaChance. Fred Anderson Collection.*

the Cape Verdean neighborhood where Paul Gonsalves would live in the thirties. In 1905, a year after their father died, Barney and his brothers started a small demolition company and soon diversified into loans, jewelry, and hardware. Although they were prosperous, it wasn't until the *Port Hunter* salvage that they became rich.

All the brothers remained bachelors except one, Harry, who increased his wealth by marrying well. Harry's bride, Cecile, was the daughter of Prussian Jewish immigrants from the Roxbury section of Boston who had made money in the family business, the Bornstein Shoe Company. A talented young artist, Cecile Bornstein had studied at Boston's School of the Museum of Fine Arts and was teaching art at a Boston high school when her family arranged her marriage to Harry Zeitz. They would have three children, the first of whom, Carl, was born in 1919 during the salvage operation.

The proceeds from the *Port Hunter* enabled Harry to construct a seventeen-hundred-seat vaudeville theater at 684 Purchase Street. He built it for Cecile and called it the Zeiterion.

At the time vaudeville houses were lavishly decorated. Not to be outdone by others, Zeitz had a massive crystal chandelier made in Czechoslovakia by Harry Winston and installed it in the central dome. In April 1923 his theater opened with the great vaudeville star George Jessel headlining. A month later, silent film heartthrob Rudolf Valentino came to town with his wife, Natascha Rambova, and tangoed at the Zeiterion.

In the midst of this whirlwind year for the Zeitzes, Harry and Cecile had their second child, Elaine Ruth. Thirty-three years later, Columbia record producer George Avakian would attach this caption to her photo on the *Ellington at Newport* LP: "The gal who launched 7,000 cheers."

All through the twenties, her father's kingdom expanded, fueled by lucrative real estate deals. Harry had moved Cecile and the family to Fairhaven, just across the Acushnet River bridge to the east of New Bedford. Later in the decade they moved to a palatial home opposite St. Luke's Hospital in the posh part of New Bedford. Virtually every night Harry's bachelor brothers dined with Harry and Cecile, and they positively doted on Elaine and her two siblings.

Five months after its vaudeville opening, Harry Zeitz closed the Zeiterion and reopened it as a silent-movie house with a new name, the State. It was a time when Massachusetts was a key player in the film business, both in finance and distribution. By the end of the twenties, Elaine's father had become one of the region's distribution pioneers. Eventually the Zeitzes would own a small chain of eight independent theaters. In addition to the Zeiterion/State, they acquired the New Bedford Theater, an old opera house, the Empire, and Paramount's Olympia and Capitol. Farther afield they added three others: the Academy in nearby Fall River, Newport's Paramount, and the Civic in Portland, Maine.

In 1927 when Warner Bros. released the first talkie, *The Jazz Singer,* Harry Zeitz was ready. He equipped the State for sound to run the Al Jolson classic. Sound conversion was an expensive proposition for theater owners. Studios saw the introduction of sound as a means to control distribution and thus wrest power from regional owners like Zeitz. At the outset many studios adopted a Western Electric sound-on-disc format for film sound, but the enterprising David Sarnoff wanted his RCA to get a piece of the action. RCA quickly developed optical sound-on-film technology. In 1929 Sarnoff allied with Joseph P. Kennedy to form his own studio, which became RKO Pictures. Zeitz remained a regional force by allying himself with Kennedy and RKO.

Harry and his cosmopolitan wife moved into the center of the regional entertainment world, hosting film stars, producers, and studio executives in their mansion. They were also a presence in New Bedford's Jewish community. Although Harry attended synagogue only on high holidays, Cecile was president of the Hadassah, the women's Zionist service and educational organization. In that role she was wont to feature her daughter and her talent that emerged in earliest childhood.

"My mother wanted to make a great dancer out of me," Elaine recalled. "From the time I was three years old, I took lessons." Among her first performances were dance recitals for Cecile's Hadassah teas and lunches.

Elaine Ruth Zeitz (Anderson). A portrait of the dancer as a child, c. 1930. ::: *Fred Anderson Collection.*

By her mid-teens Elaine was accomplished in ballet, tap, and toe. Once in high school, her taste in dancing expanded to embrace modern trends, and she befriended another keen dancer who was a year behind her: Carol Haney.

The pair would become lifelong friends. Haney wanted a professional dance career and would later become a talented actress, dancer, singer, and choreographer working in the golden years of Hollywood musicals in the late forties and early fifties.

Haney's approach to dance fully embraced swing. Sarah Woodcock, Haney's niece who is currently writing a biography of the dancer, said that just after high school Haney once went to see Count Basie play for a mainly African American audience at the Taunton Roseland. Midway through the evening, Haney connected with a tall, slim African American zoot-suiter and hit the dance floor. When the black and white couple kicked into high gear, the sea of jitterbugging dancers parted, and Haney and her partner put on a floor show. The spontaneous display was so compelling that Basie extended the solos. Their performance ended with rapturous applause and appreciative hoots, which brought the house down and stopped the show.

Buoyed by her friendship with this kindred dancing spirit, Elaine began thinking of a career in dance. As she matured, she began exploring interpretative dance and claimed as her main influence the work of Isadora Duncan, for some the mother of modern dance.

An alchemical solo dancer who viewed her art as sacred, Duncan choreographed ballets that interpreted inspirational works such as Beethoven's Ninth Symphony. At a time when British playwright Oscar Wilde, German composer Richard Strauss, and American vaudeville had been popularizing Salome and her mythical dance of the seven veils, Duncan drew on a number of traditions from skirt dancing—where the dancer manipulated fabric—to vaudeville and burlesque. Duncan saw dance as movement to free the soul.

Isadora Duncan impressed this precocious daughter of a New Bedford theater-chain owner, not just with her dancing but with her intellect and rebel stance. Like Duncan,

Elaine was at heart antiestablishment. For her, as for Duncan, dance was art, a means of expressing herself and her emotions. Having little interest in marriage, Elaine continued to harbor her desire to go professional. The idea appealed to her expressive and exhibitionist nature, perhaps inadvertently groomed by her mother.

Although she had encouraged Elaine to dance as a child and showcased her before her friends, Cecile now yanked the reins. "When I had the chance to go professional, my mother cut my throat," said Elaine. Cecile, whose own artistic aspirations had been cut short by an arranged marriage, faced a college-age Elaine—beautiful, smart, and accomplished—the spoiled darling of her doting bachelor uncles. The two were locked in an archetypal competition.

Cecile somehow sabotaged Elaine's application to Wellesley College. Harry tried to wield his influence to get Elaine into a fallback school, Simmons, but she balked and at sixteen went instead to Mount Ida, a junior college outside of Boston. After two years at a very progressive Mount Ida, she returned home with a sharpened intellect, only to continue butting heads with Cecile. As much out of a desire to escape the matriarchal grip as for love, Elaine married at eighteen. For once, a decision of hers met the unqualified approval of her mother, who turned her hand to gather the bridal trousseau. The groom was Lawrence Anderson, son of the leading textiles manufacturer in Fall River, northwest of New Bedford.

Larry Anderson's father was Jewish Ukrainian. Family lore has it that he was standing behind a bunch of Swedes at Ellis Island and couldn't speak English. When they asked him what his name was, he just pointed to the guy in front of him, and they told him he was Anderson.

Larry was born in 1917 and went to the University of Pennsylvania. Before graduating he returned to help run the family business that had expanded from raincoats to men's suits as Anderson-Little. The Little was the Italian Bostonian Al Little, brother of famed Columbia football coach Lou Little. In 1942 Larry and Elaine had a wartime marriage, and in early 1943 they had the first of three sons, Frederick. That summer Larry entered the Army Air Corps and left for air cadet training in Buffalo, New York. In the autumn he got orders to Southern California and the Santa Ana Army Air Field, the aviation cadet classification center for the West Coast. Santa Ana was the only base to give pilot, navigator, and bombardier preflight training; Larry was training to be a bombardier.

With little Frederick and a nanny in tow, Elaine followed her husband out west. Conveniently, she managed to land in Hollywood. More supportive than Cecile of his daughter's abiding aspiration to dance, Harry Zeitz had given her introductions to a number of his Hollywood contacts. One was Charles Koerner, RKO's head of production.

When Elaine got in touch with Koerner, he invited her to his studios. "What are you doing out here?" he asked her over lunch.

"Well, I came out here to be with my husband, but I found out when I got here that I can only see him from Saturday at twelve noon to Sunday at twelve noon."

"So what are you going to do?"

A Radio Pictures "candid" of Elaine Anderson, c. 1943, posed as if a Hollywood hopeful waiting to be discovered at Sunset Boulevard's Schwab's drugstore. ::: *Fred Anderson Collection.*

"I don't know. I have a baby, and Larry wants me to stay."

It wasn't hard for Koerner to recognize the screen potential in his business associate's daughter sitting across the table before him. Elaine was a petite five feet three inches, on the short side for a dancer. Yet she was a very physical, lissome beauty whose features were clearly photogenic. "Let's do a screen test," Koerner finally said.

Elaine's head shot, titled "Starlet," c. 1944. ::: *Fred Anderson Collection.*

Elaine tested, and Charlie Koerner gave her a seven-year contract for $150 dollars a week.

"I made three terrible movies," said Elaine. Shooting on her first film began in January 1944. The film was *Step Lively,* a musical with Frank Sinatra. "It was one of his very, very bad movies," she said. The second was *A Night of Adventure,* an undistinguished courtroom drama starring Tom Conway, whose renown came from a four-year run as the Falcon in the RKO film series of the same name. The last was *Seven Days Ashore,* a wartime musical about a sailor with three girlfriends, starring, among others, Virginia Mayo and pianist Dooley Wilson of *Casablanca* fame.

Sometime in 1944, Elaine's childhood chum Carol Haney joined her in Hollywood. Elaine, now pregnant with her second child, sought to help her friend, whose star was not yet rising, by providing introductions at RKO and taking her to the studios. Her own moment in the Hollywood limelight, however, was coming to an end. "My second child, Richard, ended my career," she said.

On completion of his bombardier training, Larry Anderson was assigned to the new B-29 bombers and ordered to the Pacific to ready for missions over Japan. After her brush with Hollywood glamour, Elaine spent the rest of the war with her parents in comparatively dreary New Bedford. At war's end Larry and Elaine returned to his hometown, Fall River. A third son, Bruce, was born in 1948.

Larry's textile company exploded during demobilization as GIs returned home looking to exchange their uniforms for suits. Seizing the opportunity, Anderson-Little put together a sales office near the loading dock. Lines began to form, and they grew longer by the week. In time, the sign on the door read "Anderson-Little Factory Direct to You," and a whole factory floor was devoted to selling suits. It was one of the first integrated manufacturing operations to retail directly to the customer. Anderson-Little eventually expanded into the largest clothing store chain in the New England region, with more than three hundred stores.

In the late forties and early fifties, the New Bedford Zeitzes and the Fall River Andersons were two of the wealthiest families in the region. Larry and Elaine lived in a comfortable manse at the top of the hill in the Highlands, the nicest area in Fall River, otherwise a predominantly industrial landscape. They were the stars of the local social scene—he the handsome retail tycoon, she the beautiful, vivacious wife with an unlimited expense account who could play golf with a ten handicap. Their friends included Teddy LeSavoy of Fall River and Eddie Capuano from Providence. LeSavoy and Capuano were partners in the Newport Finishing Company, which shrank and dyed the material Larry used to make his suits.

The Capuanos and the LeSavoys both had houses in Newport, Capuano being a neighbor of the Lorillards. Whenever possible, Elaine and Larry would travel, often with the LeSavoys. Among their more exotic ports of call were two cities renowned for dance, music, and nightlife: Havana and Rio. Their particular favorite was Havana's Tropicana, then reputedly the largest nightclub in the world. Located on a large estate, the Tropicana

Elaine (front, center) and her family in the early fifties. On Elaine's left is her mother, Cecile. In the white dinner jacket just behind is her father, Harry. Over Elaine's right shoulder is her husband, Larry. Over her left is her sister-in-law, Betty, and Elaine's brother, Bob Zeitz. ::: *Photo by Arlan's Studio. Fred Anderson Collection.*

boasted two stages with catwalks extending among the trees on the grounds along which a chorus line of fifty dancers enticingly performed to rhythmic voodoo themes. During the 1954–55 mambo craze, Elaine was inspired to master that demanding and athletic dance.

"I was a showoff," Elaine said. "Whenever we had parties and it got toward the end of the evening, I danced. Everybody looked forward to Elaine having too much to drink, and suddenly the Hollywood came out in me."

"Elaine would dance at the drop of a hat," said her brother Bob. "No man in her group had the talent to dance with her. She would be out there dancing by herself. She would dance the mambo. She would dance Broadway musical comedy, like Ann Miller or Cyd Charisse. She was a beautiful young lady. A lot of people would say she looked like Ginger Rogers."

Larry's party trick was the saxophone, although he was far from accomplished. His musical tastes were exclusively jazz. "I was into jazz as well as classical," said Elaine, "but I couldn't force that on him. On Sundays when we sat around the fireplace, and it was

Elaine, probably in 1952, dancing at a cocktail reception for the New Bedford premiere of *What Price Glory*. ::: *Fred Anderson Collection.*

snowing, I would play some jazz, and I would throw in a few Beethovens."

The drumbeat of jazz initially came into Elaine's life during wartime after she returned home from Hollywood, courtesy of her then fifteen-year-old brother. "I was a jazz nut all my life," said Bob Zeitz, "way more so than Elaine. Right next to the Zeiterion was a twin ballroom, a dance hall. I used to hang out there. I saw Stan Getz when he was playing in Stan Kenton's big band, and Woody Herman, Artie Shaw, Charlie Barnet, Count Basie."

Zeitz was being groomed to succeed his father in the theater-management business. As he got older, he started frequenting Cape Verdean venues like the Monte Pio and the halls along Acushnet Avenue. Soon he was booking local bands for dance parties, high school hops, bar mitzvahs, and finally into his father's theaters, particularly the Olympia. Zeitz got to know personally many band members who were friends of Paul Gonsalves: Jimmy Lomba, the Monteiro brothers, Joe Livramento, Duke Oliver, and Jedge Marita Senna. Zeitz's closest friend in the Cape Verdean music scene was tenor sax man Eddie "Stack" Ames, whose group played gigs all around New Bedford and as far away as Newport. Zeitz booked Stack for many of his own family functions.

By the early fifties Elaine and Larry had become avid jazz aficionados, hitting clubs as far afield as Storyville and the High Hat in Boston. In 1952 Dave Brubeck played at Storyville. For the Andersons' social set it was a milestone. "I brought [our] whole crowd up to Boston," Elaine recalled. "They had never heard that kind of music in their lives."

Elaine, Larry, and their friends also frequented nearby jazz venues. "When the jazz groups came to Boston, they always had gigs in Providence, and in between they would gig in this terrible club called the Martinique in Fall River. We used to go there, and they were all so loaded we would bring them back to our house and feed them. That's how we got so friendly with them."

Elaine and Larry hosted many of the greats—Buddy Rich, Roy Eldridge, Gerry Mulligan, Stan Getz, Illinois Jacquet, and others. "One night Buddy Rich was playing," said Elaine. "He was so stoned it was unbelievable. My youngest, Bruce, came downstairs and said, 'What's going on here?' This wonderful jazz musician said, 'Let me teach you how to play the drums,' and sat him down and tried to get him to play the drums!"

In early 1954 Carol Haney arrived in New York, fresh from a string of dance successes in Hollywood. In the late forties she had broken into MGM, where she teamed with the studio's famed Jack Cole, a father of theatrical jazz dance. She danced for him in the movies and became the lead dancer in his nightclub act, the Jack Cole Dancers. Haney was a chorus girl in the 1950 Doris Day film musical *Tea for Two*. In 1952 she dubbed the taps for Gene Kelly's famous "Singing in the Rain" sequence in the film of the same name. Paired the following year with an up-and-coming Bob Fosse in *Kiss Me Kate*, she would have a major influence on Fosse's evolving choreographic style. In May 1954 Haney opened in the Broadway production of *Pajama Game* and became an instant star with her performances of "Steam Heat" and "Hernando's Hideaway."

Elaine and Haney had maintained contact through the years. With Carol now in New York, Elaine was sharing in the excitement of a career not her own. "To amuse herself," said her son Rick, she began making weekly trips to New York, getting her hair done at Helena Rubenstein, staying at the Anderson-Little suite at the Waldorf Astoria and gathering with Carol when and where the star's busy schedule permitted. The more Haney went from success to success, the duller Elaine's life in Fall River seemed to grow. As she approached thirty, Elaine was wrestling with an uncomfortable truth: her dance performances seemed destined to remain no more than party entertainment.

When Newport held its first jazz festival in the summer of 1954, Elaine took heart. The Andersons, Capuanos, and LeSavoys helped to sponsor the festival and bought a box at the Casino. They didn't know any others in the boxes, however. "Our names were never put up," Elaine said, "because the money went to Mr. Capuano. Teddy and Larry gave Eddie the money to give to Elaine [Lorillard]." Thereafter for the first four or five years of the festival, the three couples went every night to hear the music.

Elaine and Robert Wagner at the premiere reception for *What Price Glory*. ::: *Fred Anderson Collection.*

Routinely joining them was her brother Bob, who traded off his access as manager of the Newport Paramount, the Zeitzes' local theater. "I employed a high school girl who worked the box office at the Paramount who was dating Gordon Sweeney, George Wein's on-site stage manager. I got backstage passes."

Elaine's childhood friend, Broadway dancing star Carol Haney, with the Anderson boys—*from left:* Fred, Bruce, and Rick—probably in 1954, during the run of *Pajama Game*. ::: *Fred Anderson Collection.*

Their embrace of the regional jazz scene was just one reflection of how the prewar traditional kinship ties of New Bedford and Fall River no longer applied to many of Elaine and her brother's generation. The emerging postwar mass society and New England's decaying industrial culture were generating a personal rebellion that found expression in many ways. One novel of the time, Herman Wouk's 1955 best-selling *Marjorie Morningstar* articulated fears and longings with which Elaine identified. "Who is Marjorie?" *Time* magazine asked in a cover story. "Marjorie Morningstar is an American Everygirl who happens to be Jewish."

For Elaine this life in the cosmopolitan world beyond was becoming more real than parochial Fall River. She had come from a regional culture, with its own tensions between its residual WASP and rising immigrant traditions. In the 1950s southeast New England was making the transition to a mass, transcontinental culture fed by magazine and book publishing, the movies, radio, records, and television. Its lily pads were mythic places like New York, Las Vegas, Hollywood, Havana, and the Florida wintering spots of her parents. In the forties and fifties Harry and Cecile had a summer apartment in Hollywood Beach, just north of Miami, where they would frequent the racetracks at nearby Gulfstream and Hialeah with their film-business friends, in particular the head of distribution at Warner Bros.

It was a short ride from there to Miami's plush new Hotel Fontainebleau, famed for its stairway to nowhere, which led to a nondescript cloakroom. After checking their coats, bejeweled dinner guests would parade down the sumptuous spiral staircase before the awed gaze of crowds in the lobby. It was a symbolic gestalt—a luminous waltz into a prosperous and affirming new world where stars ruled the galaxy. Morris Lapidus, the Fontainebleau's owner, described his hotel's style as the "architecture of the American Dream."

Sometime in early 1956 Carol Haney took a break from *Pajama Game* to appear with Ellington arranger Luther Henderson at the Fontainebleau's La Ronde Room. Elaine caught one or more of Carol's Miami shows and doubtlessly internalized what she saw. As the jazz musicians played from the bandstand, Haney began her performance in the audience, among the tables, with an improvised solo dance that concluded with her gliding up the treads and onto the stage.

At her Fontainebleau performances, Haney shattered what in theater is called the fourth wall: the imaginary fourth side of the traditional proscenium stage that separates audience from performer. With jazz everyone moves, however slightly. Having descended the stairway to nowhere as celebrities for an evening, the La Ronde audience found Haney in their midst, encouraging them to respond to the music with more than just applause. That spring night in Miami, Elaine was put in touch with a reality far beyond the bleak Fall River winter to which she was obliged to return.

In the summer of 1956, Haney's career was in overdrive. One major engagement that came her way was a TV booking for a July 15 NBC Steve Allen musical special, *The Bachelor,* with Jayne Mansfield. By contrast, Elaine was losing touch even with her immediate family. In March her eldest son, Frederick, had his bar mitzvah in Fall River. "Elaine walked away from it," recalled her son Rick. "Her life was pretty good, but she'd rather stay in New York than come back to Fall River." Elaine put it more indelicately: "I always used to say, if they were going to give this country an enema, they'd stick it in Fall River."

That summer Hollywood came to New Bedford. The State theater hosted world premieres of five movies, including John Huston's *Moby Dick,* starring Gregory Peck. There were celebrations for ten days, with a parade and a costume ball with everyone in whaling garb. Elaine returned from New York to attend the ball, the premieres, and the events her parents hosted at their home. For her father she had chaperoned the contract stars who came through New Bedford, among them Robert Wagner, Anthony Quinn, Ava Gardner, and Ann Miller.

Notwithstanding her fleeting screen career, Elaine was ambivalent about the hoopla. "Those people never interested me, because I'd been in Hollywood, and I knew what they were like. That really wasn't my scene. It was my mother's."

Elaine Anderson was projecting her interior life onto the dancing Doris Day in *Tea for Two,* in which Haney had appeared. When Ellington played "Tea for Two" during his earlier set, an apparition appeared before her. Doris Day's Nanette was a wealthy heiress and wannabe Broadway actress who at one point in the film invites the cast and crew of her Broadway show to her Westchester estate for a weekend. Cecile hosted movie stars; Elaine hosted jazzmen.

"She could have gone to a four-year college and could have gone on to do a hell of a lot more than she did," said her son Rick, "but her mother wouldn't let her, and society wouldn't let her. Married at eighteen and three kids by the time she was twenty-four, she could have had a career. So there was a lot of bottled up talent and indeed frustration."

Betty Friedan wrote of the fifties woman in her 1963 book *The Feminine Mystique*. "It was a strange stirring, a sense of dissatisfaction, a yearning that women suffered in the middle of the twentieth century in the United States. Each suburban wife struggled with it alone. As she made the beds, shopped for groceries, matched slipcover materials, ate peanut butter sandwiches with her children, chauffeured Cub Scouts and Brownies, lay beside her husband at night, she was afraid to ask of herself the silent question—'Is this all?' "

While not exactly that kind of suburban wife, Elaine felt similarly stifling dissatisfaction and asked of herself that same silent question. "They are in a trap," Friedan continued, "and to escape they must, like the dancer, finally exercise their human freedom, and recapture their sense of self."

On the night of July 6, 1956, seven years before the appearance of Friedan's seminal work, Elaine Anderson made her escape and danced.

14

Not Just Patterns in the Air

An Audience Performs

The fourth wall is a state of mind, separating those in the performance from those witnessing. Theoretically inviolate, the fourth wall has compelling power. It admits the audience to a theatrical performance yet separates that audience from the performers. In some instances it preserves order, enabling a performance to continue when an audience grows rowdy or threatens to mob the stage.

In musical performance, however, the fourth wall can be too impenetrable. A traditional concert stage is often too remote. Swing bands of the thirties and forties preferred dance halls, where they could enjoy connecting with an audience, watching the dancers. Reveling in the effect that dance engagements had on his musicians, Ellington once said, "When they see people moving around the floor, they've got to put snap and ginger into their work." The bop groups of the forties and fifties came to experience highs in the more intimate setting of clubs that enabled them to interact face-to-face with a listening audience.

Paul Gonsalves crashed the fourth wall on that Sunday afternoon in Boston when he left the Savoy stage while blowing the solo to "Flying Home" and led his audience to the corner of Columbus and Massachusetts. Carol Haney high-stepped through it at the Fontainebleau, after starting her dance amid the audience and then carrying her performance onto the stage.

For his concert stage at Newport, club owner George Wein facilitated intimacy—and inadvertently put a crack in its fourth wall—by allowing photographers into the area in front of the box seats. With the audience but not of them, free to stand, move about, and rest their cameras on the edge of the stage, so close to the feet of the jazz greats, the photographers provided a psychic bridge between performers and listeners. Working in the middle ground between stage and seating, visible both to performers and audience, the photographers had the power to concentrate focus like a limelight every time they took aim with their cameras. With each shot, they gave for all almost corporate affirmation to what was happening onstage—or off.

And then there was Jo Jones, the former carnival performer who never made distinction between stage and audience, a tap-dancing percussionist who delighted in drumming on any surface, onstage and off. Jones savored his role as a leader of communal celebration and rites. His enthusiasm during the "Diminuendo" was infectious. Visibly drumming in the wings with his *Christian Science Monitor,* Jones reinforced that psychic bridge built by the photographers. Neither onstage nor off, he occupied another middle ground, acting as if he were a Newport version of the New Orleans second line. His performance became a conversation, not just with the band but with the audience as well.

And when Elaine Anderson joined that conversation, together they shattered the fourth wall, setting the mythic seven thousand shouting and dancing through the scattered pieces.

Recalling the genesis of her dance, Elaine placed it before Gonsalves's solo—when Jones began to drum sometime in the fourth or fifth chorus of the "Diminuendo." "Jo was sitting there, and he takes a rolled-up newspaper in his hand. He is beating it on his palm, and he says, 'Come on, Elaine. Let's get this thing off the ground. We're dying here.'"

At least, that's what she imagined—that Jones was speaking to her directly. Her response was to grab Teddy LeSavoy's proffered hand. "And I got up and started to gyrate and dance. Now you've got to remember: People do that all the time today, but this is a long time ago. Nobody ever did that there. Nobody."

In her mind she was the only one dancing. Certainly that was—and had always been—true in the boxes. Farther back in the center of the main seating section, however, Jack Heaney and Eileen Farrell could see people starting to dance in the side aisles. "The driving rhythm was so infectious," Heaney recalled, "that those couples only represented in motion what everyone was feeling: the sheer joy of the moment." Already on their feet but with the crowd pressing forward, they had no room to move, much less dance. They just grinned and swayed along with everyone around them. "It was one hell of an experience."

With his eyes closed, Paul Gonsalves probably didn't see Elaine dancing, but Ellington, who in Dan Morgenstern's words "had an almost telepathic response to anything involving women," must have. Duke did indeed mention her in *Music Is My Mistress,* writing, "One lovely society matron broke through her veneer of discretion, and jumped her thing for all twenty-seven choruses, adding a cherry and whipped cream topping to our sundae morning."

Elaine started to catch fire as she worked the crowd like a pro, choreographing her performance from head to toe. Her platinum hair swirled in ripples left and right across

Elaine dances in the aisle. Teddy LeSavoy between her and the stage. Note the crowd, most with their backs to the stage facing her, along with the other photographers in the ring shout. ::: *Fred Anderson Collection.*

her cheeks; her expressive throat, bare to a button-edged and plunging vee-neckline; her sleeveless shoulders revealing her sinewy arms with every hand gesture; her full-skirted cocktail dress—it was actually brown, not black as it appeared in all the monochrome photos—fanning from her hips every time she twirled. Right hand lifting her ruffled petticoat and skirt of her dress, she high-stepped in her backless white high heels, to the delight of the young collegians who quickly moved forward and surrounded her.

From his box seat in front of Duke, John Monteiro saw Ellington watching the audience reaction. At some point the bandleader had to have spied Elaine. The sight would have been just the thing to get him going. Like so many other women during Ellington's performances over the years—like that Newport woman thirty summers before who had risen from her wheelchair, claiming the music had gotten into her bones—this expressive dancer would give him energy to pump the groove.

With all the cameras and microphones surrounding his band, Ellington had himself a media event comparable to his radio broadcasts from the Cotton Club and elsewhere in the late twenties and thirties and on AFRS in the forties. Indeed, this event was on a much grander scale. At Newport he had wires not only for Avakian's Columbia recording but also for the NBC Monitor radio broadcast to the nation and VOA broadcast to the world. Finally, Ellington had a solid news peg for his cover story for *Time*.

Still early in her dance, Elaine was joyously interacting with the crowd and was well aware of the scene around her. "I'm sure [Ellington saw me] out of the corner of his eye," she said.

"It was a turn-on for Duke," recalled her brother Bob. "He and Paul and the band had the place in a frenzy." Zeitz was now on his feet with LeSavoy and the rest of their party in the box, clapping and cheering along with Stack Ames, Jimmy Lomba, and the large group of Cape Verdean and New Bedford fans crowded against the back rail of the boxes just behind them.

Underneath Gonsalves, Ellington continued to drum dissonant chords on his piano. Flashing his hands as he had learned from Luckey Roberts in the twenties, Duke played the primitivist magician, as if to conjure some ecstatic spirit transplanted from the voodoo rituals of New Orleans's Congo Square.

For his part Gonsalves was not consciously playing the showman but rather was expressing himself through his sound. Wailing on his instrument with eyes closed, he could generate only so many camera shots, and presently the photographers started looking for others in the audience reactions.

Photographer Bob Parent moved to the right of the stage to shoot the scores of young collegians now crushing against the stage. From that perspective he could immediately see the commotion around Elaine in the distant box section across the field before the left side of the stage. More people, scores with their backs to the stage, were now surrounding her, shouting as she moved up and down the aisle among the boxes. Hastily, Parent threaded his way through the crowd to the general seating area just behind her.

Elaine Anderson high stepping (Bob Parent in background). ::: *Photo courtesy of Paul "Buck" Hoeffler.*

Elaine Anderson. Teddy LeSavoy clapping. Note Cape Verdean contingent just to the rear of the boxes. ::: *Photo courtesy of Paul "Buck" Hoeffler.*

Among the first professional photographers to join the veritable ring shout now formed around Elaine, Parent entered from behind her and began clicking as she worked the aisle. Shooting without a flash, he captured her and LeSavoy, who was standing in the aisle between her and the stage, their forms silhouetted by stage lights. His shots stop her in decisive moments—the bright light catching her blonde hair fanning from her face, her bare arms pumping skyward, then her right arm thrust to Parent's left, and finally directly toward him.

On the other side of the ring, between Elaine and the stage, was the *Providence Journal*'s Buck Hoeffler, working with a flash. Moving around LeSavoy, he snapped a shot of Elaine high-stepping, provocatively flashing the skirt of her cocktail dress with her right hand as she cavorted with a young crew-cut collegian in a sport coat. The light from the flash reveals dozens of rapt faces in the crowd watching her. Another Hoeffler photo shows LeSavoy clapping with his eyes on the stage while an exuberant Elaine casts a glance at her box, urged on by the Cape Verdean American contingent in the background. Over her left shoulder is a bespectacled and smiling Bob Parent readying a shot.

Parent slides to his left. Now facing away from the stage lights, he captures an image of Elaine moving down the aisle, mouth open, arms forward, and the muscles in her bare left shoulder betraying a crease of tension. Elaine began to internalize her performance.

George Wein, some of the stage staff, and the Pinkerton security team were getting edgy. Newport had seen dancing only at the margins, notably on the first night of the '55 festival when Louis Armstrong had fans dancing down the side aisles. Tonight, the young at the head of the aisles were spilling into the photography pit and into those boxes that had emptied earlier in the evening. As more and more pressed forward, the last vestige of order collapsed, as a human wave pushed folding chairs askew and out of line, tipping many sideways to the ground. On many empty chairs, young fans were precariously standing to get an unobstructed view of the stage. Wein now worried about injuries.

Ellington's own take was incisive. "George Wein was walking up and down in front of the stage," he wrote in *Music Is My Mistress*, "walking in time with the music, with his face serious on the police side and smiling on our side."

While elderly VIPs vacated the boxes, Elaine Lorillard resolutely remained in her front-and-center box, regardless of the surge of people. Turning for a moment to her right, she noticed Elaine Anderson. "I was looking straight at her as she was dancing down the middle aisle. No one was jumping on her. No one was screeching. A couple of people here and there would get up and sort of follow her, but they didn't interfere with her. Nobody was dancing, except maybe people in the rear. Whatever [the kids] were doing, it wasn't frightening. It was perfectly calm, but for a happy bunch of people who were applauding her. She kind of floated. You had been watching the stage, and maybe the lights did it, because she was very visible and pretty, but all of a sudden this pretty creature is coming down, like an angel blowing down the aisle."

Though aware of Elaine Anderson's dancing, Jack Heaney was more focused on Gonsalves onstage. By that time the soloist was beginning to repeat his trademark riffs, but

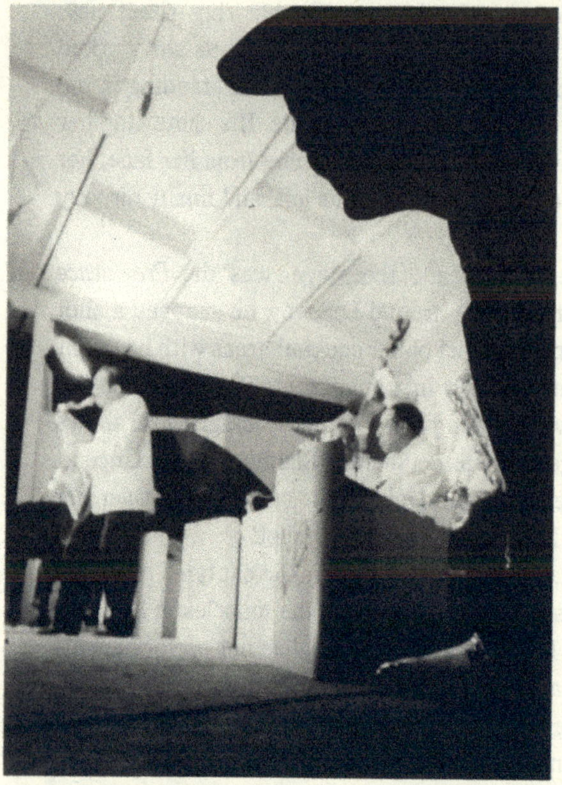

Paul Gonsalves at the mike, with George Avakian silhouetted in the foreground. ::: *Photo by Don Hunstein. Courtesy of Sony BMG Music Entertainment.*

it didn't matter, Heaney recalled. "The primary thing was the swinging rhythm, just the right tempo, and Gonsalves rode it beautifully."

John Monteiro, on the other hand, was so transfixed by his fellow Cape Verdean American's solo that he carried in his mind's eye an inaccurate image of Ellington walking off the stage and band members rising and climbing into the trumpet section where they stood to give the whole stage to Paul. "The blonde I remember, but it wasn't anything that I would've stored in my memory, 'cause there was so much excitement," said Monteiro. "Oh, the clapping, the yelling! Nothing was disorderly. It was just enthusiasm for that kind of energy coming out with that musical beauty."

At the other side of the field, Bill Farmen and the Falmouth lifeguards continued to push their way forward along the crowded stage-right aisle. Like Monteiro's, his focus was entirely on the pulsating energy emanating from the stage.

Yet for Lorillard and her section of boxes, "Everybody had their eyes on Elaine going up and down the aisle."

About seven minutes into the "Diminuendo" and interval, George Avakian first became aware of the commotion Elaine was generating with her dance. Suddenly she materialized in his field of vision, directly in front of the stage. "If she had taken five steps forward and I had taken three, I could have reached down and shaken her hand."

Notwithstanding the earlier exodus of weary ticket holders, crowds outside the gate were clamoring for admission, some threatening to storm the wickets when refused. One group was exploding firecrackers, elevating tension throughout the crowds surrounding the park. By this time George Wein had made up his mind that security needed to intervene. "I don't remember if he came out on the stage or whether he was down below," Elaine Lorillard said. "It all happened so quickly, but he was probably over on the right side. George was screaming, 'Get the Pinkerton men!' As Elaine [Anderson] was dancing, he was calling the Pinkerton men to come over, shouting at them to go into the crowd to stop her."

Lorillard turned to her husband and nudged him hard. "Don't let him stop this!" she yelled in Louis's ear.

Columbia photographer Don Hunstein was on the stage beside Jo Jones. He snapped some shots of George Avakian in his baseball cap, visibly relaxed now, smiling at Gonsalves. Then Avakian turned and peered into the crowd. When Hunstein followed his eyeline and saw Elaine dancing, he seized his chance. Jumping off the stage, he began elbowing his way toward her, hoping that she'd still be dancing when he got closer.

By this time Elaine's dancing was surely an impetus to the extended choruses. "The more I danced, the more Paul Gonsalves got going, and the more Paul went, the more I went, until it got to a fury that you couldn't believe. I wasn't doing this to get attention. I was just carried away. I have no idea whether he saw me. I don't think anybody saw me, except the people behind me egging me on, and the more I did it and Gonsalves was playing, I just went crazy."

"[Duke] wasn't going to stop it, because everybody was popping," said her brother Bob. "I mean, he was in show business."

By now the mikes were capturing a lot of the band's excited chatter as well as the mounting rumbles coming from fans. Some started whistling. Others were clapping. Onstage the band members were yelling their support, and all the while Gonsalves was blowing away, with Ellington, Woodyard, and Woode behind him.

By the time Hunstein joined the ring of photographers and fans around her, Elaine was more exercised. Like Hoeffler, Hunstein worked with a flash. His first photo has her glancing sideways and down, hair falling across her cheek, right arm angled as if it were an armature pumping a driving wheel. Another crew-cut college boy in a sport coat extends his right hand to her. In the next shot she turns away, skirt flying, left hand on the box railing. Three shots later she's dancing toward the camera, but in the foreground a stiff right forearm interrupts her. A large white cuff and ostentatious cuff link protrude from a suit sleeve, a tense index finger blocks her advance.

"I think we were asked to leave. I don't remember," Anderson said. "Yeah, I think George Wein wanted to cut it off, because it was becoming wild."

Elaine Lorillard was livid. "I was against her being thrown out. She was not doing any harm. We all knew she was a nice person, and it was a nice crowd." Grabbing her husband Louis, she marched from her box to confront Wein.

"Don't you dare turn anyone out of here!" she ordered, but to little effect.

At that point Louis intervened directly with the Pinkertons. "Let her go," Louis told them. "Let her dance down there."

"It was wonderful," Elaine Lorillard observed with satisfaction. "The Pinkerton men didn't take her out. I had no idea that something very special was happening. All I knew was: Don't change. Don't try to suddenly make a scene and take her out. This was before the era of rock and roll riots. We weren't worried. That was why I didn't want them to stop it, because it seemed so nice."

With that impediment removed, Elaine Anderson cut loose, riding on Gonsalves's

Elaine Anderson. ::: *Photos by Don Hunstein. Courtesy of Sony BMG Music Entertainment.*

R&B riffs, and together this New Bedford duo improvised across the fourth wall. The Cape Verdean community knew Paul Gonsalves, the soloist on tenor sax who gave voice to their American experience and spoke for them all. As for Elaine's social set, the LeSavoys, the Capuanos, and countless others, they knew her dancing. It was nonpareil.

Hunstein snapped a shot of Elaine in full fly, arms outstretched, back arched, chin skyward. Just behind her right shoulder, getting ready for a shot, was a tall, bespectacled African American photographer, the great visual interpreter of jazz Roy DeCarava. The year before, DeCarava had hit it big when his work was included in Edward Steichen's seminal collection of images of the Harlem Renaissance, *The Sweet Fly Paper of Life*, with text by Langston Hughes.

Hunstein and DeCarava captured Elaine in controlled abandon, at the peak of ecstasy, but from opposite perspectives. Hunstein's succession of shots now show his subject deep within herself, oblivious to everything but the music. She arches backward, this time with an open-mouthed youth just over her left shoulder mimicking her move. Hunstein's flash lights her face against a black sky—she's looking left, eyes closed, neck muscles taut, mouth open in a scream, fingers of her left hand splayed against her face. Then she's facing right, arms forward, hair swept back, eyes still closed, mouth open unmistakably expressing pure, sensual pleasure. She is beautiful. She turns to him. Now her eyes are cast down, hair across her face, arms pumping—left angled high, right, low.

She's gone. Hunstein is close now. His flash captures her in stark black and white, highlighting the blonde hair that frames her still-closed eyes. Her left forearm masks her lips. Her right hand gestures upward, palm open, almost reverently.

It was this photo that would come to grace the back of the Columbia LP, that would transform the dancer into a jazz history icon, "the gal who launched 7,000 cheers." Then another close-up. Elaine is looking up, eyes slightly open, hair flowing from her brow, mouth wide, clearly in the middle of a forceful and joyous scream, just behind the shadowy face of a spellbound youth seen in earlier shots. Then another, hair back, eyes now open wide, she is gazing up, her right arm stretched to the darkness above, blackness all around, and a scream of release. Joy.

"Elaine was oblivious to everything," said Avakian, "but the music." "I don't know how she lasted," said her brother Bob Zeitz. At last, she returned to the moment. A final Hunstein shot has her eyes fully open, looking above his lens. She's wearing an open smile that resembles forties singer and fifties TV hostess Dinah Shore's. A man whispers, perhaps suggestively, into her ear, his hands cupped together, as if pleading. Behind them are two youths with exuberant expressions in full scream at the stage. Gone.

Roy DeCarava glimpsed a slightly darker side of Elaine's response to the Gonsalves interval. In his legendary collection of jazz images and poetry eventually published as *The Sound I Saw,* DeCarava included six photos of Newport '56: a photo of Ellington at the keyboard, another of the crowd in front of the stage and a remarkable four photos of Elaine in the shadowy throes of her expressive dance. DeCarava captioned all six images in verse: "With Duke reminiscing in tempo at festival junction with sophisticated lady and jack the bear in a flippant flurry to take the a train to the upper manhattan medical group and the lush life of rocking in rhythm."

One of these four images shows Elaine in a lost moment before her release. She is turned toward the photographer, arms outstretched, yet this time her face—eyes shut, an open-mouthed grimace—betrays pain. It is as if, in that moment, she is experiencing what swing musicologist Gunther Schuller called "the struggle, the torment, and the anguish" of the composition at that instant propelled by Ellington's dissonant rhythms and Gonsalves's driving riffs. Was it a glimpse into her future? Or was it an exorcism of

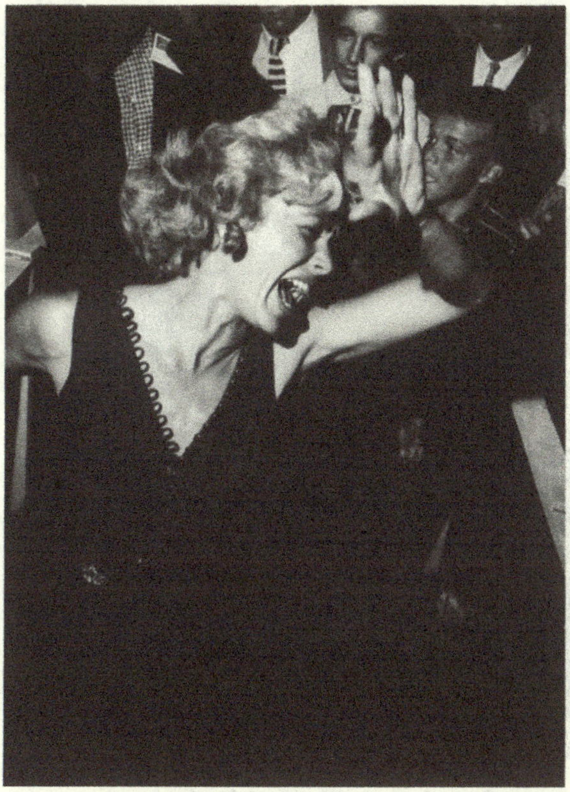

her past? Who were the apparitions floating through her darkness? The mother who blocked her career? The husband who made her a young mother? Isadora Duncan, Carol Haney, Marjorie Morningstar, Doris Day, or the unreachable platinum blondes in the decade's ubiquitous Clairol ads—"Does she, or doesn't she?"

The father of theatrical jazz dance, Jack Cole, once said that in the theater "you want to see real people doing real things, expressing valid emotions in an artistic, meaningful way, disclosing bits of insight that will transfix you and make you understand something about life, and about yourself. . . . I just try to touch the dancer at the center of his emotion. I try to remind him of what he is—a dancer, an actor, a real person. If you're ashamed of this or that emotion, you can't dance. You yourself may not behave in a certain way as a person, but when you dance you must bring real emotion to whatever you're doing. Isn't that what dancing is all about—emotion, life, and not just patterns in the air?"

Almost nine minutes into "Diminuendo and Crescendo in Blue," the whistles and claps were as much a part of the musical conversation as the notes and the beat. The intensity was exploding everywhere in the field.

"Don't stop now! Don't stop!" Ellington screamed to his soloist.

"Woo! Woo!" from the stage.

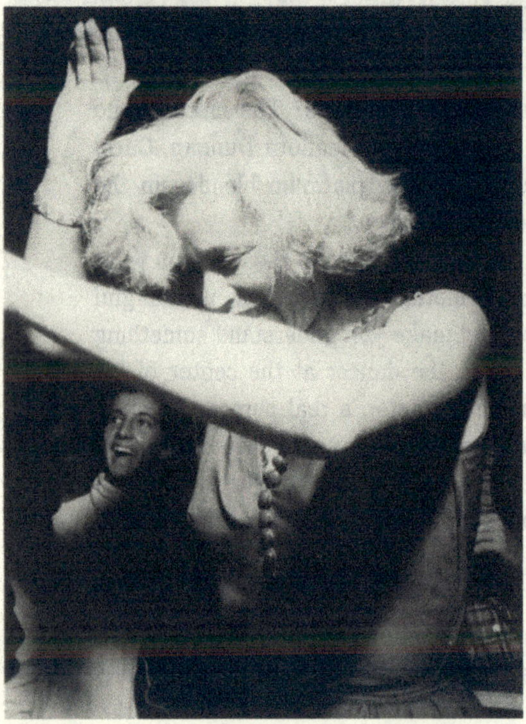

Photo used on the back cover of the Columbia LP. ::: *Photo by Don Hunstein. Courtesy of Sony BMG Music Entertainment.*

"Yeah! Yeah! Yeah!" And more whistles.

Hearing Gonsalves fading and beginning to repeat himself, Ellington started his chording. "Duke would throw [Paul] the cue," said Avakian. "The idea was that he should just keep playing until Duke would cue him to go out." Speculating that the cue was probably the chording, he added, "It's possible that at the point he might have even glanced at Duke." Gonsalves grabbed a high note and held it. Ellington broke for him and then lay back to let him finish.

Some ten minutes into the performance, after twenty-seven solo choruses, Gonsalves was done. As the soloist returned to his perch next to the piano, Ellington concluded the interval with a second piano interlude. Hitting the keys with a series of discords and blues wrinkles, he lowered the tension. From the crowd the whistles continued, along with a low-level roar like distant traffic.

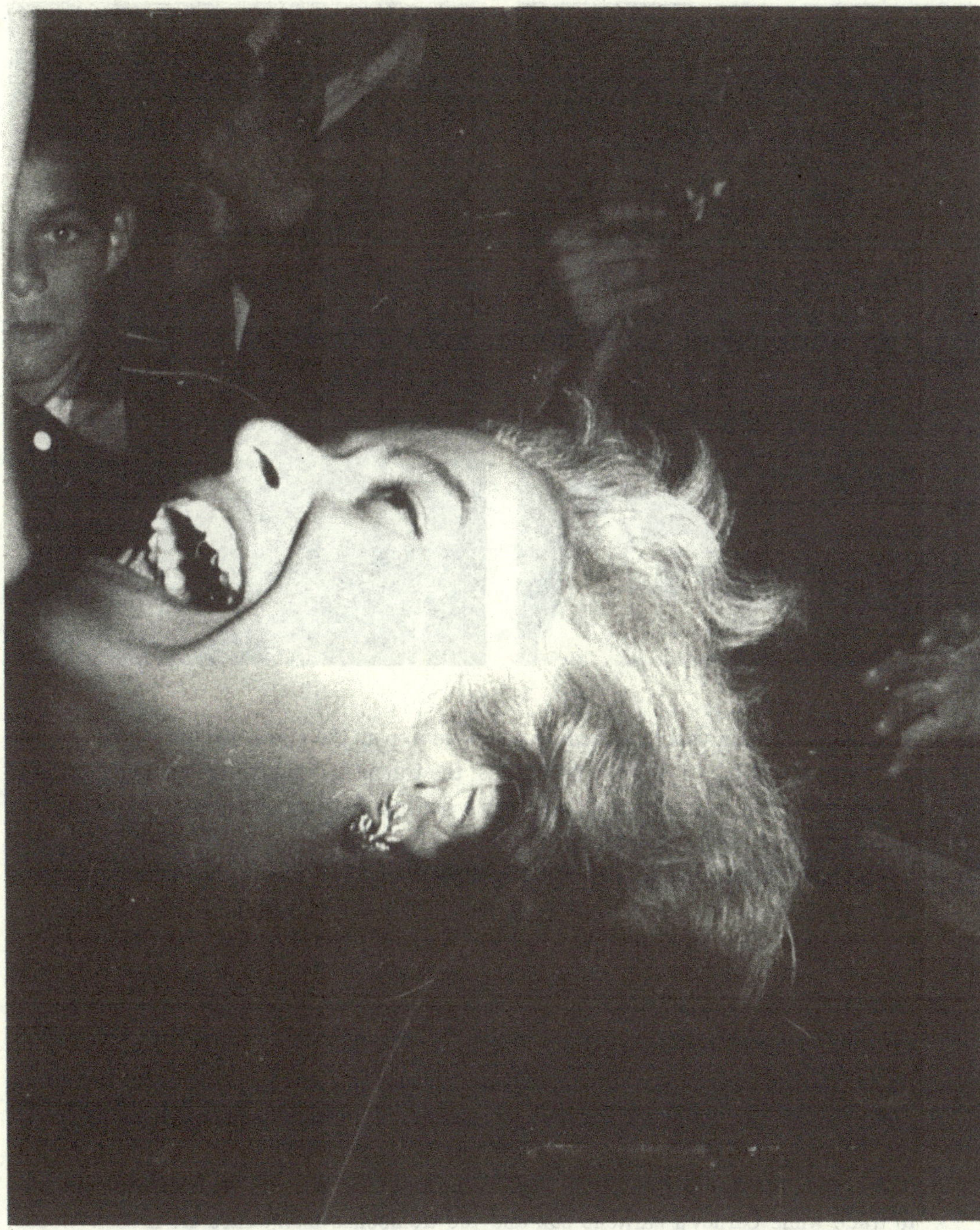

A minute later the reeds hit and the "Crescendo" began. Then the trombones entered, followed by stuttering trumpets, and soon the three sections were trading notes in call and response.

"When we were doing the 'Crescendo' I could just feel the excitement," said Sanders.

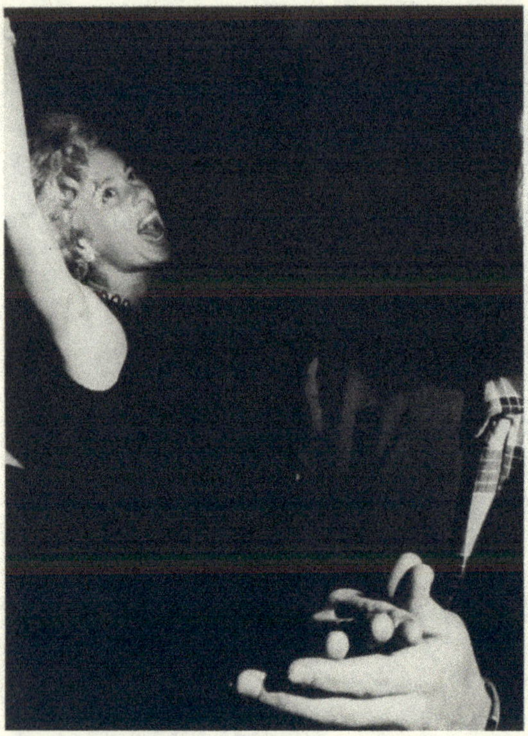

"You had to contain yourself, because you have to play the notes. We have our little solo parts, the reeds, the brass—the trombones, the trumpets—but we are an orchestra. And I think that night, at that point, there was a oneness between everyone, and we brought it to a climax. It was a peak moment."

"Analogies don't always work," he continued, "but one night a conductor goes out on the stage with an orchestra. How many times has it played a Brahms, a Beethoven, or a Tchaikovsky symphony? But what happens on this particular night, at this particular concert hall? They play it like they have never played it before. Something transpires between conductor and orchestra and orchestra and conductor. And maybe someone writes it up that he's never heard this Brahms, or that Beethoven, or the Tchaikovsky ever played so. The conductor and orchestra are transformed and are at one with the music. And they give a performance that was just wonderful. Newport was such a night."

Trumpets and trombones—the brass together—traded with the reeds in close harmony, rising to the upper registers. Once at the top, the reeds and the trumpets continued to trade while Carney's baritone sax and the trombones maintained an anchor. Woode, forcefully attacking his bass runs, and Woodyard, now with both feet jamming on the pedals of his two bass drums, drove the beat like a speeding express train.

When Ellington nodded his cue to Cat Anderson, the crowd became ecstatic. As the Sabby Lewis veteran made his way to the solo mike, young people were screaming themselves hoarse. Many were leaping. Others stood in awe. In the distance the dancing

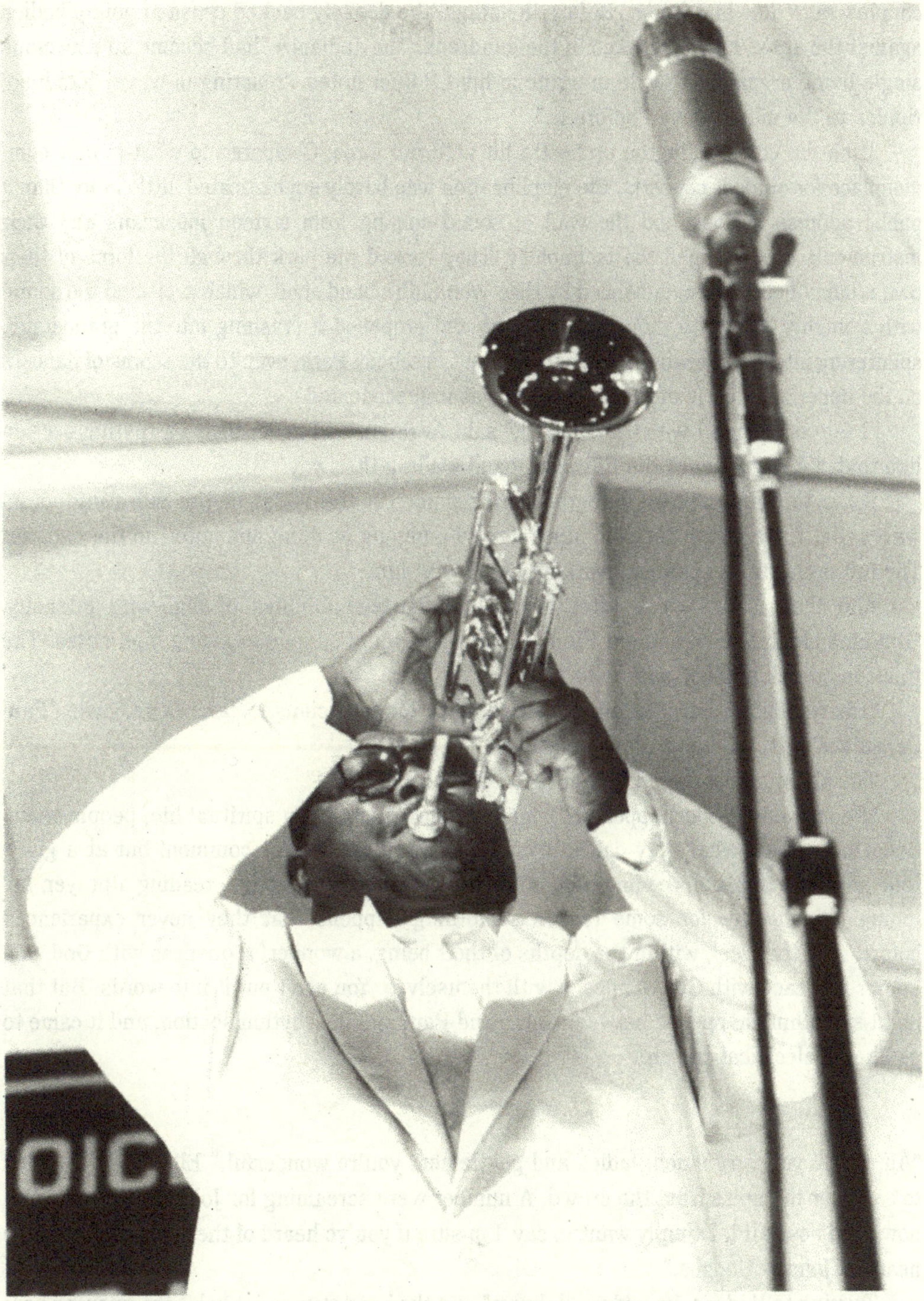

Cat Anderson hits the high note. ::: *Photo courtesy of Paul "Buck" Hoeffler.*

couples were now in a frenzy. Before the stage, the densely packed crush of young bodies against the apron now numbered in the hundreds. The audience "had become an enormous single living organism," Avakian wrote in his LP liner notes, "reacting in waves like huge ripples to the music played before it."

Then the entire Ellington orchestra hit with full force. Compared to what is now commonplace for outdoor concerts, the amplification was hardly sophisticated, little more than a public address system, and the wall of sound coming from sixteen musicians and their instruments overwhelmed the technology. They rocked the park through the force of their own unamplified volume, enhanced by Hsio Wen Shih's band shell, which projected the sound with a mighty blast into thousands of faces and propelled it crashing into the grandstand, splintering into reverberating waves throughout Freebody Park, even to the scores of dancers on the uppermost levels of the stadium. It was unprecedented.

"I felt as though I was transported," said Avakian. "I'd never heard a rhythm section like that. I'd never heard the Ellington band wailing that way."

Some thirteen minutes into the performance, in the midst of the pulsating sound waves, Cat Anderson at the solo mike started pumping, walking his notes up the register. The full orchestra responded, walking along with him.

And then it was over. After more than fourteen minutes of high-wire intensity, "Diminuendo and Crescendo in Blue" climaxed with Cat's last screaming high notes. The frenzied crowd let loose with wild yells.

"Everybody!" Ellington called, motioning to his musicians to take their bows. "Paul Gonsalves! Cat Anderson! Paul Gonsalves!"

The shouting continued, refusing to ebb. "More! More!"

"People ask, 'What happened?'" mused John Sanders. "In spiritual life, people sometimes experience what they call a mystical experience. It's not common, but at a given time and a given place, reading a book, reading a scripture passage, reading a prayer, listening to a homily, for some reason something happens that they never experienced before. And they feel, within the depths of their being, a wonderful oneness with God, you know? At peace with God. At peace with themselves. You can't put it into words. But that night something happened between Duke and Paul and the rhythm section, and it came to us like an electrical current."

"Ah, thank you very much, ladies and gentlemen, you're wonderful," Ellington struggled to say over the noise from the crowd. A number were screaming for Johnny Hodges. "And now. And now, all I, I simply want to say, I'm sure if you've heard of the saxophone, you've heard of Johnny Hodges."

Turning to Hodges, he added, "Johnny," and the band then quickly hit the opening bars of "I Got It Bad (And That Ain't Good)." Ellington had written the number in 1941 for Hodges, and according to Sanders he featured it regularly after Rab's return in late 1955. Hodges opened with a squeak from his reed as he bent a note upward, followed by muted trumpets and the saxes. Hodges promptly squeaked his second time around but slid into a beautiful series of solo statements with the sax section anchoring behind him and Duke introducing the occasional blues wrinkle on the keyboard.

Rapt young fans—in the hundreds—crowded in staggering row upon row, pressed against the apron of the stage. Just behind, the Anderson contingent made its way from the box. Exasperated by his wife's public display, which perhaps violated some final taboo in his eyes, Larry hurried her from the field. At various times through the night, he might have watched her dancing to a different drum, adopting another totem, finding power in other fetishes. For in photographer Buck Hoeffler's recall, "The famous 'Bedford Blonde' was seen dancing in the audience, earlier during this evening, before Ellington's famous combustible explosiveness." For better or worse, Elaine's dance—the one that the photographers captured for all time—would prove to be a turning point in her marriage.

Onstage, Harry Carney's baritone and the rest of the saxes continued to anchor the song and the crowd. Ellington sparingly filled around Hodges. Then came the finish with the trombones and muted trumpets. Though engaged, the crowd still had a restlessness and excitement beneath the surface. It was still noisy. When the number finally came to a close, appreciative applause poured forth.

Hodges remained at the mike, and Duke went right into the piano introduction to "Jeep's Blues" with the full band behind him. Dating from 1938, it was another of Duke's numbers for a Hodges solo, which originally had also featured solos by trumpeter Cootie Williams, trombonist Lawrence Brown, and Harry Carney. When the performance settled, it was just Rab and the rhythm section, Woodyard riding his cymbals with punctuation here and there from his twin bass drums. Ellington filled with his wrinkles, and the alto soloist started with his sultry wail.

Duke took a backseat for Hodges. "He knew when to lay it on heavy," said John Sanders, "or when to just kind of pull back. And he would do that. You could hear him on the ballads. He wouldn't get in the way. There'd be a tinkling on the piano, and the soloist would be just carrying it all the way with a light rhythm."

Ellington then went into dissonant chording around Hodges's runs. He growled, "Hey! Hey!" Hodges then soloed with Woode's sparse bass runs and Woodyard's cymbals. Then came the reeds, and Hodges started bending his notes. He played a mood that conjured the image of shadowy lovers sharing a cigarette after a long and mutually satisfying bout of lovemaking, smoke curling in neon colors from the light of a second-story saloon sign across an alleyway.

It was another kind of emotional high for the evening, so apt and well-chosen in terms of mood, personnel, and performance. Said Dan Morgenstern, "It was a great choice, and, hey, that's one of Johnny's featured pieces. As we know, Johnny Hodges had been away from the band and had come back and is perhaps in Duke's mind and in the public's the biggest individual star in the Ellington band." That night Hodges had with him his ten-year-old son, Johnny Junior. "He had his special showcase," continued Morgenstern, "and it would always be placed strategically on an Ellington program. ['Jeep's Blues' is] a

Ray "Floorshow" Nance teasing a most willing audience for a response during "Tulip or Turnip."
::: *Photo by Don Hunstein. Courtesy of Sony BMG Music Entertainment.*

perfect choice for bringing the level of all that excitement down, but it also is a very intense piece. Ellington would have been thinking Johnny is going to be somewhat overwhelmed by this terrific response to Gonsalves. Not that there was jealousy, but there are egos involved. It was the perfect choice musically and psychologically, because that performance has a lot of weight, and Johnny plays beautifully because he is also up. I mean, they are all up for this thing."

Ellington brought it back down with his wrinkles. The reeds traded for a moment, and then Hodges, Ellington, Woode, and Woodyard returned. And finally it was the finish with shading from the trombones and then all the brass. Exquisite.

Hodges had certainly calmed the crowd, but Ellington could see that they were far from satiated and not yet spent. Hodges's metaphorical cigarette had recharged their batteries. The applause continued over Hodges's acknowledgments and then became insistent. "Oh, we got a lot more," Ellington quickly reassured them. "We got a lot more. We got a lot more."

He then called Ray Nance and "Tulip or Turnip." Light and somewhat of a novelty number, Ellington and Don George had written it in 1946 for Floorshow. It had a beat great for dancing. "Well, I think again that's Ray Nance," said Morgenstern. "Ray's one of Duke's favorites in there at that particular point in time."

Nance excited the young at the stage apron as he growled through his verses. The band broke, and Nance started to dance, moving to stage right, to the delight of Jonathan Yardley and his Groton friends, who were now right beneath him. The crowds all around started to hoot and whistle. The energy returned. Dancing broke out behind the crush. One very bohemian couple, the young man wearing a Ben Hogan gold hat, ubiquitous at the time, started to jitterbug, catching the attention of Bob Parent and Buck Hoeffler, who were shooting nearby.

Nance went into his trumpet solo, alarming Wein and his security team, if not the Newport police. It was now evident that Hodges had not played encores. Well past the midnight curtain time, Wein was now faced with a show that was apparently gathering steam again and a seemingly rowdy crowd that had reenergized. The old timers were long gone. The kids were now ruling the night, and Nance was playing to their rowdiness. The collegians by the stage vociferously interacted with him as he twirled his trumpet and danced in circles, at times dancing with his back to the crowd. The photographers were having a field day. Parent captured Yardley three deep from stage right with a look of joy and awe on his face.

Collegiates to the rear. ::: *Photo courtesy of Paul "Buck" Hoeffler.*

The band climaxed to high applause. It was a very late 12:50. From stage right Wein crossed in front of Ellington to grab the microphone. "Duke Ellington, ladies and gentlemen. Duke Ellington." The crowd sensed a stage hook and was not at all pleased. Ellington resisted. "That, that's it! No! No! No, Duke! That's it, Duke!" Boos from the fans began to build. Ellington tried to interject. "I mean it now! That's good night!" screamed Wein. The crowd became intense. "No! No! No! I mean it now!" Ellington tried to get Wein to let him calm his audience with another number. The boos, whistles, and shouts became more insistent, almost defiant. "Let me tell them good night," Ellington suggested diplomatically to Wein. "Can I tell them good night?" After a long minute, the crowd noise subsided as Ellington stepped to the mike. Woodyard lightly cued a couple of taps on his drum kit. "Thank you very much, ladies and gentlemen," he said coolly. "We have a very heavy request for Sam Woodyard. And 'Skin Deep.'"

"Duke was a master of handling crowds for forty years by then," Duke's nephew Michael James observed about the exchange with Wein. "You want to bring 'em down? You just have Rab play a ballad, then bring 'em back up. Duke faked him out and then went into 'Skin Deep.'"

Cheers and cries of joy greeted the announcement. Ellington led from the front. The band rolled into the intro, and Woodyard went into a solo break with the reeds and brass

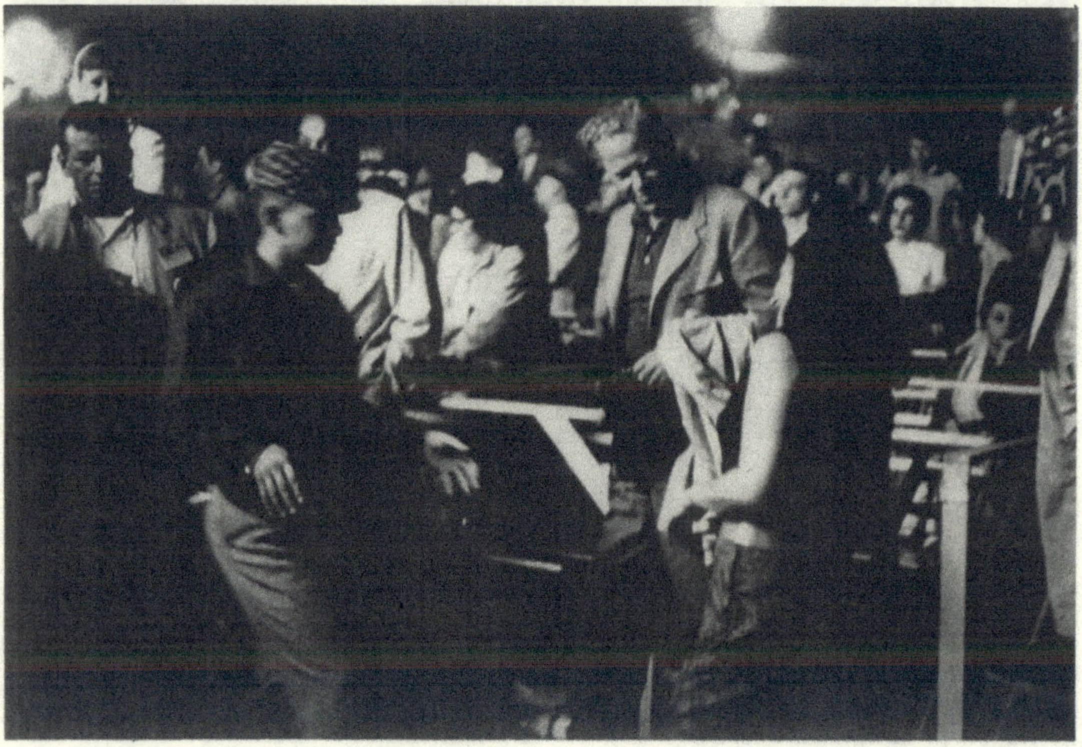

Bohemian couple put on their own show during "Tulip or Turnip." ::: *Photo courtesy of Bob Parent.*

The young audience on its feet, in no hurry to leave. ::: *Photo by Don Hunstein. Courtesy of Sony BMG Music Entertainment.*

following in sequence. Drummer Louis Bellson's "Skin Deep" was a standard Ellington crowd pleaser throughout the early fifties from the time Bellson was with the band. Ellington routinely placed it at the end of a concert. "Of course, it's Sam," said Morgenstern. "Yeah, 'cause Sam had so much to do with driving that night."

As was intended, Woodyard did a wild and lengthy over-the-top drum solo that finally spent the crowd. First drumming them into silence and then into submission, Woodyard finished with slashing cymbals which presaged a full orchestral build. Finally satiated, the fans returned hearty applause, short of the earlier abandon. "Sam Woodyard!" said Ellington. "Sam Woodyard! Sam Woodyard!"

The sax section introduced the first few bars of "Mood Indigo," and the audience continued to calm and quieten. They knew it was over. One o'clock, "on the nose," as critic Leonard Feather observed.

"Ladies and gentlemen, we certainly want to thank you for the wonderful way you've inspired us this evening." "Oh, no!" several voices sighed in the crowd. Quickly, Duke continued, "You're very beautiful, very sweet, and we do love you madly. As we say good night, we want to give you our best wishes and hope we'll have this pleasure again next year. Thank you very much." "Thank you, Duke," said a female voice. Appreciative whistles and

Young fans in the crush against the apron at once marvel and capture the experience. ::: *Photo by Don Hunstein. Courtesy of Sony BMG Music Entertainment.*

applause accompanied the band members as they made their exits, many to continue the frenzy at bars and nightspots, some of which remained open until four in the morning.

The band was totally exhausted, Jimmy Woode recalled. "It was too emotional. I thought I would die or have a heart attack. . . . It was so exciting. The ambiance was so great for the public. . . . Oh, what a great experience!"

"Hey, way to go, Duke!" someone shouted as Ellington crossed to the stage-left steps. There he saw an exhausted George Avakian. "Was the 'Suite' alright?" Duke asked the producer as he descended the steps. "Yes," Avakian replied wearily, following him into the backstage tent. "We had some problems with the big mikes, but we'll patch it up, and it'll be OK." "Well, you only heard the piece once, and I can tell you we've got a lot of work to do. What about 'Diminuendo and Crescendo?'" "A great performance, but we'll have to do something to salvage it." "Maybe we could have Strayhorn write out the first few bars and have it done in the studio. Maybe overdub it again." "I don't think it's possible." "Well, let's give it a try," said Ellington.

After conferring with Irving Townsend and recording an interview with Willis Conover in the VOA trailer, Ellington may have spent the night at the Viking Hotel. The band, however, repaired to the Casino Tennis Club, where, according to Burt Goldblatt, a "barracks-like room" with cots had been erected over the tennis courts. The photographer recalled sleeping among the band and next to baritone saxophonist Harry Carney, Ellington's driver.

Once his engineers had packed and secured their gear, Avakian made his way to the Viking Hotel and tried to sleep. It was not an easy rest. Reflecting on the defects in the recording, he thought seriously of not releasing it but instantly dismissed the thought. As for George Wein, he came to appreciate Duke's handling of the crowd at the end of his set. "I learned a lot from Ellington that night," he said almost fifty years later. "That was very good."

"I do remember," said Buck Hoeffler, the *Providence Journal* photographer, "security had to deal with a young man after the Ellington concert. The crowd had almost dispersed and gone home, and this lanky, quite casually dressed young fellow, not quite a hippie and obviously slightly incoherent, was intent on climbing onto the stage; he seemed convinced that he had to perform with his flute, and show what could be done. A couple of security guards very nicely tried to deal with his one-sided direction, he persisted, and 'bam' was grabbed and hustled away without ceremony. I was just a few feet away, and did not photograph this. This was the only unruliness which I saw contrasted to the gangs of disruptiveness bent on disruptiveness, a couple of years later."

Bill Farmen remembered the return drive to Falmouth in his buddy's Buick. Such drives tended to be lonely for the driver as the other three passengers usually slept. That unforgettable night, the energy was so high not one crashed. All down the highway the foursome replayed the whole evening, every note, in an on-the-road conversation that continued till dawn.

"I've been lucky," said Jonathan Yardley, reflecting on that experience more than fifty years ago. "Apart from my own private life, nothing has had the staying power of Duke Ellington at Newport that night. It was the night of my life."

Where It All Went

15

As Though You Were There

The LP

"I heard the buzz," recalled Dan Morgenstern, then a student on the GI Bill at Brandeis. "People came back who had been to Newport, and they would say, 'Hey, you should have gone.'"

Morgenstern had been attending summer school that July. Having already spent his saved allowances on catching the jazz names at their Boston engagements, he was "pretty broke. So I couldn't get there that year. I really wanted to kick myself for having missed this thing."

The repercussions from the Ellington performance were not just traveling by word-of-mouth within the close-knit jazz community. Photos and the story of the Gonsalves solo and the anonymous blonde dancer ran in numerous publications, from the local newspapers to the trade press. Critic Whitney Balliett in the *Saturday Review* characterized Ellington's second set as a "magnificent frenzy" and tagged the saxophonist's interval as "honest, old-time rhythm and blues—a bomb that blew the crowd to its feet, to dancing, to rushing crazily at the bandstand."

Similarly crediting Gonsalves with producing a "surprise revival meeting," the September 1956 *Metronome* reported, "There was dancing in the aisles, shouting, clapping and a madly romping Ellington band, aware of the feeling it was generating." Leonard L. Levinson in *Variety* wrote how Ellington "stripped the decorum off the crowd as they kept blowing until 12:50 A.M."

With a cropped Bob Parent photo of the dancing bohemian couple, *Down Beat*'s Leonard Feather wrote:

> For three nights, the Festival audience had been intent, frequently enthusiastic and seldom bored. But when Duke and his men roared across the Sunday night horizon, the audience suddenly fused into a heatedly unified, pulsating congregation. Sporadic dancing broke out all over Freebody Park and continued to spread in wide varieties of happily improvised choreography. Most of those who weren't dancing, stood on chairs, cheering or wide-mouthed in silent, graphic pleasure. Duke's men, catching the fever in turn played as the set spiraled into full-scaled rocking rapport between a participating audience and a blowing band. Duke, dominating the scene and the Festival, appeared to grow in size as he dug into the piano, playing with a smile that grew wider and wider. The set lasted until 1 a.m. and left everyone satisfyingly spent.

"The industry buzz [on Ellington] really began after all the write-ups about the 1956 event," said George Wein. "When he got the cover of *Time* magazine, it gave him a second life."

Ellington's *Time* cover story didn't hit the street immediately, however. As a rule, *Time* cover stories responded to current events. The Ellington piece was to be a so-called back-of-the-book story. Even though it did not have to be tied to breaking news, it still needed some sort of news peg. Earlier in the spring, Duke had suggested his July 12 date with the New Haven Symphony Orchestra. With the Newport triumph, Joe Morgen, the Ellington publicist who had mooted the Ellington cover story in the first place, suddenly had the ideal peg. Three weeks after the festival, at an all-night party at critic Leonard Feather's in Manhattan, Morgen pitched his idea to Carter Harman, the *Time* writer who had been developing the Ellington story. Harman agreed to run it by his editors.

When to publish a cover story was a decision made by Otto Fuerbringer, assistant managing editor. Fuerbringer chaired weekly cover conferences and had that proverbial nose for news. With every passing week, the Newport angle was less of a hook.

The first post-Newport cover had been David John McDonald, the president of the United Steelworkers of America, newsworthy because of the ongoing U.S. steel strike. The rest of the month featured the frontrunner Democratic presidential candidate, Adlai Stevenson; Rex Harrison, star of the hit Broadway musical *My Fair Lady;* and Indian prime minister Jawaharlal Nehru. Internationally, increased attention was going to simultaneous crises in Eastern Europe and the Suez.

Within a week after Harman had put forth Newport as the hook for the Ellington cover story, Fuerbringer made the decision to go with it for the August 20 issue, which hit newsstands on the thirteenth. Ellington was appearing among some hefty notables. Greek shipping tycoon Stavros Niarchos was Fuerbringer's choice for the first August cover, followed by former president Harry Truman for the second. Then came Ellington, with Egyptian president Gamal Abdul Nasser, instigator of the worsening Suez Crisis, finishing the month.

Time had access to freelance photographer Bob Parent's fourteen rolls of film, which he took that night. Two of Parent's photos, one of the young crowd, arms uplifted, crushing the stage, captioned "Jazz buffs digging Ellington at Newport Festival," accompanied Harman's copy.

> Ellington's Paul Gonsalves was ripping off a fast but insinuating solo on his tenor saxophone, his fancies dandled by a bounding beat on the bass and drums (Jimmy Woode and Sam Woodyard). The Duke himself tweaked an occasional fragment on the high piano. Gradually, the beat began to ricochet from the audience as more and more fans began to clap hands on the offbeats until the crowd was one vast, rhythmic chorus, yelling its approval. There were howls of "More! More!" And there was dancing in the aisles. One young blonde woman broke loose from her escort, and rioted solo around the field, while a young man encouraged her by shouting "Go, go, go!" Festival officials began to fear that something like a rock 'n' roll riot was taking place. One of them was pleading with beaming Band-leader Ellington to stop. When the fellow's entreaties got too emphatic, Duke wagged a soothing finger at him and said mildly, "Don't be rude to the artists."
>
> The event last month marked not only a turning point in one concert; it confirmed a turning point in a career. The big news was something that the whole jazz world had long hoped to hear: the Ellington band was once again the most exciting thing in the business. Ellington himself had emerged from a long period of quiescence and was once again bursting with ideas and inspiration.

Ellington and Columbia seized on the promotional value inherent in the cover story, both for the maestro's comeback and the album. It suited all parties concerned to have it that the Newport performance inspired *Time* to do the cover story, but it was merely the hook. Still, *Time* was not a niche jazz magazine but a national one. As Columbia was selling albums to a national audience, the cover story was a timely blessing for Ellington's appearance in the label's September catalog.

The Ellington material was to be part of George Avakian's four-volume offering of Columbia artists who were performing at the festival. "I expected it to be something like that," said the record producer. "Separate jackets. All four packaged in a box. You could buy them separately, or get the volume in a box. But I didn't know what I would get."

Volume 1 would be Louis Armstrong on side 1 and Eddie Condon on side 2. The second volume was Dave Brubeck and trombonists Jay and Kai, each with a side. The third volume was one side with four tracks of Duke Ellington from his second set of the night, along with side 2 of the Buck Clayton All Stars with Coleman Hawkins. The fourth volume was all Ellington, with the three movements of the "Suite" on side 1 and "Jeep's Blues" and "Diminuendo and Crescendo in Blue" on side 2.

"As it was," said Avakian, referring to the Ellington content on volume 3 of the set, "I had to pad out Duke's portion with some 'repeat' repertoire I did not want. I wanted to avoid spill-overs of two artists on one side of an LP because of a lack of fresh repertoire.

When I had to do so anyway with Duke, I correctly figured I would get away with it because Duke had dominated the Festival and there would be no protests."

Immediately following Newport, the Ellington band faced a full set of road bookings. The next day, they were scheduled to perform at Danceland, Ocean Park, New London, Connecticut. Then it was a return to New York for Duke to participate in a Monday night jazz forum at the Overseas Press Club. Tuesday, the tenth, they hit the road for the rest of the month through New England and Canada. As it had been for decades, it was a nonstop summer. Whatever the stakes for Duke personally, for the band, Newport had been only one gig among many. The only window for any studio rerecording of the Newport material had been the Monday morning, otherwise the band's off-day in New York. The initial 9:00 A.M. call for the band at Columbia's Studio D was understandably not well received by some of the musicians.

George Avakian arrived at Studio D at 8:00 for the setup and a preview of the concert tapes. On the Friday, when he had booked the session by phone from Newport, he hadn't needed to prep his studio team. "I did not talk to the re-mixing engineer George Knuerr. Not necessary, because from past projects I knew what George and I could do. Nor did I talk to the studio engineers, Harold Chapman and Fred Plaut, for the same reason. All I had needed to do was book the time and leave word in general terms of what I thought we would do. We had a great team.

"My goal was to save Duke's neck, pride, and reputation by salvaging what was the most important element in his mind of the performance at Newport—the 'Suite,' which, God knows, we could not release with glaring mistakes, and could not refuse to release after all the pre-concert publicity. It was Duke's first extended composition in so many years, not to mention what it would've done to the festival itself. It would have made Duke a laughing stock."

Duke and Strayhorn ambled into the studio around 10:00. Avakian and the pair listened to the "Suite" tapes first to determine what needed fixing. The producer recalled thinking the tapes had recorded performances that were "good enough" and proposed that he "just make patches."

"Oh no, no," said Ellington. "You really don't know the composition. Let's remake the whole thing and then decide afterwards."

"As Duke pointed out to me," Avakian recalled, "there were many more corrections needed than I was aware of, and by rerecording long sections, I would not have to sweat matching short inserts. He was absolutely right."

Sometime around eleven thirty, the band members began arriving.

The first track they tackled was the "Diminuendo and Crescendo in Blue." Although Avakian appreciated the need for studio work to fix Ellington's acknowledged problems with the "Suite," he knew that a recording capturing "Diminuendo and Crescendo in Blue" would alone make for a hit LP. Because Gonsalves had begun and continued to play his solo into the VOA mike—or at least off the Columbia mike—the recording engineers, Ad Theroux and Buddy Graham, had to boost the gain to bring forward his sax.

Although the VOA mike was found to have captured the solo fully, Gonsalves may not have played into it in error, despite what many have come to believe. In concert, recalled both Ellington nephew Michael James and Gonsalves fan John Monteiro, the saxophonist would frequently and expressively move with his whole body as he dug into solos. As such, Gonsalves might often play off-mike as a way of eliminating the distraction of any thought of his hitting the mike or the stand with his instrument. Ellington had a different assessment of his performance style, writing that Gonsalves was "shy, hates microphones, and loves *au naturel.*" Hence, it may have been that the VOA mike just happened to be more directionally focused toward or nearer to where Gonsalves happened to be moving with his horn. As for the Columbia mike, when Theroux and Graham boosted the gain, along with the signal of the solo came a rising torrent of ambient noise with catalytic shouts from Duke, the band, and a surging audience.

In any event in the studio that Monday, "the first thing Duke wanted to do was to try to have Gonsalves play over the start of his solo," said Avakian. "I think Duke had the band and Gonzales play the beginning of it, and after listening to the tape itself agreed."

In his 2004 interview with Phil Schaap, trumpeter Willie Cook similarly remembered Ellington trying to re-create the performance in the studio.

"It's hopeless," Ellington said in the control room after comparing what he heard live in the studio to what was on the Newport tape. "Let's forget it."

"I know one thing: We didn't run any tape," said Avakian.

What they did run were attempts to augment Ellington's grunted exhortations from the piano. Schaap, while producing the 1999 reissue of *Ellington at Newport 1956 (Complete),* and Sony engineer Mark Wilder found a number of studio dubs of Ellington shouting "Go Paul!" Said Schaap, "There were many, many attempts to make it sound like it was that night." Bandsmen Russell Procope and Paul Gonsalves separately told him that Columbia wanted Ellington to rerecord the whole concert performance. Duke was quite steamed. Moreover, "Ellington was disputing the contract," said Schaap, "and the contract wasn't signed until either later that day or later in the week, and Irving Townsend was the agent of its being signed."

Ellington and his producer now turned their attention to the "Suite," which the band rerecorded along with Johnny Hodges doing alternate takes of his intro of "I Got It Bad" and "Jeep's Blues." The former number in the concert recording was marred by two serious squeaks as Hodges bent his reed during his first phrasings. Acceptable in the gritty, one-time reality of the actual performance, it would not bear repeated listening as a live performance on record. The corrected "I Got It Bad" would appear on the third volume in the Newport box set. Despite the studio recording of "Jeep's Blues," they would go with the original concert version as the first track on side 2 of volume 4. Giving the live LP its own dramatic flow, Avakian chose to put "Jeep's Blues" before the "Diminuendo," reversing the night's running order, thus ending the side with the explosive climax of Cat Anderson's high-note trumpet over the full sixteen-member band and the cresting roars of a truly ecstatic audience of seven thousand clamoring for more.

As for the decision made to include "Jeep's Blues" and the "Diminuendo," "there was never any doubt that was going to be on the album, come what may," said Avakian. "I don't know if Duke listened to all of those. He was interested in the big composition. Strayhorn, I think later on, maybe not even the same day, listened to everything with me, because I was so concerned to make sure that this was going to be just what Duke wanted, because he was so worried about the entire project. I don't think he had any input particularly in what should be put on there or not. He was worried about the big work and getting as decent a sound as possible on the Gonsalves solo. But that was definitely secondary to the long composition."

Avakian still had to compress Father O'Connor's rambling introduction of the band, which in any case had been for the opening of the first set, after Duke and his men had played the national anthem. On side 1 of the record, O'Connor's edited introduction would be followed by Ellington introducing the first section of his "Suite." Ellington's remarks and those introducing the second section had to be rerecorded. At Newport, Ellington had struggled with the introductions, looking for words and saying vaguely that both movements had been "tentatively titled." On the record, Ellington says casually—without stumbling—that the sections are "titled" "Festival Junction" and again (as the lead-in for track 2) "Blues to Be There."

On Tuesday Avakian started his editing. It was still the prestereo era and well before multichannel recording technology that would have made his job far easier. "Apart from tape splicing by hand and limited overlaying, the only tools we had were changing equalization, emphasizing or reducing sound level in narrowly selected frequencies, and the use of echo. The toughest job was to match the live sound."

The problems Avakian would have with the Ellington set were the same as he would have for the whole Newport project, particularly for the Louis Armstrong performance. At least, the Ellington band comprised the only artists Avakian would have to bring into the studio.

Avakian credited the Ellington musicians on the second side of the third disc of the set, "because that is the right place to do it." "I made a point of listing all the soloists who played in the 'Suite,' including even in the kind of buried passages."

Editing on the Ellington material took at least a week. When Avakian finished Ellington, he tackled Brubeck, then Armstrong, and finally the other Columbia artists, which he recalled altogether took "about another week."

His next task was to focus on promoting and marketing the four-volume Newport set, for which he was responsible, "one hundred percent from idea to point of sale." "After all, I knew more about the potential market than anyone else in the company." His strategy was to stress "the uniqueness of the venue and the event, as well as the excitement of the performances—the first time anything like this ever happened, and such events cannot ever be duplicated. As one can see, the emphasis after the fact was on 'Diminuendo and

Crescendo in Blue.' It was the most salable thing in the whole package. The other five artists could not compete for attention."

As soon as he completed the masters, Avakian started writing his liner notes. It was standard that he would write them, although he wouldn't do so for every release he produced. "I just wrote liner notes for the ones that I felt like writing. That was perfectly normal. Basically I was the editor. I had a very free hand. I didn't even have a recording budget, because the top albums, once they really got started, were so successful that I could do anything I wanted to. Literally. That's why I didn't have any trouble planning this, because if I wanted to do it, 'That's fine. George knows what the hell he is doing. Look at the money that's coming in.' The money that came in eventually in the pop album department was unbelievable. The profits ran in the millions of dollars."

Columbia considered *Ellington at Newport* a pop album. "Not only that, we didn't separate the jazz releases from the pop releases," Avakian continued. "They all came out in one release. No separation within the release, once a month. We put out maybe fifteen to eighteen albums a month."

"Diminuendo and Crescendo in Blue" would be Avakian's hook. "Overshadowing everything else," his liner notes began, "including the introduction of a new work written expressly for this recording at Newport, Duke Ellington's performance of 'Diminuendo and Crescendo in Blue' in the last set of the 1956 Festival turned into one of the most extraordinary moments in the history of this annual event.

"Within an hour, reporters and critics were buzzing about it. By next morning, it was generally conceded to have been one of the most exciting performances any of them had ever heard. All agreed that it was a triumph of the good old rocking (R&B, if you will) blues beat which has been too often missing in jazz in the last fifteen years."

For Avakian's generation the performance was a throwback to the prewar salad days of the Swing Era. For others it captured the mood of the summer and like another set of performances, Elvis on television, the future direction of pop for a new generation of maturing baby boomers. Perhaps, erroneously after years of bebop and its successor jazz subgenres, Avakian was subconsciously rather hoping that jazz-as-swing would make a comeback as America's pop music.

"Neil Fujita [Columbia director of design and packaging] had everything ready for the covers around July 24." A studio close-up of Ellington graced the cover. On the flip side, six of Don Hunstein's photos were arrayed above the copy visually telling Avakian's story beneath. To the right of the track listings was an afternoon shot of Ellington in the backstage area and another, a head shot of drummer Jo Jones, captioned "Jo Jones—unsung hero?" Just below was a string of four photos: Paul Gonsalves before the mike, with a recognizable Avakian in silhouette in the foreground, with the caption beginning "Gonsalves digs in." Another two were of Ellington, one with him onstage, leading before the reed section, and the other, a shot through two microphones while he talks to Willis Conover in the VOA remote truck. On the far left was a close-up of Elaine Anderson in the throes of her dance. Said Avakian simply of the decision on that particular photo: "She was a very photogenic girl. She was an integral part of the moment, and that is why she went on the album."

Columbia added *Ellington at Newport* and the other three festival albums to the regular September release on a rush basis. "The buzz from the festival was already going into the magazines right away," said the producer. "There was the *Time* magazine. We had a great launching pad there. We knew that we had a strong product, and we pushed it. I think that the concentration had to be on [the *Ellington at Newport* volume], because it was the most spectacular thing that everybody had already written about already."

The album was "the most promoted jazz release of the year. All of them." As it was a first-time outdoor live recording for an album, it was technically noteworthy, a "historical event. That was it," Avakian continued. "When the push started for Christmas, the promotion was basically aimed at the entire four-volume set. But very quickly, everybody started talking about 'Diminuendo and Crescendo,' and so people began to think of *Ellington at Newport* as one LP."

Ellington at Newport remained on the charts into July 1957 and eventually became the top selling record of Duke's career.

Gary Giddins, in his *Visions of Jazz: The First Century,* pressed home the significance of the Newport '56 audience as a legitimate artistic element in the recording of "Diminuendo and Crescendo in Blue":

> Consider Ellington's 1956 Newport triumph: Was it the amazing twenty-seven-chorus blues intermezzo by Paul Gonsalves that landed Ellington on the cover of *Time,* or was it the crowd's response to it? When the album was released, producer and annotator George Avakian seemed to have no doubt when he included one photo of the young woman whose spontaneous dancing started the cheering and another of Jo Jones, who used a rolled-up newspaper to incite the rhythm section. The album was designed to make you feel as though you were there; as good as the music is, the energy of the *event* pushed it over the top—and would have been unthinkable within the isolation of a recording studio.

In reviewing the album for *Down Beat* in 1956, Nat Hentoff wrote:

> Then came the deluge, the "Diminuendo and Crescendo" with the 27 rocking choruses in between by Paul Bunyon Gonsalves that turned the final Newport night into Dionysian rites and convinced nearly everyone present, including me, that a memorable event was occurring. Hearing the phenomenon several months later, away from the charged open air volcanic atmosphere, I feel that the emotional brush fire that ignited and united the audience remains an indelible memory. . . . It's also kicks to hear and feel Duke's vitality on piano and in his vocal

exhortations. And certainly, there is a gripping, rising excitement in the remarkable length and spare consistency of Gonsalves' solo over a rhythm section rocking in a uniquely heated groove (and aided by the coxswain-strength of Jo Jones, an assist the notes explain). And the long, climbing ensemble close over a gyrating, shouting audience of 7,500 is also an experience that will chill you.

Not to say Hentoff's review was a complete rave. "I am afraid the music that caused the conflagration doesn't wholly hold up," he wrote, adding later that Gonsalves "wasn't saying too much except rhythmically."

Whatever the quality of the recording, the music, or the solo, the album was more. It was a documentary record of the transformative and defining experience that for many was Newport '56. Like the hot collectors of the thirties, many postwar fans valued their records, as serious readers value their books and almost define themselves and others by their important ones. LPs by Baez, Miles, Dylan, or the Dead served as totems in their passage to postadolescent or in some cases an enduring adult identity. Moreover, only a label like Columbia, a division of the CBS media conglomerate, could give such a totem a mass effect truly continental.

The release of *Ellington at Newport* coincided with Arlene Avakian's start as a freshman psychology major at Alfred University, in distant and rural western New York.

At the time not a serious student, Arlene, now professor and director of women's studies at the University of Massachusetts, Amherst, defined herself as a jazz fan with a record player to boot. Few students, including her music-major roommate, had phonographs or listened to music in their dorm rooms. They were, she said, "more into the Frank Sinatra kind of pop, not the rock and roll stuff. I don't remember people listening to Elvis Presley, but we used to go to this bar to dance, and there was a lot of rock and roll there." The next autumn, Arlene and her friends were dancing to calypso star and later civil rights advocate Harry Belafonte's "Island in the Sun," from the film of the same name about interracial romance, and the following winter the smash hit instrumental "Tequila."

"But I'd been to Newport," she boasted. "If people didn't know about it, that was their loss. I was so consoled by the idea that here I had been on this kind of ground floor for jazz that I was very assertive. I listened to jazz. I was a missionary for jazz."

Listening to *Ellington at Newport* enabled her to relive and hold on to a piece of a weekend of wonder. "I think this is particularly true, because I had been so really ostracized when I was in high school in New Jersey. So it was really important that I had this place where I felt like these are my people."

The record also served her missionary purpose. In December 1957, midway through her second year, Ellington played a dance engagement at Alfred. To prepare his way, Arlene played the record for two solid weeks in advance of the Maestro's coming. " 'Listen,' " she recalled announcing to the unknowing. " 'You have to understand who's coming. Let's understand who's coming. You don't understand, this is Duke Ellington. He is fabulous. You have to listen to this record.' Oh, they thought I was a little crazy, but they listened to it."

The particular track that would capture them was "Diminuendo and Crescendo in Blue." "I played it endlessly. Once Ellington came and went, and people respected him, I remember saying to them, 'See?! See?! See how great he is?!' I was really a missionary, and this was my Bible. The 'Diminuendo and Crescendo in Blue' was my Bible."

16

The Columbia Formula

From Niche to Mainstream

In 1955 Columbia Records had introduced its Walking Eye logo, which replaced the magic notes and microphone, for decades staple Columbia images on its records, advertising, and promotion. The legs depicted a phonograph stylus, the eye a record, but in a manner refraining a teaming with a secular omniscience—CBS Television's Eye logo, which the network, the label's parent, first aired in 1951 during station breaks. The logo decision, taken the same year that Columbia launched its record club, was indicative: Columbia was positioning itself far above the niche music labels, branding itself as a media conglomerate's division with national reach into the mainstream suburban markets.

George Avakian was ready to leave Columbia by the fall of 1957. He made his exit in early '58 to join his friend and West Coast jazz producer Richard Bock as a partner in Bock's Pacific Jazz Records as it became World Pacific Records. One of Avakian's projects was to produce pianist, band leader, and arranger Gil Evans, with whom he had worked at Columbia with Miles Davis. The album was *New Bottle, Old Wine*.

The following year, two of his former Columbia colleagues, Jim Conkling and Hal Cook, had moved to Warner Bros. to launch that film studio's record label. While still at Columbia, Conkling had become in 1957 the first president of the newly formed National Academy of Recording Arts and Sciences, now famous for its Grammy awards. Conkling was a force in music; hence, his and Cook's Warner label held promise for the producer. When Avakian came aboard, his task was principally to build the pop catalog. The film studio wanted to record its contract actor Tab Hunter, and Avakian produced the young star for the record division's first charted single, "Jealous Heart." He also brought to the label rockabilly stars the Everly Brothers and stand-up comic Bob Newhart. In the jazz category he signed drummer Chico Hamilton, who with his Newport '56 performance of the haunting "Blue Sands" had primed the audience for Ellington's extraordinary second set.

In 1962 Avakian went to the pop album division of RCA. There he signed and recorded Brubeck saxophonist Paul Desmond, who had the freedom to record as a free agent, and New Orleans jazz and pop trumpeter Al Hirt. Perhaps his greatest coup for RCA was to return tenor saxophonist Sonny Rollins to recording after three years of self-imposed retirement. Avakian produced this serious and somewhat mystical talent's dramatic classic *The Bridge,* noteworthy among other things for John Hall's smooth guitar in place of a more familiar piano accompaniment.

By the end of 1963 Avakian left recording. On occasion he would work for small jazz labels, notably Chiaroscuro Records, while producing independently for Columbia and the Ertegun brothers at Atlantic. He then moved into management, first for tenor saxophonist and flutist Charles Lloyd and later for a former member of Lloyd's quartet, the cryptic pianist Keith Jarrett.

In the nineties Avakian worked for Columbia Legacy on reissues of many of his Columbia sessions from the fifties. Among the familiar reissued titles were *Armstrong Plays Handy, Miles Davis and Gil Evans: The Complete Columbia Studio Recordings,* and *Miles Davis and John Coltrane: The Complete Columbia Recordings,* to which he contributed annotations. Throughout his later life he maintained a working interest in Avakian Brothers, the family's carpet business, and to this day has remained a frequent interviewee and lecturer on the jazz circuit worldwide.

The Columbia Records that Avakian left behind was poised for greater glory as recording technology advanced from the era of hi-fi to stereo. Before leaving the label, he produced *Miles Ahead*. Originally released in May 1957, it was Davis's first album with Gil Evans. The following year, it was remixed in stereo when Columbia began stereo recording.

Cal Lampley, Avakian's assistant and Newport '56 veteran, produced with Teo Macero Davis and Evans's follow-on collaboration *Porgy and Bess.* The trumpeter and arranger would collaborate on a third album, *Sketches of Spain,* also produced by Macero. Earlier, when Lampley left Columbia to join Avakian as his assistant at Warners, Macero produced with Irving Townsend the Davis 1959 classic *Kind of Blue*.

Released in August 1959, *Kind of Blue* was Davis's best-selling album and the all-time best-selling jazz record, certified triple platinum in sales by the Recording Industry Association of America. For many, it is the greatest jazz album ever.

The year 1959 also saw the release of the Dave Brubeck Quartet's *Time Out,* which similarly provided Columbia with major critical and commercial success. Also produced by Macero, its cover an original abstract artwork by art director Neil Fujita, *Time Out* was musically noteworthy for its unusual-for-jazz time signatures. On release, however, critics gave it negative reviews. It was not until 1961, its best year of sales, that the album went platinum, reaching number two in *Billboard's* pop chart. At the same time Paul Desmond's

Gil Evans (left), George Avakian, and Miles Davis in the studio, probably during the 1957 recording of *Miles Ahead*. This photo was taken by Dennis Stock, New York Magnum photojournalist who apprenticed to *Life*'s Gjon Mili and was known for his images of James Dean. ::: *Courtesy of the Institute of Jazz Studies at Rutgers University and Sony BMG Music Entertainment.*

title cut charted number five as a single in the adult contemporary category. Like *Kind of Blue, Time Out* became another best-known and best-selling jazz offering. It was also a perennial sixties favorite on the Columbia Record Club list, generating huge sales. After eight years of operation, the club in 1963 accounted for 10 percent of all record music revenue, giving Columbia deep penetration into suburban homes.

The monumental success of these two jazz classics makes for a textbook case in mainstream marketing, arguably prototyped by Avakian and *Ellington at Newport.* With Davis and Brubeck the label had validated his gambles four years earlier with a business model for pulling niche artists and music into the younger edge of mass-market mainstream jazz fans born during the war. Yet as huge and as successful as it was, the 1950s Columbia was principally characterizing and catering to an older suburban mass market, at its heart the aging swing generation, whose tastes had been changed by the war and the postwar prosperity.

The bitter truth was that the core pop business of the label was not jazz but what would later become known as MOR, middle of the road, a creature of the late forties and fifties business model proven by Columbia Records president Goddard Lieberson and his pop division chief Mitch Miller. MOR was best reflected in the standard offerings of the Columbia Record Club: Rogers and Hammerstein and Lerner and Lowe musicals (and film sound tracks), notably *West Side Story, Camelot,* and *The Sound of Music;* easy listening artists like the Ray Conniff Singers, bandleader Percy Faith, and soloists like club singer Jerry Vale and Broadway star Robert Goulet. Perhaps most notable was Johnny Mathis, who joined the label in 1956, left in 1963, and returned in 1968, whose time with Columbia was the longest of any of its recording artists. Similarly positioned in 1962 was Tony Bennett, whom the label broke into the mainstream with his epic "I Left My Heart in San Francisco."

By the end of the fifties, Lieberson's corporate higher-ups had studied the demographics and concluded that the increasing purchasing power of record-buying baby boomers born after the war would not support his model into the sixties. Lieberson thus looked to a producing friend from the thirties who wrote the book on transforming niche into mainstream taste, a proven visionary one beat ahead of the pulse of American popular music: John Hammond. The producer rejoined Columbia in 1959, voicing disgust at the label's purveyance of what he called "bland music for the masses." For just over five years, Hammond had been outside the channel circulating in the eddies, producing jazz for the niche label Vanguard Records, which among other things would break folksinger Joan Baez and later record Hammond's son, the amplified blues guitarist John Hammond Jr. For Columbia Records Hammond would serve as producer, director of talent acquisition, and vice president.

When Hammond returned to Columbia, he applied his talent-spotting gift not to jazz but to black gospel. His first production effort with the label was a throwback to his late thirties recordings of the "From Spirituals to Swing" concerts. The record, *Shakin' the Rafters,* was a live recording of Newark, New Jersey's Abyssinian Baptist Church choir. While moving around the gospel circuit, he discovered the following year the young Aretha Franklin, then a teenage soloist from Detroit fronting for her minister father's church choir. Hammond recorded her and unsuccessfully tried to position her as a pop-jazz artist, but her two Columbia records didn't sell. The professional relationship never fully gelled. Franklin moved to Atlantic Records, where the Erteguns were better able to position her to become in time the soul diva for the sixties generation.

Hammond's next foray drew from his continued involvement with the Newport Jazz Festival. In 1959 George Wein added a full day of folk music to his jazz offering and the following year held a separate weekend of folk, the first official Newport Folk Festival. The political message of the folk revival was civil rights. Not surprisingly, Hammond was excited by the same confluence of politics and art in sixties folk music as he'd experienced in thirties swing. In 1961 Hammond signed the veteran folk Pied Piper and long-neck, five-string banjoist Pete Seeger, who, blacklisted during the McCarthy era, had been recording for Moses Ache's niche folk label, Folkways, and playing the college circuit. The time was right. The nation had moved forward into a new decade with a new administration in Washington and its young charismatic leader, John F. Kennedy.

Seeger was more a traditional folk purist than a contemporary songwriter. It would be a younger, rising talent through which Hammond would help define the pop music of the new decade. Notwithstanding Lieberson's support, Columbia executives, unimpressed by the sluggish sales from his first album, tagged this new voice "Hammond's folly." The world would know him as Bob Dylan.

In the years to come, Columbia signed other folk talents deemed to possess pop potential, notably the singing duo Simon and Garfunkel. Hammond nurtured another folk songwriter, the Canadian poet and vocalist Leonard Cohen, and moved him into the pop mainstream. As Columbia had demonstrated for jazz with Davis and Brubeck, the label had the corporate clout to elevate its artists to become pop, as opposed to merely cult, icons. Columbia was in a class by itself in comparison to Vanguard, Electra, Prestige, Verve, and Folkways, to name a few labels that carved a niche in folk. While Vanguard can be said to have had relative success with folk guitarist and singer Joan Baez, none of these labels had a national market penetration like Columbia to fashion their artists into mainstream stars with a crossover into pop.

As the decade advanced, Hammond would have one major jazz find in guitarist George Benson. He produced in the mid-sixties two albums: *It's Uptown* and the follow-on, *The George Benson Cookbook*. Columbia, however, would not go so far as to embrace the cutting-edge jazz movement of the time, free jazz, perhaps because the sound was too inaccessible to be commercially viable for a national audience.

Into the seventies Hammond would recycle his Dylan model of the singer-songwriter. The pitch would be the same: "the new Dylan." He first tried with the darkly quirky Loudon Wainwright with one album noted for its hit novelty song "Dead Skunk." Wainwright did two more albums for the label but was too much in the Greenwich Village mold. The nation had moved beyond the acoustic sensitivities of Downtown Bohemia. The locus of vision in the seventies was across the Hudson amidst the amplified and cinematic fantasies of the blue-collar Jersey suburbs. There Hammond hit the jackpot with an electric guitarist, Bruce Springsteen.

The Boss was Hammond's last find as a Columbia man. In 1975 he retired to become an independent record producer, consultant, and chairman of the board of Hammond Music Enterprises. His final discovery came in the eighties via his blues-playing son in the form of an Austin, Texas, electric blues guitarist, Stevie Ray Vaughan, whom he brought to his former label.

Columbia applied the niche-to-mainstream model in other genres. In the late fifties it took *Louisiana Hayride* country radio star Johnny Horton into pop, using as a vehicle a number of so-called saga songs. Two capitalized on high-profile film releases. The first, the 1959 chart topper "The Battle of New Orleans," followed the success of Cecil B. DeMille's *The Buccaneer,* which climaxed with a battle scene said to last longer than the actual engagement itself. The second was his 1960 ode "Sink the Bismarck," which coincided with the distribution of the British war film of the same name. A third was "North to Alaska," the signature song of John Wayne's similarly titled film, released in November 1960 just after Horton died in a car crash.

Columbia's greatest country star was Johnny Cash, who signed in 1958 and remained until 1986. The 1968 album *Johnny Cash at Folsom Prison* revitalized his career, made him an international star, and popularized the genre. From that album came the celebrated crossover hit "Folsom Prison Blues," at a time when rock sales finally buried those of jazz and all other forms—the year the greatest bulge of baby boomers attained their majority.

The label had been slow to embrace the youth market. In 1961 it made a fitful attempt when it signed white doo-wop star Dion DiMucci of Dion and the Belmonts. Two years later its West Coast office brought aboard Columbia's first rock and roll group, Paul Revere and the Raiders, produced by Doris Day's son Terry Melcher.

Another Melcher-produced band utilized the crossover strategy to leverage the folk scene to commercialize Bob Dylan's music for a wider audience, indeed paving the way for Dylan himself to make the break into a national audience in his own 1965 LPs and the single "Like a Rolling Stone." The group was the Byrds, who in early '65 recorded an electric version of Dylan's "Mr. Tambourine Man" with their signature folk-rock sound. Columbia released the debut album of the same name featuring electric covers of a number of Dylan songs. In June the single topped the U.S. charts, as did the album.

Columbia thus finally entered the rock business. Observers have it that the corporate driver behind the entry was Clive Davis, a lawyer who shifted from the legal department to the pop division in 1964. Three years later the label fully embraced rock when Goddard Lieberson was kicked upstairs and Davis rose to the Columbia Records presidency. During 1967's Summer of Love, Davis attended the seminal Monterey Pop Festival, held at a venue made famous by nine years of Monterey Jazz Festivals, and immediately signed festival showstoppers Janis Joplin and Big Brother and the Holding Company. During his tenure Columbia followed suit, signing among others such sixties stalwart aggregations as the blues band Electric Flag, the Latin blues band Santana, the rock big band Chicago, and the R&B band Earth, Wind, and Fire, plus pianist-singer-songwriter Billy Joel. After three years of Davis's reign, the company doubled its market share. By the time he left, he had increased the label's rock volume from 15 percent in 1967 to more than 50 percent in 1973.

Davis continued the crossover strategy into the late sixties and seventies as rock completed its domination of pop music. Bob Dylan and Johnny Cash recorded Dylan's "Girl from the North Country," which in 1969 appeared on *Nashville Skyline*, Dylan's first country album. The label also applied the strategy to jazz during the 1967–75 jazz fusion period. Noteworthy was the jazz fusion band Blood, Sweat & Tears and the 1969 release of the Miles Davis LP *Bitches Brew*, which blended his trumpet with electric guitar and synthesizers to perform a music of blues structures and modal improvisation. Also crossing into rock and pop was jazz pianist Herbie Hancock with his 1973 Columbia release *Headhunters*. The Davis era imploded in 1973 when Columbia fired him amid government investigations into financial irregularities in the record industry.

When the decade of the seventies began, jazz accounted for far less than 10 percent of all record sales, while the pop genres were in the 70 percent range and above. Riding now on pop, Columbia moved into the eighties, during which it enjoyed worldwide success with the number-two biggest selling album of all time: Michael Jackson's *Thriller,* released in 1982 through its Epic Records division. In 1988 Sony acquired CBS Records and its Columbia Records unit, becoming in 1991 Sony Music Entertainment.

Recording technology advanced from vinyl records to magnetic tape cassettes in the mid-sixties, first as eight-track and then as the familiar Philips cassettes. In 1982 the first digital audio five-inch CD discs appeared, foreshadowing the merger of the music and computer industries. In 1988 CD sales surpassed sales of vinyl, finally ending the era of the LP.

In 2004 Sony merged its music division with Bertelsmann AG's BMG unit to form Sony BMG. Ironically, BMG had acquired Columbia Records' fifties rival RCA in the mid-eighties, making for what now is a media conglomerate that is truly global.

The LP *Ellington at Newport* figured in the 1999 Duke Ellington centennial, although not by design. Three years earlier Phil Schaap, who had already won Grammys for work on reissues, pitched to Sony the idea of a remixed CD of the Newport concert. At the time he and Sony's catalog division, Legacy Recordings, which reissues classic LPs for Columbia, were releasing his Miles Davis–Gil Evans collection, which would win him two more Grammys.

Schaap and other jazz researchers knew that VOA had recorded at Newport festivals. In 1995 Larry Appelbaum, the Library of Congress jazz specialist and studio engineer who is also a Washington deejay, discovered the festival recordings while preserving the VOA collection after the library received the broadcast agency's archive of cultural programs. Appelbaum passed the word. A number of interested parties including George Avakian, Dan Morgenstern, and jazz musician and scholar Loren Schoenberg made the trek to Washington to hear the tapes. "I remember Loren Schoenberg's reaction quite clearly," said Appelbaum, "especially the look of joy on his face when he heard Gonsalves' solo."

Schaap, who knew Appelbaum from his own research at the Library of Congress, also came and left with the intent to pitch Sony on the remix. "But I knew from the flat transfer of 'Diminuendo and Crescendo in Blue' that the VOA tapes needed help sonically," said Schaap, "and that could only be done with the equipment Mark Wilder [Sony's transferring and mastering engineer] had here at the Sony studios in New York. So the difficult part of the process was the delay in getting the material released by VOA, and then the courier process and getting it returned."

"Once permissions were obtained, Sony/Columbia asked for copies of the entire concert," Appelbaum related. "They preferred to use their studios to do the transfers. So I hand-carried the tapes up to New York and back."

Schaap and Wilder married the VOA material and George Avakian's original Columbia tapes to produce *Ellington at Newport 1956 (Complete),* in effect blending two mono releases into one stereo. As for the celebrated "Diminuendo and Crescendo in Blue," the

Schaap remix relies on the VOA mike to bring forward the Gonsalves solo. For better or worse, what is missing in the 1999 CD is what Dan Morgenstern called "the ambiance of the event, the response to the music," which in his view "is more apparent on the [1956 release]." Listeners will have their own preferences for their own reasons. Whatever one's preference, each rendering captures a driving performance with all its mythic intensity.

17

Sleeping under a Fur Coat

No Longer the Rich Mrs. Anderson

One day, several months after her celebrated dance at Newport, Elaine Anderson received a phone call from a young friend who was a Fall River record store owner. "Elaine, I have a record here with your picture on it."

A photo of a clearly identifiable Elaine, Marilyn Monroe–like in the throes of her dance, had appeared on the front page of the *Newport Daily News* just after the festival, providing conversational fodder for those who knew her. News of a photo on the flip side of the Columbia LP promised her a national notoriety of sorts. When she first saw the photo, Elaine felt a measure of disappointment. A likeness it was not. Columbia had selected a photo in which her left forearm masked her features. The notoriety proved to be anonymous. The caption read: "The gal who launched 7,000 cheers."

Meeting George Avakian for the first time at Newport '57, Elaine asked the Columbia producer, "Why didn't you use a better picture?" "The lawyers were afraid if we used one where you could be identified, you would sue for violating your privacy." "Sue?" she replied. "I would've loved it."

Taken by her moxie, Avakian continued the conversation and recalled gallantly saying, "Watching you, I was dazzled." Their exchange began a lifelong association. Elaine and Larry Anderson mingled with Avakian during the 1957 concerts and spent a noteworthy after-hours evening with trumpeter Roy Eldridge. Having attended every festival since the first in 1954, Elaine, Larry, and their friends the Capuanos and LeSavoys were part of the in-crowd of locals who socialized with the organizers and musicians. Teddy LeSavoy in particular had become drinking buddies with Eldridge, pianist Erroll Garner, and former Basie and JATP tenor sax man Illinois Jacquet.

Data

[illegible]ises 5:20 Sets
[illegible]:09 A.M. 10:22
[illegible].M. 3:56 P.M.

[illegible]tures - high 73

Newport Daily News.

Vol. 112—NO. 231 NEWPORT, R. I., MONDAY, JULY 9, 1956 SIXTEEN [illegible]

BLONDE REALLY CATCHES JAZZ MOOD—Young spectator at Freebody Park gets caught up in rhythm of the sensational windup of the Newport Jazz Festival on Saturday, while audience stands on chairs in background for better look at excitement. (Daily News Photo).

THE DUKE IN ACTION—Duke Ellington, pianist-composer leads his band in a rousing finale at the Newport Jazz Festival. (Daily News Photo).

Ellington Brings Festival To Rip-Roaring Windup While Fans Shout, 'More'

By JAMES T. KAULL JR.

The third annual Newport Jazz Festival passed into history at 1 a. m. yesterday with an enthusiastic crowd of diehards still screaming, "More, more"

The windup Saturday night saw another 10,000-plus attendance, equalling and perhaps surpassing the jam at Freebody Park on Friday night. Counting the cut-down crowd during Thursday's rainy program and the "gates" at the afternoon forum and concert sessions, the overall attendance for the festival was close to 27,000.

Orderly madness reigned as the midnight hour passed at Freebody, with Duke Ellington and his big band scoring a smash hit. While Paul Gonslaves of Pawtucket was wailing away on a long blues number, the audience suddenly let loose with pent-up emotions.

Almost everyone stood up on seats There was general dancing in the aisles and on the uppermost levels of the concrete stadium. The crowd forced it way down near the stage, where roars of delight greeted every offering by the Ellington band.

By that hour, a good half of the audience had left the park, but those remaining were young enthusiasts who would willingly have stayed all night. The Duke declined Producer George Wein's nervous invitation to call it quits. Instead, he presented drummer Sam Woodyard in a rip-roaring finale which ended at 12:53 a. m. The field lights had long since been turned on, casting a glare through the chilly fog that had crept over the park.

With a final "Hope to see you all next year!" Ellington swung the band into its closing "Mood Indigo" theme and the 1956 festival ended.

Setting new records for any spector events in Newport, the final night had been an exciting one. Musically, it was perhaps tops for the three-night bill, with a tremendous critical success chalked up by Ellington and by the Teddy Wilson trio.

The crowd was a much more lively one, to say the least. Among the 10,000 fans (equal to one-quarter of the population of Newport), there were perhaps 50 who chose to make a nuisance of themselves. About a dozen of those became police problems including an out-of-town trio involved in a stabbing that could be blamed on drink, rather than an anything connected with jazz music.

Outside the gate, a crowd of late comers clamored for admission, but there were no more seats to be sold. At one point, a group of young hoodlums threatened to storm the wickets, but they were dispersed. Two firecrackers were set off outside with a loud bang.

For the most part, the frenzy was an exuberance of spirits that harmed no one, as young jazz-lovers bounced in their seats or exhorted performers onward with cries of "Go, go!" It was by far the liveliest scene of any of the annual festivals, with the uproar at the end even topping the excitement during the impromptu jam sessions at the Casino in 1954.

After the "ball" was over, Newport and the surrounding towns continued to throb as the patrons dispersed or sought entertainment in night spots, some of which stayed open until 4 a. m.

The Jamestown Ferry ran until 2:30 a. m. cleaning up stragglers. It had still been disgorging festival-bound passengers as late as 9 p. m. Saturday.

Throughout the city, restaurants, hotels and lodging houses were swamped Friday and Saturday. In fact, some jazz fans had spent Thursday or Friday night sleeping in the city police station, out in Middletown at St. Columba's Cemetery or in cars at beaches and on side streets.

Traffic on island highways was extremely heavy, as an estimated 4,000 cars sped patrons to and from the festival. Parking on Saturday night was again a problem near Freebody Park.

No one earned more credit than the police department, which had a score of patrolmen on duty inside and outside the field for three long nights. Traffic control was well-handled and the rush inside the park was better directed than in the festival's two previous years.

Firemen were also on duty at the park all three nights, helping to keep the aisles clear and standing by with Engine 5, which was in place at the northeast corner of the field at all times.

The big-league event got underway exactly at 8:30 p. m., with

(Continued on Page 4)

Cover page of the July 9, 1956, issue of the *Newport Daily News*. Photo of Elaine Anderson with caption reading, "BLONDE REALLY CATCHES JAZZ MOOD—Young spectator at Freebody Park gets caught up in rhythm of the sensational windup of the Newport Jazz Festival on Saturday, while audience stands on chairs in background for better look at excitement." ::: *Fred Anderson Collection.*

Sometime early in the '57 festival, Elaine also crossed paths with George Wein. "He asked me to behave myself," she recalled. On another occasion, George Avakian brought her to one of festival founder Elaine Lorillard's after-concert parties, where she sat for a long time with Erroll Garner. The apparent intimacy between the two irritated Martha Glaser, Garner's manager. "I thought this woman was going to kill me. I think Elaine [Lorillard] asked George to take me away. She didn't want any problems."

Elaine Anderson tended to remember contrarian vignettes. One such was the Sunday of the 1957 festival, when gospel singer Mahalia Jackson was preparing to sing at Newport's Trinity Episcopal Church along with a number of other gospel greats. "She was very nervous, and she said she had to have some cognac. In Rhode Island, you couldn't buy a bottle of cognac on a Sunday if you were God! Teddy LeSavoy went to his house—he had a house in Newport at the time—and gets this gorgeous bottle of cognac and gave it to Mahalia. I think she drank the whole thing in one gulp."

"Newport '56 had to be a seminal event for my mother," observed her son Rick, "although it wasn't at all a 'Whoops, I've now come out of my shell,' or what have you." Elaine was already a gifted extrovert in her own way. Her dance was more the tipping point in her high suburban life in Fall River and her million-dollar marriage.

By the winter of 1957–58, that marriage showed signs of fraying. Elaine's trips to New York and jaunts to joy spots in Miami, Havana, Rio, and elsewhere were not just failed cures for a cabin fever. In industrial Fall River her spirit was now imprisoned. In the spring of 1958, Larry agreed to let her represent her father at the annual convention of the Variety Club in London, England. A pioneer member, Harry Zeitz prevailed on his fellow members in Boston to allow his daughter to serve as his stand-in, although a Variety Club member she herself was not. Meeting some resistance, her benefactors, who included film director John Frankenheimer, saw to it that she was chosen, "much to the chagrin of a lot of the other women—wives—who were very angry."

In April 1958 Elaine thus joined the 956 attendees and Prince Philip, the head of London's Variety Club, for the twenty-second annual convention at the Savoy Hotel. It was a giddy time for her. At the Variety Club tea party at Windsor Castle, she was chosen to be one of a few women to be presented to Queen Elizabeth.

From London Larry had planned for her to join him at the 1958 Brussels World's Fair, which had opened just prior to her arrival in London. "That wasn't my cup of tea," said Elaine. "I skipped it. I went to Paris instead."

It proved to be a fateful getaway. On the plane to France, Elaine found herself sitting next to "probably the most gorgeous human being you'd ever want to meet in your whole life." The woman, a European, was in tears, apparently unwilling to "open up" and remaining "very secretive" for most of the flight. Yet just before landing, the dark-haired beauty offered to Elaine a measure of intrigue.

"Would you take my jewel case and take it through customs?" she asked an initially skeptical Elaine. "They know me in customs, and they always bother me. Just take it, and I'll meet you on the other side." Casting prudence to the wind, Elaine agreed, thereby

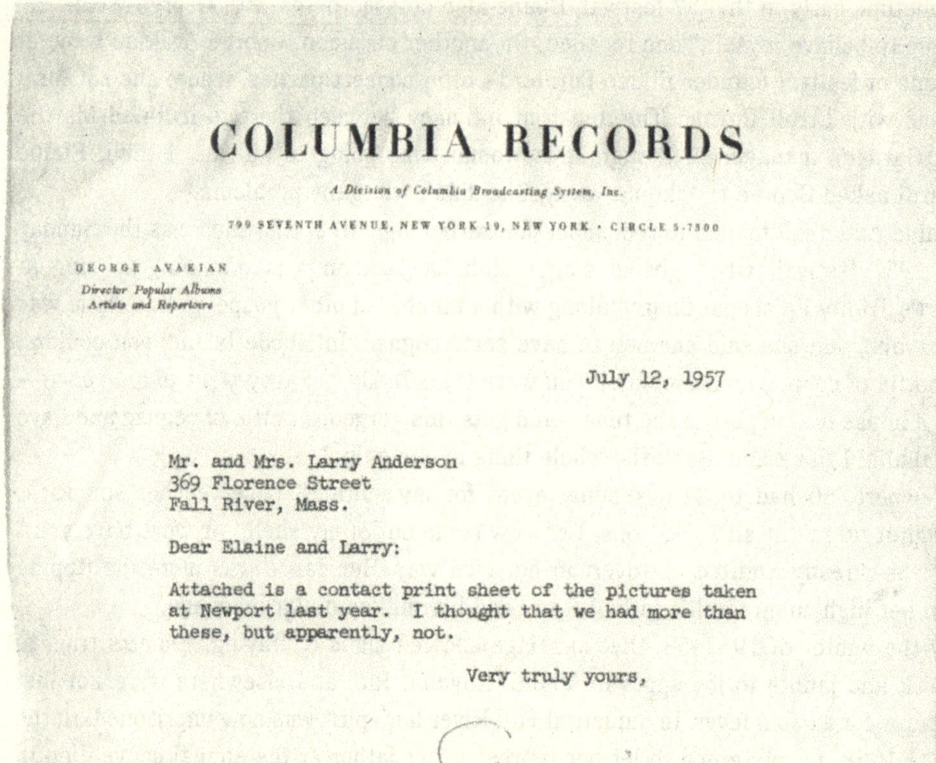

COLUMBIA RECORDS

A Division of Columbia Broadcasting System, Inc.

799 SEVENTH AVENUE, NEW YORK 19, NEW YORK · CIRCLE 5-7300

GEORGE AVAKIAN
Director Popular Albums
Artists and Repertoire

July 12, 1957

Mr. and Mrs. Larry Anderson
369 Florence Street
Fall River, Mass.

Dear Elaine and Larry:

Attached is a contact print sheet of the pictures taken at Newport last year. I thought that we had more than these, but apparently, not.

Very truly yours,

George

GA:ec

Am sending some LP's in the mail, separately — hope you enjoy them and thanks again for everything!

George Avakian's July 12, 1957, letter to Elaine and Larry Anderson following his discovery of her identity a year later, at Newport '57. ::: ***Fred Anderson Collection.***

embracing an uncertain promise of adventure. Clearing customs without a hitch, she found the woman and returned the case. Whether recognizing Elaine as a fellow vagabond or simply a mark, this most attractive vision asked about her arrangements in Paris. "I'm staying at the George V." "Why do you want to spend all that money?" "It's all been paid for." "We'll get your money back, and we'll move around the corner, and you can stay for two or three months with all the money you would've spent on that hotel."

A deal was thus struck, and Elaine was now on the lam. When the pair arrived at the Hotel George V just off the Champs-Elysees, Elaine's savvy companion went to the front desk and somehow managed to get all her money refunded. From there they skipped away to the Avenue Pierre, where she then booked them into the more modest Hotel Queen Elizabeth.

Elaine soon discovered that this mysterious European beauty was Swiss, one Francine Brandt, a sometime actress. One of her notable appearances had been in the Franco-American TV series *Captain Gallant of the Foreign Legion,* with Buster Crabbe. Filming in North Africa in 1954, she had played Tala, a sheik's daughter, in "Tala's Secret," the series' third episode. In real life, however, she played a somewhat different role: Francine Brandt was a courtesan. "I would call her," said Elaine, "the most expensive call girl in the world."

Brandt moved in a fashionable European circle already characterized as the jet set. Among her acquaintances were the Franco-Russian filmmaker Roger Vadim and the British playwright John Osborne, whose individual creative successes had thrust both into prominence in 1956. Vadim, the son of a diplomat and one of the founders of the French New Wave in cinema, owed his sudden fame to his film *And God Created Woman,* which starred his young wife, Brigitte Bardot, and made her one of the faces of the fifties. Osborne was also basking in fame as one of Britain's Angry Young Men, the new generation of writers who were upending upper-middle-class arts and letters with their working-class sensibilities. In 1956, the year of the Suez Crisis, which signaled for many Brits the end of empire, Osborne's seminal play *Look Back in Anger* changed the face of London theater.

"He found me fascinating," Elaine maintained; "would you believe that?"

Osborne and Brandt had begun their two-year affair when the playwright was in New York that winter during the Broadway run of his play. Trysts continued in Beverly Hills, Jamaica, Geneva, London, and Paris. In Paris Osborne evidently projected onto Elaine what he saw in Brandt. Elaine was in no way a naif. Vivacious to a fault, she could easily trade on the showbiz associations of her father, as well as those from her own wartime Hollywood acting career. By Elaine's account, during one long walk along a Parisian boulevard, Osborne offered that he didn't understand how she could accept living in a provincial American town and not a European capital. He felt she belonged elsewhere. Perhaps with a measure of theatricality, he proclaimed, "You're a courtesan."

In some ways Elaine could see herself wearing the same mantle as Francine. Both had acting careers of sorts. Both could be seen as kept women—she by Larry, but without the apparent freedoms enjoyed by Francine, whose stage was the world.

Elaine Anderson in Paris, May 1958. This photo was taken by Bill Crespinel, who later took photos for *Penthouse* magazine. *Fred Anderson Collection.*

From Paris Elaine continued her spree by accompanying Brandt to the Riviera and Rome. In the south of France Brandt introduced her to such personages as the British actor Sir Lawrence Olivier, Dominican playboy and race-car driver Porfirio Rubirosa, and American Express president and CEO Ralph T. Reed. Brandt's circle extended to the

Greek shipping tycoon Aristotle Onassis. At some point in the late spring, Onassis was entertaining the former British prime minister and wartime leader Sir Winston Churchill aboard his yacht *Christina.* Brandt went, but Elaine didn't.

Elaine's extended fling was winding down. She and Brandt had joined Vadim and Bardot, who was in Rome finishing work on a film, possibly *En cas de malheur* with the prewar French star Jean Gabin. "I was on the set with her at five o'clock in the morning," Elaine recalled. She also connected with the irreverently witty Ava Gardner, who had just broken up with Frank Sinatra and was living in Spain. Elaine had met Gardner some years before, when for her father she chaperoned the star while she was in New Bedford for a Zeiterion film premiere. In 1958 Gardner was in Rome finishing *The Naked Maja,* a film about the Spanish painter Goya and his muse, the Duchess of Alba, the subject of two of his famous works.

Elaine was evidently quite visible amongst this fast company. "I was written up in one of those awful, awful paparazzi magazines." Yet her season in the Roman sun was coming to an end. Her money was spent. For whatever reason, Elaine chose not to try to earn it herself nor to follow Brandt any farther. She called Larry. "He told me, 'Come home.' "

Returning to Fall River in time to attend the '58 festival, she resumed the familiar routine of escapes to New York. Her friend Carol Haney was working on the choreography for the Broadway musical *Flower Drum Song.* On one of her trips, Elaine joined Haney while she conducted a rehearsal. According to Elaine, Haney at one point had trouble expressing a concept for her dancers. Sharing a similar approach to dance and having a mutual trust and regard for each other's work, she asked for input. "Elaine, I can't get this. It's really important to get this."

Invited to enter the rehearsal process, Elaine demonstrated some extended movements, offering, "You should do this with your hands." At that moment, producer and lyricist Oscar Hammerstein appeared and caught a glimpse of Elaine as she moved and gestured. Taken by what he saw, he whispered to Haney, "Tell her she should be in the show." Whatever the sincerity of the statement, Elaine chose to remember taking the idea to Larry and being met with his refusal to let her pursue it.

Elaine's and Larry's lives were just not going in the same direction. Her three sons were beginning to leave for the world of fashionable New England prep schools, Rick to Massachusetts's very traditional Deerfield Academy.

The stress fractures in the marriage continued to worsen as the Andersons and America entered a new decade. Constraint was going out the window. Excess was in the wind. The whole Anderson family went to Newport '60, when rioting blew the lid off the festival. Son Rick Anderson began his junior year at Deerfield, but at home sometime before the end of the school year, his parents officially separated. Elaine was finally riding out of town.

"She was a very smart person," he said, "somebody who finished all the *New York Times* Sunday crossword puzzle usually by noontime. The only problem was that she had no judgment. She took the wrong horse to leave with."

Elaine as a country-club golfing champion. From 1957 to 1960 she was a familiar face on the local sports pages in Fall River.
::: *Fred Anderson Collection.*

The ride was on a bounder in the stamp redemption business, one Paul Warren, from Marblehead, Massachusetts, where he and Elaine first made their home. In 1963 Elaine divorced Larry. She and Warren married and later moved to Tiburon, California. In no time the relationship exploded. Warren proved to be a womanizer. "She ended up kicking him out of the house, and he'd come back," said Rick. "And this went on for a number of years."

By late 1965, the time Elaine met with Ellington in San Francisco at his First Sacred Concert, she and Warren were in the throes of separation and divorce. Once free of Warren, Elaine moved to Los Angeles. "This," said Rick, "was her survival period."

Two years later, Elaine was the weary prodigal ready to come home. Sometime in 1967, she came East to stay with her parents, now retired in Florida. There a relationship deepened with another who was twice divorced, Otto John Kralovec, a retired architect from Chicago. Kralovec had been a student of the great modernist Ludwig Mies van der Rohe when he was head of the architecture school at what is now the Illinois Institute of Technology. Kralovec later specialized in urban renewal, which took him and his family all over the country. His last job had been in Oregon, where he had a house on the coast. After his second divorce he went to Europe before landing in Florida in Del Ray Beach.

The couple may have met earlier when Elaine was in Tiburon and Kralovec was in Oregon, said his youngest daughter Etta Kralovec, now an associate professor of teacher education at University of Arizona South. "Their love for San Francisco was the only thing they had in common."

After a marriage in Chicago, they settled in Del Ray Beach, where Kralovec had a home. Since she and her three older siblings had already left the nest, Etta recalled that Elaine and her father "moved around. Both were in a very reclusive period in their lives."

The marriage lasted only seven years, and sometime in 1975 after her third divorce, Elaine made her way to Boston. There at age fifty-one, she started putting a life together as a working single woman. Settling in Back Bay, the leafy, historic nineteenth-century residential neighborhood of three- and four-story brownstones, she took a job with Sepp Firnkas, a structural engineering firm specializing in reinforced concrete. Firnkas supported one main client, which built hotels and motels worldwide. The expanding firm finally afforded Elaine an opportunity to parlay her intelligence and talents, and for sixteen years she served as Firnkas's office administrator.

Despite Elaine's divorcing her father, Etta Kralovec remained close to her stepmother. While a graduate student, she often stayed with Elaine in Boston. Short of money, Elaine moved frequently from rental to rental. Etta recalled one occasion arriving at a new apartment to see "four champagne glasses and not a stick of furniture." Having not yet

Elaine in Mill Valley, California, August 1971, during her third marriage. ::: *Fred Anderson Collection.*

Elaine in Boston in the 1980s. ::: *Fred Anderson Collection.*

unpacked the linens, Elaine pointed to a bare mattress and handed Etta a fur, saying, "If you haven't slept under a fur coat once in your life, you haven't lived."

Etta remembered her stepmother as "a keen intellect, gracious, vivacious. Even when down, she was still the life of the party. When you were around Elaine, she took up most of the space in the room."

During the eighties Elaine returned to taking her junkets to New York, this time to visit her youngest son, Bruce, who was working for the Metropolitan Opera. During this period her love for opera matured. Etta recalled frequently rendezvousing with Elaine with tickets provided by Bruce for performances at the Met.

Although Elaine Anderson had moved forward in her life and in her musical tastes beyond Newport '56, she remained "very proud of that event. That night was a signature moment for her," said Etta Kralovec; "she gave me a signed copy of the album."

In 1992 Elaine went to work for a local nonprofit, the Neighborhood Association of the Back Bay, a community-based organization established by residents in 1955. As its only paid employee, she served as the administrator of an association that had grown to number some seventeen hundred members. Her primary tasks were to coordinate fund-raisers and events. One of her great joys was to host and cook for the monthly meetings of the association board.

In early 2003 she left the association and in April moved to Charleston, South Carolina, intent on a retirement filled with tennis and opera at the city's annual spring Spoleto Festival. The enjoyment was a single season all too brief. Early the following year, she was diagnosed with pancreatic cancer. With her characteristic what-the-hell attitude, Elaine Zeitz Anderson braced for the end, which came quickly in April. At eighty, the gal who launched seven thousand cheers took her final exit.

Sometime during her mid-sixties survival period in Los Angeles, Elaine was living in Beverly Hills. One night at the Beverly Rodeo Hotel, she met Ellington, who was in town to give a lecture at UCLA. Recognizing her, he asked, "What are you doing here?" "Well, I live in a little dump around the corner."

A sympathetic Ellington was moved to invite her to the lecture and a gathering afterward at the home of Quincy Jones. Elaine recalled it as one of the best evenings of her life, which concluded with an after-party with Ellington and others at his hotel suite.

"I was a bad girl in those days," Elaine confessed, "and I used to hang around that hotel all the time. I called down to the kitchen and said, 'Mr. Ellington wants a vanilla ice cream and a Coke, and bring it up right away.' They thought I was crazy. He used to like vanilla ice cream and a Coke, and I got it for him."

As the Maestro devoured his after-midnight ice cream, the fallen socialite who sat before him transformed perhaps into another weary incarnation of "Sophisticated Lady." "Elaine," he finally asked, "what do you miss most, not being the rich Mrs. Anderson?"

"I don't have a record player," she replied. "I miss my music." Two days later arrived "the most beautiful portable record player and records like you couldn't believe—with no card."

Whatever else she may have been or done, Elaine's improvised dance at Newport '56 was the pinnacle of her interior life as an artist. An odd triumph, it was one she didn't parlay, but should have. "If you asked anybody," concluded her son Rick, "I mean, does this woman know how to dance? She knew how to dance."

18

The Brotherhood of the Jam

On the Road with Paul and Duke

"When 'The St. Louis Blues' was written," began its author W. C. Handy in a quote from Albert Murray's *Stomping the Blues,* "the tango was in vogue. I tricked the dancers by arranging a tango introduction, breaking abruptly into a low-down blues. My eyes swept the floor anxiously, then suddenly I saw the lightning strike. The dancers seemed electrified. Something within them came suddenly to life. An instinct that wanted so much to live, to fling its arms and to spread joy, took them by their heels."

Blues music was created for "dance-beat-oriented people," Murray wrote. "Dance, after all, not only antedates music, but is also probably the most specific source of music and most of the other art forms as well."

Elaine Anderson's dance and Paul Gonsalves's interval built into a ritual seemingly without end because of what Murray would call "the context of the performance." It's "the primary consideration underlying the length of riff-chorus compositions," he wrote. Referring to jam sessions among Kansas City musicians before the war, the cultural critic continued, "Jo Jones said it was not at all unusual for a number to be jammed for an hour and a half in those days."

Although more a matter of minutes than hours, the dance-interval during "Diminuendo and Crescendo in Blue" was a moment of individual triumphs expressed for all who were together in the eternal now that night, as well as for all who have viscerally responded to the recording ever since. "What the customary blues-idiom dance movement reflects is a disposition to encounter obstacle after obstacle as a matter of course," Murray maintained. "Indeed, the improvisation on the break, which is required of blues-idiom musicians and dancers alike, is precisely what epic heroism is based on."

Both Elaine and Paul were riding on what Murray identified as Ellington's "unchallenged supremacy," that is, his "most comprehensive assimilation, counterstatement, and elaboration of most, if not all, of the elements of blues musicianship." The Newport '56 audience epically participated in the performance of "Diminuendo and Crescendo in Blue." It joined an infectious conversation among Ellington and his band, who themselves were refraining the hypnotic drum talk of New Orleans's Congo Square. To paraphrase Murray, it was as if listeners were hearing "so many talking drums, some voiced as . . . pianos, trumpets, trombones, saxophones, clarinets. . . . The incantation [was] so percussion oriented that it dispose[d] the listeners to bump and bounce, to slow-drag and steady shuffle, to grind, hop, jump, kick, rock, roll, shout, stomp, and otherwise swing the blues away."

Referring specifically to "Diminuendo and Crescendo in Blue," Murray wrote that "not only do the trumpets and trombones extend the shouting and hey-saying voice of the downhome church choir, but they also take the lead in doing the drum work and drum talk at the same time."

Ellington discographer Eddie Lambert believed that "Diminuendo and Crescendo in Blue" is "certainly one of the most imaginative twelve bar blues in the history of jazz music." Lambert listed and critiqued many of the recordings of the composition in its variations. After 1937's original 78 release, the next known recording was of a June 9, 1945, Toledo, Ohio, performance that has survived as one of six recordings in the Duke Ellington Treasury Series. Referring to the forties "Diminuendo and Crescendo in Blue," plus interval as triptych versions, Lambert noted that the piece went under the title "Blues Cluster." Of the Toledo record, Lambert wrote, "The opening of 'Crescendo in Blue' has a magic quality as the clarinet and trombones enter in hushed dialogue." The July 7, 1945, Radio City Studio recording was his favorite because it did not finish with a high note trumpet at the microphone that otherwise would have masked the orchestral detail. The October 13, 1945, version, also at Radio City, he noted, "has Sidney Catlett on drums, an unusual and fascinating feature."

The intervals for the three 1945 recordings were all Ellington compositions: "Rocks in My Bed," "Carnegie Blues," and "I Got It Bad." In 1946 Ellington began using Kay Davis singing "Transbluency" for the interval, which continued, save two recorded exceptions, into 1947.

The first of the other three Treasury Series recordings was the January 20, 1946, evening concert at the Chicago Civic Opera House that was broadcast on the Armed Forces Radio Service, AFRS. The second was what Lambert tagged the "most rousing" recording: the May 4, 1946, Dartmouth College performance "topped by some exciting Cat Anderson high note trumpet," during his first stint with the band. The third was an August 3, 1946, San Francisco broadcast performance.

Lambert cited a 1946 Musicraft studio version of "Diminuendo in Blue" without "Crescendo" and in his view "a rather poorly recorded" version from an April 30, 1947, concert at Cornell University. Then, of course, came the June 30, 1951, recorded broadcast from Birdland, the first with a Gonsalves solo, and another with Paul on Gene Norman's March 30, 1953, recording of the Pasadena concert.

The post-Newport July 28, 1956, recording from Fairfield, Connecticut, features an on-mike Gonsalves solo that runs for thirty-eight choruses, which Lambert wrote was "undoubtedly" the best recording of his interval. The discographer noted two others: one a Carrolltown, Pennsylvania, date in June 1957 and a November 1958 recording thought to be in Stockholm but actually in Göteborg, Sweden, both of which he believed were better recordings of the solo and band than at Newport.

Lambert wrote that when Ellington seemed to have tired of performing the work, he began in 1959 to alternate the full composition with one consisting of "Diminuendo in Blue" and the Gonsalves solo with band accompaniment at the end and no "Crescendo in Blue." By the early sixties, Ellington replaced the full version completely by dropping the "Diminuendo" and leaving only the tenor improvisation under the title "Blow by Blow." "Later still," concluded Lambert, "this became a three-way tenor saxophone battle entitled 'In Triplicate,' but by then the thread with the 1937 'Diminuendo and Crescendo in Blue' was effectively broken."

This discography aside, the confluence of personalities, event, and time made the improvised break during the Newport '56 performance of "Diminuendo and Crescendo in Blue" the performance of legend. Phil Schaap recalled George Wein himself stating in the late sixties his opinion that the performance was the greatest moment of the Newport Jazz Festival. For Paul Gonsalves and Elaine Anderson it was the defining moment in their lives. When Elaine improvised her response, it rebounded onto the stage, energizing Duke, who in turn energized Paul, the band, and ultimately the mythic seven thousand.

"Maestro was very energetic that night," Clark Terry recalled, "and when he was energetic and feeling good he could transfer all that feeling into the players. He was amazing at that. He was in control, man. Yeah, he was not nervous at all. The more he gave of himself, the more he got from the band."

It was a moment expressing heroism for all. Two Americans with immigrant roots—one German Jewish, the other Cape Verdean, both with ties to nearby New Bedford—reached deeply into their very beings to bring forth their innate dance-beat dispositions. And riding on the percussive statement in the music, together they interpreted Duke Ellington's inclusive but distinctively Negro American cultural idiom to express arrival in postwar America. The break was a transformative experience at the highest aesthetic for soloist, dancer, and audience alike, the foretaste of the more generalized mass symbiosis of the sixties, when popular musical expression would become for a thrusting, rebellious counterculture not just entertainment but a way of life.

In his 1961 interview with Stanley Dance, Paul Gonsalves spoke of "a real competitive feeling in the band" that night at Newport '56. Gonsalves seemed to be recalling the welling impatience of a big bandsman having to sit through some of the posturing introspection of the small modern combos on the program before returning to the stage. "Paul

Desmond [Dave Brubeck's lead sax player] told me shortly afterwards, 'What you and the band played was the most honest statement that night.'"

"He is well featured in the band," said Dan Morgenstern of Gonsalves, "but he had never had a showcase like that, because needless to say it is very unusual under any circumstance to have this kind of marathon solo in a big band context. I mean, that solo by itself is longer, I think, than all the combined solos on 'Sing, Sing, Sing.' But in a way, as happy as Paul would have been about getting this fame out of that, it became a bit of an albatross."

"Ellington remained particularly beholden to Gonsalves afterward, tolerating the saxophonist's errant behavior, including abuse of drugs and alcohol, indulging him like a prodigal son," wrote Tom Reney, Amherst, Massachusetts, jazz deejay and freelance writer researching a book on Duke Ellington in New England. Reney recalled attending a Sunday afternoon benefit for the local hospital guild at the Webster, Massachusetts, town hall. Locals in the audience knew a nearby body of water, Webster Lake, by its original Nipmuck Indian name, roughly translated as "You fish on your side, we'll fish on our side, and no one fishes in the middle." Ellington introduced Gonsalves as having been born "just to the east of Lake Chargogagogg Manchaugagogg Chaubunagungamaugg." By Reney's account, the locals responded "with delight," and thereafter, Ellington would introduce Gonsalves as being "from Newport, Rhode Island."

"From his Birdland gig in '51, Duke understood how Paul's tenor completed the 'Diminuendo,'" said Ellington nephew Michael James. "He knew the effect, which enabled him to choreograph that Newport performance." James identified a "purification ritual" in the composition that expressed "the melding of the sacred and the secular in Duke, because he felt God blessed him. Duke used to tell me, 'Mike, we've been liked longer than most people been liked.' He appreciated Paul for what he gave him. So when anybody asked, 'Why you putting up with this stuff?' [referring to Paul's nodding off onstage at the very end of his career] Duke wouldn't pay any attention. It was his way of giving back."

The two men were very close, a fact noticed by others in the band. James remembered tenor saxophonist Harold Ashby, who in the sixties replaced clarinetist Jimmy Hamilton, telling him that the band came to call Gonsalves "Teacher's Pet." Beyond music, both men shared another artistic sensitivity: as teenagers both had considered careers in commercial art. Gonsalves had a natural gift for caricature, which infrequently would manifest itself. "In seventy-four when Duke was in the hospital," said James, "Paul came over to my place for dinner one night and on a pad of hotel telephone stationery drew a one-line sketch—like Picasso—of Duke wearing his blue velvet velour hat."

Just before Newport, in the spring of 1956, while the band was playing the Flamingo in Las Vegas, Gonsalves met a shapely and dark-haired showgirl whom he would later marry. A single mom with a young daughter, Joanne was a most attractive German American from a family originally from the Midwest but transplanted to Long Island. Their courtship began while Paul was staying in a hotel cabin with Willie Cook in the Dust Bowl, the African American section of Las Vegas. A smitten Joanne would arrive at the cabin in her Volkswagen to take Paul on afternoon drives into the desert. Not long after the festival, Joanne was pregnant with Paul Junior, their first child together; they married, and Paul, Joanne, and her daughter, Collette, initially took residence in Harlem at the Cecil Hotel, famous for its physical connection to Minton's Playhouse at West 118th and St. Nicholas. There Paul and Joanne would hang with fellow residents Ray Nance and his former-model wife Gloria. After their time at the Cecil, they moved to an apartment in Jackson Heights, Queens, in suburban Long Island.

Gonsalves friend and fan John Monteiro remembered how Paul was determined to buy a house next to Illinois Jacquet on 179th Street in the nearby St. Albans section of Queens, a neighborhood filled with jazz stars. He got close when he was later able to move to what he called a two-family house elsewhere on Francis Lewis Boulevard. Joanne left show business, and the couple eventually had another child, a daughter, Marlena. Joanne later would return to work as a schoolteacher. Paul Junior inherited one of his father's three saxophones. Many years ago he connected with saxophonist David Murray, who agreed to teach him to play on the instrument.

Into the sixties and seventies, Gonsalves cut more than twenty LPs featuring primarily his reflective ballad work—sometimes with Ellingtonians, sometimes not. *Gettin' Together* was an issue from a somewhat bopish 1960 session with Nat Adderley supporting him on cornet. Another was a 1962 recording, *Duke Ellington and His Orchestra, Featuring Paul Gonsalves,* on which Ellington gave Gonsalves a solo on every track.

Paul had a twenty-four-year tenure with the band and was truly beloved. According to Michael James, his best friends were Sam Woodyard, his main drinking buddy; Willie Cook, his roommate on the road, whom he knew from their time in Dizzy Gillespie's band; Ray Nance; and Clark Terry, his partner from their Basie years. In tours through New England, Terry would often accompany Gonsalves on visits to the family home in Pawtucket. "Where's boy-a Clark-a Terry?" he remembered Paul's mother, Maria, greeting her son every time he followed him through the front door. The trumpeter could recall each of the Gonsalves siblings by their skin tones, widely varying like that of most Cape Verdeans: Joe, the eldest, short and dark; John, tall and light-skinned, and his wife, Tilly; and their sister Julie, a light-brown beauty.

Gonsalves was a broad musical interpreter who expressed his own ideas through his choruses to "tell a story," as he put it to Stanley Dance. The breadth of his music appreciation extended beyond jazz. Dance noted an instance during an Ellington gig at Storyville, when Paul took friends to the downstairs stage to hear the blues duo, pianist Memphis Slim and bassist-songwriter Willie Dixon, announcing, "This is authentic." Another time, recalled John Monteiro, Paul played an engagement at the historic Rhodes on the Pawtuxet in Cranston, Rhode Island, and stopped the show with an especially moving interpretation of "Days of Wine and Roses."

Gonsalves was, in Dance's words a "sacrificial image," a master at satisfying "the public conception of the frenzied, driving tenor man." In *Music Is My Mistress* Duke called him "the strolling violins," in reference to his penchant for hopping off the stand to serenade an audience—breaking the fourth wall—as Monteiro recalled his doing that

Paul Gonsalves in the studio. Jimmy Hamilton in the background. ::: *Photo by Roy DeCarava. Duke Ellington Collection, Archives Center, National Museum of American History, Smithsonian Institution.*

postwar night at Boston's Savoy. In his 1946 "Flying Home" solo, Paul was identifying with the GIs in his audience because as a vet himself he was telling his own story. Some two decades later in that Rhode Island ballroom, Monteiro heard him voice with some pathos his later story, sacrificial indeed.

"Paul never took care of business," said Terry. "On the road, I used to have to write his mother postcards and have Paul sign them."

Monteiro and the Cape Verdean community rightly regarded Gonsalves as one of their own. When his seafaring cousins and other Cape Verdean merchant seamen would come ashore in New York, he and Livramento routinely would gather with them for a meal at the Grant Cafeteria on Forty-second and Broadway. Michael James, however, remembered his frustration when non-showbiz civilians from his past, family and friends, arrived in town and "wanted to hang." No doubt, Gonsalves felt a conflicted loyalty to both worlds. "He was into the brotherhood of the jam," said James. Recalling the September 1964 Monterey Jazz Festival, James made the point with a description of a joyous Gonsalves in the musicians' hotel "going from room to room, greeting old friends and then hugging them all over the festival grounds, the Heaths [Jimmy and Percy], Miles, Buck Clayton, Mingus."

Like Ellington, Gonsalves preferred the road. Said James, "Paul would get depressed when the band bus returned to New York and he'd see the Manhattan skyline and the skies getting low."

Clark Terry remembered one night at Beefsteak Charlie's on Fiftieth Street after a record date when road manager Al Celley paid a thoroughly inebriated Paul in cash. Since he lived in Corona, a section of Queens adjacent to Jackson Heights, Terry put him into his cab and delivered him to Joanne at the door, along with a fistful of bills. It was an all-too-typical scene.

Joanne tried to run a strict household. She had wanted Paul to come off the road and take steady nine-to-five work as a studio musician. He wouldn't. In 1973 they finally separated, and Paul moved into the Edison, the musicians' hotel at Forty-seventh and Broadway. Several floors above him was Ellington's son Mercer, who had succeeded Celley as the band's road manager in 1964.

In the spring of 1974, Gonsalves and his fellow band members were resting, each coming to terms with an unsettling truth: life on the road with Duke was over. Maestro had literally been lifted from his piano stool at the end of his final performance and within days was at the Harkness Pavilion of Columbia Presbyterian Hospital receiving treatments for terminal lung cancer. Gonsalves spent his time with Michael James, coming to his East Side apartment to visit and cook Cape Verdean cuisine. James remembered his last day with Paul, sometime in late April. Finding Gonsalves at the Edison short of cash, James accompanied him to Mercer's room to help obtain a draw. They entered as his cousin was finishing a telephone conversation with Duke. When Ellington heard that they were together, he asked them to come visit.

When they arrived in his hospital room, each "got the two kisses from Maestro," said James. Seeing Gonsalves, Ellington brightened and his mood turned playful. "Now that I am in the hospital, you're the one with the charisma," Ellington told his saxophonist. Duke roused himself, and the pair lifted him from his bed to a wheelchair. It was the first meeting either had had with Ellington since the cancer had forced him off the road that winter. According to James, Gonsalves was the only band member to see him in that condition, a testimony to the close bond between the men. Having trouble maintaining eye contact, James was emotionally paralyzed by the sight of his uncle. Gonsalves, however, looked Duke straight in the eye, gamely continuing to make conversation, talking about his father's recipe for shrimp creole. Ellington extracted a promise that he would bring him some. After some thirty minutes, it seemed time to leave, but a tiring Duke insisted they remain. "One doesn't have to apologize to friends," he told them. For another half-hour as he drifted in and out of sleep, they silently read newspapers until the nurses arrived to take Ellington for a cobalt treatment for his metastasizing cancer. Although Duke continued insisting they remain, the staff refused. "I'm sorry, fellas," James recalled Maestro finally saying to them as he was wheeled down the corridor. "It was as if we were three boys hanging on the street who are told they have to go home, and one of them says, 'We can't play anymore.'"

Once on the street, James was moved to remark, "Things don't look good for the old man." "Well, Mike," came Gonsalves's pensive reply, "life's a cycle."

That night Paul returned to the Edison and at the bar met some Dutch musicians who invited him to join them for a well-paying two-week gig in Holland. Gonsalves went. Instead of returning home, he binged and caught a plane to London, landing in a distressed condition but with a pocketful of cash. Immigration held him at the airport until representatives from Ronnie Scott's club came to collect him. Once among friends at the premier Soho venue, he was able to secure an offer to crash at the flat of jazz fan Jackie Sharp and his girlfriend. Several days later, on the morning of May 15, Gonsalves failed to emerge from his room. The girlfriend found him, collapsed. One account has it that he died while taking a bath.

Shortly after he heard the sad news from London, Michael James was at Duke's bedside with his mother, Ruth Boatwright; Ellington's companion on the road, Fernanda de Castro Monte; and a nurse's aide. With only a few days remaining himself, Ellington awoke for a moment. "Where's *o cozinheiro?* " he asked his nephew, recalling his request for Paul's shrimp creole. No one—to that moment or in his few days remaining—had the heart to tell him Paul had left.

"I've always considered myself a success as a musician," Gonsalves once said as befitting an epitaph. "Two things I wanted to do: play the saxophone and play with Duke Ellington."

In *Music Is My Mistress*, Duke Ellington credited Paul Gonsalves as one of the "three heroes," along with his two rhythm section partners, of Newport '56. "Paul Gonsalves, Jimmy Woode, and Sam Woodyard lifted that stone-cold audience up to a fiery, frenzied, screeching, dancing climax that was never to be forgotten."

Paul Gonsalves soloing with Duke at one of the Sacred Concerts. ::: *Duke Ellington Collection, Archives Center, National Museum of American History, Smithsonian Institution.*

Ellington and Gonsalves doing the twist, August 1962. This photo was taken by New York jazz photographer Jack Bradley, known for his association with Louis Armstrong, for founding the New York Hot Jazz Society, and for cofounding the New York Jazz Museum. ::: *Courtesy of the Institute of Jazz Studies, Rutgers University.*

Woode left Duke in 1960 and went to Europe, first to Sweden and then to Germany, where he joined bebop drummer Kenny Clarke in a collaboration that ran to 1973. The bassist would live and gig all over Europe until the late nineties, when he returned and settled in New Jersey. He would continue to gig in both the United States and Europe until his death in 2005. Woodyard remained with Ellington and with interruptions played until 1968. The drummer left to join Ella Fitzgerald's band for a time and then variously played, recorded, and toured until moving to Paris in 1975. He remained a fixture in the Parisian scene until his death in 1988.

As for Maestro himself, after Newport '56 he would enter a lengthy and most creative period in his career. Ellington's three-year contract with Columbia Records and Irving Townsend, whom he tagged as his "wonderful" A&R man and a "very sensitive musician," took him and his band to 1959, when he signed another three-year renewal extending him to 1962. Wrote Ellington biographer John Hasse, it was a time of stable recording with a major label that allowed him the freedom to compose new extended pieces. In the opinion of Eddie Lambert, it was "six very fruitful years with the company. In these years he recorded twenty-four LPs of superb music." The pace did not slacken—then or later to the end of his life. The continued touring schedule meant that Ellington composed on the road.

Not two months after Newport, in September 1956, he recorded his composition *A Drum Is a Woman,* tagged by Hasse "a satirical history of jazz." In a revised and expanded version, it aired as a dance performance on the May 8, 1957, CBS Living Color broadcast of a *U.S. Steel Hour* special, one of the first television programs performed exclusively by African Americans. One number, "Congo Square," per Hasse, "offers sensuous, minor-key chords in an undulating rhythm supporting Ellington's story of a pretty girl arousing passions in the crowd." The year 1957 also saw *Such Sweet Thunder,* a work commissioned for the Stratford Ontario Shakespeare Festival. Two years later, Duke composed a musical score for Otto Preminger's film *Anatomy of a Murder,* starring Jimmy Stewart. In 1960 he scored another film, with stars Paul Newman and Sidney Poitier: Martin Ritt's *Paris Blues.* (The performance of the theme song played on the sax by the Newman character was dubbed by Gonsalves.) For that year's Monterey Jazz Festival, the third, he and Billy

Duke Ellington playing a *bal pare* in Munich, 1965. ::: *Courtesy of the Institute of Jazz Studies, Rutgers University.*

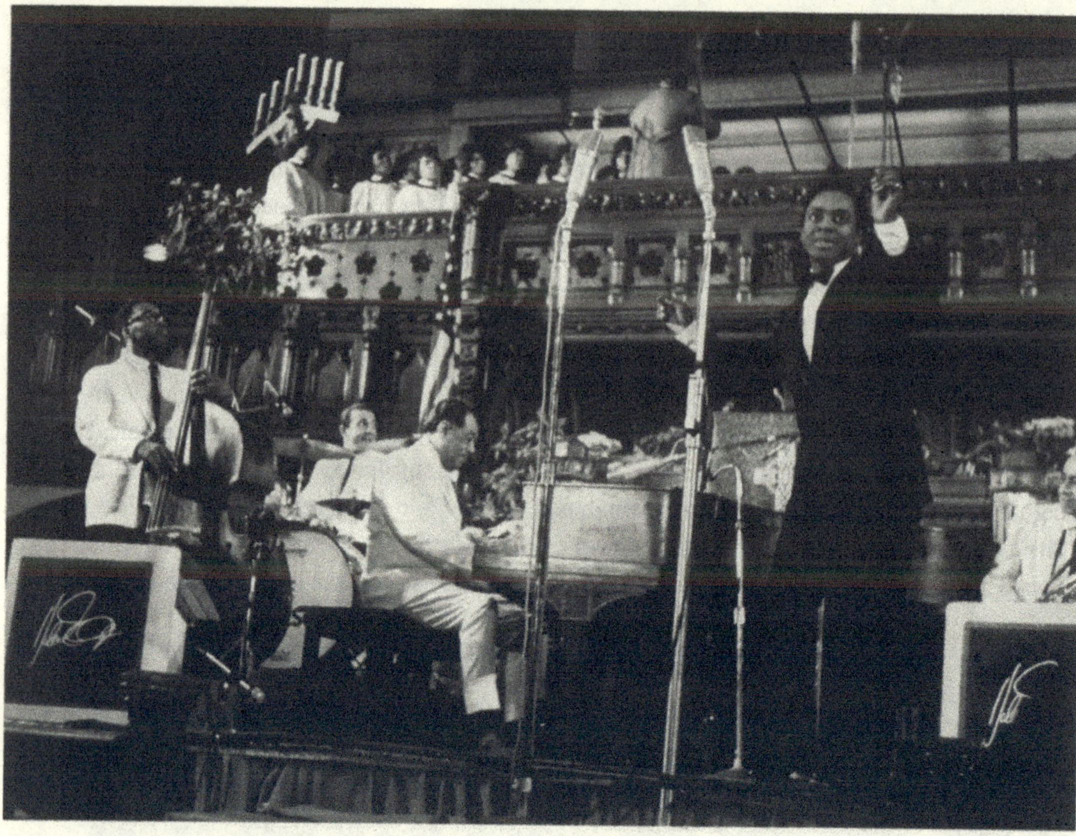

First Sacred Concert, December 26, 1965, at Fifth Avenue Presbyterian Church, New York. With Bunny Briggs dancing, Louis Bellson on drums, John Lambe on bass, and Paul Gonsalves off right. ::: *Courtesy of the Institute of Jazz Studies, Rutgers University.*

Strayhorn wrote "Suite Thursday," after John Steinbeck's novel *Sweet Thursday*. The pair followed that with a composition based on Tchaikovsky's "Nutcracker Suite."

While in Las Vegas for that year's engagement, Ellington met Fernanda de Castro Monte, a fortyish Portuguese chanteuse who had sung all over Europe. A tall and strikingly beautiful blonde of worldly sophistication, she had also lived in Algeria and Brazil and could speak five languages. Johnny Hodges tagged her "Contessa." Duke would introduce her as "Countess." While Evie Ellis remained his unmarried partner in their West Side apartment in New York and was sometimes introduced as Mrs. Ellington, de Castro Monte would become his romantic companion on the road to the end of his life.

When Ellington finally left Columbia, he ventured into a number of creative recording sessions, notably those with Coleman Hawkins, John Coltrane, and Charlie Mingus. It was a time when Maestro was moving into the role of elder statesman. In 1963, the centennial year of the Emancipation Proclamation, he composed "My People" for Chicago's Century of Negro Progress Exposition. It was a big year for overseas touring with a tour of Europe and another of the Middle and Near East. The band was on the road for 174 days. The following year, he was again in Europe and later the Far East. The latter tour inspired compositions with Strayhorn that he eventually would combine into his 1966 work "The Far East Suite."

In the years of the rock explosion and the British invasion led by the Beatles, Ellington and his band proved they could survive. They toured Europe again in 1965. Britain's *Melody Maker* critics' poll voted Ellington musician of the year and the winner in big band, arranger, and composer categories. That summer, however, the Pulitzer Prize advisory board in a very controversial decision refused him a special prize. Duke was undeterred. In September he premiered his *First Sacred Concert*, whose opening number, "In the Beginning, God," would win the 1966 Grammy for best original jazz composition. That year saw release of a third motion picture with an Ellington score, the Frank Sinatra adventure film *Assault on a Queen*. More important for Ellington, throughout the year he continued to perform the *Sacred Concert*, which that December finally came to his hometown Washington with a performance at the august DAR Constitution Hall, just down Seventeenth Street from the White House.

By 1966, in the opinion of biographer John Hasse, the creative period that began in 1956 had peaked. For Ellington the stage was beginning to empty. That year his estranged wife, Edna, died. His creative alter ego Billy Strayhorn would die of cancer in 1967, a death Ellington took especially hard.

Duke soldiered on, garnering acclaim. During the Johnson years he performed at the White House seven times. In 1969 at his seventieth birthday tribute at the White House, where his father had butlered a lifetime before, President Richard Nixon bestowed on him the Presidential Medal of Freedom, the nation's highest civilian decoration. In the course of his life, Duke Ellington would receive honors and awards from all over the world. More than three hundred such formal recognitions, including seventeen honorary doctorates, are in the Smithsonian Ellington Collection. According to Hasse no American composer has been honored so widely—nationally and internationally.

Ellington's many awards, displayed at his sister Ruth Ellington Boatright's Park Avenue apartment. ::: *Courtesy of the Institute of Jazz Studies, Rutgers University.*

In January 1968 Ellington premiered his *Second Sacred Concert* at New York's Cathedral of St. John the Divine. That year, he toured South America and Mexico. The following year, Newport impresario George Wein took him to Europe. Also in 1969 he toured the Far East. In 1970 he composed "The New Orleans Suite" for the New Orleans Jazz Festival. The next year he went with Wein to the Soviet

Union and again to Europe. In 1972 it was the Far East for a third time and Southeast Asia. In 1973 he wrote his memoir, *Music Is My Mistress,* and painstakingly composed music for his *Third Sacred Concert.* He would also tour Europe with a foray to Ethiopia and Zambia. In October he premiered his *Third Sacred Concert* at London's Westminster Abbey to honor the founding of the United Nations.

"And so the program rolls on until it is time to bid farewell . . . ," concludes Duke's act 1, scene 1 of *Music Is My Mistress*. In the spring of 1973 he had been diagnosed with lung cancer, but he kept rollin' on the road. In January 1974 he collapsed at a Washington

Paul Gonsalves and Duke in the Soviet Union, 1971. ::: *Courtesy of the Institute of Jazz Studies, Rutgers University.*

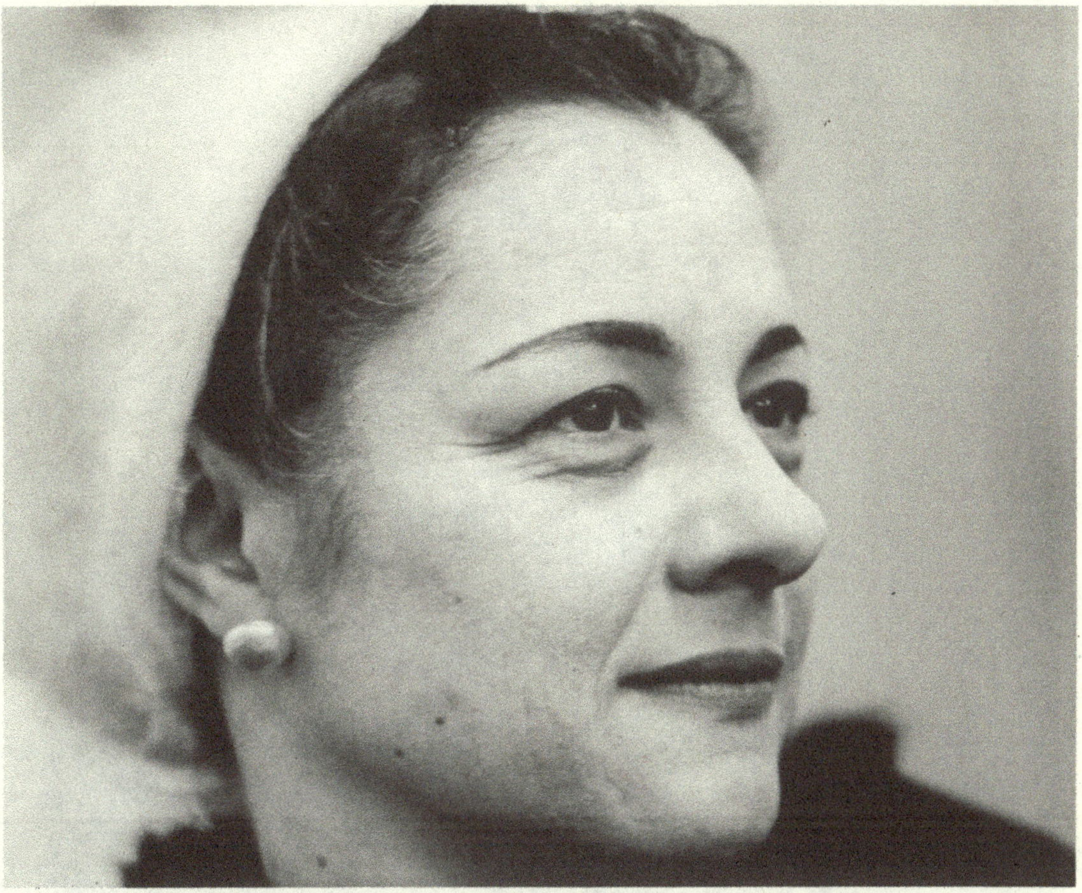

Evie Ellis, c. 1960s. This photograph was taken by Arnold H. Meyers, who photographed Ellington in the sixties. ::: *Courtesy of the Institute of Jazz Studies, Rutgers University.*

concert. After treatments at Columbia Presbyterian hospital, he was able to tour intermittently until March, when he left the road for good and returned home to his apartment with Evie. That month she, too, was diagnosed with lung cancer and once hospitalized would remain so until her death two years later. Although the couple would communicate regularly by phone, they would never again be in each other's company. In early April Duke returned to hospital, where for a time at an electric piano beside his bed he was able to continue work on revisions to his *Third Sacred Concert*. After a few weeks he was bedridden. The cancer was now metastasizing rapidly beyond all treatment. Pneumonia finally took root in his lungs, and on May 24, without words, Edward Kennedy Ellington bade his last farewell and left.

Duke was taken to Third Avenue's Walter B. Cooke funeral home at Eighty-fifth Street on Manhattan's East Side, where he was not alone. There his body lay with the bodies of two of his musicians. One was Tyree Glenn, who six days before had passed. An out-

Duke Ellington, the statesman. This photo was composed and shot by Louis Fabian Bachrach, midcentury America's premier portrait photographer. Bachrach said, "I do not believe that the average person wants a 'map' of his face—I believe he wants to be idealized." ::: *Duke Ellington Collection, Archives Center, National Museum of American History, Smithsonian Institution.*

standing trombonist from the late forties band, Glenn had replaced Tricky Sam Nanton on the plunger mute and as a soloist. Also a vibraphone player, he had played with Cab Calloway. Glenn left the band to serve as a studio musician. For a time he had a stint on Ted Steele's TV show, and in the late sixties supported Louis Armstrong.

With Glenn was another, Duke's beloved hero from Newport '56: Paul Gonsalves.

The funeral service was three days later at St. John the Divine, Memorial Day 1974. Some ten thousand attended. Former Ellington valve trombonist and scorer, now Monsignor, John Sanders read the epistle, passages from Romans 8, among which was the twenty-eighth verse, which had particular poignancy for a life of such grandeur and contradiction, a life indeed beyond category: "We know that in everything God works for good with those who love him, who are called according to his purpose."

Sanders had left the band in 1959 and in 1965 decided to enter the priesthood. He started seminary the same month Ellington performed his *First Sacred Concert* in San Francisco. Sometime afterward, when Duke had returned to New York and was playing Lewisohn Stadium, Sanders visited with him backstage. "You know," confided Ellington to his former bandsman, now seminary student, "we're on the same team, John."

In February 1973 at the Church of St. Pius V, Jamaica, in Queens, Sanders celebrated his first mass. At the reception afterward it was his turn to receive a visitor from his jazz past. Duke Ellington had made time to come off the road to be there early on a Sunday morning for his colleague and friend. Some thirty years later, the Monsignor fondly recalled how the Maestro eased himself from the predictable limelight of attention. Shifting focus with a touch of humility, he simply offered, "This is *John's* day."

A year later the priest would see his former bandleader for the last time. The band was playing a concert at the Shakespeare Theatre in Stratford, Connecticut, and Ellington knew Sanders was in the audience. After the performance, the Monsignor and his party went to his dressing room. "Duke was gracious, as always," he related, "but he was obviously very ill."

After the concert was over and the band took its final applause, Ellington had crossed the stage to his piano. The musicians remained in their chairs, their instruments on their laps. Dedicating what he was about to play to Sanders, Duke sat down and very gently phrased the ascending chords to Strayhorn's "Lotus Blossom." It was a composition he maintained was the number Billy most liked to hear him play. It was also a solo track on the elegiac 1967 LP *And His Mother Called Him Bill,* on which he similarly conjured the apparition of his then recently departed friend, somehow recorded as the band was taking a break. That night at the 1974 concert, all were spellbound as he continued the piece. Said Sanders, "Duke played it like a meditation."

Duke Ellington did not write endings. So with "Lotus Blossom" he chose a composition not his own, one through which he could simply say good-bye.

19

Someone Else's Freedom

The VOA Broadcast

From the moment they began planning for the 1956 Newport Jazz Festival, Elaine and Louis Lorillard and John Hammond intended to find a means for its liberating music to have an international impact. In late 1955 they saw how that goal might be achieved during the U.S. government's embrace of the spirit of Geneva, the West and the Soviet Union's attempt at thawing the cold war through cultural exchanges in the wake of that year's Swiss summit and ministerial meetings. The Lorillards and Hammond thus pursued a course to take a festival tour to the Soviets, and they had a precedent.

In December 1955 Robert Breen's Everyman Opera began its historic tour of George Gershwin's *Porgy and Bess*. Chronicled by Truman Capote in his *The Muses Are Heard*, the Everyman tour was the first by an American theater company in the Soviet Union since the Bolshevik Revolution. The State Department had refused to fund the tour in line with the Eisenhower administration's restriction on the use of any such funds behind the Iron Curtain. However, the Soviet Union came forward to pay Breen's costs within its borders.

Into early 1956 Louis Lorillard and Hammond looked for ways to cover costs of a festival tour to the Soviet border. Hammond had made a summer 1947 trip to precommunist Prague for Keynote Records, where he had discovered a thriving jazz scene. Now, eight years later, he reckoned on using his contacts with the head of the Czech Composers Alliance, Emil Buron, and critic Emanuel Ugge to make viable a ten-day tour in Czechoslovakia. Although he knew that festival advisory committee member Robert Schnitzer's American National Theatre and Academy would not support an Eastern European tour, Hammond hoped that he could bring pressure on the State Department to change its funding policy.

For a time Hammond was confident that he could enlist support from his friend Harlem Democratic congressman Adam Clayton Powell Jr. In 1955 the African American legislator had attended a gathering of nonaligned states at Indonesia's Bandung Conference of African and Asian nations. He returned to Washington to argue for an American foreign policy supportive of anticolonialism and more responsive to the needs of what was being called the Third World. Possessed with a vision of sending jazz into communist-oriented countries, Powell helped facilitate the 1956 Dizzy Gillespie worldwide tour, the State Department's first sponsored tour of a jazz artist. In November 1955, State had also approved funding for Armstrong's May 1956 tour to Accra, a year in advance of Ghanaian independence, the first for a former Sub-Sahara African British colony.

Hammond intended to play the Powell card in the effort. He also believed that Powell was going to make a run for national office in November 1956. In the end Powell broke Democratic ranks, charging that the civil rights plank in the party platform was too weak, and threw his support behind President Eisenhower's reelection.

Louis Lorillard was already talking to State, "with the person who holds the strings on the actual disbursements," as he told a meeting of the festival advisory committee in December 1955. The festival's nonprofit status, he believed, could support a case for getting department funds for a Western European tour.

Without any realistic business plan, Elaine Lorillard opposed attempting to go through Western Europe as a commercial venture. Instead, she wanted to go directly to the Soviet Union. "I am in communication with Russia," she told the festival advisers that December. "Why not just send musicians to Russia for a commercial deal to bring up the precedent of the Festival? That is my point. . . . I think the very fact of going behind the Iron Curtain is terrific."

Her approach was to work on Rhode Island senator Theodore Francis Green. As a senior Democrat on the Senate Foreign Relations Committee, Green, Elaine believed, was in a good position to try rewriting the legislation restricting State funds for use behind the Iron Curtain. "We have one asset which no other group can claim," she boasted, mindful of touring efforts undertaken by ANTA, impresario Norman Granz, and others. That asset was the remarkably well-connected Dr. Carleton Smith, founder, president, and director of New York's National Arts Foundation. Smith was a man for all seasons: a music history professor who taught at Oxford in the thirties; music editor for *Esquire*; European correspondent for the *New York Herald Tribune*, who interviewed Hitler, Mussolini, and Stalin; a musicologist whose sleuthing through Middle Europe in the late forties recovered many priceless music manuscripts lost during the war; NBC vice president; personal friend of President Harry Truman; and latterly a PR man known for organizing VIP lecture tours. Similarly inspired by the spirit of Geneva, Smith had returned from an October trip to Moscow, where he was putting together with the Soviets an exchange of dancers, musicians, and singers. Said Elaine, "Carleton Smith has the personal 'okay' from the Russian Cultural Attache. He said, 'I don't think jazz is cultural, but the Russian people would like it.' Therefore, we have that 'go ahead.'"

After pondering this proposal, Hammond was ready to seize on what could be a propaganda angle for the Soviets. "We might not get too much, but possibly we could play State against the Russian cultural attaches on this deal and come up with both of them trying to pay for it."

The State Department saw jazz tours in part as a means to distinguish American modernist culture and jazz as its musical art form from the less internationally accessible classical and folk music forms proffered by the Soviets. This view aligned perfectly with the Newport Jazz Festival mantra about jazz as the American art form. It was thus easy to believe that the futures of the festival and State's touring program could intertwine. It would in fact happen. Key advisory committee member Marshall Stearns accompanied Gillespie for part of his tour and along with *New York Times* jazz critic John Wilson would serve on State's selection committee, which chose the artists for the tours. Renaming the 1956 festival officially as the American Jazz Festival at Newport would provide further leverage to secure State Department funding for an overseas tour, or so the Lorillards and Hammond anticipated.

Whatever the hopes the festival directors embraced for government sponsorship of a jazz tour, however, domestic politics intervened. While the high-level proponents of the jazz tours sought to embed them with an integrationist agenda for propaganda purposes, they failed to shield that intention from domestic segregationists. The contrary behavior of Gillespie at various points during his tour didn't help and generated sharp congressional criticism, unfortunately from members of Green's own party, in particular from New York congressman John Rooney and Louisiana senator Allen Ellender. Attacks from congressional segregationists peaked in May 1956, just as Gillespie returned and Armstrong left for his triumphant tour to Accra. Ellender later introduced legislation to zero funding for the touring program.

International politics would also intervene as the year advanced. A loosening of cultural and political restrictions, known as the thaw, had begun after Soviet Premier Joseph Stalin's death in March 1953. It intensified after his successor Nikita Khrushchev, in his secret speech to the February 1956 Communist Party Congress, revealed and distanced himself from the excesses of Stalinism and the deceased premier's cult of personality. However, the thaw came to an abrupt halt in the late spring as public agitation spread through Eastern Europe in protest against the persistently hard-line communist regimes held in place by continued Soviet military occupation.

Although a festival tour of the Soviet Union would not be in the cards for 1956, the Lorillards and Hammond could take other steps to internationalize what they now officially titled The American Jazz Festival at Newport. Mindful of how the State Department would approve of the choices, they booked three jazz pianists from abroad, two not coincidentally from two defeated World War II powers who were in 1956 symbolically important cold war allies. A third came from Austria, which until the previous year had been divided into four zones of occupation under American, British, French, and Soviet forces.

The first was Japanese, the twenty-seven-year-old Toshiko Akiyoshi. A Wein protégée introduced to jazz by old Erroll Garner records, she was trained in Joseph Schillinger's system of musical composition at Boston's Berklee School. One 1956 account read, "Telegenic and dressed in native costume, she beats out well thought-out improvisations on Porter and Rogers." The second was Jutta Hipp, a thirty-one-year-old German brought to the United States by critic Leonard Feather. The same article read that she had been recording with Blue Note and "showed a Len Tristano influence and a strong style." The third was Friedrich Gulda, a twenty-six-year-old Viennese. Better known as a classical pianist and Beethoven interpreter, Gulda was tagged the "greatest new piano talent of our generation."

John Hammond and the Lorillards were not the only ones who grasped the liberating potential of jazz, especially in Communist countries. The truth, in fact, was held at the very highest councils of the U.S. foreign policy establishment.

Overseas jazz broadcasting was evidently not as visible to the segregationists in Congress as were the jazz tours. The potential for jazz broadcasting to the Soviet Union was immediately grasped by the new American ambassador Charles E. "Chip" Bohlen as soon as he arrived in Moscow shortly after Stalin's death. One of the most powerful and most connected architects of postwar U.S. foreign policy, particularly with regard to the Soviet Union, Bohlen astutely observed a political potential to the growing counterculture among Soviet youth in the fifties.

Sometime before Bohlen arrived in Moscow, young Russian jazz lovers danced and drank in restaurants and the big hotels frequented by foreigners. To the annoyance of the Communist authorities, they dressed and swaggered in a zoot-suited manner ironically associated with the Rumanian-born Hollywood icon Johnny Weissmuller, the star of numerous Tarzan films for more than a decade. It came from his *Tarzan in New York,* which somehow passed Soviet censorship and ran in 1951–52. The youths in this Soviet subculture thereafter went by the name *Tarzantsy,* wearing their hair long to the base of the neck.

During the thaw, these and other Soviet youths, if not rebelling, at least adopted a style of rebellion. The authorities called them *stiliagi* (style hunters), and the style going into 1956 refrained that of the American zoot-suiters of the 1949 era. Inventing their own jargon, males and females referred to each other as *chuvaki* (dudes) and *chuviki* (chicks), with the more far out living a life they called *kliovyi* (groovy). Into the year, stiliagi began dressing in the cool bop mode associated with Dizzy Gillespie, who was in the midst of his well-publicized world tour. Well in advance of the London punks of the seventies, female stiliagi, their hair cut short, wore large safety pins as ornaments on their dresses. After Khrushchev's secret speech, the increasing visibility of the stiliagi became a great worry to the Stalinist hard-liners, who still were a conservative force on the new premier's right.

Despite the thaw, the Soviet ban on jazz records continued. When rock and roll later arrived with early rock and roller Bill Haley in the form of bootleg albums, which circulated on X-ray plates called *Roentgenizdat,* the Stalinists saw that these were banned as well.

Bohlen personally understood the impact of jazz. As a young diplomat stationed at the Moscow embassy in the mid-thirties, he and some of his fellow single diplomats ran with a jazz crowd around singer Vera Dneprova. Mistress to one, she benefited from hundreds of American jazz records, plied by the young envoys, which she transcribed for use by her Ladies Jazz Orchestra.

After a year of witness to countercultural ferment of the mid-fifties, Bohlen sensed a liberating potential in the wide dissemination of American jazz among these young audiences. In late 1954 he suggested an idea that was to become jazz commentator Willis Conover's *Music USA*, which would build on a previous program of live broadcasts from Fifty-second Street hosted by Leonard Feather and called *Jazz Club USA*. Conover's new program first aired in January 1955.

"*Music USA* had tremendous impact. It literally was worldwide," said one of Conover's VOA chiefs, Barry Zorthian, at the time a program manager who reported directly to VOA director Bob Button, "but it was very well focused on behind the Iron Curtain."

Zorthian, it so happened, was a Yale classmate of George Avakian. "We were the only two of Armenian extraction, both with 'I-A-Ns' at the end of our names," said Zorthian, "and I remember meeting George. He was in Jonathan Edwards College, and I was Davenport, and I said, 'We better get together.'"

If jazz was the lingua franca of dissident Soviet youth in 1956, the stiliagi style was in satellites as well, especially Czechoslovakia, Poland, and Hungary. Conover's arrival at VOA the year before led to a peaking of the stiliagi movement and an explosion of jazz combos on the campuses of universities and colleges.

"Willis always thought it had a particular impact on the Poles," said Zorthian. "The evidence on the show is available: The Poles started their own jazz clubs, and so on."

According to Art Tatum biographer Jim Lester, "Poland's best known musicians all assert that *Music USA* provided the foundation of their education in jazz. . . . Before tape recorders were available each man in a band might try to capture on paper at least two bars of a song, so that later the group could re-construct the whole piece."

Music USA with its opening theme, "Take the A Train," may have seemed an anthem for cultural identification and community, but in the context of the 1956 uprisings it may have had greater effect as a clarion call to political rebellion. As Hans N. "Tom" Tuch, cultural affairs officer in Moscow in 1956, told Soviet-era jazz historian Frederick Starr in 1979: "The whole business of jazz was a political question, not cultural."

By the summer of 1956, many of Conover's young Eastern European listeners were among those inclined to protest against their Stalinist puppet governments and their Soviet masters. Although Hungary and to some extent Czechoslovakia saw considerable and growing unrest in the late spring, the spirit of rebellion violently took to the streets first in Poland. Three weeks before Newport '56, June 18, Polish workers erupted into two days of rioting in Poznan that left seventy-five Poles dead and nine hundred injured.

In Hungary VOA specifically targeted students and intellectuals who formed for the most part the Hungarian jazz audience. Listeners relied on broadcasts from the Voice of

America, as well as the far more strident Radio Free Europe, for news of the great happenings in the West that might have a direct influence on their lives. The VOA used this curiosity about life in America to hook listeners and subtly propagandize. While Bohlen was firm in later statements that VOA and Radio Free Europe broadcasts did not overtly incite Hungarians to revolt, his was a temperament that connected the dots between liberating music and liberating politics. Indeed, in the context of civil rights, such connections at once inspired progressives like John Hammond and terrified segregationists like Allen Ellender.

Budapest had an illegal grouping of scores of young jazz aficionados called the Budapest Hot Club, which met in secret at members' flats to listen to the famously hypnotic deep and sonorous voice of Willis Conover and his jazz playlist. Among them was a young American foreign service officer, Ernest A. Nagy, who would supply them with *Down Beat* magazines, sheet music, and records. At any one meeting some twenty-five would attend, Nagy recalled, including a member of the Hungarian secret police. "He was a jazz lover," said Nagy, "who was supposed to report on the goings-on, but didn't."

In the autumn, when Hungarian composers and musicians published a manifesto that in part wanted more knowledge of Western music, the VOA Hungarian service responded on October 2 with a weekly music broadcast. That same month, VOA maintained heavy prepublicity announcing the upcoming broadcasts of Conover's coverage of the American Jazz Festival at Newport. As the month advanced, the mood in Budapest became more confrontational.

VOA aired the first program on Monday, October 15. On Thursday, October 18, listeners heard their first Ellington composition of the broadcasts, "In a Mellotone," performed by Coleman Hawkins and the Buck Clayton All Stars. The following Tuesday, October 23, one hundred thousand Hungarian students and workers took to the streets with prodemocracy banners. The uprising had begun, and a massacre ensued. On Wednesday VOA went to an emergency schedule to all Europe and the Soviet Union. It would call the uprising a freedom revolt. On Friday the twenty-sixth, tanks fired on demonstrators, killing hundreds on the same day that Hungarian rebels formed workers' and national councils. VOA broadcast that day Ellington's two numbers from his opening Newport set, "Black and Tan Fantasy" and "Tea for Two," plus Conover's interview with Billy Strayhorn.

The Soviets withdrew on Tuesday the thirtieth, and VOA aired the first numbers in the second set, "Take the A Train" and the three-part "Suite." The following day, the thirty-first, VOA aired the last program in the Newport broadcast that finished Ellington's second set. It opened with Conover's interview with Duke and then picked up the running order at "Sophisticated Lady," "Day In, Day Out," "Diminuendo in Blue and Crescendo in Blue," "I Got It Bad," "Jeep's Blues," "Tulip or Turnip," "Skin Deep," and finally "Mood Indigo."

On November 1 came the ceasefire. The Hungarian leader Imre Nagy announced Hungary's withdrawal from the Warsaw Pact, the Kremlin's military alliance with its satellite Eastern European regimes. Nagy also declared Hungary neutral and appealed to the

Willis Conover when he was a pioneering jazz disc jockey for WWDC in Washington, DC, in the forties and early fifties. ::: *Photograph by Seghers. Courtesy of the Institute of Jazz Studies, Rutgers University.*

West for support. None came. The daring attempt at independence would be over by the weekend. On Saturday, November 3, Soviet military forces surrounded Budapest and the following day reintervened with tanks to crush the uprising.

The Hungarian Uprising was a brief two weeks. The young bore the brunt. Of the tens of thousands who died, some 85 percent were between sixteen and thirty-five. Of the two hundred thousand who fled, just under three-quarters were not yet thirty.

Many of the young who fought in the streets were members of the Hungarian jazz community. A number of Budapest Hot Club members participated in the street fighting, and some were killed, said Ernest Nagy. After the uprising the foreign service officer was tasked with opening Camp Roeder, a refugee camp near Salzburg, Austria. He was able to connect with five Hot Club veterans, one of whom was the Hungarian jazz guitarist Gabor Szabo. All five eventually made it to the States.

Willis Conover interviewed Duke Ellington some fifty times, including that night at Newport before the Maestro returned to the stage for his second set. "Willis referred to that Ellington performance many times," said Terry Ripmaster, who is writing a biography on Conover, "and when it appeared on a record, it became one of his favorites on his VOA programs."

Some time ago, London-based Russian jazz producer Leo Feigin of Leo Records offered the insight of the listeners clandestinely glued to their radios, as Alexander Solzhenitsyn put it, "in the midst of Communist darkness." "Willis Conover," Feigin told National Public Radio, "was broadcasting the kind of music which personified for us someone else's freedom." For hundreds, maybe thousands of Budapest jazz fans—freedom fighters—the music of Ellington and of Newport '56, broadcast in the midst of the uprising, was nothing less than its sound track.

20

Festival Junction

From Newport to Yasgur's Farm

Newport, Rhode Island, "was front-page news again all over the uncivilized world," wrote Cleveland Amory in the August 1956 *Holiday*. "As for the civilized world, in Newport itself, one gas-station attendant admitted that he made more from three days of the Jazz Festival than he did from four months of the summer Society people. 'And,' he added meaningfully, 'I was paid in cash too.'"

Three years of jazz festivals culminating in the '56 Ellington performance had put Newport once again on the national map. The town's past image, associated with the descendants of Gilded Age society, had become just that, an image, albeit with commercial uses. In 1957 the Lorillard Tobacco Company capitalized on a branding opportunity by launching its Newport menthol cigarette, marketing it as a "fun cigarette" to appeal to the young. Now America's number-one menthol, the brand enjoys extensive popularity among African American smokers. The original pack arrived in aquamarine blue with a logo suggesting a wind-filled sail, familiar today in inverted form as Nike's swoosh. The logo was an aptly classy reference, for in 1958 the America's Cup ocean sailing competition returned to Newport after a hiatus of twenty-one years.

In post-1956 America the reality of Newport-the-town had as much—if not more—to do with the economic interests and cultural tastes of its small business community and the wealthy newcomers like the Andersons, Capuanos, and LeSavoys than with those of the old guard. Fed and linked nationally by mass media, this kind of social alliance was reaching critical mass in Newport and elsewhere and would accelerate social change into the sixties. Moreover, for better of worse, after 1956 the young in every audience came to the festival with the promise of an event—be it revival meeting or happening—occurring onstage or off, and, as much, beyond the grounds of Freebody Park.

The 1957 jazz festival opened, according to *Time*, "with the authority of an established institution." The '57 festival generated the "first substantial profit," George Wein remembered. While the *Time* article quoted Elaine Lorillard's dismissing the festival's earlier opponents among the old guard as persons "not socially secure," the accelerating change was blowing past her own best efforts. In 1957 Norman Granz and his Verve label got the rights to record the festival performances. By throwing an extravagant party at the Viking Hotel that attracted many of the musicians, the California jazz impresario upstaged her annual soiree on her own turf.

George Wein believed the Newport jazz festival of the fifties restored a national focus on jazz. In the forties "all the real jazz fans came to Fifty-second Street. But it wasn't a national thing; it was New York. If you were a jazz fan, you went to New York. You went to Fifty-second Street. There weren't that many jazz clubs outside of New York. The nightclubs were mostly on a circuit of California, Philly, New York, and Boston. The festival built up a whole new world. It became a great public-relations medium for jazz. The press picked up on it. There were radio broadcasts. Jazz was American music in a tremendous surge, which helped every artist, club, everything."

The success of the Newport jazz festival also inspired a West Coast equivalent, launched in September 1958 when San Francisco disc jockey and jazz poet Jimmy Lyons and writer Ralph J. Gleason held the first Monterey Jazz Festival, which continues annually to this day. Featured artists included Bay Area star Dave Brubeck, along with other greats like Dizzy Gillespie, Louis Armstrong, Harry James, Billie Holiday, and Gerry Mulligan.

The Bay Area was a major jazz outpost and mecca for the beat generation. Alongside the Beats and the jazz community, a folk revival was beginning to bloom and put weight under another genre heretofore outside the popular music mainstream. Reacting to growing criticism of the confrontational first wave of rock and rollers, the mainstream music business started packaging relatively vapid singers like Fabian and Frankie Avalon as latter-day Sinatras. The more discerning youth abandoned the genre for folk. A local group from Palo Alto, the Kingston Trio, broke into the pop charts and went to the top nationally with "Tom Dooley."

Back East, in Boston, George Wein had looked across the Charles River to the folkie scene in Cambridge and began booking folk acts into his Mahogany Hall at Storyville and into his Storyville on Cape Cod. For the 1959 jazz festival, he decided to book the Kingston Trio. When he grew the idea into adding a full afternoon of folk music to the weekend after the jazz festival, Wein secured the assistance of banjo troubadour Pete Seeger and the owner of Chicago's Gate of Horn folk club, Albert Grossman, later the manager of such major folk artists as Bob Dylan and the trio Peter, Paul, and Mary. For the 1960 Newport Folk Festival, Wein ran three nights of music the weekend before the ill-fated jazz festival of that year.

For both folk and jazz purists in rebellion against consumer culture, Newport had commercialized jazz. For them the Newport Folk Festival was the jazz festival's other. The difference generally between the two subcultures was in their attitude toward political

Newport Freebody Park at the 1958 festival, the year of the documentary film *Jazz on a Summer's Day*. ::: *Photo courtesy of Bob Parent.*

activism. Whereas the jazz subculture could be said to be more preoccupied with freedom of the psyche, folkies were prepared to act on their preoccupation with social freedom. Their activism, like Pete Seeger's, had roots in the Old Left of the thirties. The gathering civil rights movement amid the plenty of the fifties became the cause for folk revival, although Joan Baez maintained it was more the cry to ban the bomb.

The reaction against postwar consumer culture was already evident in some responses to the 1956 jazz festival. The previously cited 1956 *Metronome* piece opined that "the prestige and pleasure of the Festival is on the wane (regardless of its commercial success this year)." Referring to a "variety of jazz Babbitts" and the tensions evident on Marshall Stearns's Friday panel, the magazine criticized "the emphasis on the exotic *jazz entertainer* and the use of Bird's name in much the same way as politicians call upon God to support their statements and overcome their enemies." According to one commentary on the festival, what started with the intent to bring respectability to beats and Harlem music was becoming a college party.

The spirit of these years was captured on film. The story goes that Elaine Lorillard had asked celebrity photographer Bert Stern to take some photographs of the 1958 festival, but he had something more in mind. The result was Stern and film editor Aram Avakian's *Jazz on a Summer's Day,* a documentary of the 1958 jazz festival, which did not see release until early 1960.

"The Lorillards are selling both Newport residences but keeping the farm," Cleveland Amory had written in his 1956 *Holiday* piece. " 'We're moving to New York,' she concludes gaily. 'Newport, you know, is a great place to visit, but I wouldn't want to live there.' " The Lorillards that November sold Belcourt to the Tinney family, who were from Cumberland, just north of Pawtucket and Providence, for $25,000.

In fact, Elaine Lorillard's marriage to Louis did not survive. "Sour went the notes in the love song of Louis and Elaine Lorillard," reported an October 1958 *Time*. "Filing suit for separation, blonde, pretty Elaine . . . charged that Louis had locked her out of their Manhattan cooperative apartment and packed her belongings off to a nearby hotel while she was away for a weekend." In the throes of a divorce, Louis Lorillard as festival chairman had Elaine removed from the board in advance of the 1959 festival, to which she responded with a lawsuit. Yet a fixture in jazz she remained.

In 1960 Elaine gave financial support to bassist Charles Mingus to offer an alternative Jazz Artists Guild Festival on the seaside grounds of the Cliff Walk Manor hotel and restaurant overlooking First Beach and Middletown. It was known familiarly as the Newport Rebel festival. Mingus was joined by alto saxophonist Eric Dolphy, drummers Max Roach and Jo Jones, and others. Musicians slept in tents on the hotel grounds, and Mingus himself passed the hat among the some seven-hundred-fifty fans who attended. It was a response to the supposed commercialism of the regular festival.

Wein was expanding his 1960 festival to five days and nights, encompassing a weekend and leading to a planned finale on Monday night. The Saturday night program attracted fifteen thousand, the largest festival audience to date. In 1959 the bars had stayed open and resulted in a plethora of drunken college kids littering the town. In 1960 the problem had become worse. Many youthful fans and thrill seekers encamped outside Freebody Park, and some overindulged and became restless. When drunken youths rioted on Middleton Avenue and started pelting the police with bottles, firemen opened their hoses on the mob. The rampage that ensued along Bellevue Avenue was only quashed by state police intervention, with support from the National Guard and a contingent of marines.

The town suspended the rest of the festival but spared Mingus's rebel festival and Wein's Sunday afternoon blues offering. The 1960 riots led to Newport's cancellation of both the 1961 jazz and folk festivals, ending the Lorillards' nonprofit enterprise for good.

The separation squabbling between Elaine and Louis continued for a number of years. "In Middletown, R.I., Elaine and her two teen-aged children by Louis were evicted from their rented Paradise Farm home. Louis had let the lease lapse," a June 1963 *Time* reported. "Mrs. Lorillard further complains that her $700 monthly support payments have dwindled to a mere $100 a month, and she can't locate her husband, who at one point last year got the electricity turned off, plunging Paradise into darkness. 'I don't think I will ever serve dinner by candlelight again,' she said ruefully." Their divorce became final in 1964.

After his festival days Louis had returned to the travel business and moved to France in 1961. Later he relocated to St. Croix in the Virgin Islands, where he was executive secretary of the Chamber of Commerce and commissioner of commerce from 1969 to 1971. Sometime afterward, he returned to Middletown. In November 1986, at sixty-seven, he died of pneumonia.

Elaine Lorillard remained in Newport and for many years continued to produce events. Notably she played a role in the movement for jazz exchanges with the Soviet Union in the mid-to-late sixties. In 2002 the Rhode Island School of Design recognized her as a state treasure. Today in her nineties, she remains active as an artist while working on a nonprofit to establish a Newport Jazz Festival Museum.

The Newport Jazz Festival itself would continue without her. Two years after the 1960 riots and the collapse of the Lorillards' nonprofit, George Wein was able to put together the for-profit Festival Productions, Inc., ironically with support from former Newport rebel Charlie Mingus. For staging Wein engaged Chip Monck who later became famous for his lighting and stage managing Woodstock and a host of other celebrated rock events in the sixties and seventies.

The revived Newport Jazz Festival thus entered a triumphant phase. "We had the greatest years of jazz in '62, '63, '64," Wein recalled in his 2003 interview.

In 1963 Wein revived the folk festival under the nonprofit Newport Folk Foundation. The folkies themselves were the message of the festival and its identification with the civil rights movement. The musicians were unassuming, and their house parties were starkly different from the Lorillards' ostentatious Bellevue Avenue affairs of the fifties. At the 1963 folk festival the artists assembled onstage to sing the civil rights anthem "We Shall Overcome." Wein quoted writers tagging the moment as the "apex of the folk revival." A noteworthy musical bellwether was the Saturday afternoon blues program that featured among others the just rediscovered prewar Delta blues guitarist Mississippi John Hurt.

For George Wein the year of change was 1964. "The fans really weren't contaminated by rock and roll until the Beatles came along, when if you liked jazz, you were too old."

"Rock and roll," continued Wein, "didn't raise its ugly head until Chuck Berry came [to the 1958 jazz festival]. And, well, Chuck Berry was brought on especially, because John Hammond wanted him. And Ray Charles I brought on, because my friends the Erteguns [brothers Ahmet and Nesuhi, founders of Atlantic Records] played his record for me, and when they first signed him, I flipped over him."

Although young people had been sleeping on beaches at earlier festivals, the volume at the 1964 festivals led Newport to ban future festivals at Freebody Park. For the 1965 festivals Wein was able to secure a site on the north side of town on private land between the naval base and the hillside to Miantomoni Memorial Park. The festival erected a permanent stage, and the site came to be known as Festival Field. While the 1965 jazz festival featured a high-profile performance by Frank Sinatra, who, in the fashion of an immortal, came and went by helicopter, history best remembers that year's folk festival as the moment when John Hammond's Columbia folk star Bob Dylan went electric. When Dylan sang his final number, "It's All Over Now Baby Blue," Wein and others inferred in the performance the troubadour's farewell to folk and his embrace of rock, which led to the demise of the folk festival. Wein also read in a backstage fisticuffs between folk purist Alan Lomax and folk entrepreneur Albert Grossman the conflict between folk idealism and commercialism. The following year the folk festival for the first time lost money.

Wein was another who felt that 1968 was the year when rock overtook pop music and the music world generally and when jazz lost relevance in the pop cultural mainstream. The national mood was turning ugly amid an unpopular war and the coming of age of a rebellious new generation intent on writing its own script.

Wein discovered the saving grace of sponsorship with the Joseph Schlitz Brewing Company when he was able to take the festival on the road that year with the Schlitz Salute to Jazz tour. He also expanded his operation to the Big Easy with the first New Orleans Jazz and Heritage Festival. Back in Newport in 1969, Wein included rock on the Friday night, July 4. It was chaotic and led to the Newport City Council outlaw of rock at future festivals.

That August saw Woodstock. In the autumn came two huge Washington antiwar demonstrations. Youth had gone confrontational. Wein put together a strictly jazz program for the 1970 festival, which passed without incident. For 1971, however, he ill-advisedly booked the Allman Brothers, a southern blues band, for his Sunday night fare. As distinct from the 1960 crowd of drunken collegians, Wein found this crowd "obsessed with protest." A riot erupted, cancelling the show and killing the festival once and for all.

The following year, Wein took the name Newport Jazz Festival to multiple venues in New York City. Calling it the Newport Jazz Festival New York, he once again engaged Schlitz to sponsor music at two venues. Wein's New York festival led to a boom in New York jazz clubs in the seventies. As for his tours, Wein would have Schlitz sponsor a number of tours and would later align with Brown and Williamson Tobacco to sponsor what became the Kool Jazz festivals.

Jazz would return to Newport when the mood of the country changed with the Reagan years. Besides, Newport was hungry. In 1973 the navy had closed much of its shore establishment and shifted its Newport-based destroyers and other ships to Norfolk, Virginia, and elsewhere as the military downsized after the Vietnam War. The economic shock was tremendous. Throughout the postwar period the navy had been the state's largest employer.

By 1981 the tourist industry was driving Newport priorities, and the festival was a proven draw. Wein returned with a daytime offering at Fort Adams State Park, on Narragansett Bay, just west of downtown. Two years later, JVC came aboard as title sponsor. In 1985 Wein restarted the folk festival and later secured for it a string of sponsorships that included Ben and Jerry's ice cream and Dunkin' Donuts. Wein's Festival Productions now holds jazz and folk offerings worldwide.

"The Newport Jazz Festival really started everything that is happening today," George Wein reminisced. "But there was a different type of camaraderie [in the fifties] that's missing from the festival today. All the musicians were brothers and sisters. Whether they were bebop or traditional, they knew the same songs, the same changes. Jamming then was more frequent. They weren't playing modal, electronic, all different styles. Now, there's so many different kinds of music. And the people who came to Newport [in the fifties] had more knowledge of what they were coming to see. They knew the performers. They knew every group. There was not that much conflict in music. There only was jazz and pop. The pop was Patti Page and Frank Sinatra, and the jazz was jazz—swing or bebop. We had a collective structure of jazz in those days. The fans came for the entire feeling."

One young fan who came for the feeling on the threshold of the sixties was Elaine Anderson's son Rick. He had inspired his Deerfield classmate, John Roberts, a Park Avenue heir to the Py-Co-Pay toothbrush fortune, to join him. Rick had attended festivals with Fall River friends in '58 and '59. In 1960 he and Roberts went with a couple of girls in his Fall River circle.

On the first night of what would become the riotous 1960 festival, the two boys decided to smuggle a couple of beers in the girls' purses. Caught by the police and "thrown in the can and as they used to do," the four were released the next morning and "were severely chastised by our dates' parents."

Sans the young ladies, the boys returned to the festival that raucous Saturday. Rick recalled how Roberts "was all excited about the whole atmosphere," as the numbers of youth swelled through the weekend. "It really started getting out of hand. It became a real scene."

Roberts was overwhelmed by the magnitude of what he had experienced at Newport '60, having lived a somewhat sheltered life between prep school and Park Avenue. From that point onward Rick would come to New York and serve as his introduction to nightlife, taking him to Midtown music venues like Jimmy Ryan's, Birdland, and the Embers, where they would smuggle into the clubs flasks of rum.

After graduating from Deerfield in 1962, Rick went to Brown, Roberts the University of Pennsylvania. The pair maintained their close friendship. Roberts was one of Rick's ushers at his 1967 wedding. Rick joined the Army Reserve and promptly went to work for helicopter manufacturer Textron at their corporate headquarters in Providence, Rhode Island.

While in New York sometime in late 1968, Rick paid a visit to Roberts at his Upper East Side apartment on Eighty-fifth Street and Third Avenue. He recalled arriving to see stacks of letters with "all kinds of wacko" proposals throughout the flat. Roberts and his roommate, Joel Rosenman, had evidently put ads in the *Wall Street Journal* and the *New York Times* touting themselves as "young men with unlimited capital" looking for good ideas.

In August, when Rick returned to his office from two weeks of Army Reserve training at Fort Smith in Blackstone, Virginia, he received "a frantic message" from Roberts calling from "somewhere in upstate New York, the Catskills, 'Please send helicopters!' "

John Roberts had succeeded in overwhelming himself with the magnitude of his own festival. The wacko proposal that he and Rosenman financed came to life as an event that for better or worse defined a generation and is recalled in a single word: Woodstock.

Notes

1. A Phrase with Six Tones—Apart, Yet Integral

5 *"the force that put his band back on the jazz map"*: Elaine Anderson, quoted in Sjef Hoefsmit, ed., "Dance to the Duke," *International DEMS Bulletin,* 02/2 DEMS 9, Duke Ellington Music Society, 02/2 August–November 2002, www.depanorama.net/dems/02dems2b.htm (accessed Aug. 26, 2007).

5 *"no industry buzz"*: George Wein, interview with author, New York, Nov. 12, 2002. Unless otherwise indicated, all Wein quotes are from this interview.

6 *Who caused the moment?* Anderson, quoted in Hoefsmit.

6 *"American culture"*: Albert Murray, *The Omni-Americans: New Perspectives on Black Experience and American Culture* (New York: Outerbridge and Dienstfrey, 1970), p. 22.

6 *"Who, seeing and hearing"*: Ralph Ellison, *Living with Music: Ralph Ellison's Jazz Writings* (New York: Modern Library, 2001), pp. 79–80.

6–7 *One view:* Ortiz M. Walton, *Music: Black, White, and Blue* (New York: William Morrow, 1972), p. 50. The consequent "group identity crises," wrote Walton, an African American sociologist who at one time was a principal bassist with the Boston Symphony, gave expression toward the end of that century to jazz that "helped to create a sense of common cultural identity."

7 *white Anglo-Saxon Protestant establishment:* Despite the rhetoric of American democracy, entrance into Anglo society remained closed. The Great War and Bolshevik Revolution—and Red Scare that followed—prompted an anxious American establishment to try to impose its own notion of assimilation. Essentially it reinforced the extensions of English social and cultural hegemony in American institutions still very much controlled by Anglo-Saxon Americans. Some called the approach Anglo-conformity. Passing through Ellis Island, many new immigrants were given new names—Anglicized. Non-English-speaking immigrants would have to learn English. Over time some would work their way into entrepreneurships and the professions.

7 *the same pot:* As cultural historian Lewis A. Erenberg put it, "Along with fashion, dance, and music, jive language bespoke a creolization of American youth culture" (*Swingin' the Dream: Big Band Jazz and the Rebirth of American Culture* [Chicago: University of Chicago

Press, 1998], p. 56). Not limiting the observation to swing, African American playwright Amiri Baraka (LeRoi Jones) took the point further, writing that jazz "was a music capable of reflecting not only the Negro and black America but a white America as well," thus creating "a common cultural ground" (*Blues People* [New York: William Morrow, 1963], pp. 149–50). Ralph Ellison went so far as to express a belief that violates a "Crow Jim" taboo when he told an interviewer in 1976, "When a black musician says he was influenced by white musicians I believe him and see no reason to doubt him. It's most American. This is a pluralistic society and culturally the melting pot really melts" (*Living with Music,* p. 25). No less than "The President" of the tenor sax, Lester Young, averred that two mid-western German Americans, cornetist Bix Beiderbecke and C-Melody saxophonist Frankie Trumbauer, were the *major* influences on his playing.

7 *social status:* The trend was already evident before the war with the advent of café society, when Newport started going to Harlem in the twenties and to Greenwich Village in the thirties. Café society was in part an aggregation of new millionaires from textiles, mass communications, and automobiles—plus the mass entertainers.

7 *"The deciders and originators":* C. Wright Mills, *White Collar: The American Middle Classes* (New York: Oxford University Press, 1953), p. 253.

7 *"manufactured loyalties and distractions":* Mills, *White Collar,* p. xvi.

8 *"nonconformist[s] in the Marlon Brando tradition":* Quoted in Peter Viereck, *The Unadjusted Man: A New Hero for Americans: Reflections on the Distinction between Conforming and Conserving* (Boston: Beacon, 1956), p. 13.

8 *"a secular, vernacular rite":* W. T. Lhamon Jr., *Deliberate Speed: The Origins of a Cultural Style in the American 1950s* (Washington: Smithsonian Institution Press, 1990), p. 152.

8 *came of age:* "Jazz audiences become age-linked," wrote Ortiz Walton; "an association is established between the age of audience, player and era of musical content." The Newport festival aspired to present its audiences with a range of jazz genres. The popular music of the early fifties was the music of the solo singer. While it may have been just what the war-weary wanted, it did not suit the unadjusted intellectuals and nonconformists.

9 *"The riff itself":* Baraka, *Blues People,* pp. 172–74.

9 *"That's the Negro's life":* Barry Ulanov, *Duke Ellington* (London: Farrar, Straus and Giroux, 1947).

10 *"The most neglected component":* Gary Giddins, *Visions of Jazz: The First Century* (New York: Oxford University Press, 1998), p. 509.

10 *"The audience expectation":* Dan Morgenstern, interview with author, Newark, NJ, Nov. 13, 2002. Unless otherwise indicated, all Morgenstern quotes are from this interview.

10 *devil in the music:* Saxophonist Paul Gonsalves began his solo with a tritone substitution, what medieval musicologists called *diabolus in musicam,* the "devil in the music." Midway on the scale, the note divides the octave into two halves. A sound completely foreign to a key, the devil in the music is extremely dissonant, a restless, ambiguous sound that creates for the ear a spiritual and mysterious tension. It is the ultimate in conjuring, a sound that awakens a sense of the miraculous. Wagner used the devil in the music as the curse motif, the spiritual context, in *The Ring of the Nibelung,* and it was found frequently in compositions of other mystical romantic composers like Gustav Mahler and Anton Bruckner. More recently, Leonard Bernstein decided to write almost all of the music for the 1957 Broadway musical *West Side Story* using tritones. The second note in the opening phrase of "Maria" is the devil in the music.

2. Ellington's Long Road to Newport

13 *"You have really given me something!"* Quoted in Stuart Nicholson, *Reminiscing in Tempo: A Portrait of Duke Ellington* (Boston: Northeastern University Press, 1999).

13 Ellington family material from Michael James, Duke Ellington's nephew, who first toured with the band as a youth, ostensibly to be tutored on the trumpet by Clark Terry. Unless otherwise indicated, all James quotes are from conversations with the author.

14 Although various ascriptions abound, Ellington himself claimed that he acquired the name "Duke" early in life from a Washington pal, Edgar McIntree. Together they frequented the corner of Seventh and T streets in the Shaw neighborhood, where they refined their bantering skills playing the dozens and smoking cigars in an adolescent effort to emulate the mustachioed silent movie star Stuart Holmes, who played opposite vamp Theda Bara in three films in 1916.

15 *"sat beside white people"*: Langston Hughes, *The Big Sea* (New York: Hill and Wang, 1993), p. 206.

15 *New Negro movement:* The larger American society characterized the prosperous post–World War I decade as the Roaring Twenties—F. Scott Fitzgerald's "Jazz Age" of miracles, art, excess, and satire, as the Irish American Princetonian would have it. Yet the Harlem of the 1920s was a place and time where a different history culminated.

In 1896, as is well known, African Americans received a setback to social advancement promised by President Lincoln's Emancipation Proclamation when the Supreme Court's *Plessy vs. Ferguson* decision enshrined the notorious "separate but equal" legal provisions for accommodating black and white citizens. Plessy, the Creole plaintiff in a discrimination case against the railroads, was ironically only one-eighth black and seven-eighths white, but under Louisiana law he was considered a Negro. The decision gave racial inequality and segregation an air of legitimacy for the next half century. The South began enacting equally notorious "Jim Crow" segregation laws across the board and all but denied African Americans voting privileges. As such, millions of African Americans began the Great Migration to the presumed more tolerant North and cities like New York, Chicago, and Washington. The first decades of the twentieth century, however, were beset with at times extreme and vicious racial violence all over the country. While lynchings occurred primarily in rural areas, they were not exclusive to the South, as some would imagine. Virtually every state in the continental United States had lynchings. The exceptions were Massachusetts, New Hampshire, Vermont, and, notably, Rhode Island. Race riots, on the other hand, were more often urban outbursts. They occurred in both North and South but were more characteristic of the North. The summer of 1919, called "The Red Summer" by James Weldon Johnson, the lyricist for "Lift Every Voice and Sing," generated the most intense period of interracial violence the nation had ever witnessed. That year, America suffered twenty-six violent race riots. On July 19, one rocked Ellington's Washington. By one reckoning, 40 were killed and 150 were wounded.

Harlem offered incipient political alternatives. One leader was Jamaican-born Marcus Garvey, founder of the Universal Negro Improvement Association and the Back to Africa movement and the first African American to get a PhD from Harvard. Another was the original Pan-Africanist W.E.B. Du Bois, editor of the NAACP's *Crisis* magazine. Later in the thirties, Langston Hughes, by then a leading Harlem literary figure, would turn radical, outraged by the effects of the Depression on African Americans and in particular the travesty of justice dealt the Scottsboro boys. In 1931 Alabama indicted and tried nine black youths for allegedly raping two white women, one of whom later recanted her testimony. While none was executed, the case took years to resolve. Throughout the thirties

Hughes consorted with Communist Party fronts and became a regular contributor to the party's literary publication *New Masses.*

The move was not unusual for the time. Howard "Stretch" Johnson, a dancer who went from performing with Duke Ellington at the Cotton Club to a youth leadership position with the Communist Party, once claimed that in late 1930s New York "seventy-five percent of black cultural figures had Party membership or maintained regular meaningful contact with the Party." The FBI even started and maintained for years a file on Ellington.

15 *primitivist chic:* In the twenties, when Ellington first arrived, the writers and artists of the Harlem Renaissance were exponents of *primitivism.* Artistically, the movement was a reaction to residual puritanism. Whites embraced the form as part of their own reaction to the hypocrisy of a European civilization that had recently allowed the mass technomurder of World War I. They were looking for alternatives. African Americans were thus in vogue. Aaron Douglas, the African American muralist, characterized the primitivist school as "spiritually earthy," a sobriquet that fits Ellington perfectly. While the movement thrived during the boom of the twenties, it would not survive the bust of the stock market crash and the Depression.

16 *"The Sugar Cane Club":* from Wallace Thurman's *Negro Life in New York's Harlem,* quoted from an extract in Amritjit Singh and Daniel M. Scott III, eds., *The Collected Writings of Wallace Thurman: A Harlem Renaissance Reader* (New Brunswick, NJ: Rutgers University Press, 2003), pp. 47–48.

17 *"primitive naked quality":* Horne quoted in Tod Olson, "Harlem Renaissance: After Midnight," "Teaching Resources." Scholastic.com http://content.scholastic.com/browse/article.jsp?id=4792.

18 Fredi Washington claim in Mercer Ellington, with Stanley Dance, *Duke Ellington in Person: An Intimate Memoir* (Boston: Houghton Mifflin, 1978).

18 *"apparitions within the music":* Ellington and Dance, *Duke Ellington in Person.*

23 *"as rhythmically sophisticated as Charlie Parker":* Quoted by Michael James.

24 *big solo singer:* Crosby had been the top male popular vocalist from 1936 to 1941 and the first crooner to work the mike. Before him were Russ Columbo and Rudy Vallee, indeed the first crooner to generate mass hysteria. Sinatra may have held Crosby as a model, but he created his own style. He once said that he fashioned his singing after Tommy Dorsey's trombone playing—a claim that is not too far-fetched given that Armstrong's trumpet was said to have inspired Billie Holiday's vocalization. On October 11, 1944, more than twenty-five thousand teenage fans jammed the thirty-six-hundred-seat Paramount for his Columbus Day concerts, the first of a five-show-a-day, three-week engagement. The bobby-soxers, by now associated with mass hysteria, rioted outside the theater. Sinatra was America's major teen pop star and remained so until 1948, when his scandalous and adulterous relationship with Ava Gardner almost ended his career.

24 *Musicraft Records:* An independent label that boasted Artie Shaw, Teddy Wilson, and Sarah Vaughan.

26 *"He always wanted a hit single again":* George Avakian, interview with author, Yonkers, NY, Nov. 11, 2002. Unless otherwise indicated, all Avakian quotes are from this interview.

27 *Biographer John Hasse:* John Edward Hasse, *Beyond Category: The Life and Genius of Duke Ellington* (New York: Simon and Schuster, 1993). I have attempted to cross-check dates against citations in Klaus Stratemann, *Duke Ellington Day by Day and Film by Film*

(Copenhagen: JazzMedia Aps, 1992). In instances where dates and citations do not correspond, I have used my best judgment along with informed advice to indicate when and where events occurred.

27 *"The band had to be broken up"*: Monsignor John Sanders, interview with author, Stamford, CT, Nov. 11, 2004. Unless otherwise indicated, all Sanders quotes are from this interview or subsequent conversations between Monsignor Sanders and the author.

27 *"The place was packed"*: Clark Terry, interview with author, Haworth, NJ, July 11, 2005. Unless otherwise indicated, all Terry quotes are from this interview.

3. Duke's Instrument

31 *"his tonal charisma"*: Duke Ellington, *Music Is My Mistress* (Garden City, NY: Doubleday, 1973), p. 118.

31 *"Writers talk"*: Cue Hodges, quoted on the CTI Jazz Web page, www.ctijazz.com/hodges.php (accessed Aug. 28, 2007).

33 *"reborn world"*: Jimmy Woode, interview with Phil Schaap, made available to the author by Michael James from his collection.

38 *"You could see"*: Willie Cook, interview with Phil Schaap, made available to the author by Michael James from his collection.

42 *Irving Townsend:* A younger protégé of John Hammond, Townsend like his mentor had gone to Hotchkiss, the fashionable Lakeville, Connecticut, prep school that dates from 1891, where they had been jazz fans. When Hammond first came to Columbia in 1939, he hired Townsend. Sometime later, Townsend went to Keynote Records to write publicity, where, after the war, Hammond landed as president. In 1977 Townsend would coauthor Hammond's autobiography, *John Hammond on Record.*

42 *"not just another bad record"*: Hodier quoted in Peter Keepnews, "Seven Decades of the Duke," *New York Times,* Nov. 21, 1993.

4. The Tiffany Label

46 *rise and rivalry:* Ever since the birth of recording, at the end of the nineteenth century, the original record division companies Columbia and Victor had been rivals. Two decades before Paley and Sarnoff, they were vying for the dictation and later music markets with two different recording machines and technologies.

50–51 *Commodore Records:* The Teagarden release led to pressings of other jazz artists and Gabler's starting another label, the United Hot Clubs of America. In 1938 guitarist Eddie Condon appeared on *Commodore Classics in Swing.* Other reissues featured Coleman Hawkins and, most notably, Billie Holiday's "Strange Fruit," her historic but previously unreleased musical statement against lynching.

5. George Avakian

53 *"exceptional school"*: Jack Kerouac, *Vanity of Duluoz* (New York: Penguin, 1994).

53 *U.S. visa:* The year 1921 was the year of the First Quota Law, an attempt to curtail immigration to America by setting limits according to nationality. Although Armenians, the Avakians were living in Persia at the time, and George Avakian's father was the last of two hundred Persians to get a visa under the law.

54 *especially meaningful:* Goodman came from Russian Jewish immigrants. Unlike Horace Mann students, however, his family had painfully modest means. He owed his early musical training to Hull House, Chicago's famous settlement house founded by Jane Addams, where he began private lessons with Franz Schoepp of the Chicago Symphony Orchestra.

54 *bandleader's entourage:* During this time Avakian first met and came to know John Hammond. They were heady days. In March 1937 Goodman began his explosive Paramount Theater booking that included a blistering five performances a day during the run. At seven in the morning on opening day, thousands of teenagers formed lines outside the theater. A full house of thirty-six-hundred screaming and cheering fans greeted Goodman and his band as they ascended on a rising stage playing "Let's Dance." The event was manic with jitterbuggers dancing in the aisles, ickies pressing against the stage, and the rest of the audience standing on seats in raucous abandon, presaging later frenzies over Frank Sinatra, Johnnie Ray, Elvis Presley, and the Beatles. The first-day attendance figure was twenty-one thousand. By the end of the opening week, Goodman had broken all attendance records. During the booking Paramount's "Negro" patronage reportedly rose from a typical 3 percent of the total to more than 15 percent. Goodman was the first bandleader to break the color line in music. Prior to the engagement, some in the press had predicted a race riot.

59 *Carnegie Hall concert:* The story of the concert is well known. Goodman's appearance was the first jazz booking at a concert hall and thus a historic event. It was a 2,760-seat sellout weeks in advance, with each ticket going for $2.75. Energy was high. Supporters of Generalissimo Francisco Franco picketed the Fifty-seventh Street entrance, angered by Goodman's support for the Spanish Republican government during the Spanish Civil War. Goodman, of course, went onstage with racially integrated lineups of musicians in orchestra, quartet, and trio settings and featured guest artists from the Ellington and Basie bands. While not as raucous as the Paramount audiences of the previous year, the crowd that night did dance and shout, while the ickies bopped at the edge of the stage.

60 *JATP:* Like Goodman and Hammond, Granz believed that the jazz experience had not just an artistic or aesthetic dimension but a social imperative as well, with its potential to serve and promote racial equality. Wartime Los Angeles had suffered through a difficult period of racial tension arising from an August 1942 murder in the Mexican American community, the police and court's mishandling of the case, and the riots that followed, pitting servicemen against zoot-suited Mexican Americans. *Down Beat* reported, "The Sunday afternoon affair, the proceeds of which will go to the Sleepy Lagoon Defense Fund (for liberation of a group of Mexican boys who were sent to San Quentin in a killing case during the 'zoot suit riots' here), was planned and sponsored by Norman Granz, local impresario for jazz performances and protagonist for racial unity." JATP was a fourth jazz performance in a concert hall venue after Goodman and Hammond's three prewar Carnegie Hall offerings but with a distinct difference. Goodman and Hammond had structured their events to educate a jazz audience with jazz history and only included jam sessions as combos in that context. Granz, however, allowed his musicians to revel in jams throughout, to the delight of the

racially mixed audience. At the first JATP was Albanian photojournalist Gjon Mili, who had made his name via his photos for a 1943 *Life* cover story on the Lindy Hop. "Warner Brothers was impressed with Gjon Mili's images," said Granz biographer Tad Hershorn, "and of course, Mili was one of the prime movers back then of strobe light photography" (Tad Hershorn, interview with author, Newark, NJ, July 10, 2003; unless otherwise indicated, all Hershorn quotes are from this interview). The studio had invited Mili to Hollywood to make a ten-minute short on any subject of his choosing. A friend brought him to the concert. Then and there, Mili found his subject, and Granz thus became technical adviser for Mili's film. Titled *Jammin' the Blues,* the short represented jams such as Mili experienced at JATP and featured Lester Young, Harry "Sweets" Edison, Coleman Hawkins, Jonah Jo Jones, and a slick tenor sax player, Illinois Jacquet. *Jammin' the Blues* won the 1944 Academy Award for best short subject. According to Hershorn, Granz believed the short "made his name."

61 *"Norman is very articulate on this":* Hershorn interview.

61 *Britain's HMV:* The His Master's Voice (HMV) concert was sponsored by the British music newspaper *Melody Maker.* Billed as "jam sessions" at EMI's Abbey Road Studios, the event featured pianist George Shearing among others whose jams entertained a wartime London audience of more than one thousand.

63 *Brubeck's San Francisco label, Fantasy:* In 1949 two entrepreneurial brothers in San Francisco, Max and Sol Weiss, were operators of a plastic molding business that included a record-pressing plant. The pair knew Brubeck from frequenting the famed North Beach jazz venue the Black Hawk. The Oakland musician had recorded with Coronet, a tiny local label, but had received no income from the records. The Weiss brothers gave him $400 to buy the masters, formed their own label, Fantasy, named after a science-fiction magazine, and successfully reissued the recordings. The label eventually pressed records for other West Coast musicians, including such comers as trumpeter Chet Baker, baritone sax player Gerry Mulligan, vibraphonist Cal Tjader, and pianist Vince Guaraldi. Later, Fantasy recorded hip comedian Lenny Bruce and beat poets Lawrence Ferlinghetti and Allen Ginsberg.

63 *"If George Avakian is smart enough":* Quoted by George Avakian in his interview with the author.

6. Outdoor Live Recording

65 *"stocky man":* Lillian Ross, "You Dig It, Sir?" *New Yorker,* Aug. 14, 1954, p. 35.

67 *Prestige:* A marvelously inspired independent, Prestige had the reputation of signing jazz junkies in need of a few bucks gleaned from a quick recording session. The criticism was perhaps unfair. It arrived on the scene in 1950, essentially as Bob Weinstock's one-man company that evolved from his initial label, New Jazz, which he started in January 1949 at the age of twenty. Weinstock was another West Coast collector turned producer like Avakian. The son of a jazz enthusiast, he had started in the business as a student who had built a solid reputation as a custom distributor to jazz collectors. His first recording was of blind pianist Lennie Tristano, a name later entwined with free jazz. Weinstock was known to be close to his musicians and allowed them the freedom to improvise in the studio. As such, he garnered a lot of cutting-edge talent and quickly began to rival the East Coast's Blue Note, a label that structured its recording sessions differently to include ample rehearsal time.

67 *"George, think about this"*: Quoted by George Avakian in his interview with the author.

69 *write a composition:* At a December 1955 meeting of the Newport Festival advisory members committee, organizers briefly had discussed the idea of commissioning new works but dismissed it. For Newport '56 several new pieces were done but not commissioned, including those from J. J. Johnson, Dave Brubeck, Charlie Mingus, the Modern Jazz Quartet, and pianist Teddy Charles, who played a Saturday afternoon spot as part of a lead-in to a discussion panel.

71 *"not particularly a jazz fan"*: John Hammond, *John Hammond on Record* (New York: Ridge Press, 1977).

71 *"she kissed Lieberson"*: Don Hunstein, telephone interview with author, Nov. 24, 2002. Unless otherwise indicated, all Hunstein and Ishlon quotes are from this interview.

72 *LP cover art:* Much of the early work came from the small independents that linked visual design and music. Blue Note, for example, was accomplished in Bauhaus-influenced design, reflecting two Germans who charted its trajectory. The label belonged to a former Berliner, Alfred Lion, who started with financial backing from a leftist New Yorker, writer, musician, and stereoscopic photographer, Max Margulis. A friend from Lion's Berlin days was photographer Frank Wolff, who arrived in late 1939 on the "last boat out of Nazi Germany." By the mid-forties, Wolff was shooting evocative monochrome studio candids during recording sessions. Lion saw the label and its music with a "missionary zeal" as part of an art form. Blue Note also enjoyed graphics from Reid Miles, whom Wolff got from *Esquire*. Again, however, it was Norman Granz who was one of the first to think of album covers as art. For his Clef and JATP covers, Granz had David Stone Martin, who had been an illustrator working for Moses Ashe, and Merle Shore. Said Hershorn, "The fact is, Norman's records had a look to them. . . . It is in keeping with Norman's philosophy that jazz was high art and should be treated as such." The 1949 *Jazz at Carnegie Hall* cost $25 at the time and included a gallery of Gjon Mili photographs on the jazz scene. "His thing was to present a real showplace of music, you know, kind of a snapshot of jazz in the late 40's." Another was the 1953, four-LP release by Fred Astaire with Oscar Peterson of the singer-dancer's musical hits, *The Astaire Story*, "which had kind of a pocket of art by David Stone Martin and photos by Mili. I think that was a $100 album. The Stone Martin drawings were reproduced on cotton rag paper."

72 *her departure:* The dismissal, coming from Lieberson himself, left her bitter. Subsequently, she went to work as director of communications for a politically well-connected French Canadian financier, Pierre Rinfret. "One of my favorite people," said Rinfret. "She worked with me for twenty-five years, edited all my stuff and contributed enormously to the company. Debbie and I never discussed her prior career, because it ended horribly!"

72 *"Look, George"*: Lieberson quoted by George Avakian in his interview with the author.

73 *"Goddard"*: Cook quoted by George Avakian in his interview with the author.

7. From the Masses to the Classes

76 *"he left"*: Elaine Lorillard, interview with author, Newport, RI, July 12, 2003. Unless otherwise indicated, all Lorillard quotes are from this interview.

77 *"We would sit around"*: Elaine Lorillard and Richard Gehman, "Hot Time in Old Newport," *Collier's*, July 20, 1956.

78 *Pierre J. Lorillard:* Cleveland Amory, a writer friend of the Lorillards, maintained that Pierre, Louis's great-grandfather, was the first to be called in print a millionaire. Louis's grandfather built the first The Breakers, one of Newport's earliest mansions, a shingled Queen Anne–style Victorian "cottage" that burned to the ground in 1892. In 1886 he founded the sportsmen's preserve of mansions in New York's Ramapo Mountains, Tuxedo Park. Louis's father, Louis Lasher Lorillard, did not, however, add to the Lorillard family wealth: far from it. He did attend Yale and tried his hand as a naval architect. "I think," said Elaine Lorillard, "he designed *one* [ship or boat]." In the 1920s the elder Lorillard took his family to Pau, just inland from Bayonne in the Pays Basque region of France, where Louis spent his childhood. He subsequently attended the Southborough, Massachusetts, Fay School, "a very fashionable school for boys who did not go to a university."

78 *Italian count:* In the early fifties Elaine and Louis would spend two weeks in the spring at Count Cerio's villa on Capri, overseeing a property that for most of the year was vacant.

78 *heavyweight lineage:* Louis Lorillard was also a member of the all-but-aristocratic Society of the Cincinnati, descendants of the officers of Washington's Continental Army and of French officers who fought with the Americans. This most select group had inspired (as a democratic counterbalance) the creation of the Tammany Societies in New York, Philadelphia, and other cities in the early 1800s.

79 *Gilded Age:* Newport as a resort for the super-rich can be said to have taken shape around the 1880s. Within two decades enormous mansions—the so-called summer cottages—would constitute a colony comprising the families of great wealthy industrialists and robber barons like Vanderbilt and others whose wealth surpassed those found on Caroline Astor's mid-nineteenth-century list of "The 400" and on Millionaires' Row, whose urban mansions lined Fifth Avenue and elsewhere on New York's Upper East Side. By most reckonings, construction of the first such cottage began in 1893. That year, Commodore Cornelius Vanderbilt's grandson, Cornelius Vanderbilt II, the chairman and president of the New York Central Railroad, commissioned the design of a seventy-room palazzo, The Breakers, the second so named on what had been the Lorillard site.

79 *old-guard colonists:* After the war many cottages were converted into summer apartments. Mansions with apartments to the west and south of town afforded short-term rentals for navy families who were following the fleet. In 1945, leading an effort to save a number from the wrecking ball, Mrs. George Henry Warren formed the Preservation Society of Newport County. Eleven years before, the youngest of Cornelius Vanderbilt II's seven children, Gladys, wife to Hungarian count Laszlo Szechenyi, inherited The Breakers on her mother's death. In 1948 she leased it to the Preservation Society for a dollar a year to serve as a museum.

79 *sell their cottages:* In 1947 the politically powerful New England Catholic establishment saw an educational opportunity in the colony's decline. The church acquired the Ochre Court, architect Richard Morris Hunt's 1891 mansion for banker and developer Ogden Goelet, to found Salve Regina, Rhode Island's first Roman Catholic women's college, known now as the coeducational Newport College–Salve Regina. By 1955 the Astor family's Chetwode had become a church and seminary. Beacon Hill, once the town's largest mansion, became a convent.

79 *dying:* "The Newport Social Register, once a must in every villa, ceased publication in 1948," wrote Gardner Dunton, who made his name as a World War I Army Air Corps aviator, in the June 12, 1955, *New York Times.* In 1930 the register boasted 462 names, but in 1955 Dunton found fewer than 200 names in an advertising folder listing summer

colonists. The younger generation summered elsewhere, he observed, and few were taking their places. "High income taxes, the servant problem and the passing of a social aristocracy are sounding the knell of Newport's exclusiveness."

81 *"To take jazz from the masses"*: Cleveland Amory, "High Society Blues," *Holiday,* July 1956.

81 *"Elaine talked a little more"*: Thomas Guthrie, telephone interview with author, Oct. 24, 2003. The accounts of Guthrie and Lorillard conform. George Wein's slightly different account is in George Wein, *Myself among Others: A Life in Music* (Cambridge, MA: Da Capo Press, 2003).

82 *WEVD:* The station was then managed by the Russian émigré Morris S. Novik to promote socialism and the labor movement. The call letters stood for Socialist Party leader Eugene V. Debs.

82 *Esme O'Brien:* She was the granddaughter of Tammany Hall judge Morgan O'Brien, and her mother was a Crimmins, the well-known New York construction family.

82 *"no particular love"*: Transcript of the Dec. 9, 1955, meeting of the Newport Festival Jazz Committee, from the Newport file of the Marshall Stearns collection at the Institute of Jazz Studies, Rutgers University.

83 *"barely surviving"*: Wein, *Myself among Others,* p. 122.

84 *Bourgeois would bring classical critics:* Wein, *Myself among Others,* p. 84.

84 *Carl W. Haffenreffer:* He was also a philanthropist and shipyard owner. In the thirties his yard built the *Enterprise* and the *Rainbow,* which defended the America's Cup in 1930 and 1934 respectively.

84 *Edward J. Capuano:* Despite his investment, Capuano did not serve on the festival committee. Yet his story provides one insight into Elaine's heartfelt sensibility, as well as the social prejudice she had to battle. "Capuano's second wife was very attractive, good looking, very handsome. And the daughter, Liz, was just Didi's age. And so, they played together. That part of Newport had very few children out there, and so Didi would invite her down to Bailey's. Didi would go down to the beach and tell Liz, who was up there in the house, to come down and play. And Didi was brought up before the board of the beach and told she was not bringing that little girl in the door. Can you believe? You see why I am a Democrat now? That was so sad. I was so cross. There was nothing I could do. I couldn't have Didi disobey the rules of the beach. But I remember I told a few people. I said, 'I think this is so sad. This little girl.' 'Oh,' they said, 'she didn't belong.' And they said, 'If she comes as a guest, she has to pay to get in.' But can you imagine this little girl having to pay? The next day, she came to me with the money in her hand."

85 *"one or two Astors"*: Lorillard interview.

8. The Most Unlikely Place

87 *"What is a jazz festival?"*: Lillian Ross, "You Dig It, Sir?" *New Yorker,* Aug. 14, 1954, p. 33.

87 *Theodore Francis Green:* A Baptist and army veteran of the Spanish-American War and member of the Society of the Cincinnati, Green became a U.S. senator in 1937 and before

that was Rhode Island's governor. Until the mid-thirties the Rhode Island senate was Republican, reflecting the rural power of the abandoned farms of the state. As then-governor and state party leader, Green engineered a governmental reorganization known as the Bloodless Revolution of 1935 that resulted, among other things, in the Democrats' control of the state senate. Beyond Rhode Island his actions drew fire. The *Chicago Daily Tribune* declared them to be unconstitutional, and its famous editor, Colonel Robert McCormick, clamored for cutting one star from the American flag on the grounds that Rhode Island was unworthy of membership in the union. In 1957 Green rose to chairman of the Senate Foreign Relations Committee, where he served for two years until Senate Majority Leader Lyndon B. Johnson removed him. In 1961 he retired at the age of ninety-three. Today, his name graces Providence Airport.

87 *"Magnificent undertaking!"* Quoted in Ross, "You Dig It, Sir?" p. 45.

89 *"in the kitty"*: Transcript of the Dec. 9, 1955, meeting of the Newport Festival Jazz Committee.

90 *"How about Elaine's personal preferences?"*: Transcript of the Dec. 9, 1955, meeting of the Newport Festival Jazz Committee.

91 *"live on benzedrine"*: In the mid-fifties the drug was a topic of the times. Overwrought during the Suez Crisis of 1956, Anthony Eden, the British prime minister, said himself that he was "practically living on Benzedrine." His dependence certainly impaired his judgment during the crisis and contributed to his physical and emotional collapse and his 1957 resignation.

92 *"a revolutionary force"*: Quoted in the *New York Times*, July 17, 1955.

92 *"brought down the house"*: *New York Times*, July 18, 1955.

93 *"insidious criticism"*: Transcript of the Dec. 9, 1955, meeting of the Newport Festival Jazz Committee.

94 *"There was a general feeling"*: Transcript of the Dec. 9, 1955, meeting of the Newport Festival Jazz Committee.

94 *"For the first time"*: Transcript of the Dec. 9, 1955, meeting of the Newport Festival Jazz Committee.

94 *"Because of the Newport Jazz Festival"*: Transcript of the Dec. 9, 1955, meeting of the Newport Festival Jazz Committee.

94 *"Basically my job"*: Transcript of the Dec. 9, 1955, meeting of the Newport Festival Jazz Committee.

95 *site options:* At various times into March 1956, press reports would appear stating that the festival organizers were looking at Westport and Bridgeport, Connecticut, the Midwest, and even Monte Carlo.

95 *"Every time"*: Transcript of the Dec. 9, 1955, meeting of the Newport Festival Jazz Committee.

96 *reported the lineups:* More than one hundred musicians were on the schedule. While Art Tatum was originally on the bill for Saturday, the great pianist was ill and under doctor's orders not to play. He would die several months later. Although Art Blakey and the Jazz Messengers were scheduled to play on the Friday, they would arrive too late to go onstage.

96 *"The great importance"*: *Ash Box*, Newport, RI, June 23, 1956.

96 *the host of* Music USA: Barry Zorthian, interview with the author, Arlington, VA, May 2003. Unless otherwise indicated, all Zorthian quotes are from this interview.

9. Newport '56

101 *"He was much more in the culture":* Arlene Avakian, telephone interview, June 4, 2003. Unless otherwise indicated, all Arlene Avakian quotes are from this interview.

107 *"This is the first jazz concert": Newport Daily News,* July 6, 1956.

108 *"a gimmick": New York Times,* July 7, 1956.

111 *"tore the place apart":* Leonard L. Levinson, "Third Newport Jazz Fete Swinging in the Rain; '400' Likes Blast 'n' Beat," *Variety,* July 11, 1956, p. 45.

10. The Saturday Night

115 *"Everyone was* up": Paul Hoeffler, conversations and e-mail correspondence with the author, April 2005. Unless otherwise indicated, all quotes from Hoeffler come from these sources.

115 *Henri Cartier-Bresson:* Hoeffler called Cartier-Bresson one of "the originals, the first generation front line of working professional photographers," among whom he included Gjon Mili, "who worked with great capacity in the arts." Said Hoeffler, "I immediately believed this was 'ethical, moral, truthful' and the *right* way to photograph" and set the standard. "This standard, coupled with the alternative magazine displays of dynamic [black and white] work by Herman Leonard with his smoke machine, William Claxton, William Gottlieb, Bob Parent made *Down Beat* and *Metronome* necessary for inspirational viewing." As for "Cartier-Bresson and 'full frame,' I still shoot that way today."

116 *Bob Parent:* A thirty-three-year-old freelancer, Parent was the son of a Chelsea, Massachusetts, sign painter and had begun a draftsman's career in his late teens. His real interests were jazz and photography. According to his nephew, Dale Parent, who manages his photo archives, after reading *Young Man with a Horn,* Dorothy Baker's novel loosely based on the life of Bix Beiderbecke, as well as after studying Gjon Mili's jazz photographs, he decided to become a professional photographer. Preferring to shoot unobtrusively, he had shot at Newport the previous year. Into the next decade and the seventies, he would photograph virtually every New York civil rights and antiwar demonstration and many in Washington. He also did a fair amount of photojournalism in Cuba, during which time he became closely acquainted with Fidel Castro.

116 *"For a while":* Jonathan Yardley, interview with the author, Washington, DC, Nov. 21, 2003. Unless otherwise indicated, all Yardley quotes are from this interview.

117 Quotes from the stage for all Newport Jazz Festival performances on the evening of July 7, 1956, are from the Voice of America recordings, RGA 0027-0029, held by the Recorded Sound Reference Center (Motion Picture, Broadcasting and Recorded Sound Division), Library of Congress.

119 *mimeographed handout:* From the Newport file in the Marshall Stearns collection at the Institute of Jazz Studies, Rutgers University.

121 *He needed another trumpet:* Some years later swing trumpeter Jimmy Maxwell stated in an October 1977 *Jazz Journal* article that he had played in the Ellington band that famous night at a time when Cook was late returning to the stand. Just when is unclear. Cook was onstage for the opening set. When the band returned for the final set, it opened with "Take the A Train." Maxwell could have covered for that number, but it is unlikely. It was a Ray Nance solo, anyway. The following number was the first section of the "Newport Festival Suite," in which Cook soloed.

122 *"old show tunes":* Leonard L. Levinson, "Third Newport Jazz Fete Swinging in the Rain; '400' Likes Blast 'n' Beat," *Variety,* July 11, 1956, p. 45.

123 *"What are you going to play?"* Account from Bobby Boyd cited in Charles H. Waters Jr., "Anatomy of a Cover: The Story of Duke Ellington's Appearance on the Cover of *Time* Magazine," *Annual Review of Jazz Studies* 6 (1993). This article is excellently annotated and is an extremely valuable source for material related to the story.

123 *"I've worked my fingers":* Wein interview.

124 *"What are we":* Quoted in John Edward Hasse, *Beyond Category: The Life and Genius of Duke Ellington* (New York: Simon and Schuster, 1993), p. 319.

125 *"A high spot":* Levinson, "Third Newport Jazz Fete Swinging in the Rain," p. 45.

125 *Buddy Collette:* Quoted in Waters, "Anatomy of a Cover," p. 39.

125 *backstage scene:* A somewhat apocryphal account of what transpired during this time originated in an article titled "Ellington in Private," which appeared in the May 1975 issue of the *Atlantic Monthly.* The author was Irving Townsend. [Townsend in *Jazz Journal,* Oct. 1976]. In 1956 Townsend was thirty-five. Duke Ellington would call him his "friendly advisor." In his *Atlantic* piece Townsend began a portrait of the bandleader with his memory of his first time alone with him: backstage in the tent before Ellington returned to the stage for his memorable second set. He started the article with a brief discussion about Ellington's next project, "A Drum Is a Woman." Townsend's recall may be suspect, however. "He was there at the festival, but he didn't take any part," said George Avakian firmly. At the conclusion of this meeting, Townsend wrote, he could hear the tromp of Harry Carney's foot above them at the first bars of "Take the A Train," cuing Ellington to come onstage. Again, his recall is suspect. In the first place, the tent was behind the stage. In the second, that famous signature tune starts with piano phrasings. If Ellington were still with Townsend, somebody else would have been on piano. This could only have been Billy Strayhorn, who of course was there. The 1999 CD version, however, does not credit Strayhorn. More telling, early in the phrasing, Ellington's growls are clearly recognizable. Yet Townsend did meet in the tent one-on-one with Ellington sometime that night, as Don Hunstein's camera recorded. The rolls on which they appear, however, are much later in the evening. The tent is fairly empty, and Ellington is wearing his overcoat.

125 *"we've all worked very hard":* Account from George Avakian, interview with author.

126 *"I don't think I know that one":* Don George, *Sweet Man: The Real Duke Ellington* (New York: G. P. Putnam's Sons, 1981), p. 118. This account may not be entirely accurate. Gonsalves had played the interval many times before Newport '56. Further, George was wrong about the key of B-flat. The "Diminuendo" modulates key four times from E-flat to D-flat, the key of the wailing interval. The "Crescendo" is in E-flat.

127 *"you sure made it hot":* Account from Buddy Collette, quoted in Waters, "Anatomy of a Cover," p. 39.

128 *Then came Terry:* Ellington used Terry's talents to help write the bopish ending to the "Newport Jazz Festival Suite." Terry said the piece was "close to 'Hot House,'" pianist-composer Tadd Dameron's bop classic. "Maestro asked me to write the ending," the trumpeter recalled in his 2005 interview, "because for him endings had a connotation that meant finality. So he didn't like to fool around with endings. You notice a lot of his tunes would segue from one thing to another? Endings were one of his idiosyncrasies. He didn't dig playing endings."

129 *"Frankly, it was boring":* Elaine Anderson, telephone interview with author, Nov. 18, 2002. Unless otherwise indicated, all Anderson quotes are from this interview.

11. A Leading Voice Supported by Many Parts

133 *"like a Mexican":* Quoted by Michael James in a conversation with the author.

133 *"The Cape Verdeans":* Ron Barboza, interview with the author, New Bedford, MA, July 11, 2003. Unless otherwise indicated, all Barboza quotes are from this interview.

136 *Atlantic crossing:* The author would like to credit historian, researcher, photographer, and consultant Ron Barboza for information provided, based on his original research into Gonsalves family immigration records.

137 *Florence Almeida:* Quoted by Ron Barboza in his interview with the author.

137 *John Monteiro:* John Monteiro, telephone interview with the author, Oct. 15, 2004. Unless otherwise indicated, all Monteiro quotes are from this interview.

138 *"so shy":* Quoted by Ron Barboza in his interview with the author.

142 *"Dope was a whole way of life":* Martin Torgoff, *Can't Find My Way Home: America in the Great Stoned Age, 1945–2000* (New York: Simon and Schuster, 2004), p. 38.

144 *In that session:* On that date they cut a Cat Anderson composition, "Night Walk"; a Tizol piece, "Moonlight Fiesta"; and another that the valve trombonist composed with Bellson titled "She." These further illustrate how Ellington offered collaborations to feature new-comers like Gonsalves, whether for composition or for soloing. Valve trombonist John Sanders had soloed when he played with Lucky Thompson. Soon after joining the Ellington band, his section mate and friend Britt Woodman encouraged him to take solos. "Duke liked the phrases," recalled the trombonist, "and wrote 'John Sanders' Blues' which I played on the slide, not the valve."

146 *"the basic lines":* Barry Ulanov, *Duke Ellington* (London: Farrar, Straus and Giroux, 1947).

146 *"the struggle":* Gunther Schuller, *The Swing Era: The Development of Jazz, 1930–1945* (New York: Oxford University Press, 1989), p. 93.

146 *GNP (Gene Norman Presents) label:* Norman was a West Coast deejay and concert promoter who ran Sunset Strip nightclubs called the Crescendo and the Interlude and was famous for recording live concerts and jams, somewhat in the vein of Norman Granz's JATP.

146 *"crowd went wild":* Quoted in Charles H. Waters Jr., "Anatomy of a Cover: The Story of Duke Ellington's Appearance on the Cover of *Time* Magazine," *Annual Review of Jazz Studies* 6 (1993): 40.

147 *"Rocket 88":* The song was also Sam Phillips's first hit, which gave him the money to start Sun Records.

147 *white teenage audiences:* These audiences had already been primed in the New York market by deejay Alan Freed.

147 *R&B sax men:* Also heavy on the beat in the genre was alto sax man Earl Bostic, who sold better in white audiences than black.

147 *"rock and roll things":* Duke Ellington, "The Future of Jazz," Newport Jazz Festival program, 1955.

12. The Rhythmic Groove of the Century

149 *"If a guy plays something":* Duke Ellington, quoted in Stuart Nicholson, *Reminiscing in Tempo: A Portrait of Duke Ellington* (Boston: Northeastern University Press, 1999).

152 *"rhythmic energizer":* Gunther Schuller, *The Swing Era: The Development of Jazz, 1930–1945* (New York: Oxford University Press, 1989), p. 49n.

152 *"rhythm ignited":* Albert Murray provides the key to unlocking insight into the moment when he speaks of so-called talking drums, "some voiced as . . . pianos, trumpets, trombones, saxophones, clarinets." The term can be misleading; talking drums are not about rhythm per se. As another musician-writer, Ortiz M. Walton, put it in his book *Music: Black, White, and Blue*: drums talk not through Morse Code but rather through changes of pitch. Ellington modulated through five keys in the "Diminuendo," whereby his instrument, his whole orchestra, served as his talking drums. Especially through *unexpected* changes of pitch was he able to generate subliminal effects to transport musicians and audience to another place, prompting all to conjure with him apparitions that demanded responses.

152 *"Jo Jones was the driving force":* Duke Ellington, *Music Is My Mistress* (Garden City, NY: Doubleday, 1973), p. 241.

154 *"just driving away":* Willie Cook, interview with Phil Schaap.

154 *piano interlude:* The "Diminuendo" is noteworthy for its rising pitch. As scored, Ellington opened it in the key of E-flat for several choruses and then modulated up a major third to the key of G. Musicologists know that a modulation of a major third (a four-semitone interval) is somewhat unexpected to the ear. While not dissonant, it's an interval of soft consonance. The ear actually expects a transition more familiar, a more predictable modulation, either up a major second (two semitones) or up a perfect fourth (five semitones) to G's subdominant, C. In any event the effect of modulating up a major third suggests a mystery. Ellington was already conjuring. But he was only teasing the ear. He remained in the key of G for only two choruses. It served as a pivot key for another modulation, which this time was predictable. Hitting a passing G7 chord, he moved up a perfect fourth to the key of C to resolve at what had been G's subdominant chord.

It was with his next modulation, however, that he chose to disorient the ear completely. When Ellington went from the key of C to A-flat, he moved up the scale a minor sixth, raising pitch via an interval most unpredictable. The impact would have been dramatic, akin to the use by nineteenth-century romantic composers like Richard Wagner of such expansive eight-semitone modulations to depict heavenly ascents to the other worlds.

Once Ellington got there, he continued in A-flat by further unsettling the mood. In his musicological analysis of the original 1937 composition, Gunther Schuller wrote that when Ellington got to the A-flat in the "Diminuendo," he chose notes in a scale that was "highly chromatically altered." Put another way, he was using a scale that emphasized blue notes throughout the choruses played in that key. As for the emotional effect on the audience, it was the point where the ear would have been subliminally cast adrift in a musically unresolved sea of blue.

Summarizing, Schuller wrote that Ellington constructed in his 1937 "Diminuendo" dramatic blues changes for texture within choruses. The material in the work's elongated fourteen bars was in motifs, as opposed to complete melodic themes. The modulations, Schuller wrote, were often abrupt, startling shifts in tonality, certainly the case with the second and fourth modulations.

Although the rhythmic groove was constant, Ellington was providing fragments of speech, of conversation. In Schuller's view, "it was not exactly conducive to easy finger-snapping listening." On the contrary, it is disorienting, akin to the mixes in the clubs of today or a succession of televised sound bites, unlike a melody and beyond thoughtful reflection at the moment one hears them. Ellington was rather prompting an emotional discussion to take his performers and audience to another place to romp among their apparitions, to appease, do battle, exorcize, make love, expiate . . . demanding them to make their own associations and express them.

He did not leave his audience adrift forever. With his fifth modulation he called them together on a plateau, when to finish the "Diminuendo" he rose another perfect fourth to resolve the piece in D-flat, what would have been A-flat's subdominant chord. The audience, however, was only momentarily resting. They had been taken on a ride through five modulations of rising pitch, two of which unhinged them, which had lifted them upward to an unsteady precipice. Ellington had taken the blues changes and applied polytonal concepts to his composition that enabled the band in the performance to create in the audience strong, unsettled emotional responses. To the ear the tonality conveyed a sense wholly unfamiliar. It's safe to assume that very, very few people in the audience that night had heard the piece before, either on record or in performance.

Igor Stravinsky had achieved the same effect in 1913, when Parisians rioted during the premiere of his "Rite of Spring." The piece relied on tritone intervals, diminished fifths (six restless semitone leaps forward), which by most accounts led to the popularizing of polytonal approaches in twentieth-century music. Similarly, the "Diminuendo" confounded the ear with an air of mystery and substance. The audience was pulled in two directions: on the one hand by the earthy rhythms and fragmentary blues motifs within the choruses, on the other by the modulating language of the spiritual. Altogether, Ellington had indeed constructed a "spiritually earthy" piece with added profundity.

154 *began to blow:* Gonsalves seized on the polytonal possibilities Ellington handed him and made a bold improvisational choice when he started blowing with a G in his opening phrase. A most accomplished improviser, the saxophonist departed from the text and created his own, impromptu. He chose to build on the tritone in D-flat. Similar to what Ellington had done with his key changes in the "Diminuendo," he did not choose to begin with the predictable D-flat root note, G-flat subdominant, or A-flat dominant. He went with a note three tones from the D-flat root note, the restless, highly dissonant pitch between the subdominant and dominant in that key. His choice bordered on the mystical. His style was highly chromatic. While the band was in D-flat, he was using the tritone G as the root of the chord he was building.

The use of tritones in solos had been well established by Charlie Parker and Dizzy Gillespie, so his choice was certainly not anything new. But it was a different choice than he had made in two previous recordings. On the 1951 Birdland recording, he launched on a B-flat, nine semitones up, which was probably his routine. The pitch on the Birdland recording is actually sped up. Ellington and the band sound as if they are playing in the key of D instead of D-flat, and Gonsalves sounds as if he is starting with a B. On Gene Norman's 1953 Pasadena recording, Gonsalves starts on E, three semitones up.

Unlike these two previously cited recorded intervals, where Gonsalves attacked the solo by launching in the middle to upper end of his register, at Newport Gonsalves started low, which allowed a *tessitura*, a range of notes, to give him ample room to raise pitch as he built his many choruses to a climax. The choice would have momentarily knocked the audience sideways. Elaine Anderson, an engaged listener with a classically trained ear attuned to Beethoven, the transitional giant between the classical and romantic eras, would have subliminally responded. Very early in the solo, if not in the opening phrases, what she heard tore her from her seat and propelled her to interpret in dance. Continuing in this dissonant way, Gonsalves got everybody else on their feet and moving, building chorus after chorus, until Ellington's chording brought him out with an exit that he almost casually tossed off as he finished his twenty-seventh.

154 *"What's going on?"* George Avakian's account in his interview with the author.

157 *Woodyard started to swing:* As for the rhythmic aspects of the Gonsalves interval, Ellington's nephew Michael James has compared the Newport solo and the drumming behind it to those at Birdland and at the Pasadena concert. Observing that the 1937 recording was a two-beat rhythm stiffly played by drummer Sonny Greer, he said that in the Birdland recording Louis Bellson played a straight ride beat (as opposed to a backbeat) that was solid, enabling Gonsalves to play a looser solo. "It was a totally jazz crowd," said James, "and Paul was playing a 'steady four' with some very interesting ideas."

At Pasadena, James continued, drummer Butch Ballard swung more than Bellson but still played with no backbeat. "The pulse is stronger than [Ellington's Newport drummer Sam] Woodyard's. It has a freer rhythm, not as locked in. He uses rim shots, off-beat accentuation on the bass drum, so Paul's solo could be a little more polyrhythmic." The bassist for both performances was Wendell Marshall, who, according to James, would "lock in" with his drummers and was stronger on the bass than Jimmy Woode.

As for Newport, "Woodyard sensed Duke wanted to groove the crowd and seize the moment," offered James. "He swings. He's locked into a back beat which allows Paul to play to the crowd."

157 *"As the mood swelled"*: Jack Heaney, interview with the author, Washington, DC, April 20, 2004.

13. Elaine Anderson

159 *salvage rights:* Zeitz family lore has it that those rights had been arranged by a prominent power broker in Boston Jewish circles by the name of Bernard Drucker, who was close to the young Joseph P. Kennedy Sr. and other regional movers and shakers in the Democratic Party.

160–161 *Zeiterion:* Stylistic inspiration came from the Boston-based B. F. Keith and Edward F. Albee, the regional giants, with their KAO vaudeville chain.

161 *Valentino:* As part of their engagement, Valentino and Rambova judged dancing and beauty contests for their dance tour sponsor, Mineralava Beauty Clay.

161 *key player:* "Theater owners had more of the whip hand in the wheeling and dealing in those days," said Harry's son Bob, who subsequently managed Zeitz theaters. The New

Bedford, Empire, and Civic were also vaudeville houses where they billed double features in between the stage shows. Bob Zeitz remembered booking many stars in the fifties: Armstrong with Ella, Basie, Sammy Davis Jr., and Danny Kaye, to name a few. In the early twenties the silent film epic *Down to the Sea in Ships,* starring a teenaged Clara Bow, later of "It" girl fame, put New Bedford decidedly on the entertainment map. In August 1921 the city's board of commerce approved a charter for the Whaling Film Corporation to produce the film. For the next year filming was underway in New Bedford, Fairhaven, and nearby Dartmouth, providing employment for numerous locals as actors, technical consultants, and construction workers. On September 25, 1922, the film had its world premiere at the Olympia Theater. As the excitement surrounding *Down to the Sea in Ships* waxed and waned, Harry Zeitz was completing construction of the Zeiterion. Today a performing arts center, it was one of a half dozen New Bedford vaudeville houses.

161 *Sound conversion:* Kennedy had lured Boston vaudeville magnate Edward Albee into the alliance and then absorbed him, converting Albee's thirty-one KAO vaudeville houses into a cinema chain. The result was RKO Pictures, whose first film was *Syncopation.* RKO required independent producers to shoot with the Photophone, Sarnoff's sound technology, if they wanted an RKO distribution, and theater owners had to install Photophone sound heads for their projectors if they wanted to run RKO product.

162 *Sarah Woodcock:* Sarah Woodcock, telephone interview with the author, Sept. 24, 2003.

167 *"Elaine would dance":* Bob Zeitz, telephone interview with the author, April 21, 2005. Unless otherwise indicated, all Zeitz quotes are from this interview.

169 *"To amuse herself":* Rick Anderson, telephone interview with the author, Nov. 16, 2002. Unless otherwise indicated, all Rick Anderson quotes are from this interview.

171 *"a strange stirring":* Betty Friedan, *The Feminine Mystique* (New York: Norton, 1974).

14. Not Just Patterns in the Air

173 *"When they see people":* Quoted in Stuart Nicholson, *Reminiscing in Tempo: A Portrait of Duke Ellington* (Boston: Northeastern University Press, 1999).

174 *"The driving rhythm":* Jack Heaney, in Sjef Hoefsmit, ed., "Dance to the Duke," *The International DEMS Bulletin,* 02/2 DEMS 9, Duke Ellington Music Society, 02/2 August–November 2002, www.depanorama.net/dems/02dems2b.htm.

174 *"telepathic response":* Dan Morgenstern, interview with the author.

180 *"The primary thing":* Heaney, in Hoefsmit, "Dance to the Duke."

181 *ostentatious cuff link:* Whose arm is unknown. However, it is possibly her husband, Larry's. In one of the family photos of her dancing that night, the cuff link is visible on the arm of a seated gentleman in her box.

184 *"With Duke reminiscing":* Roy DeCarava, *The Sound I Saw* (New York: Phaidon Press, 2001).

184 *"the struggle":* Gunther Schuller, *The Swing Era: The Development of Jazz, 1930–1945* (New York: Oxford University Press, 1989), p. 93.

185 *"you want to see real people":* Jack Cole, interview in *Dance Magazine,* 1968; repr. at www.theatredance.com/choreographers/cole.html (accessed Sept. 21, 2007).

187 *"Crescendo" began:* To enter the "Crescendo," Duke did a quick pass, playing block chords from D-flat up an expansive minor sixth to A, then up a perfect fifth to the dominant E, and finally up a major seventh to rest at E's leading note, E-flat, whereupon the band joined the conversation. From here without modulation, the piece continued to build with heavy repetitions of rhythmic motifs. With layer on layer of sound, Ellington had his sections trade with each other, as Schuller described the 1937 recording, "in *bolero* fashion."

Although the English critic Max Harrison famously regarded the '56 performance as "rape and murder," he wrote that "Diminuendo and Crescendo in Blue," along with several others, "makes demands that not even top-level jazz players were normally expected to face." Through its fourteen-bar phrases, twelve bars plus two-bar extensions, the well-oiled precision '56 band delivered a powerful sound that spiraled upward through the "Crescendo" until finally Cat Anderson's high-note trumpet blew the lid off the night.

196 *"It was too emotional":* Jimmy Woode, interview with Phil Schaap.

197 *"barracks-like room":* Burt Goldblatt, *Newport Jazz Festival: The Illustrated History* (New York: Dial Press, 1977).

15. As Though You Were There

203 *"Jazz buffs":* Carter Harman, "Mood Indigo & Beyond," *Time,* Aug. 20, 1956, p. 55.

205 *"shy, hates microphones":* Duke Ellington, *Music Is My Mistress* (Garden City, NY: Doubleday, 1973), p. 221.

205 *"It's hopeless":* Account from George Avakian, interview with the author.

205 *"many, many attempts":* Phil Schaap, telephone interview with the author, Feb. 11, 2007. Unless otherwise indicated, all Schaap quotes are from this interview.

208 *"Consider Ellington's 1956 Newport triumph":* Gary Giddins, *Visions of Jazz: The First Century* (New York: Oxford University Press, 1998), p. 510.

16. The Columbia Formula

214 *Vanguard Records:* Founded in 1950 by Seymour and Maynard Solomon as a New York independent label, its first commissioned recordings were of five Bach cantatas. In the 1950s it recorded singer Paul Robeson and the folk group the Weavers and other performers blacklisted during the McCarthy era. The success of the recording of the Weavers' 1955 Christmas concert at Carnegie Hall prompted the label to increase its footprint in folk, which led to its becoming the major folk label of the sixties.

217 *"I remember":* Larry Appelbaum, e-mail to the author, Mar. 1, 2007.

17. Sleeping under a Fur Coat

219 *"I have a record":* Elaine Anderson, interview with the author.

219 *"a better picture":* George Avakian, interview with the author.

226 *"Their love"*: Etta Kralovec, telephone interview with the author, Jan. 20, 2007. Unless otherwise indicated, all Kralovec quotes are from this interview.

18. The Brotherhood of the Jam

231 *"When 'The St. Louis Blues'"*: Albert Murray, *Stompin' the Blues,* 2nd ed. (Cambridge, MA: Da Capo Press, 2000), p. 139.

232 *"certainly one"*: Eddie Lambert, "Duke's 'Diminuendo and Crescendo in Blue,"* *Coda,* Dec. 1985–Jan. 1986.

233 *"a real competitive feeling"*: Quoted in Stanley Dance, *The World of Duke Ellington* (New York: Charles Scribner's Sons, 1970), p. 173.

234 *"Ellington remained"*: Tom Reney, correspondence with the author.

235 *"the strolling violins"*: Duke Ellington, *Music Is My Mistress* (Garden City, NY: Doubleday, 1973), p. 221.

241 *"a satirical history"*: John Edward Hasse, *Beyond Category: The Life and Genius of Duke Ellington* (New York: Simon and Schuster, 1993).

19. Someone Else's Freedom

250 *"with the person"*: Transcript of the Dec. 9, 1955, meeting of the Newport Festival Jazz Committee.

250 *"I am in communication"*: Transcript of the Dec. 9, 1955, meeting of the Newport Festival Jazz Committee.

251 *"We might not get"*: Transcript of the Dec. 9, 1955, meeting of the Newport Festival Jazz Committee.

252 *"Telegenic"*: Leonard L. Levinson, "Third Newport Jazz Fete Swinging in the Rain; '400' Likes Blast 'n' Beat," *Variety,* July 11, 1956, p. 45.

253 *"Poland's best known musicians"*: Jim Lester, "Willis of Oz," unpublished article on Willis Conover, made available to the author by Mr. Lester.

253 *"The whole business"*: Quoted in S. Frederick Starr, *Red and Hot: The Fate of Jazz in the Soviet Union, 1917–1980* (New York: Oxford University Press, 1983), p. 244.

254 *"a jazz lover"*: Ernest A. Nagy, telephone interview with the author, Mar. 16, 2007.

256 *"Willis referred to that Ellington performance"*: Terry Ripmaster, telephone interview with author, Sept. 20, 2003.

256 *"in the midst"*: Quoted in Lester, "Willis of Oz."

20. Festival Junction

259 *"the prestige and pleasure"*: "Newport Jazz Festival Story," *Metronome,* Sept. 1956.

261 *"apex of the folk revival"*: George Wein, *Myself among Others: A Life in Music* (Cambridge, MA: Da Capo Press, 2003), p. 322.

Bibliography

Primary Sources

Interviews

Anderson, Elaine. Telephone interview, Nov. 18, 2002.
Anderson, Rick. Telephone interview, Nov. 16, 2002.
Avakian, Arlene. Telephone interview, June 4, 2003.
Avakian, George. Yonkers, NY, Nov. 11, 2002.
Barboza, Ronald. New Bedford, MA, July 11, 2003.
Farmen, Bill. McLean, VA, July 20, 2005.
Glaser, Martha. Telephone interview, Dec. 5, 2002.
Guthrie, Thomas. Telephone interview, Oct. 24, 2003.
Hasse, John Edward. Washington, DC, Oct. 1, 2003.
Heaney, Jack. Washington, DC, Apr. 20, 2004.
Hershorn, Tad. Newark, NJ, July 10, 2003.
Hoeffler, Paul. Conversations and e-mail correspondence, Apr. 2005.
Hunstein, Don. Telephone interview, Nov. 24, 2003.
James, Michael. Telephone interviews and conversations, June 2005–Aug. 2007.
Kralovec, Etta. Telephone interview, Jan. 20, 2007.
Lorillard, Elaine. Newport, RI, July 12, 2003.
Monteiro, John. Telephone interview, Oct. 15, 2004.
Morgenstern, Dan. Newark, NJ, Nov. 13, 2002.
Nagy, Ernest A. Telephone interview, Mar. 16, 2007.
Panagio, Leonard. Newport, RI, July 13, 2003.
Parent, Dale. New Castle, DE, Jan. 13, 2003.
Ripmaster, Terry. Telephone interview, Sept. 20, 2003.
Sanders, Monsignor John. Stamford, CT, Nov. 11, 2004.
Schaap, Phil. Telephone interview, Feb. 11, 2007.
Terry, Clark. Haworth, NJ, July 11, 2005.
Wein, George. New York, Nov. 12, 2002.

Woodcock, Sarah. Telephone interview, Sept. 24, 2003.
Yardley, Jonathan. Washington, DC, Nov. 21, 2003.
Zeitz, Robert. Telephone interview, Apr. 21, 2005.
Zorthian, Barry. Arlington, VA, May 19, 2003.

Archival Material

Newport Jazz Festival Committee. Transcript of meeting, Dec. 9, 1955, pp. 1–61. Institute of Jazz Studies, John Cotton Dana Library, Rutgers University.

Secondary Sources

Books

Aasland, Benny H. *The Wax Works of Duke Ellington.* Hollywood: Duke Ellington Jazz Society, 1954.

Ake, David Andrew. *Jazz Cultures.* Berkeley: University of California Press, 2002.

Altschuler, Glenn C. *All Shook Up: How Rock 'n' Roll Changed America.* New York: Oxford University Press, 2003.

Amory, Cleveland. *The Last Resorts.* New York: Harper, 1948, 1952.

______. *The Proper Bostonians.* New York: E. P. Dutton, 1947.

______. *Who Killed Society?* New York: Harper, 1960.

Baraka, Amiri (LeRoi Jones). *Black Music.* New York: William Morrow, 1967.

______. *Blues People.* New York: William Morrow, 1963.

Barboza, Ronald, ed. *A Salute to Cape Verdean Musicians and Their Music.* New Bedford, MA: Documentation and Computerization of the Cape Verdeans, 1989.

Cantwell, Robert. *When We Were Good: The Folk Revival.* Cambridge, MA: Harvard University Press, 1996.

Carr, Ian. *Miles Davis: The Definitive Biography.* New York: Thunder's Mouth Press, 1998.

Collier, James Lincoln. *Jazz: The American Theme Song.* New York: Oxford University Press, 1993.

Cook, Richard. *Blue Note Records: The Biography.* Boston: Justin, Charles, 2003.

Crouch, Stanley. *The Artificial White Man: Essays on Authenticity.* New York: Basic Civitas Books, 2004.

Dance, Stanley. *The World of Duke Ellington.* New York: Charles Scribner's Sons, 1970.

DeCarava, Roy. *The Sound I Saw.* New York: Phaidon Press, 2001.

Ellington, Duke. *Music Is My Mistress.* Garden City, NY: Doubleday, 1973.

Ellington, Mercer, with Stanley Dance. *Duke Ellington in Person: An Intimate Memoir.* Boston: Houghton Mifflin, 1978.

Ellison, Ralph. *Living with Music: Ralph Ellison's Jazz Writings.* New York: Modern Library, 2001.

Erenberg, Lewis A. *Swingin' the Dream: Big Band Jazz and the Rebirth of American Culture.* Chicago: University of Chicago Press, 1998.

Forman, Joel, ed. *The Other Fifties: Interrogating Midcentury American Icons.* Urbana: University of Illinois Press, 1997.

Friedan, Betty. *The Feminine Mystique.* New York: Norton, 1974.

George, Don. *Sweet Man: The Real Duke Ellington.* New York: G. P. Putnam's Sons, 1981.

Giddins, Gary. *Visions of Jazz: The First Century.* New York: Oxford University Press, 1998.

Gioia, Ted. *The History of Jazz.* New York: Oxford University Press, 1997.

Goldblatt, Burt. *Newport Jazz Festival: The Illustrated History.* New York: Dial Press, 1977.

Gordon, Milton M. *Assimilation in American Life: The Role of Race, Religion, and National Origins.* New York: Oxford University Press, 1964.

Hadju, David. *Lush Life: A Biography of Billy Strayhorn.* New York: Farrar, Straus and Giroux, 1996.

______. *Positively 4th Street: The Lives and Times of Joan Baez, Bob Dylan, Mimi Baez Fariña, and Richard Fariña.* New York: Farrar, Straus and Giroux, 2001.

Halberstam, David. *The Powers That Be.* New York: Alfred A. Knopf, 1979.

Hammond, John. *John Hammond on Record.* New York: Ridge Press, 1977.

Hasse, John Edward. *Beyond Category: The Life and Genius of Duke Ellington.* New York: Simon and Schuster, 1993.

Heble, Ajay. *Landing on the Wrong Note: Jazz, Dissonance, and Critical Practice.* New York: Routledge, 2000.

Heilpern, John. *John Osborne: The Many Lives of the Angry Young Man.* New York: Alfred A. Knopf, 2007.

Hughes, Langston. *The Big Sea.* New York: Hill and Wang, 1993.

Jewell, Derek. *Duke: A Portrait of Duke Ellington.* New York: Norton, 1977.

Kerouac, Jack. *Vanity of Duluoz.* New York: Penguin, 1994.

Korall, Burt. *Drummin' Men: The Heartbeat of Jazz: The Swing Years.* New York: Oxford University Press, 1990.

Lawrence, A. H. *Duke Ellington and His World.* New York: Routledge, 2001.

Leonard, Neil. *Jazz: Myth and Religion.* New York: Oxford University Press, 1987.

Levine, Lawrence W. *The Unpredictable Past: Explorations in American Cultural History.* New York: Oxford University Press, 1993.

Lhamon, W. T., Jr. *Deliberate Speed: The Origins of a Cultural Style in the American 1950s.* Washington, DC: Smithsonian Institution Press, 1990.

Lipsitz, George. *Dangerous Crossroads: Popular Music, Postmodernism, and the Poetics of Place.* London: Verso, 1994.

______. *Time Passages: Collective Memory and American Popular Culture.* Minneapolis: University of Minnesota Press, 1990.

MacAdams, Lewis. *Birth of the Cool: Beat, Bop, and the American Avant-Garde.* New York: Free Press, 2001.

May, Lary, ed. *Recasting America: Culture and Politics in the Age of Cold War.* Chicago: University of Chicago Press, 1989.

Mills, C. Wright. *The Power Elite.* New York: Oxford University Press, 1956.

______. *White Collar: The American Middle Classes.* New York: Oxford University Press, 1953.

Morrison, Toni. *Playing in the Dark: Whiteness and the Literary Imagination.* Cambridge, MA: Harvard University Press, 1990.

Murray, Albert. *The Omni-Americans: New Perspectives on Black Experience and American Culture.* New York: Outerbridge and Dienstfrey, 1970.

______. *Stompin' the Blues.* 2nd ed. Cambridge, MA: Da Capo Press, 2000.

Nicholson, Stuart. *Reminiscing in Tempo: A Portrait of Duke Ellington.* Boston: Northeastern University Press, 1999.

O'Meally, Robert G., ed. *The Jazz Cadence of American Culture.* New York: Columbia University Press, 1998.

Packard, Vance. *The Hidden Persuaders.* New York: David McKay, 1957.

______. *The Status Seekers.* New York: David McKay, 1959.

Porter, Eric. *What Is This Thing Called Jazz? African American Musicians as Artists, Critics, and Activists.* Berkeley: University of California Press, 2002.

Poutain, Dick, and David Robins. *Cool Rules: Anatomy of an Attitude.* London: Reaktion Books, 2000.

Prial, Dunstan. *The Producer: John Hammond and the Soul of American Music.* New York: Farrar, Straus and Giroux, 2006.

Rampersad, Arnold. *The Life of Langston Hughes.* 2 vols. New York: Oxford University Press, 1986.

Rawnsley, Gary D. *Radio Diplomacy and Propaganda: The BBC and VOA in International Politics, 1956–64.* New York, St. Martin's, 1996.

Schuller, Gunther. *The Swing Era: The Development of Jazz, 1930–1945.* New York: Oxford University Press, 1989.

Shipton, Alyn. *Groovin' High: The Life of Dizzy Gillespie.* New York: Oxford University Press, 1999.

______. *A New History of Jazz.* London: Continuum, 2001.

Singh, Amritjit, and Daniel M. Scott III, eds. *The Collected Writings of Wallace Thurman: A Harlem Renaissance Reader.* New Brunswick, NJ: Rutgers University Press, 2003.

Starr, S. Frederick. *Red and Hot: The Fate of Jazz in the Soviet Union, 1917–1980.* New York: Oxford University Press, 1983.

Steed, Janna Tull. *Duke Ellington: A Spiritual Biography.* New York: Crossroad, 1999.

Stratemann, Klaus. *Duke Ellington Day by Day and Film by Film.* Copenhagen: JazzMedia Aps, 1992.

Szatmary, David P. *A Time to Rock: A Social History of Rock 'n' Roll.* New York: Schirmer, 1996.

Taraborrelli, J. Randy. *Sinatra: Behind the Legend.* Secaucus, NJ: Birch Lane Press, 1997.
Torgoff, Martin. *Can't Find My Way Home: America in the Great Stoned Age, 1945–2000.* New York: Simon and Schuster, 2004.
Tucker, Mark, ed. *The Duke Ellington Reader.* New York: Oxford University Press, 1993.
Tucker, Mark. *Ellington: The Early Years.* Urbana: University of Illinois Press, 1991.
Ulanov, Barry. *Duke Ellington.* London: Farrar, Straus and Giroux, 1947.
Viereck, Peter. *The Unadjusted Man: A New Hero for Americans: Reflections on the Distinction between Conforming and Conserving.* Boston: Beacon, 1956.
Von Eschen, Penny M. *Satchmo Blows Up the World: Jazz Ambassadors Play the Cold War.* Cambridge, MA: Harvard University Press, 2004.
Walton, Ortiz M. *Music: Black, White, and Blue.* New York: William Morrow, 1972.
Ward, Geoffrey C., and Ken Burns. *Jazz: A History of America's Music.* New York: Alfred A. Knopf, 2000.
Wein, George. *Myself among Others: A Life in Music.* Cambridge, MA: Da Capo Press, 2003.

Articles

Amory, Cleveland. "High Society Blues." *Holiday,* July 1956, pp. 50–51, 92–97.
Chambers, Jack. "Sweet as Bear Meat: The Paradox of Johnny Hodges." *Coda,* July–Aug. 2001, pp. 16–20.
Cook, Willie. Interview by Phil Schaap. Stockholm, 1994. Made available to the author by Michael James from his collection.
Deveaux, Scott. "The Emergence of the Jazz Concert, 1935–1945." *American Music* 7, no. 1 (spring 1989): 6–29.
Fredell, Tomas P. "Newport Up: An Ellington Suite," pp. 1–17, www.utexas.edu/cola/depts/ams/Jazz/Jazz2/Fredell.html (accessed Dec. 22, 2003).
Harman, Carter. "Mood Indigo & Beyond." *Time,* Aug. 20, 1956, pp. 54–63.
Hoefsmit, Sjef, ed. "Dance to the Duke." *International DEMS Bulletin,* 02/2 DEMS 9, Duke Ellington Music Society, 02/2 Aug.–Nov. 2002, www.depanorama.net/dems/02dems2b.htm (accessed Aug. 26, 2007).
Lambert, Eddie. "Duke's 'Diminuendo and Crescendo in Blue,'" *Coda,* Dec. 1985–Jan. 1986.
Lester, Jim. "Willis of Oz." Unpublished article on Willis Conover. Made available to the author by Jim Lester.
Levinson, Leonard L. "Third Newport Jazz Fete Swinging in the Rain; '400' Likes Blast 'n' Beat." *Variety,* July 11, 1956, p. 45.
Nagy, Ernest A. "Willis Conover, the VOA, and Jazz: A Retired FSO Recalls a Broadcasting Legend's Pivotal Role in Thawing the Cold War in Hungary in 1956." *Foreign Service Journal,* Nov. 2002, pp. 31–33.

Ross, Lillian. "You Dig It, Sir?" *New Yorker,* Aug. 14, 1954, pp. 31–55.
Waters, Charles H., Jr. "Anatomy of a Cover: The Story of Duke Ellington's Appearance on the Cover of *Time* Magazine." *Annual Review of Jazz Studies* 6 (1993): 1–64.
Woode, Jimmy. Interview by Phil Schaap. Stockholm, May 22, 1994. Made available to the author by Michael James from his collection.

Index

About the Author

John Fass Morton began a career in theater, film, and writing in London in 1974 where much of his work involved music. Following a starring role in a West End musical, he made appearances in major films, including *The Empire Strikes Back*.